# Register Your Book

## at ibmpressbooks.com/

Upon registration, we will send you electronic sample chapters from two of our popular IBM Press books. In addition, you will be automatically entered into a monthly drawing for a free IBM Press book.

Registration also entitles you to:

- Notices and reminders about author appearances, conferences, and online chats with special guests
- Access to supplemental material that may be available
- Advance notice of forthcoming editions
- Related book recommendations
- Information about special contests and promotions throughout the year
- Chapter excerpts and supplements of forthcoming books

## Contact us

If you are interested in writing a book or reviewing manuscripts prior to publication, please write to us at:

Editorial Director, IBM Press
c/o Pearson Education
800 East 96th Street
Indianapolis, IN 46240

e-mail: IBMPress@pearsoned.com

Visit us on the Web: ibmpressbooks.com

# A Practical Guide to
# Trusted Computing

# IBM Press

## COMPUTING

**Autonomic Computing**
Murch ▪ ISBN 013144025X

**Business Intelligence for the Enterprise**
Biere ▪ ISBN 0131413031

**Grid Computing**
Joseph and Fellenstein ▪ ISBN 0131456601

**Implementing ITIL Configuration Management**
Klosterboer ▪ ISBN 0132425939

**Inescapable Data**
Stakutis and Webster ▪ ISBN 0131852159

**Mainframe Basics for Security Professionals**
Pomerantz, Vander Weele, Nelson, and Hahn ▪ ISBN 0131738569

**On Demand Computing**
Fellenstein ▪ ISBN 0131440241

**A Practical Guide to Trusted Computing**
Challener, Yoder, Catherman, Safford, and Van Doorn ▪ ISBN 0132398427

**RFID Sourcebook**
Lahiri ▪ ISBN 0131851373

**Service-Oriented Architecture (SOA) Compass**
Bieberstein, Bose, Fiammante, Jones, and Shah ▪ ISBN 0131870025

## RATIONAL AND SOFTWARE DEVELOPMENT

**IBM Rational® ClearCase®, Ant, and CruiseControl**
Lee ▪ ISBN 0321356993

**IBM® Rational Unified Process® Reference and Certification Guide**
Shuja and Krebs ▪ ISBN 0131562924

**Implementing IBM® Rational® ClearQuest®**
Buckley, Pulsipher, and Scott ▪ ISBN 0321334868

**Implementing the IBM® Rational Unified Process® and Solutions**
Barnes ▪ ISBN 0321369459

**Outside-in Software Development**
Kessler and Sweitzer ▪ ISBN 0131575511

**Project Management with the IBM® Rational Unified Process®**
Gibbs ▪ ISBN 0321336399

**Requirements Management Using IBM® Rational® RequisitePro®**
Zielczynski ▪ ISBN 0321383001

**Software Configuration Management Strategies and IBM® Rational® ClearCase®, Second Edition**
Bellagio and Milligan ▪ ISBN 0321200195

**Visual Modeling with IBM® Rational® Software Architect and UML™**
Quatrani and Palistrant ▪ ISBN 0321238087

## INFORMATION MANAGEMENT

**An Introduction to IMS™**
Meltz, Long, Harrington, Hain, and Nicholls ▪ ISBN 0131856715

**DB2® Express**
Yip, Cheung, Gartner, Liu, and O'Connell ▪ ISBN 0131463977

**DB2® for z/OS® Version 8 DBA Certification Guide**
Lawson ▪ ISBN 0131491202

**DB2® SQL PL, Second Edition**
Janmohamed, Liu, Bradstock, Chong, Gao, McArthur, and Yip
ISBN 0131477005

**DB2® 9 for Linux®, UNIX®, and Windows®**
Baklarz and Zikopoulos ▪ ISBN 013185514X

**High Availability Guide for DB2®**
Eaton and Cialini ▪ ISBN 0131448307

**The Official Introduction to DB2® for z/OS®, Second Edition**
Sloan ▪ ISBN 0131477501

**Understanding DB2® 9 Security**
Bond, See, Wong, and Chan ▪ ISBN 0131345907

**Understanding DB2®, Second Edition**
Chong, Wang, Dang, and Snow ▪ ISBN 0131580183

## WEBSPHERE

**Enterprise Java™ Programming with IBM® WebSphere®, Second Edition**
Brown, Craig, Hester, Pitt, Stinehour, Weitzel, Amsden, Jakab, and Berg
ISBN 032118579X

**Enterprise Messaging Using JMS and IBM® WebSphere®**
Yusuf ▪ ISBN 0131468634

**IBM® WebSphere®**
Barcia, Hines, Alcott, and Botzum ▪ ISBN 0131468626

**IBM® WebSphere® Application Server for Distributed Platforms and z/OS®**
Black, Everett, Draeger, Miller, Iyer, McGuinnes, Patel, Herescu, Gissel, Betancourt, Casile, Tang, and Beaubien ▪ ISBN 0131855875

**IBM® WebSphere® System Administration**
Williamson, Chan, Cundiff, Lauzon, and Mitchell ▪ ISBN 0131446045

**WebSphere® Business Integration Primer**
Iyengar, Jessani, and Chilanti ▪ ISBN 013224831X

## LOTUS

**IBM® WebSphere® and Lotus®**
Lamb, Laskey, and Indurkhya ▪ ISBN 0131443305

**Lotus® Notes® Developer's Toolbox**
Elliott ▪ ISBN 0132214482

## OPEN SOURCE

**Apache Derby—Off to the Races**
Zikopoulos, Baklarz, and Scott ▪ ISBN 0131855255

**Building Applications with the Linux® Standard Base**
Linux Standard Base Team ▪ ISBN 0131456954

**Performance Tuning for Linux® Servers**
Johnson, Huizenga, and Pulavarty ▪ ISBN 013144753X

## BUSINESS STRATEGY & MANAGEMENT

**Can Two Rights Make a Wrong?**
Moulton Reger ▪ ISBN 0131732943

**Developing Quality Technical Information, Second Edition**
Hargis, Carey, Hernandez, Hughes, Longo, Rouiller, and Wilde
ISBN 0131477498

**Do It Wrong Quickly**
Moran ▪ ISBN 0132255960

**Irresistible!**
Bailey and Wenzek ▪ ISBN 0131987585

**Mining the Talk**
Spangler and Kreulen ▪ ISBN 0132339536

**Reaching the Goal**
Ricketts ▪ ISBN 0132333120

**Search Engine Marketing, Inc.**
Moran and Hunt ▪ ISBN 0131852922

**The New Language of Business**
Carter ▪ ISBN 013195654X

## Visit www.ibmpressbooks.com for a complete list of IBM Press books

Challener, David.
A practical guide to
trusted computing /
c2008.
33305213298940
la            04/01/08

# A Practical Guide to Trusted Computing

David Challener
Kent Yoder
Ryan Catherman
David Safford
Leendert Van Doorn

IBM Press
Pearson plc
Upper Saddle River, NJ • Boston • Indianapolis • San Francisco
New York • Toronto • Montreal • London • Munich • Paris • Madrid
Cape Town • Sydney • Tokyo • Singapore • Mexico City

Ibmpressbooks.com

The authors and publisher have taken care in the preparation of this book, but make no expressed or implied warranty of any kind and assume no responsibility for errors or omissions. No liability is assumed for incidental or consequential damages in connection with or arising out of the use of the information or programs contained herein.

© Copyright 2008 by International Business Machines Corporation. All rights reserved.

Note to U.S. Government Users: Documentation related to restricted right. Use, duplication, or disclosure is subject to restrictions set forth in GSA ADP Schedule Contract with IBM Corporation.

IBM Press Program Managers: Tara Woodman, Ellice Uffer
Cover design: IBM Corporation

Associate Publisher: Greg Wiegand
Marketing Manager: Kourtnaye Sturgeon
Publicist: Heather Fox
Acquisitions Editor: Greg Wiegand
Development Editors: Kevin Howard, Chris Zahn
Managing Editor: Gina Kanouse
Designer: Alan Clements
Project Editor: Michelle Housley
Copy Editor: Water Crest Publishing
Indexer: WordWise Publishing Services LLC
Senior Compositor: Gloria Schurick
Proofreader: Lori Lyons
Manufacturing Buyer: Anna Popick

Published by Pearson plc
Publishing as IBM Press

IBM Press offers excellent discounts on this book when ordered in quantity for bulk purchases or
special sales, which may include electronic versions and/or custom covers and content particular to your business, training
goals, marketing focus, and branding interests. For more information, please contact:

  U.S. Corporate and Government Sales
  1-800-382-3419
  corpsales@pearsontechgroup.com.

For sales outside the U.S., please contact:

  International Sales
  international@pearsoned.com.

The following terms are trademarks or registered trademarks of International Business Machines Corporation in the United States, other countries, or both: IBM, the IBM logo, IBM Press, DB2, Lotus, Rational, Tivoli, WebSphere, Notes and AIX. Java and all Java-based trademarks are trademarks of Sun Microsystems, Inc. in the United States, other countries, or both. Microsoft, Windows, Windows NT, and the Windows logo are trademarks of Microsoft Corporation in the United States, other countries, or both. Intel, Intel logo, Intel Inside, Intel Inside logo, Intel Centrino, Intel Centrino logo, Celeron, Intel Xeon, Intel SpeedStep, Itanium, and Pentium are trademarks or registered trademarks of Intel Corporation or its subsidiaries in the United States and other countries. UNIX is a registered trademark of The Open Group in the United States and other countries. Linux is a registered trademark of Linus Torvalds in the United States, other countries, or both. Other company, product, or service names may be trademarks or service marks of others.

This Book Is Safari Enabled

The Safari® Enabled icon on the cover of your favorite technology book means the book is available through Safari Bookshelf. When you buy this book, you get free access to the online edition for 45 days. Safari Bookshelf is an electronic reference library that lets you easily search thousands of technical books, find code samples, download chapters, and access technical information whenever and wherever you need it.

To gain 45-day Safari Enabled access to this book:

- Go to http://www.awprofessional.com/safarienabled.

- Complete the brief registration form.

- Enter the coupon code YFR8-IKQP-5NMX-CDP7-XR27.

If you have difficulty registering on Safari Bookshelf or accessing the online edition, please e-mail customer-service@safaribooksonline.com.

*Library of Congress Cataloging-in-Publication Data*

Challener, David.
  A practical guide to trusted computing / David Challener, Kent Yoder.
     p. cm.
  Includes index.
  ISBN 0-13-239842-7
  1. Embedded computer systems. 2. Programmable controllers. 3. Computer security. I. Yoder, Kent. II. Title.
  TK7895.E42C4533 2007
  005.8—dc22
                                    2007038929

All rights reserved. This publication is protected by copyright, and permission must be obtained from the publisher prior to any prohibited reproduction, storage in a retrieval system, or transmission in any form or by any means, electronic, mechanical, photocopying, recording, or likewise. For information regarding permissions, write to:

Pearson Education, Inc
Rights and Contracts Department
501 Boylston Street, Suite 900
Boston, MA 02116
Fax (617) 671 3447

ISBN-13: 978-0-13-239842-8
ISBN-10: 0-13-239842-7

Text printed in the United States on recycled paper at R.R. Donnelley in Crawfordsville, Indiana.

First printing December 2007

*This book is dedicated to all the people who worked so hard to make the TPM and TSS specifications what they are today.*

*It is also dedicated to my wife, Ruth, who allowed me the time to work on this book.*

*—David Challener*

# Contents

# Part IV:  Appendixes                                        291

# Preface

We hope you enjoy our book, *A Practical Guide to Trusted Computing*. This is the first book available that guides you through the maze that is the Trusted Platform Module (TPM) now shipping from all major PC vendors. It also enables you to actually use the TPM.

## What This Book Is About

This book is about the increasingly important discipline of Trusted Computing. As the number of viruses, Trojans, and spyware has increased over the last several years, so has the need for a way to provide safety to users. Although a number of books have been written that discuss the philosophy of trusted computing, this is the first one that gets down into the nitty gritty of what solutions can be afforded by making use of the Trusted Platform Modules (TPMs) and discussing how to code them. This book covers the basic capabilities of the TPM and how to write code that accesses those capabilities using the standard TCG Software Stack. It also provides example problems and discusses solutions that could be coded using TPM capabilities.

During the writing of this book, several of the authors were also working on the extension of the TSS 1.1 specification to the TSS 1.2 specification. The latter provides access to new functionality afforded by the 1.2 TPM. This book covers the new capabilities in the 1.2 TPM in Chapter 14, "Administration of Trusted Devices," so that people who want to write code that will work on any TPM can avoid that chapter, and those who want to use the new functionality of the TPM 1.2 can use Chapter 14 along with the rest of the book.

The authors of this book are truly experts in the field, having either worked on the specifications, written TSS stacks for use by software, or written software that uses the TPM itself. Several have given seminars, taught classes, or written papers on the use of the TPM.

## What You Need to Know Before Reading This Book

The code in the book is all based on the C language, so skill in reading C is a requirement for understanding any of the coding examples. Additionally, it is important that the reader have some understanding of cryptography—particularly the difference between symmetric and asymmetric keys, and cryptographic hashes. There is some discussion in the book about these concepts, but a detailed description of the algorithms used is not included. Bruce Schneier's *Applied Cryptography* is a good reference for those who wish to go deeper into that area. If the reader wants merely to find out what TCG is good for, Parts I and III of the book are recommended. If the reader has a particular project in mind, all sections of the book are likely to be helpful.

## Who You Are and Why You Should Read This Book

This book does provide the specific details needed to write applications that take advantage of the TPM. If you are unfamiliar with Trusted Computing and want to write code that will use the capabilities of the TPM, all of this book will be valuable to you. If you want to learn about the reasoning behind the design choices in the TPM, Parts I and II of the book are the ones to concentrate on.

### For a Software Engineer

The authors have tried to write a book that would include everything they would have liked to know about programming with TPMs. As a result, we have included sample code that we have compiled to make sure it works. We give examples that do real things, not just using defaults everywhere. We explain the choices we make in designing the code, and the code is commented, so it is clear about what it does.

If you want to understand how big the problem is that needs to be solved, read Chapter 1, "Introduction to Trusted Computing." If you want to learn about the capabilities of the TPM, read Chapter 2, "Design Goals of the Trusted Platform Module," and Chapter 3, "An Overview of the Trusted Platform Module Capabilities." If you want to find out what kinds of problems can be solved using the capabilities of the TPM, read Chapters 11–13. If you already understand the capabilities of the TPM and want to write programs that use TPM 1.1, read Chapters 4–10. If you want to use the expanded capabilities in the TPM 1.2, read Chapter 14.

### For a Software Project Manager or Technical Leader

A software project manager needs to understand the capabilities of the TPM and also the architecture of projects he is leading. In any security program, it is particularly important that the architecture be established well before coding begins. Architectural design flaws lead quickly to security flaws.

This book should help you understand the issues necessary to design a secure program architecture that takes advantage of the TPM. Chapters 1, 2, 3, 11, 12, 13, and 14 should be particularly useful for the project manager.

## For a Computer User Interface Designer

Ease of use and security have been at odds ever since the first lock was designed. At first glance, they seem adamantly opposed to one another. The designs in Chapters 11, 12, and 13 may provide information necessary for the computer user interface designer to improve the usability of the solution.

## For Those Interested in Trusted Computing

If a person is considering using the TPM, Chapters 1–3 and 11–13 provide the best reading. They provide a good overview of the problems that trusted computing tries to solve and how they are (architecturally) solved.

## For Experienced Users of TPMs

If you are a long-time user of TPMs and are interested in what more you can do with the functions used in the TPM, this book—particularly Chapters 11, 12, 13, and 14—may provide you with inspiration. Sometimes just seeing how other people approach a problem is sufficient to provide the solution to a grating problem.

## How the Book Is Organized

This section provides you with an overall view of how the book is organized, including a brief summary of all the chapters.

## Part I: Background Material

Part I provides an overview of Trusted Computing, including what was the impetus that caused its creation, what problems it was trying to solve, and a functional view of what is provided by a Trusted Platform Module.

- **Chapter 1, "Introduction to Trusted Computing"**

    Historically, hackers have focused on the network, then the server, and now the client. This chapter gives an overview of the security attacks that are focused on today's client and their severity, and then explains why a TPM is ideal for solving such problems. It also discusses privacy issues and gives recommendations to the programmer to avoid causing privacy problems.

- **Chapter 2, "Design Goals of the Trusted Platform Module"**

    When the security experts who generated the original TPM got together, they had a number of features they wanted to make sure were included in the specification. This chapter discusses what they were trying to accomplish. Having this broad view of what a TPM was designed for will help the reader with background information necessary to understand how the actual features that were implemented were intended to be used.

- **Chapter 3, "An Overview of the Trusted Platform Module Capabilities"**

  This chapter describes the actual features implemented in the TPM 1.1 design and how they work. This provides an architectural view of the design of the specification. After reading this chapter, the reader should have an idea of what types of problems the TPM will help solve. Additionally, it provides some discussion as to why certain features were omitted from the specification.

## Part II: Programming Interfaces to TCG

Part II includes chapters for the programmer. It provides an in-depth view of the interfaces that are available in the software stack, with examples of how they are used. It starts out with the lowest level—talking to the device driver. Next, it looks at the boot sequence for a computer and how that can be enhanced with a TPM. This is followed with a section on the core services provided by the software stack, along with a brief discussion of talking directly to this interface, as when a remote application is using a TPM. Following this, the next few chapters are about using the TPM at the highest level: the application interface

- **Chapter 4, "Writing a TPM Device Driver"**

  This chapter provides the reader with the information necessary to write a device driver to communicate with the TPM. This is important to the person who wishes to use the TPM with an operating system other than those (Windows, Linux) that already have device drivers available.

- **Chapter 5, "Low-Level Software: Using BIOS and TDDL Directly"**

  This chapter provides the reader with the information necessary to talk directly to the chip in the absence of a TSS stack. This is important to a person writing code that runs in BIOS, or for writing a TSS stack for a new operating system, or in a memory constrained environment. This chapter is based on work originally done for Linux, but has been deliberately written in an OS neutral format. Additionally, this chapter will provide to the user a real appreciation of the work done for him when he is using the TSS stack.

- **Chapter 6, "Trusted Boot"**

  This chapter describes using the chip in one of the most exciting forms—to measure the security state of a platform. There are two means of doing this in the Trusted Computing space: the 1.1 Static Root of Trust and the 1.2 Dynamic Root of Trust. Both are described in detail, and example code is given showing how they are implemented. This is one of the few places in the book where 1.2 code that has been tested can be given, as these interfaces do not require nonexistent 1.2 TSS stacks.

- **Chapter 7, "The TCG Software Stack"**

  The TSS API is the most commonly used interface to access the TPM. This chapter describes the architecture of the TSS, conventions used in the API, and software object types and their uses. It will also walk you through some simple programming examples using the TSS API and clarify the differences in programming for the 1.1 API versus the 1.2 API.

- **Chapter 8, "Using TPM Keys"**

  Key management is one of the most difficult things to achieve in a security program, and one of the areas where a TPM excels. This chapter describes and gives examples of how keys can be created, stored, loaded, migrated, and used. Special keys are described, including identity keys, storage keys, and signing keys, along with examples of their usage.

- **Chapter 9, "Using Symmetric Keys"**

  This chapter explains the richness of facilities provided by the TPM to exploit symmetric keys in applications. The reader who is interested in using the TPM to enhance the security of any application that does bulk encryption will want to read this chapter to find out, with examples, how to exploit TPM features.

- **Chapter 10, "The TSS Core Service (TCS)"**

  The core services underlie the normal application interface APIs. It is important that an application developer have some idea of what these services provide, so that he can understand exactly what is happening when an API is called. Additionally, if an application writer wants to create a client server application, and a TPM needs to be asked to perform services remotely, the core services are the application layer that is called. This chapter provides insight into the core services and some sample code for doing remote calls.

- **Chapter 11, "Public Key Cryptography Standard #11"**

  This chapter provides a real example of coding using the TSS. It provides a complete working example of a PKCS#11 stack that links to the TSS stack to provide middleware services to applications. The code is commented and is available open source for use.

## Part III: Architectures

This section of the book is intended to give the reader a flavor of the richness of applications that are enabled with the Trusted Computing software stack. It will provide the reader with an idea of the target applications that the specification writers had in mind when they designed the architecture. Even if the reader is not interested in writing these particular applications, reading these chapters will help explain why design decisions were made the way they were.

- **Chapter 12, "Trusted Computing and Secure Storage"**

  The TPM provides capabilities for storing data securely in two commands: BIND and SEAL. This chapter provides a number of examples of how those commands could be used to provide useful functions to an end user. It also discusses some of the problems that need to be solved to have a secure implementation. Reading this chapter will help the reader understand why the commands were designed the way they were.

- **Chapter 13, "Trusted Computing and Secure Identification"**

  The TPM provides capabilities for doing secure signing internal to the chip itself. This chapter gives a number of examples of how those functions can be used to provide practical applications that solve real user problems. Reading this chapter will help the reader understand why the signing commands were designed the way they were.

- **Chapter 14, "Administration of Trusted Devices"**

  When companies start deploying TPMs in large numbers, it becomes particularly important that they find ways of administrating them. This chapter is concerned with how to use the migration commands to provide administration applications that will allow remote administration of a TPM.

- **Chapter 15, "Ancillary Hardware"**

  The TPM could not, by itself, solve all security problems. It is by design an inexpensive device. However, it does provide a number of capabilities that allow it to hook into other security devices. This chapter describes some of the ways this can be done to provide enhanced security for a client.

- **Chapter 16, "Moving from TSS 1.1 to TSS 1.2"**

  The TSS 1.2 specification has recently been released. In this chapter, we describe the new capabilities that are in the new specification, and give code examples of how each one can be used. These new capabilities include CMK, Delegation, DAA, new PCR behavior, Locality, NVRAM, Audit, Monotonic counter, Transport, Tick, and Administrative commands This section is aimed at those who want to take advantage of these new features to write code that will work ONLY on clients that include 1.2 TPMs.

## Part IV: Appendixes

We have also included several useful appendixes. If you are just trying to find out an API that will provide a specific function, these appendixes give a quick way of finding the APIs in question. For those looking to talk to the hardware directly, a TPM command reference is given. For those looking to talk to the Trusted Computing Software Stack, a TSS command reference is given. These references provide a quick description of the command and a list of how they are typically designed to be used.

- **Appendix A, "TPM Command Reference."**

  A list of TPM-level commands, where they were intended to be used, and a brief description of what they do.

- **Appendix B, "TSS Command Reference."**

  A list of TSS-level commands, where they were intended to be used, and a brief description of what they do.

- **Appendix C, "Function Library."**

  A list of proposed helper functions which would help the user in creating programs using the TPM, along with a description of their function.

- **Appendix D, "TSS Functions Grouped by Object and API Level."**

  This appendix breaks down the functions by the internal TSS object that they affect and by the API level at which they interact. This information can be used as a quick table for determining which APIs are available while writing code.

Some reviewers have noted that considering possible uses for the TPM helped them understand the reasoning behind the design of the TPM. The authors hope that this book will not only help in that understanding, but promote the exploitation of the resource that is now so widely deployed.

# Acknowledgments

Special thanks to the reviewers who gave valuable advice on changes that needed to be made to the text, especially David Grawrock, Ken Goldman, Sean Smith, and Emily Ratliff, and to the many others too numerous to name who helped by encouraging us.

# About the Authors

**David Challener** went to work for IBM® in East Fishkill after graduating with his Ph.D. in Applied Mathematics from the University of Illinois, (Urbana-Champaign). After helping design the first TPM (representing IBM), he became chair of the TCG TSS committee. When the IBM PC division was sold to Lenovo, he became a Lenovo employee, where he has represented the company on the TCG Technical Committee, TPM workgroup, and many other groups, while continuing to chair the TSS committee. Currently he is the Lenovo Board Member for TCG.

**Kent Yoder** has been working for the IBM Linux® Technology Center since graduating from Purdue University with a degree in Computer Science in 2001. He has represented IBM on the TCG TSS committee and has helped write and maintain TrouSerS, an open-source TSS library that implements the TSS software specification for the TCG TPM hardware.

**Ryan Catherman** was a member of the Trusted Computing Group, including active memberships in the TSS and TPM working groups while employed at IBM. He was also coauthor of the IBM implementation of Trusted Computing software at its inception and originator of Unix versions of this software. Currently, he works for Opsware Incorporated, a recent HP acquisition, and holds a masters in Computer Engineering

**David Safford** is a researcher at IBM's T. J. Watson Research Center in Hawthorne, New York. There he has led security research in numerous areas, including ethical hacking, threat analysis, security engineering, intrusion detection sensors, vulnerability scanning, cryptography, and operating system security. Prior to coming to IBM in 1996, he was Director of Supercomputing and Networking at Texas A&M University, and an A-7 pilot in the United States Navy.

**Leendert van Doorn** is a Senior Fellow at AMD where he runs the software technology office. Before joining AMD he was a senior manager at IBM's T.J. Watson Research Center, where he managed the secure systems and security analysis departments. He received his Ph.D. from the Vrije Universiteit in Amsterdam where he worked on the design and implementation of micro-kernels. Nowadays his interests are in managed runtime systems, accelerated computing (AMD's name for heterogenous and homogenous manycore computing), security, and virtualization. In his former job at IBM he worked on FIPS 140-2 level 4 physically secure coprocessors, trusted systems, and virtualization. He was also actively involved in IBM's virtualization strategy, created and lead IBM's secure hypervisor and trusted virtual data center initiatives, and he was on the board of directors for the Trusted Computing Group. Despite all these distractions, he continued to contribute code to the Xen open source hypervisor, such as the integrated support code for AMD-V and Intel® VT-x. When conference calls and meetings are getting too much for him, he is known to find refuge at CMU.

# PART I

# Background
# Material

# Introduction to Trusted Computing

This book is designed to provide the reader with a practical understanding of how to use the new embedded security subsystem built into many computers: TCG (Trusted Computing Group)'s Trusted Platform Module (TPM). The book does not limit itself to a mere description of the capabilities of the TPM and the standard Application Programming Interfaces (APIs). Through multiple examples, it provides the reader with an understanding of what problems the TPM can be used to solve, and the motivation behind the design decisions made in the specifications. After reading this book, the reader should better understand the security problems facing PC clients today—and how to use the capabilities of a TPM, via the standard APIs, to solve many of those problems. Let's first look at what the TPM can do for client security.

In this chapter, we want to make three major points:

- Current security threats are severe.
- Software alone *cannot* defend against these threats.
- The TPM is specifically designed to defend against these threats.

We also briefly discuss the role of the TPM in maintaining privacy as well as security.

## Computer Security Attacks Are Staggeringly Expensive

Although it is impossible to know exactly how high the financial losses are to cybercrime, there are estimates based on some known data and on surveys. Estimated statistics on cybercrime are alarming:

- "Cybercrime proceeds in 2004 were $105 billion, greater than those of illegal drug sales."—Valerie McNiven[1]

- "Identity fraud reached $52.6 billion in 2004."—Javelin Strategy & Research[2]
- "Dealing with viruses, spyware, PC theft, and other computer-related crimes costs U.S. businesses a staggering $67.2 billion a year."—FBI[3]
- "Over 130 major intrusions exposed more than 55 million Americans to the growing variety of fraud as personal data like Social Security and credit card numbers were left unprotected"—*USA Today*[4]

These are just some of the statistics and estimates that show the magnitude of the problem. All too frequently, the authors have talked to individuals and companies who have bank accounts emptied by fraudulent access to electronic banking. Who *hasn't* had to spend hours reloading PC operating systems because they had become infested by a virus or spyware? Too many individuals have had their identity stolen due to computer fraud, such as phishing and pharming, which exposed their private information, such as their Social Security numbers. Many of these threats that are focused on the client PC have changed and grown dramatically in recent years. Let's take a look at some of the threats and trends.

## The Changing Threats to Computer Security

A popular trend for hackers focuses on attacking the client. In the 1980s, hackers attacked the network by sniffing passwords and hijacking network sessions. As applications encrypted data going across the network, hackers began attacking servers by taking advantage of misconfigured or buggy services, like web servers. Companies responded to these attacks with firewall intrusion detection and security auditing tools to protect their servers. Thus, hackers have increasingly turned to unprotected clients.

The hackers are interested in client PCs for many reasons. First, they are an easily available source of machines from which to launch high-bandwidth attacks, such as Distributed Denial of Service (DDoS) attacks and mass spamming. Hackers now focus also on collecting usernames and passwords used to target and access servers. An early example of this type of attack is the QAZ virus, which targets client machines through email and windows file shares, and which has a payload that captures usernames and passwords, and emails them off to the hackers. With the rise of online banking, stolen usernames and passwords have enabled attackers to steal large amounts of money electronically out of business and personal accounts.

What are the modern security threats? There are many categories of problems the hackers use to attack a system. Six of the most significant categories are the following:

- Vulnerable programs (coding bugs, buffer overflows, parsing errors)
- Malicious programs (spyware, Trojans)
- Misconfigured programs (security features not turned on)
- Social engineering (phishing/pharming)

- Physical theft (laptops)
- Electronic eavesdropping (capturing email)

In the following sections, we examine each of these problem areas.

## Vulnerable Programs

*Vulnerable programs* are ones whose requirements, designs, or implementations are inherently unsafe. Examples of unsafe design include telnet and ftp, which normally send usernames and passwords over the network unencrypted. Hackers can easily record the username and directory passwords as they go over the network, and replay them to steal a person's access. Another example is rlogin; this uses the sender's IP address for authentication, which is easily forged. These programs were not designed with security in mind, and are inherently exploitable by hackers.

Buggy programs are ones that are designed and configured properly, but which have implementation or coding flaws that can be exploited remotely by the hacker, who sends carefully crafted malicious data that exploits the bug. The two most common program vulnerabilities are buffer overflows and parsing errors.

A *buffer overflow* is a programming error in which the programmer creates a fixed-size buffer to store remote input data, but fails to check the length of the input data to make sure it fits in the buffer. The remote hacker can then send more data than can fit in the buffer, in which case the excess data overwrites whatever follows the end of the buffer. The malicious data will typically include malicious executable code, which gives the remote hacker access to the machine. Buffer overflows have been well understood for more than 30 years, and are easily avoided, yet they consistently are the most frequently discovered and exploited vulnerability.

*Parsing errors* occur when the contents of remote input data are not properly checked. For example, a web server accepts requests to view html files by name, verifying that the specified file is allowed to be viewed. If the parsing of the filename is not done correctly, the server may improperly allow the hacker to view data (such as the password file).

Buffer overflows and parsing errors can easily be used to break into systems that have been set up incorrectly. Because it is difficult to set up software correctly, hackers can also take advantage of software that won't default into a correct setting. Since software is widespread, and identical on every CD, cracks found on one system are likely to replicate across all of them.

One alarming trend in security is the increasingly rapid rate at which new vulnerabilities are discovered and exploited. The chart displayed in Figure 1.1, based on cert.org statistics, shows that vulnerabilities are being discovered at ever-increasing rates, and that this rate was roughly 6,000 per year, or 16 for every day in 2005! From the perspective of the vulnerability of software, the problem appears to be continually growing, and certainly not getting better.

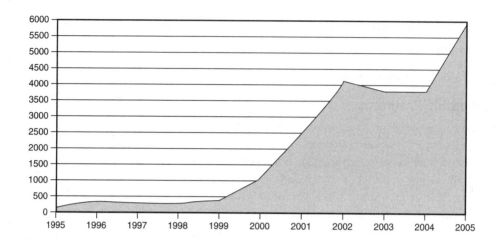

**Figure 1.1**   Vulnerabilities discovered per year (CERT).

The chart displayed in Figure 1.2 shows the rapid increase in the ability of hackers to translate the newly discovered vulnerabilities into practical attacks on actual systems. In 2004, it took on average only six days from publication of the vulnerability to actual exploitation. So not only are vulnerabilities being discovered more and more rapidly, the exploitation of these vulnerabilities also follows more rapidly. As such, it is increasingly more difficult to protect client software from compromise, even with automated patch download and installation. If the trends continue, we are not far from a situation in which even automated download and installation of patches are not fast enough to defend against new attacks. Already some studies have shown that a new Internet-connected PC can be compromised faster than all the needed patches can be downloaded and applied.

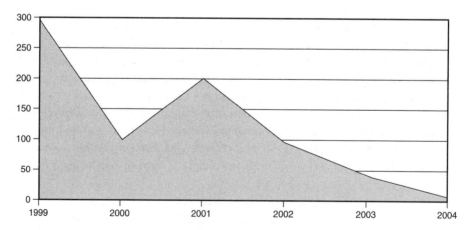

**Figure 1.2**   Days from patch to exploit (information security, July 2004).

## Malicious Programs: Viruses and Spyware/Adware

In addition to exploiting vulnerable programs, attackers can write malicious programs, and then try to get the user to install and run them. Malicious programs can be transmitted as email attachments, made available as innocent-looking downloadable programs, such as games or screensavers, and installed invisibly merely by playing a music CD on your computer. Malicious programs have been transmitted as email attachments that look quite convincingly as security patches for the operating system.

Many viruses and Trojan horses today use social engineering to spread. They try to trick a user into downloading and executing a file, upon which action the executable will scour the user's address box and try to send a copy of itself to everyone in that file. The email will appear to come from the user, and as such will be trusted by the sender of the email. Although it is easy to tell users not to execute files that they were not expecting to get, it doesn't seem to do a lot of good in the real world. Users need to be protected from themselves. While there are numerous software programs that have been used to mitigate this problem, including antivirus programs, adware programs, and personal firewalls, there is no known way in software even to detect the attacks reliably.

## Misconfigured Programs

*Misconfigured programs* are ones that have adequate security features, but that require the features to be turned on or configured properly. For example, NFS can be configured to export a file system in read-only mode, which is very safe, but it can also be configured to export a file system read-write to everyone, which allows the hackers to break in easily. 802.11 wireless networks can be configured securely to protect the clients and the network, but by default these features are typically turned off.

## Social Engineering: Phishing and Pharming

> *"Three can keep a secret, if two of them are dead." —Benjamin Franklin*

People are bad at keeping secrets. Unfortunately, if one of those secrets is a password for online banking, failure to keep the secret can lead to having one's bank account stolen. Social engineering attacks try to trick users into giving away a secret, such as their banking password.

Phishing and pharming are the most frequent methods of social engineering. In *phishing*, the attacker sends an email to the user that typically appears to be from the user's bank. This email asks for account-related information, such as the account name and password. These phishing emails can be very difficult to distinguish from actual email from the bank, even for security experts, as they use sophisticated techniques of concealing the true address information. Phishing email attacks are not new (one large-scale attack happened more than 20 years ago), but the combination of them with online banking has lead to recent large-scale financial attacks. Phishing emails often provide links to malicious web sites carefully constructed to look like the real bank's site.

*Pharming* is a similar attack method, but it is more difficult to detect as it uses the correct address/link for the bank, but redirects the email or link on the network by inserting false information into the domain name system (DNS). The bottom line is that it can be difficult or impossible for the user to determine whether or not an email or web site is authentic.

## Physical Theft of Data

With the rise of laptops, many people now are keeping extremely valuable data on their laptops. Some executives are even rumored to have their laptops targeted, due to the value of the data on the laptop. And the laptop itself can be a valuable commodity.

There are three techniques that can be used to protect against theft. The first is to make the system a brick, if someone other than the owner tries to use it. This brick technique usually uses BIOS passwords stored in non-volatile RAM, and hard disk passwords released by BIOS to the hard disk once appropriate authorization is given to the BIOS during power up. The latter protects against someone extracting the hard disk data by placing it in a different system and reading it out. Protection against password hammering is done by requiring the machine to power off after three successive incorrect attempts to boot. When this is successful, a thief can only sell parts of the laptop, at a much reduced value.

The second technique is to encrypt the data on the hard disk. Although this does not make the hardware unusable, it does protect the data on the hard disk. Because the OS is presumably up and running when the decryption takes place, much better user interfaces are available for decryption, including the use of pass phrases, proximity badges, fingerprints, and so on.

The third technique is theft recovery. In this case, the owner attempts to locate the machine after it has been stolen using lojack-like solutions. Software may periodically "call home" over a phone line or over the Internet, trying to tell the owner where it is, either using ANI, IP addresses, or (in extreme cases) GPS.

## Electronic Eavesdropping

There are a number of forms of electronic eavesdropping, including broadband eavesdropping and sniffing of email.

### Broadband Eavesdropping

Whenever a new computer is connected to the broadband, it lets other people on the network connect to that computer. A firewall is necessary to protect the user from hackers trying to use that access to get into the guts of his computer. Although a firewall cannot prevent viruses and Trojan horses from getting into the client via email or email attachments, it can prevent an outside computer from connecting to a client via NetBIOS, and using NAT (network address translation), it can prevent a number of direct attacks against clients behind the firewall.

However, email and web browsing can sometimes be monitored by other folk on the same subnet, if the network supports "promiscuous" mode in which one computer can see all the traffic on the local network.

### Sniffing Email

Some estimates state that more than 80% of the email sent to either lawyers or accountants is being monitored by hackers. If you want your email to be private, it needs to be encrypted before it is sent. If you want it to have provable integrity when it gets where it is going, it needs to be signed. Another alternative is simply to not use the Internet. In a small intranet, a switch can be used to provide some level of privacy as well.

## Can Software Be Made Completely Secure?

Probably not.

Why can't the current client software be fixed? There are many reasons, including complexity, compatibility, and compromise.

First of all, modern systems are incredibly complex. A typical Unix or Windows system, including standard applications, represents something around 100 million lines of source code. Large applications often also have hundreds of millions lines of code. All together, there are *billions* of lines of code in use today. Several recent studies have shown that typical product-level software has roughly one security-related bug per thousand lines of source code across its lifetime. Thus, a typical system will potentially have a hundred thousand security bugs. It is not surprising that we are finding six thousand of these bugs per year, and that the rate of finding them has increased so dramatically.

Second, compatibility requirements in the client space make a complete break from the commitment to the current system architecture unlikely. Even if we could build secure software systems, the amount of effort needed to replace the billions of lines of code in and for existing operating systems is simply prohibitive.

Third, without hardware support, it is likely *impossible* to detect the presence of malicious code in a system. This question is still an active area of research; but so far, all attempts to detect malicious changes in software (compromise) without hardware support have ultimately been circumvented. In contrast, with a little bit of hardware support, it is quite easy to detect compromise.

## How Can the TPM Help?

In January 2000, Roger Schell and Michael Thompson wrote a paper, "Platform Security: What Is Lacking,"[5] which analyzes the modern Internet threats, and shows how the lack of platform defenses impede important potential applications, such as electronic commerce. The article goes on to suggest minimal hardware along the lines of TCG, which can help defeat these threats. Roger's paper is well worth reading, as it goes into more technical detail than we can in this introduction.

In Trusted Computing, the goals are to protect the most sensitive information, such as private and symmetric keys, from theft or use by malicious code. Trusted Computing assumes that client software is going to be compromised at some time during its life, and provides protection for its sensitive keys in case this should happen. The TCG TPM was designed to provide an anchor in the sea of software in which a client floats. The TPM has rather limited functionality, but that is an advantage when it comes to certifying that it works as designed. And the design has been made deliberately flexible so that it can be applied to almost any problem that occurs in the security field.

The TPM has been designed to protect security by ensuring the following:

- Private keys cannot be stolen or given away.
- The addition of malicious code is always detected.
- Malicious code is prevented from using the private keys.
- Encryption keys are not easily available to a physical thief.

The TCG chip accomplishes these goals with three main groups of functions, as follows:

- Public key authentication functions
- Integrity measurement functions
- Attestation functions

The *public key authentication functions* provide for on-chip key pair generation using a hardware random number generator, along with public key signature, verification, encryption, and decryption. By generating the private keys in the chip, and encrypting them anytime they are transferred outside the chip, the TPM guarantees that malicious software cannot access the keys at all. Even the owner of the keys cannot give the private keys away to phishing or pharming attacks, as the keys are never visible outside the chip unencrypted. Malicious code could *use* the private keys on the TPM, so some way needs to be provided to ensure that malicious code cannot use the keys either.

The *integrity measurement functions* provide the capability to protect private keys from access by malicious code. In a trusted boot, the chip stores in Platform Configuration Registers (PCRs) hashes of configuration information throughout the boot sequence. Once booted, data (such as private keys) can be "sealed" under a PCR. The sealed data can be unsealed only if the PCR has the same value as at the time of sealing. Thus, if an attempt is made to boot an alternative system, or a virus has "backdoored" the operating system, the PCR value will not match and the unseal will fail, thus protecting the data from access by the malicious code.

The *attestation functions* keep a list of all the software measurements committed to the PCRs, and can then sign them with a private key known only by the TPM. Thus, a trusted client can prove to a third party that its software has or has not been compromised.

These functions defend against all the threats described earlier.

Malicious programs, such as spyware and Trojans, will be detected by changes in the PCR measurement, which can then cause the TPM to refuse to unseal sensitive data, or to refuse to use private keys for signing or decryption. If vulnerable or misconfigured programs are exploited, any changes they make to files can similarly be detected, and sensitive data protected. Any attempts to gain authentication secrets, such as by phishing or pharming, will fail, as the owner of the authentication private keys cannot give the keys away. Data encrypted under keys sealed by the TPM will be much harder to access in the case of theft, as the attacker would need to open up the chip to get its storage root key in order to be able to unseal the protected keys. (While possible, this is really difficult and expensive.) Similarly, encrypted communications are much more immune to eavesdropping, if the encryption keys are exchanged or stored by a TPM.

# Privacy and Recovery—Special Considerations for Hardware

Privacy is a different issue from security. Security keeps confidential data under the control of the owner of that data. Privacy is concerned with keeping private data under control even after it has been given to an outside group. As such, although security concerns are important for keeping private data private, they are not sufficient to address the privacy issue.

One hot button in the privacy community has been remote identification. A *New Yorker* cartoon that is often cited shows one dog telling another dog, "No one knows you're a dog on the Internet." This anonymity of surfing is a key characteristic of Internet browsing, and one that has been under attack since the beginning. The business value of knowing a lot about the buying and browsing habits of a person is quite large, and so there have been a number of attempts to extract this information from the public without its knowledge.

Quite rightly, a number of organizations have sprung up to defend the public's right to anonymity, and they have been vociferous in complaining and explaining about various technologies, such as cookies, and software that keeps track of a person's behavior without his knowledge. The "without their knowledge" is the key point here, and an important one. There is no question that occasionally it is important for a user or customer to be able to identify themselves. When doing online banking, or purchasing, or getting into a remote intranet, it is important that impersonation not be a practical option. However, identification should not be done by default, without the user's involvement, and it should not provide more information about a user than he is willing to provide.

One problem with authentication technologies is the possibility of it being used without the owner's knowledge in order to identify him. Because one of the functions of a TPM is to provide a means for the owner to securely identify himself or his machine, the design had to be done in a way that would not expose such privacy concerns. Throughout the design specification process, the technical committee kept these concerns in mind and consulted with numerous privacy groups to make certain that all privacy concerns were addressed. Some of the solutions to these privacy concerns were just common sense, but some were quite clever.

We strongly recommend that any software designed to use the TCG TPM be likewise careful to avoid privacy concerns. It is okay to use the TPM for authentication if the user has the default option of setting it up so as to require an overt action on the part of the user to provide that authentication. Set up user interfaces to make this action non-onerous for the user, so he isn't led into turning off this feature. Users should never have to choose between ease of use and privacy.

Key recovery is a particular concern for hardware-based keys. If a hardware TPM fails, any keys locked to that chip are no longer available. If you lose a private key that is being used for authentication to your bank, you can always get a new TPM, create new keys, and register the new public keys with the bank. If, however, the TPM is being used to seal encryption keys, then failure of the TPM would lead to loss of all data encrypted under those keys. Clearly this is not acceptable. Fortunately, the TPM specification explicitly provides the owner of a key the secure ability to move keys from one TPM and back to the same TPM (key backup and restore), or from one TPM to a different TPM (key migration). These key movement functions are secure, because they allow movement of keys only from one TPM chip to another TPM chip. In transit, the keys are safe because they are always encrypted. On each end, both TPMs provide the same hardware protection of the private key.

## Summary

In this chapter, we discussed the severity of the modern electronic threats, how difficult or impossible it is to make software immune to these attacks, and how the TPM chip provides a hardware base sufficient to help defend against the attacks. In addition, the chip was designed with privacy, backup, restore, and migration of protected data firmly in mind.

## Endnotes

1   Reuters News Story by Souhail Karam, November 28, 2005.

2   Joris Evers, CNET News, January 19, 2006. http://news.com.com/Computer+crime+costs+67+billion%2C+FBI+says/2100-7349_3-6028946.html?tag=nefd.top

3   Ibid.

4   CNNMoney, "Record bad year for tech security," December 29, 2005. http://money.cnn.com/2005/12/29/technology/computer_security/index.htm

5   Roger Schell and Michael Thompson, "Platform Security: What Is Lacking," Elsevier Science, Information Security, Technical Report, January 2000.

# CHAPTER 2

# Design Goals of the Trusted Platform Module

In addition to privacy support, the Trusted Computing Group (TCG) technical committee had a number of design goals for the Trusted Platform Module (TPM). It was important that the design have the capability to do the following:

- Securely report the environment that booted
- Securely store data
- Securely identify the user and system (without encountering privacy concerns)
- Support standard security systems and protocols
- Support multiple users on the same system while preserving security among them
- Be produced inexpensively

Of course, "secure" is a relative term. Given enough resources, anything can be hacked. The relative security of personal computers (PCs) prior to TCG was fairly low, so any improvement was considered worthwhile. Although it is not required by the specification, it is expected that most TPMs will be designed as chips securely attached to the motherboard of a PC together with a secure BIOS. It is expected that most designs will also be both FIPS 140-2 and Common Criteria (EAL3) certified, to provide an independent lab's view of the security of the module. (In 1.2, the EAL level is being raised to EAL4+ in order to enable eCommerce in the European Union.)

Due to the requirement that a TPM be relatively inexpensive, a number of features that would have been nice to embed in the specification were left out. These include a real-time clock, an SSL accelerator, a symmetric encryption engine, support for elliptic curves, and support for extended secure hash algorithms. All of these would have been nice to have, and aren't specifically excluded, but were not deemed necessary. Some of them may appear in later versions of the specification.

However, the design that was settled on is flexible, and as a result a number of features not in the design can be emulated using features that are in the design or using software supported by the chip. This chapter will go over a number of these features in the 1.1 specification. Those interested in the new features in 1.2 TPMs should go to Chapter 16, "Moving from TSS 1.1 to TSS 1.2."

## Securely Reporting the Environment: Platform Status

One of the first design goals of TCG was to provide a trusted way to measure and report on a platform's environment. This is difficult, because if software is asked the question "Are you software I can trust?," you can trust the answer only if the software has not been subverted—leading to a circular kind of argument. The software can be trusted to answer the question, only if it is trusted software. Hardware tokens—such as Smartcards, USB keys, iButtons, and the like—are much harder to subvert, but typically are not integrated into the platform, so they have little ability to measure what is going on in the platform.

There is a difference in kind, rather than just in packaging, between security token solutions (such as smart cards and USB fobs) and a chip embedded in a PC. Designs that use portable security devices cannot count on tokens being persistently connected to a PC. Security tokens by their very nature are meant to be moveable between systems. They also can't count on trusted connections made between tokens and various system components. Because they are connected through a reader or port, there is no a priori way of determining how the token is connected to the system. The TCG committee wanted to take advantage of new capabilities, such as Platform Configuration Registers (PCRs), enabled by having a persistent and defined connection between the security chip and the platform. One of the design goals of the TPM was to provide a way to remotely determine the trusted status of a platform. Why is this important? The following are some examples. More are in the following chapters of the book devoted to TPM scenarios:

- Chapter 6, "Trusted Boot": A user may want to determine that a machine has not been subverted.

- Chapter 8, "Using TPM Keys": An owner of a key may or may not want to allow use of that key depending on the trusted status of a machine.

- Chapter 11, "Public Key Cryptography Standard #11": A user may want to access the trusted platform module capabilities from legacy software.

- Chapter 12, "Trusted Computing and Secure Storage": A user may want to secure data so that if it is accessed on a different computer, it cannot be decrypted.

- Chapter 13, "Trusted Computing and Secure Identification": An administrator may want to give network access to a machine based on the trusted status of a machine.

### Storing a Record of the Boot Sequence

TCG uses the boot sequence to determine the trusted status of a platform. This includes the BIOS, the installed cards that may assert control during boot, the boot loader, the OS kernel, and other things that are user selectable (such as the first program run by the OS).

The phrase "boot a computer" comes from the notion of "pulling oneself up by one's own bootstraps." When a system is booting, first the BIOS is in control. That system establishes enough subsystems to do basic input and output and initialize cards. Then it transfers control to the BIOS of various installed cards and receives control back. After this is done, control is passed to the boot loader, which in turn passes control to the OS kernel. The OS loads various device drivers and services and then may start up a program, or be asked to start a program by the end user.

By the time the end user can finally direct the OS to do something, control over the machine has transferred between a number of different items. In this situation, how can a user know that the system has not been hacked any number of times to allow a cracker access to everything he is doing?

TCG handles this problem with a daisy chain design. It starts with a small root of trust that is the first thing that gets control of the system. This root of trust is a small subset of the BIOS. It records which BIOS is being used to boot the system before passing control to the full BIOS. The BIOS then records which card's BIOSes are given control before passing control to them. The boot loader is recorded before control is passed to it. The boot loader records the kernel being used before passing control to it, and finally the kernel may record what things it gives control to before passing control to them. The TPM is used to store all these records and then report on them securely.

Because the TPM is attached directly to the platform in a defined way, the daisy chain design allows it to take advantage of the almost infinite storage for keys residing on the hard disk. Additionally, because the TPM can be guaranteed to be present during the boot sequence, the BIOS can rely on its being present, and store measurements in the PCRs of the chip very early on in the boot sequence, before an OS is loaded. Portable security tokens cannot be relied upon to be present this early, so reports from them as to the boot sequence cannot be trusted.

There is an obvious problem: The TPM can't possibly store all the information in the previous paragraph—if it had enough memory to store the OS kernel, it would cost too much to manufacture. The TPM solves this problem by storing a digest of this information instead of the information itself. These digests are stored in *Platform Configuration Registers* (*PCRs*).

PCRs are a new thing for PCs. These values are stored in memory locations in the TPM and can only be changed via an *extend* operation. This operation takes the current value in a PCR, appends an input value, takes a Secure Hash Algorithm 1 (SHA-1) hash of the resulting concatenation, and then replaces the current PCR value with the output of this operation. SHA-1, which can be found at the NIST site (www.nist.gov), is an algorithm that takes as input any size file and outputs 20 bytes of data. It is known that if one bit of the input data is changed, on average half the bits of the resultant output will change. This hash was designed to be non-invertible.

During the boot sequence, the PCRs are filled with digests of each executing program in sequence before it executes. Thus, before the BIOS hands over control to a boot loader, the BIOS hashes the boot loader and extends the resultant value into a PCR. Before the boot loader passes control to an OS kernel, the kernel would be hashed, and the value extended into another PCR. Thus, the root of trust records the status of the BIOS, the BIOS records the trust status of the card firmware and the boot loader, the boot loader records the trust status of the kernel, and so on. By examining the values kept in the PCRs, you may determine if those values correspond to trusted programs. If you trust the BIOS corresponding to the recorded PCR value, then you can trust the extensions to the PCR made by the BIOS. If you trust the boot loader, then you can trust the PCR extensions made by the boot loader. In this way, the trust boundary extends from the root of trust all the way to the kernel of the operating system (or beyond). This is illustrated in Figure 2.1.

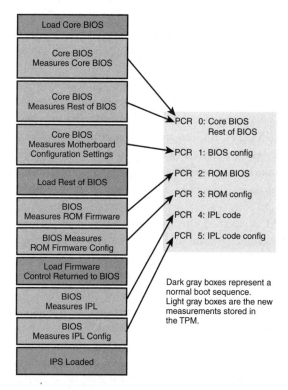

**Figure 2.1**    Dark gray boxes represent a normal boot sequence. Light gray boxes are the new measurements stored in the TPM.

A history of the extend operations performed to a specific PCR value is kept outside the TPM. The sequence of extends on the history file must be done by software outside the TPM and then compared to the current PCR value in the TPM. Thus, the history file does not need to be protected, because the PCR values can be used to verify the accuracy of the history file.

What happens if a nefarious cracker manages to change the boot loader? The same sequence will go on, and the cracked boot loader may very well lie about which OS it is loading! However, the digest of the cracked boot loader will be recorded by BIOS before it is given control, and when the TPM is asked for the record of the boot sequence, one of two things will happen. Either the history file will match and verify that the boot loader used was not the one that was expected so that the boot will not be regarded as trusted, or the history file will not match, in which case the history file (and hence the boot) will not be regarded as trusted.

This is the difference between a secure boot (which will allow the machine to boot only into a trusted state) and a trusted boot (which securely reports on the state of the boot). The TPM does not prohibit booting into an insecure OS or using an insecure boot loader. It merely records information that can be used to determine if a boot sequence was performed by a trusted set of components. If an implementer wanted to enforce a secure boot, he could use the information in the TPM to do this by changing firmware, but this could be done without the TPM's help as well. Trusted boot—being able to prove that you booted in a secure way—is a much more interesting ability: The user is not restricted in how he boots and is able to prove that he booted in a particular way.

## Reporting the Boot Sequence Record

How can a person connecting to a remote computer over the Internet be sure that the values of the PCRs (which represent the boot sequence) he gets from the TPM are the current values? There are two answers to this question. The first involves identities, described later in this chapter, which provide the means for a TPM to sign the PCR values as coming from itself. However, the tester needs to know that he is getting current values, and not values that were recorded from a previous boot.

This is solved easily: Using a nonced query made to a system, you can receive an identity signed set of current PCR values. A *nonce* is a nonsense string or a random number that is sent as part of a challenge. By including the nonce in the signed return value, the challenger can be sure that the resultant signature is fresh. Use this technique to allow secure remote checking of the boot sequence that a system went through. A good use for such a query would be when a client is connecting to a remote server—the client will want to be sure the remote server has not been compromised and might transmit a virus to it. A remote system administrator will also be able to use this technique to check that a server has not been compromised. It should be noted, though, that remote verification can be done only by those authorized by the system's owner in order to protect privacy.

There are more slots for PCRs on a chip than are necessary for just secure booting, and additional PCRs can be used for other things. Some examples would be to verify that the machine ran a particular program as the first program run or to verify that an antivirus program was run with the current set of virus signatures. Once entered, any additional PCR values can also be queried remotely (with authorization).

This solution works fine for a remote user—but how does one do the same thing locally on one's own system? If you're at the keyboard, you may want to verify that the system is booted into a trusted state. Although you can use the same procedure as you would remotely, you have a different challenge. In a remote state, you're sitting at a secure computer presumably, asking it if a different system is in a secure state. If you're sitting at the keyboard, you are asking your computer if it has been hacked. If it has been hacked, it may very well lie about it. Verifying a signature is rather labor intensive, so it is unlikely that you will sit down and verify a signature by hand. However there are other techniques available in the TPM design to solve this problem, involving locking keys to a system state.

In addition to being used for simple reporting, signing keys and data can be "locked" to a PCR register (or registers) by indicating at creation which PCRs and what values they should have in them for that key or that data to be available to the user. This process is known as "sealing" the data to the system state. Because any PCR register can be extended at any time, it is possible to use this to allow an operating system or end user to gain access to data early in the process and then lock out access after the data is used. This is valuable, because early in the process, the PCR values are a pretty good guarantee that everything is behaving as it should. Additionally, a secret can be locked to PCRs that represent a secure boot. If you want to verify that the machine has booted securely, you can ask the computer for the encrypted value. If the encrypted value is released, then you know that the PCRs are in the correct state. This avoids having to verify a signature on a piece of paper.

Another capability of PCRs should be mentioned. When data is locked to a set of PCRs, the value of the PCRs is also recorded. Therefore, at a later time, it is possible to query what the status of a machine was when data was locked to the PCRs. This technique is like a signature, which can be used to pass data between two secure boots of a system, allowing the unsealing "machine state to determine the state the machine was in when the data was sealed."

Sealing can also be used to store encryption keys, which are used by a file system to encrypt/decrypt files. This then allows one of the other main uses of a TPM: enabling secure storage.

## Secure Storage

A second design goal of the TCG was to provide a means for storing both data and signing keys in a secure fashion. There are two different techniques used to store data objects. The first involves using a separate storage medium to store the data objects. In such a design, access control is exerted on the input and output pipes that lead to this storage, as in a bank vault. The second technique uses encryption to store data, and encryption and decryption to control access to that data. The first technique provides better control over denial of service attacks, as the data cannot be erased without access to the data. The second technique can be used to provide virtually unlimited amounts of secure storage and is much cheaper than the first technique. The second technique is the one we chose.

Although a TPM is somewhat similar to a smart card chip, one difference is that it is attached (through the PC) to a large amount of persistent storage. As a result, you can store a large amount of encrypted data that is associated with the TPM. One of the design goals for secure storage was to take advantage of this persistent storage to provide that the number of private keys, symmetric keys, and data that can be stored behind those keys by a TPM is virtually unlimited. If the PC has a persistent connection to the intranet/Internet, then remote storage may also be used.

This solution may appear to have a major problem, though. Whenever the amount of data that is locked to a single point of failure goes up, a design needs to take into account disaster recovery and upgradeability of the design. The TPM architecture provides for solutions to these problems, which are discussed later in the book under "Migratable and Non-Migratable Keys."

## Storing Data and Symmetric Keys

Although the TPM itself can store only small amounts of data in an encrypted blob, the symmetric key storage that is available can be used to extend the amount of data stored in a virtually unlimited way. You can store either asymmetric or symmetric keys in encrypted blobs. Asymmetric keys can be RSA keys of 1024 or 2048 bits. Symmetric keys of up to 256 bits can be stored in encrypted blobs by the TPM. These keys then can be used by software to encrypt files of any size. The symmetric algorithm that will use this key is the choice of the developer, but 256 bits was chosen so as to guarantee that AES (the Advanced Encryption Standard) could be used. Of course, any smaller amount can also be stored, so DES, 3xDES, RC4, Blowfish, and keys for any AES candidate can also be used. Although the specification was being written, AES had not yet been selected, but Rijndael has now been chosen for AES, and the free source code is available on the NIST web site at http://csrc.nist.gov/encryption/aes/rijndael/.

Hammering is an attack hackers use to try to get by security restrictions. It involves trying one password after another until eventually they try the correct one. Because of the anti-hammering capabilities of some 1.1 TPMs (and ALL 1.2 TPMs), using the TPM for storing these keys is much more secure against this attack than storing them hidden on the hard disk. The additional authorization techniques used to release a key also provide for some interesting possibilities for applications, which are detailed in later chapters—especially Chapters 6, 7, and 8.

Keys are formatted using PKCS#1 V2.0 (an algorithm well known to be resistant to cryptoanalytical attack), encrypted under a 2048-bit RSA storage key before being sent out of the TPM for storage on the hard disk. This provides strong protection when the keys are not inside the TPM.

Why doesn't the TPM do symmetric encryption or decryption of files rather than releasing the key to the general purpose processor to do the work? The answer is that it would not provide additional security. An attacker is not after the key. The attacker is after the contents of the file. If an attacker is in a position to grab a symmetric key once it is released from a TPM (with authorization), then the attacker is also in a position to grab the decrypted file, even if the TPM decrypted the file securely. As a result, there is no added security in having the TPM decrypt the file internally. (Actually, if the same symmetric key were to be used to encrypt large numbers of files, there would be an exposure—but standard security practice declares that every file should be encrypted with its own ephemeral key.) There could be added speed, but CPU speeds are increasing so rapidly, that it is unlikely that a TPM could keep up with the processing power embedded in the CPU. Further, accelerated symmetric key encryption such as that employed in IPSec can be handled well on the NIC card, thus providing guarantees that the IP traffic that leaves the system is encrypted.

## Storing Asymmetric Keys

Several kinds of asymmetric keys can also be stored using the TPM. These include 512-, 1024-, and 2048-bit RSA keys, keys generated outside the TPM, keys generated inside the TPM, keys that can be cloned and migrated to other TPMs (with permission, of course), and keys that cannot be migrated to other systems. Only keys that are generated in the TPM can be non-migratable, which are more secure. Migratable keys can also be generated in the TPM, though they are inherently less secure. Non-migratable keys can never be decrypted except by a TPM, and their use for signing can only take place inside a TPM. Keys are stored using a minimum of 2048-bit RSA public keys, which can only be used for storing keys and sealing data. The format used to store a key is PKCS#1 V2.0.

## Authorization

A TPM enables different kinds of authorization for different capabilities, but at first the TPM specification appears to be inflexible in its design. However, by mixing and matching the different authorization, one is able to accomplish many types of authorization that at first glance appear to be missing. Even "no-auth" keys can be created (keys that can be used without providing an authorization), though those are required to actually have an authorization due to the way one of the protocols (the Object Specific Authorization Protocol or OSAP) works. To handle this problem, there is a "well-known secret" specified in the header file. In order to produce a key that requires a single authorization per boot (which does not appear to be a capability in the specification), one can lock a key to an unused PCR value equaling a value obtained by extending a password into that PCR.

The defined "well-known secret" authorization value allows software to use a known-auth valued key by merely knowing this value, which resides in the header file. This allows a number of interesting structures to be built. For example, consider the structure of a daisy chain in which one storage key, associated with a user, has a nontrivial password. That key has a child storage key that has a known-auth password. All of the user's other keys are nonstorage keys and are stored under the child storage key.

In this case, upon booting, the user has to provide his password to load the child storage key. But once the child storage key is loaded into the chip, no further passwords are required to LOAD other keys (using them is a different matter). Of course, if the base storage key is evicted from the TPM, then authorization will be required to load it again—unless the TPM supports a function called "SaveContext," which is optional in the 1.1 specification but mandatory in the 1.2 specification.

As a result, a key manager can do its work without requiring a user's intervention to keep keys loaded in the chip before they are used. Upon a power cycle, the child key would disappear and would have to be reloaded, requiring you to re-enter his password. The concept to remember here is that loading a key is an operation authorized by the parent key, not the child key, since the user is using the parent private key to load the child key.

As a result, we now have key structures that can provide any of the following:

- Require authorization every time a key is loaded or used.
- Require a key only for use (not for loading).
- Require a key once per power on.
- Do not require a key.

After the TPM has determined that authorization of a key is necessary according to policy, there are different kinds of authorization that can be required. There is a usage authorization, which is sort of like a 160-bit pin. The 160 bits were chosen to be directly compatible with the SHA-1 (Secure Hash Algorithm 1) hash of a pass phrase. Additionally, the TPM may require that certain PCR of the TPM contain specific values. These PCRs were discussed earlier in this chapter under the section "Securely Reporting the Environment: Platform Status."

We now have an even more complicated set of possibilities: a four-parameter set with each parameter able to take on two values—yes or no. This leads to 16 possibilities, not all of which are useful. The four parameters are as follows:

- Is a PCR needed to load the key?
- Is a PCR needed to use the key?
- Is usage authorization information (a pass phrase) needed to load the key?
- Is usage authorization information (a pass phrase) needed to use the key?

A realistic usage model is presented in Table 2.1.

**Table 2.1**  Usage Model

| Key Type | Loading | Usage |
| --- | --- | --- |
| Storage | Null | Null |
| Signature | Null | Pass phrase (each time) |
| Signature | Null | PCR locked |
| Signature | Null | PCR locked and pass phrase (each time) |
| BindKey | Null | PCR locked |
| BindKey | Null | Pass phrase (each time) |
| BindKey | Null | PCR locked and pass phrase (each time) |
| BindInternalUsageKey | Null | Null |

In this way, storage keys are used to control the loading features of the other keys, and the keys themselves control the usage of those keys. This is one common usage model, although some designs only have controls on the base storage key. Once that has been authorized, all other keys can be loaded and used without requiring authorization.

One more note here: You may want to have your base SRK key require authorization to provide a defense against a power analysis attack if the system is stolen. However, because the SRK key is used a lot, it would be annoying to the end user if he had to input authorization every time the SRK is used. So, it would be ideal if you could create an SRK that only required authorization one time per boot sequence. This can be accomplished by a trick: You lock the SRK to a

PCR (for example, 15 for 1.1 or 16 for a 1.2 TPM). You choose the value to lock the SRK to be the result when a password is extended into that PCR. Now during or after the boot sequence, you ask for the password, extend it into the PCR, and from then on, the SRK is useable without asking for an additional authorization. This trick can be used to apply to any key; however, you then have to protect the PCR from being further extended by other software, probably by asking the OS for help.

Another way of accomplishing the same thing for a key lower in the tree than the SRK can be done with a different trick. A storage key that requires a pass phrase is used to store a storage key or use key that does NOT require a pass phrase. Then when the system is booted, the pass phrase is necessary to load the first storage key, but not the second storage key. In the event that one is using a 1.2 TPM, the second key can then be cached out of the TPM and reloaded without requiring the first key to be loaded in the chip.

In addition, for certain specialized functions, such as migration, more authorization is required, as control for the operation is split between the owner of the TPM and the owner of another key. Migration is broken into two different pieces: authorization to migrate a key, and authorization for the public key to which it is being migrated. Although this made the design of the TPM more difficult, it generates a number of opportunities for third-party vendors to back up data without the owner of the data worrying about it being susceptible to exposure.

Allowing migration of keys is an operation that inherently creates some risk of private key exposure, but the split authorization design helps protect even migratable keys. Even the owner of a key cannot recover his private key without the cooperation of the owner of the TPM using migration data blobs.

Asymmetric keys can be authorized in many ways, but not all of them can be authorized to do the same things. Additionally, the TPM checks to make certain that a key itself is allowed to perform a particular operation.

## Secure Signatures

Asymmetric keys come in many flavors. One way to differentiate between keys is via their usage. Some keys are used to store other keys, while some keys store data. They are called storage keys or binding keys, and they cannot be used to perform signatures. It is considered bad form to use keys for both storage and signatures because in some sense, storing a key with the public portion of a key and signing data with the private portion of a key are inverse operations. A design that allows for both operations to be performed by a single key pair needs to be careful that data cannot be decrypted by signing the encrypted version of the data. Although the TPM design does allow for a key blob to be used for both storage and signing (for use with "legacy keys"), the design was still made resistant to this type of attack. However, it is recommended that legacy keys not be used unless they are required to retrofit to already designed software.

The security of a signing key also comes in many flavors. First, there is the strength of the key itself. For backward compatibility and for speed reasons, the TPM will support smaller key sizes for signing keys (not for storage keys). However, 2048-bit RSA keys (which were only used by the military when the spec was written) are fully supported. Migratable keys are inherently less secure than non-migratable keys, because migratable keys can, with joint authorization of the TPM owner and the key owner, be migrated to other TPMs or to insecure keys, thus exposing them to attack.

Keys that are imported into the TPM obviously are viewed as suspect by the TPM, no matter how securely they were generated. Thus, they are marked as migratable keys, and they cannot be certified by the TPM.

Non-migratable signing keys are linked to the platform on which their TPM exists. As a result, they can be used to identify the platform on which they are being used. However, there needed to be a way to make that linkage clear to a remote entity. This was done with a secure identity key.

## Secure Identity

During the generation of the TPM specification, it became obvious that for a TPM to be used to the greatest extent, it was necessary that it be possible to prove a given key was a non-migratable TPM key. There is value in having a signing key for a TPM that can be proven to have only existed for this TPM and never outside this TPM. This was tricky for a number of reasons:

- No signing keys are in the TPM until generated at the bequest of the end user.
- Privacy restrictions keep signing keys from being associated with a given system.

The final solution involved having each TPM generate a unique endorsement key, which was in turn certified by the manufacturer. Endorsement keys can be a privacy problem, but these are hamstrung so that they cannot be used either for signing or for encrypting. Instead, they can only be used to decrypt certificates of other TPM-generated keys, and this can only be done at the request of the owner of the TPM cooperating with a certificate authority (CA).

These latter keys, called identities, in turn can only be used for two purposes: to create certificates for other non-migratable keys or to sign PCRs, to prove they are the correct and current values. Although the CA could theoretically keep track of a 1:1 correspondence between identity keys and endorsement keys, an end user can choose his CA to be one that promises not to. Additionally, he can hide his request with multiple requests to a CA with the same identity but multiple endorsement keys, only one of which is real. And once the identity certificate is created, it does not have any link back to an endorsement key.

Identity keys are used to identify a platform, but if their authorization is known only to one user, they also can be used to identify a user, to give him access to a service. This then requires a means of isolating the keys used by different users on the same system.

## Isolation of Users in a Multiple User Environment

Here's one question that often comes up when discussing the TPM design (and particularly non-migratable keys): Why can't the end user get access to the base encryption key in the TPM (known as the SRK or Storage Root Key)? The reason for this fundamental design decision was twofold. The first reason is that one of the main attacks hackers use to get into a system is a "social attack," where the hacker convinces the end user to give him something that defeats their security. If the end user doesn't know the base secret, he can't give it away. Similar reasons are used to keep private keys in smartcards from being exposed to their owner.

The second reason is to provide protection to the end user against a rogue IT administrator. Multiple people may be using a system, and it is important that they not have access to each other's data (and especially keys). If one person had access to the SRK, he would also therefore have access to all the keys on the system! There is also a more subtle security problem: If you know one or more passwords a user is using, it is likely that you can figure out the pattern they use to create passwords—and then the passwords they use for their personal bank account may be compromised.

One use case we considered was the situation where a company gives a laptop to an employee to use when traveling. Because it is unlikely that the traveler will bring two laptops along with him (one for business and one for personal business), it is more than likely that the end user will use the business computer for personal business. In that case, the personal data stored on that computer should not be accessible to the business. In particular, things like bank account numbers, passwords, and so on are not any concern of the business. All the architects of the TPM specification have laptops and are very familiar with this concern. In this case, the TPM design protects the user's privacy from the IT administrator.

Another use case is that of the "kiosk" computer that you rent for a set period of time. This computer may be compromised. It is particularly important that such a computer have a way of using secure data in a secure way. If a user's keys are used on a TPM on such a computer, the keys remain secure even if the machine's software has been compromised.

A third problem is "hotelling." In this situation, a company has 500 employees but only 300 PCs. Thus, when an employee needs to use a computer, he sits down at an empty computer and wants to use it as though it is his own. In this case, it is important that the employees have access to their OWN keys securely—but that employees don't have access to each other's data.

There are other reasons as well to have keys that are not externally accessible. One is to use a key to identify the machine as opposed to the person using it. Consider a network in which certain computers exist behind guards and locked doors. In this case, knowing the computer doing communication can give the user some idea of the security of that computer. If the key were knowable, then there is no way to trust that the computer is the one which has a known security state.

For keys to be secure, they need to be securely generated. There is an old joke that the only truly random number is 17. However, if all the keys generated by a TPM were from a small subset of those possible, the keys could be easily broken. It is clear, therefore, that the TPM needs to have an internal random number generator.

## Internal Random Number Generation

In order to generate keys internally, it is necessary for the TPM to have an internal random number generator (RNG). Typically, instead of having a true random number generator (which is difficult to do), many TPMs will have pseudo random number generators (PRNGs) that are periodically fed with entropy from timing measurements or other sources of entropy within the TPM itself. This entropy is then distilled into the current seed, so entropy is always increasing. The output of the PRNG or RNG is used to generate keys, nonces, and seeds in the PKCS#1 V2.0 blob creation.

However, random numbers have a more general applicability than simply being used to generate keys. In particular, random numbers have a very good use in Monte Carlo routines, which use random changes in possible solutions to quickly determine a "good enough" solution to very hard problems. One very useful problem that can only be solved this way is determining the route that a school bus should take in picking up children and dropping them off at a school. That problem is often solved using a simulated annealing procedure, which mimics the motion of the atoms in a metal as they find their strongest position as a metal is annealed. The random motion of the atoms is similar to the changes in the solutions produced by random numbers.

Nevertheless, there are a couple of things that need to be kept in mind when using the TPM random number generator. First, it should be kept well fed with entropy. For example, every time the TPM is used, the time can be fed into the TPM random number generator. This may not be necessary, but security guys tend to have a healthy paranoia. Second, the generator is not likely to be particularly fast, so it probably won't be possible to feed a Monte Carlo routine from it directly. Some manufacturers may cache random numbers for internal uses, but it will not be particularly good at streaming random numbers such as is required by a Monte Carlo routine. Instead, it is better used to create periodic seeds into a software pseudo random generator, which in turn is used by the Monte Carlo routine. This provides both additional randomness for the routine, and also speed.

## Features Not Included

During the design, a number of features were considered and then dropped from the requirements for one reason or another. One of these was a secure clock. Although it would have been a useful feature for the TPM to have, a secure timing feature was dropped due to cost concerns. It has been resurrected (in part) in the 1.2 design, though it needs to be reset every time power is lost. No requirement for the TPM to have a battery is ever likely to be in any specification. A symmetric key engine also fell by the wayside. It would not have provided additional security to a PC to have symmetric key decryption done inside the chip, and it would have made export and input of the chip difficult. Algorithms that are considered secure are not secret, and the output of the decryption, which is the thing an attacker should really be interested in, would be in the clear in any event. One possible advantage to a symmetric engine would be speed, but the new AES candidates (and Rijndael, the selected one) are all designed to run fast in software, much mitigating the need for a symmetric accelerator.

There are also concerns with providing generic bulk encryption in a piece of hardware because of export and import regulations. For this reason, all symmetric operations performed by the TPM are not easily usable by the end user for basic bulk encryption, but rather are specific to the function being performed.

Missing also is a secure location in which to run arbitrary code. Although this is a nice feature (and one provided in Javacards), it was considered expensive, and also it might lead to fairly easy DRM use cases—something some of us wanted to avoid.

There is no inherent signing key in the chip. An end user can't boot a system with access to a signing key with a 1.1 chip at all. Such a key has to be loaded into the TPM before it can be used. In 1.2, it is possible for the owner to fix a key inside the TPM so that it can be used later.

Additionally, it isn't possible to use elliptic curve cryptography with a TPM, and the hash algorithm used internally to the TPM is fixed to be SHA-1. Both of those things are likely to change in the future.

## Security Analysis

In order to provide a proper evaluation of the security of various protocols described herein, it is helpful to have some notation available to keep track of vulnerabilities. In Table 2.2, we define different types of knowledge an attacker may have and how it can affect the vulnerability of various keys. Table 2.3 presents the types of attacks in which an attacker may engage.

**Table 2.2**   Types of Knowledge

| Symbol | Description |
| --- | --- |
| $A_c$ | Administrator of chip, c |
| $O_k$ | Owner of key, k |
| $U_k$ | User of key, k |
| $P_k$ | Passphrase to use key, k |
| $M_k$ | Passphrase to migrate (a migratable) key, k |
| $AU_c$ | Passphrase used to authorize a target migration public key for a chip, c |
| $R_k$ | Random number used to complete migration of a migration blob for key, k |
| $W_k$ | Wrapped key blob for key, k |
| $MB_k$ | Migration key blob for key, k |
| $PR_k$ | The private portion of a key, k |
| $PA(k)$ | Parent of key, k |

**Table 2.3**   Types of Attacks

| Symbol | Description |
| --- | --- |
| $T_1$ | Type 1 attack: Attacker gains knowledge of $P_k$ |
| $T_2$ | Type 2 attack: Attacker gains knowledge of the private key $PR_k$ |
| $T_3$ | Type 3 attack: Attacker gains ability to track a PC without the user's knowledge |

Although it is possible that a user of a key may also be both the owner of the key and the administrator of the chip, this may not always be the case. In general, the following are statistically true statements. (It is theoretically possible to violate some of these, but it appears to be computationally infeasible.)

1. $O_k$ knows $P_k$ and $M_k$ (if it is a migratable key) and $R_k$ (if it is migrated key).
2. $A_k$ knows $AU_c$.
3. $U_k$ knows $P_k$.

Table 2.4 presents the knowledge necessary to attack keys in the TPM.

**Table 2.4**   Table of Knowledge Necessary to Attack Keys in the TPM

| $W_k$ | $P_k$ | $M_k$ | $PA(k)$ | $PR_k$ | $MB_k$ | $R_k$ | $AU_k$ | $P_{PA9(k)}$ | T1 | T2 |
|---|---|---|---|---|---|---|---|---|---|---|
| X | | | | | | | | | | |
| | x | | | | | | | | | |
| | | x | | | | | | | | |
| | | | x | | | | | | | |
| | | | | X | | | | | I | I |
| | | | | | x | | | | | |
| | | | | | | x | | | | |
| | | | | | | | x | | | |
| | | | | | | | | x | | |
| X | x | | | | | | x | | I | |
| X | C | C | x | C | | | | | I | I |
| X | x | | | | | | | | | |
| X | | | | | | | | X | | |
| | x | | | | | | | x | | |
| X | C | x | C | C | | | x | x | I | I |
| C | C | C | x | C | x | x | | | I | I |
| | x | x | x | | x | x | x | | | |
| X | | | | | x | x | x | | | |
| X | x | | | | x | x | x | | I | |

Table of attacks for migratable keys: x represents initial data; C = consequent data; I = implied attack.

A number of things become clear immediately. If an administrator of the chip and the owner of a migratable key collaborate, the key is not secure. However, an administrator and a user collaborating cannot recover the key. (A user can, of course, give other people the ability to use the chip.)

The table of attacks for non-migratable keys, k, is much more simple: If you can load a key and know its usage password, you can use it. There is no way to obtain the private key short of a hardware attack. Any hardware attack that can retrieve any private non-migratable key can by implication also unwrap and expose any non-migratable descendent key.

Strangely enough, this does not imply that any migratable key is exposed. If a key is locked per the section on super secure migratable storage, it is not possible to expose that key without also knowing a random string.

## Summary

The design goals of the TCG committee in designing the TPM took advantage of its location inside a system in two ways. It used the other facilities of the platform to provide unlimited secure storage, and it used its unique position so that the platform could record its boot sequence in the TPM in a trusted way. Once these two major decisions were made, the rest of the design decisions were made so as to create maximum flexibility for the design. Both asymmetric and symmetric keys can be securely packaged by the chip, and use can be locked to one of system state, authentication data, or the use of a parent key. In order to have strong keys, a random number generator was incorporated. In order to implement secure signatures, signing could take place inside the chip. Last, in order to provide a means to prove to a remote entity that your system was secure, secure identities were added to the design. In the next chapter, we will see how these ideas were actually implemented.

# CHAPTER 3

# An Overview of the Trusted Platform Module Capabilities

Now that we have had a chance to look at the design goals of the TPM, we next turn to discussing how they were implemented in the design. There were several key issues that needed to be decided. These included the following:

- **Secure storage:** How the TPM can use an unlimited number of keys with a small chip using a daisy chain design. This design shows the environment in which the TPM was assumed to be running, so it is important to understand.

- **Migratable and non-migratable keys:** How keys can move from PC to PC—or not.

- **Key types:** The types of keys the TPM can use and create.

- **Platform status:** How a Trusted PC utilizes the TPM to securely record and report the platform status using Platform Configuration Registers.

- **Maintenance:** How to recover keys in case a machine dies.

- **Identity keys with privacy:** How to prove remotely that records reported by a TPM come from a TPM.

- **Secure signatures:** How to keep signatures secure and private.

Each one of these topics is discussed in detail in this chapter.

## Secure Storage: The Storage Root Key

When a TPM comes to a new user, it typically does not include anything other than an endorsement key (EK). (The EK is used by a user when he wants to prove to a second party that a key generated in the TPM was generated in a genuine TPM.) This is for both security and privacy reasons. Shipping with an EK provides a service to the end user only if it also comes with a certificate from the TPM vendor and/or the platform vendor. If no certificate is provided with the EK, then there is no added security when compared to a TPM where the end user will initiate creation of the EK himself.

Upon activating the TPM (or upon reset), the TPM will use its random number generator to create a new base 2048-bit RSA key. This key is special, as it is the only key that is guaranteed to always be present in the chip. It is non-migratable and a storage key. We decided to call it a storage root key (SRK) instead of a root storage key, because we didn't like the acronym RSK (risk) applied to security. SRK (Shark) sounds much better. The SRK is required to be non-migratable and to be a 2048 (or greater) storage key, but other parameters are left to the end user. This includes whether authorization is required to use the key and what that authorization is. This can also include if any PCRs are required to use the key (although this would make the design pretty inflexible).

The SRK is the root of all the key chains described later; if it is lost, all the non-migratable and non-migrated keys are consequently lost. In order to mitigate loss of the SRK, there is a maintenance procedure that can be done with the cooperation of both the owner of the TPM and the manufacturer of the TPM, which can restore the SRK to another system. However, there are some caveats to this maintenance procedure, as follows:

- The maintenance procedure is not a required TPM function.
- The capability to perform this maintenance procedure can be turned off by the owner.
- Once turned off, the only way to restore the maintenance facility is to reset the TPM to a virgin state.
- The manufacturer will not perform maintenance unless he is convinced the first TPM is dead.
- Neither the manufacturer nor the owner is able to perform the migration alone.
- The recommended procedure does not expose the actual SRK to either the manufacturer or the TPM owner.

Although this is an allowable procedure in the spec, it is optional, and no one has (so far) implemented this part of the spec.

Storage keys are keys that are used to store other keys. They store keys by encrypting a new key and its attendant header information with the public portion of a storage key. Storage keys can be used to store other storage keys or signing keys, as shown in the daisy chain chart. However, they cannot be used to sign. For a storage key to be used, it needs to be resident in the TPM. Only the SRK is guaranteed to always be in the TPM.

Figure 3.1 shows the basic setup of keys inside a TPM. In the figure, if Key 2 is directly below Key 1, then Key 2 is encrypted (wrapped) with the public key corresponding to Key 1. Thus, we see that User 1 migratable storage is wrapped with the platform migratable key, which is in turn wrapped with the SRK. User 1's non-migratable storage key is also wrapped with the SRK.

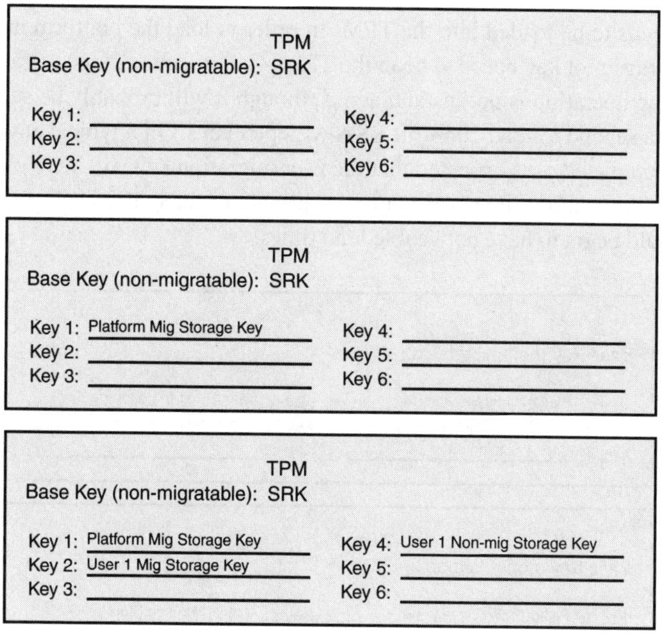

**Figure 3.1**   Basic key structure

Initially, only the SRK is loaded in the TPM. In this design, it and all general-purpose storage keys will not require authorization to use them. It is a non-migratable key stored in non-volatile storage (usually NVRAM) inside the TPM chip. The first key that gets loaded into the chip after the machine is booted is usually a platform migratable key. This key, usually owned by the system administrator, has the well-known secret for its authorization, but requires the system owner's authorization to migrate. If it is migrated, all other migratable keys (which in this design will be children or grandchildren of this key) will also be migrated.

After the platform migratable key is loaded, a user can load his base migratable storage key and his base non-migratable storage key because the TPM now knows the private portion of the platform migratable key necessary to decrypt the user migratable key.

If a user wants to move just his own keys to a new platform, the user base migratable key is the only key that needs to be migrated. This key will not require authorization to use but will require authorization to migrate. There is no base platform non-migratable storage key—the SRK is used in its place. There is, however, a base user non-migratable storage key. This is used to organize all the non-migratable keys owned by a particular owner.

This daisy chain structure is only three deep, but there is no theoretical reason it could not be much, much deeper. However, there is a practical reason not to make the structure too deep. In order to load User1 binding key 1 at the bottom left of Figure 3.2, the User 1 migrate storage key has to be loaded into the TPM. In order to load the User 1 migrate key into the TPM, the platform migration key needs to be loaded into the TPM. In order to load the platform migration key into the TPM, the storage root key needs to be in the TPM—but of course, it is guaranteed to be in the TPM. The loading operation is not instantaneous, though it will probably be sub-second. (Older TPMs may take a second to load 2048-bit RSA wrapped keys.) In a typical environment, by the time a logon is completed, it is expected that the user migration key will be loaded into the TPM, ready for use, so the loading time will not be noticeable to the end user. But a very deep daisy chain of keys could begin to have noticeable load times.

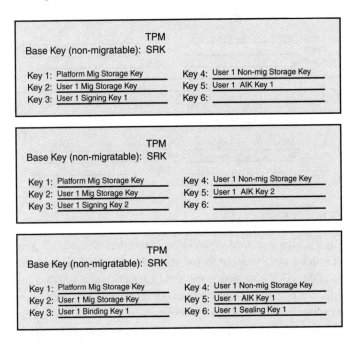

**Figure 3.2**    Example "leaf" keys

Once these three keys are loaded into the TPM, any other user keys can be loaded into the TPM. These keys, called "leaf" keys, are used to sign data or messages, or decrypt symmetric keys. Of course, it may be the case that there isn't enough room to load all the keys into the TPM simultaneously, but in that case the TSS will evict keys as necessary and reload them when necessary.

Figure 3.1 also illustrates that a software designer will typically design the key hierarchy so that the TPM will typically have two daisy chain structures hanging from it. The one on the left consists entirely of migratable keys, described in detail in the next section. The one on the right consists mainly, but not necessarily entirely, of non-migratable keys. That will also be described in some detail in the next section. The important point is that the daisy chain structure depicted in Figure 3.1 need not be followed exactly. Figures 3.3 and 3.4 depict other uses.

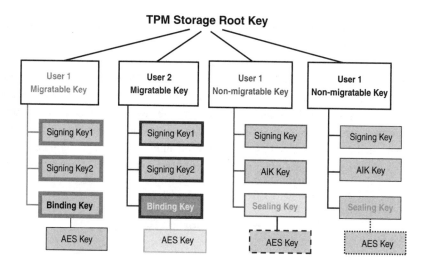

**Figure 3.3** TPM storage root key

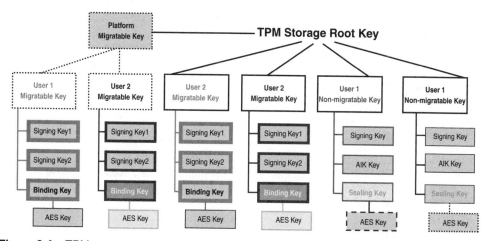

**Figure 3.4** TPM storage root key and platform migratable key

In Figure 3.3, we see a multiple daisy chain structure, with each user having control over the migration of his own keys. The advantage of this structure is exactly that: There is no IT administrator who owns the platform migratable key in the previous structure and who can migrate all the keys willy-nilly. The disadvantage to this structure is that if the machine dies, each user will have to have acted the part of an administrator and have migrated and saved his root key for migration to a new system.

In Figure 3.4, we see a mix of the two styles. Here we have keys that an administrator who owns the platform migration key can move, some user migratable keys that the user is responsible for, and of course some non-migratable keys. Which structure is picked depends on what you need to accomplish. If you have a single user machine, with the user also being the owner, a very simple structure is probably ideal. If a machine is shared among a large number of employees, but owned by an IT organization, Figure 3.4 is probably ideal. Because the TPM doesn't know (or care) how the keys are created, it is even possible for different software to see different key hierarchies.

In Figure 3.5, we see a variation on an earlier structure. Here we have a key owned jointly by User 1 and a vendor. When creating a virtual dongle, a key could be locked inside a specific user's chain of non-migratable keys and yet be a migratable key whose migration is controlled by the owner of the software. The owner of the software would not typically ever migrate from the copy of the key on the user's platform, so the migration authorization data might be 160 bits chosen randomly. (This usage is described in more detail in Chapter 13, "Trusted Computing and Secure Identification.")

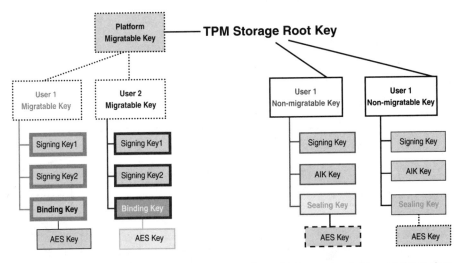

**Figure 3.5**    Prominent in all these architectures are keys that are migratable and those that are non-migratable. The differences between the keys lend flexibility to the architecture in solving different kinds of problems.

## Migratable Versus Non-Migratable Keys

Migratable keys are meant for two purposes. The first is to provide a quick way to transfer keys from one platform to another in the event that a user is changing systems, either because of upgrade or other reasons. The second is to provide the capability for more than one system to use a key. Keys can be valuable if they have associated certificates, or store a lot of data, so this is a requirement. For example, if a key is used for signing e-mail, a person might want to use it at home and at work or on multiple systems. A key that is used to store symmetric keys might be shared among a group, so only members of that group have access to the keys necessary to decrypt a shared file.

Migration entails having the TPM unwrap the private portion with one parent key and rewrap it with a different parent key. The TPM can tell a migratable key from a non-migratable key and will refuse to migrate a non-migratable key. Only the owner of the TPM (typically the administrator) can choose the new public key, but the TPM will only migrate a key if the owner of the key itself authorizes the action using the `migration_auth` of the key being migrated.

Migratable keys can be generated inside or outside the TPM and wrapped with any storage key, migratable or non-migratable. The design in Figure 3.5 is nice because all the migratable keys in the left-hand tree can be migrated by the simple migration of the platform migratable key. This saves an end user from needing to migrate all his keys individually. However, it also means that the end user has to be careful to understand who owns all of the ancestor keys of a key he is creating. If any ancestor key is migrated, then the descendent keys are also effectively migrated at the same time. Of course, if an end user uses a non-migratable key for his parent key, he need not worry about unauthorized migration of his key—his newly created key becomes the root migratable key of the key string in which it exists.

Control of public keys to which a key is migrated is important because the TPM has no way of checking if a public key it is given corresponds to a safely hidden private key. It is the responsibility of the owner of the TPM to decide what public keys are safe for usage as the new wrap key. In the event that the keys are simply being migrated between TPMs, this is easy. But in the event that a machine dies, a backup migration key can be used to migrate first to a middle machine and then to a final machine—a two-step process that can still be done in a secure manner.

Non-migratable keys have to be generated inside a TPM. Upon generation by the TPM, they are marked by the TPM in such a way that the TPM can recognize them as its own non-migratable key wrapped with a non-migratable key. (Clearly, non-migratable keys cannot be wrapped with migratable keys, as they would then become migratable.) This is enforced by the TPM as non-migratable keys that can only be created by the TPM and only when the parent key is present.

Non-migratable keys can be used for multiple purposes. They can be used to identify a machine. They can be used to store migratable keys in such a way that they cannot be further migrated. They can also be used as identities of people. Indeed, in any application where the security of the private key needs to be guaranteed by the TPM, only non-migratable keys can be used in the ancestry of that key.

Of course, this extra security comes with a price tag; if the machine is ever upgraded, new non-migratable identities and storage keys will have to be generated.

Non-migratable keys are also not meant to be clonable, so it is not possible to have a non-migratable key on two separate systems simultaneously. It is possible that such keys could be used as virtual dongles, to ensure a one-to-one correspondence between software and hardware, but this would require a lot of software on top beyond what the TPM itself can do.

## Types of Keys

Although keys can be broadly characterized as migratable or non-migratable, they also can be classified by other aspects of their functionality. It is well known in cryptographic circles that it is a bad practice to use the same key to provide two different functions. There have been famous cracks of cryptographic systems due to a key being used for both storage and for signing. The TPM keeps track of what functionality a key is intended for when it is created, to avoid these types of cryptographic breaks. Here we describe the various types of keys that can be created and distinguished by a TPM.

## Storage Keys

*Storage keys* are keys that are used to store other things, be it another storage, binding, or signature key. They do not store symmetric keys. Storage keys are 2048 bit-RSA private keys and can be either migratable or non-migratable. Storage is normally done via PKCS#1 V2.0, but in some cases, for backward compatibility, a legacy key can be used for storage using PKCS#1 V1.5. In this case, a key is created especially to handle this interface. This storage key will NOT store data using PKCS#1 V2.0, as there is a security concern if a key is to be used for both PKCS#1 version 2.0 and version 1.5.

## Binding Keys

*Binding keys* are keys that are meant to be used to store symmetric keys. They can be used to store a single symmetric key or to store many symmetric keys. The point is that a binding key is meant to do basic RSA encryption and as such, it doesn't make sense to encrypt anything other than a symmetric key.

## Identity Keys

*Identity keys* are special non-migratable signing keys that are generated inside the TPM and then provided with a certificate via the long involved process that preserves privacy of the owner. Identity keys have only two functions: to sign PCRs when a request is made to the TPM and to sign other keys as being non-migratable. This provides a daisy chain of certificates: the first certificate from the CA that guarantees the identity is a TPM identity, and the identity key provides a certificate that the second key is a non-migratable TPM storage key.

Identity keys are always created with the SRK as the parent, as this further guarantees that the identities only exist for the given TPM. The obvious point to note here is that when the owner is cleared in the TPM, the identities are also destroyed.

## Signature Keys

*Signature keys* are standard RSA signature keys, which can be of a variety of lengths. The largest size a TPM is guaranteed to be able to handle is 2048 bits, which should be well above the size necessary to guarantee security unless there is a major breakthrough in cryptanalysis or a large quantum computer becomes feasible.

At this point, you may wonder if all the functionality of a TPM is present in a security token. After all, many security tokens (such as the common access card used by the U.S. Government) contain a public/private key pair. If this were the case, a TPM would still provide cost advantages of not requiring a reader for the token, but in fact there are other advantages to having a TPM in a PC.

# Platform Integrity

One distinct difference between a PC with an embedded TPM and a PC that has a removable crypto token inserted is that the TPM can be guaranteed to be present when the machine is booted. As a result, it is possible to use the TPM to validate a log that is a record of how the machine booted. The TPM was designed specifically to allow this, using Platform Configuration Registers. In addition, when a new owner takes over a machine, there needs to be a way to reset a TPM, through a handoff procedure. This preserves the privacy and secrecy of the original owner. A third difference is that with the TPM attached to a motherboard, no reader is necessary. The user isn't required to put his security token into an untrusted reader device that may be using power analysis or RF analysis to extracts its secrets. If the LPC bus on which the TPM exists is tampered with, it is highly likely that the user will know. Of course, this also means that the driver may be sniffed by bad software—but the design of the chip prevents any of the data so gained to be useful to an attacker.

A fourth difference is that with the TPM attached to a motherboard, there is the possibility that the motherboard will die. In this case, some users may require that a maintenance action be taken that could re-enable all their keys. Of course, they would want to make certain that the procedure did not expose any of their secrets. This was also implemented in the specification but as an optional set of commands. (This procedure requires the user to make a doubly encrypted backup of his SRK—once with his own encryption and once with the manufacturer's public key.) After this, the manufacturer decrypts the outer encryption, and then re-encrypts the result with the SRK of a new TPM. The manufacturer sends the result to the user. The user then passes this encrypted blob to the new TPM, along with information allowing it to internally decrypt the old SRK, which is used to replace the new one. The end result is a procedure that does not expose the SRK to either the user or the manufacturer.

## Platform Configuration Registers

Platform Configuration Registers (PCRs) are memory regions on the TPM. When the machine is first powered on, they register all zeros. However, they can be changed through an "extend" operation, which concatenates a value to the current value of the PCR, and then performs a SHA-1 hash of the concatenation, replacing the current value of the PCR with the result of the operation. A history file is kept externally of the values that have been extended into the PCR. Because a SHA-1 hash is essentially irreversible, the value in the PCR can be used to verify the values stored in the history table.

A TPM is guaranteed to have at least 16 PCRs, though it may have more. Theoretically, a TPM would only need one PCR value for verifying all the values in a history table, but PCRs are used for more than just the verification of the history table, so several of the PCRs are used during the booting process.

Various platform-specific specifications from TCG define what some of the PCRs are to be used for. In a PC, they are defined as in Table 3.1.

**Table 3.1**  Platform Configuration Register Standard Usage

| PCR | Use |
| --- | --- |
| 0 | Core BIOS, POST BIOS, Embedded Option ROMS |
| 1 | Motherboard configuration |
| 2 | Option ROM code |
| 3 | Option ROM configuration data |
| 4 | IPL code |
| 5 | IPL configuration data |
| 6 | State transition (sleep, hibernate, and so on) |
| 7 | Reserved for OEM |
| 8–15 | Not assigned |

PCRs can be used in a fashion similar to passwords in that the TPM will refuse to use a signing key or release a symmetric key unless the PCRs have a value that matches the value inside the TPM. Unlike a password, the value is easily read but not easily set.

On a PC, when the boot finishes and the kernel of the OS has control of the system, the kernel can verify if it is in a known state by reading a value (or using a key to sign a random value) that is locked to a known PCR value or set of values. If this value is available (or this key can be signed with), then the OS can conclude the PCR values are in the required state.

It is possible to infer that a machine is in a state consistent with a certain set of PCR values if it is able to decrypt a particular value that was locked to that PCR state. It is also possible to prove it is in that state by obtaining a signature signed with a nonce. Signing is stronger than the value release, though, as it might be possible for a rogue person to obtain the released data during an earlier session and pretend to decrypt the value locked to the PCR values. The private key is never released, however, so a signature cannot be spoofed.

Of course, the OS or any user can request the TPM to give it a signed statement as to the values in the PCRs. Because this uses a nonce, it is known as a "fresh" value of the PCRs and not a stored value that has been replayed.

After the OS has finished loading, the PCR values can still be extended. This can be used to lock away values that were read during boot or keys that were available during the boot sequence. After a PCR is extended, it is in a different state, so its keys and data locked to the previous state will no longer be accessible from the TPM. Of course, any copies of data released by the TPM would have to be erased or held in another secure place if they are to be truly inaccessible.

The preceding example illustrates the transition from a PCs POST to an OS loader to the OS itself. The concept can be used in any system where the control is passed from one module to the next. Before the module is handed control, the module is measured. Any module in the chain of control can "quote," or sign the PCRs, which reflect the current state of the system to determine if the state is a good value.

In order that the values stored in the PCRs can be trusted, a daisy chain of trust is created among the PCR values. The first PCR value refers to a section of the BIOS that gets control first, and is considered immutable. It is called the "static core root of trust of measurement," or CRTM (or SRTM). This code records the value of the next section of code into PCR0 before it passes control of the CPU on to that section of code. Similar record/handoff takes place with code all the way up to the handoff to the kernel of the OS. In this way, the PCRs can be regarded as a historical record of the state of the system.

In version 1.2 of the TPM specification, new PCR values 16–23 have been added; they are used similarly for measuring trusted code that is loaded later in the system. This measurement is done by a dynamic root of trust of measurement, also known as a DRTM.

## The Handoff Procedure

The handoff procedure between different owners of a TPM can be done in a number of ways. The easiest and most secure, but most radical, method is to reset the TPM. By doing this, the TPM will erase its SRK, after which it will no longer be able to load any keys that previously worked on that TPM. The new owner could then create a new SRK and new owner pass phrase for the TPM. Migratable keys could be migrated to the new SRK. If the reset were to be done accidentally, and if the owner had made a maintenance backup (assuming the TPM allowed a maintenance backup), then the TPM could be restored to its former state. This would be a rather lengthy process and would have to involve the manufacturer of the system in addition to the owner of the system. However, reset is unlikely to happen by accident—it is a function that is generally available only during the boot sequence and may require physically moving a jumper. There are currently only two ways to reset a TPM. One way requires owner authorization and the other requires physical presence, which on a PC is typically done by an administrator physically at the system.

Another technique would be to simply pass control of the TPM from the old owner to the new owner. Then the new owner would establish a new password to control the system using the TPM_ChangeAuthOwner command, and continue working with the system. Of course, any migratable keys would still be at risk, so they should be replaced; but non-migratable keys should be unaffected by the change over.

Maintenance backups, as mentioned previously, can be used for disaster recovery. However, the procedure is complex.

## Maintenance

Maintenance is a tricky subject, and it consumed a fair amount of the committee's time. If two machines simultaneously have the same SRK, then they will also simultaneously be able to report the current boot information of two different machines. The recipient of this information would then not know which machine was being reported on, so the report would not be trustworthy.

Additionally, if the SRK is ever exposed outside a TPM, all secrets the TPM stores would be exposed. Therefore, the requirements were set out as follows:

- Support of maintenance is not required in a TPM.
- If support for maintenance is put into a TPM, there must be a mechanism for an owner to shut off the capability.
- If the owners shut off the capability, the only way to restore the capability would be to reset the TPM (thus wiping the SRK).
- It must not be possible, given the maintenance blob, for an end user to use it to clone his system.
- It must require both the manufacturer and the end user to cooperate to perform maintenance.
- The information given to the manufacturer must not be sufficient for the manufacturer to read the SRK in the clear.
- The information given to the end user must not be sufficient for the end user to read the SRK in the clear.
- After the manufacturer does his part of the recovery mechanism, what he passes back to the end user must not be sufficient for the end user to either clone or read the SRK in the clear.

The details of how this is done can be read in the specification. They entail an OAEP wrap followed by XORing with a random string, followed by a standard PKCS#1 V2.0 wrap using the manufacturer's public key. If maintenance is not to be allowed, and maintenance is a feature of a TPM, the maintenance lock should be performed directly after the SRK is established. Otherwise, it should probably be performed directly after the maintenance blob is created and the maintenance blob stored in a safe place (such as a safe).

Because maintenance is an optional function, and most manufacturers seem to NOT be implementing it, perhaps it is less interesting today. But in the future, maintenance may very well start to be implemented. However, indications are that it may change in the next revision of the specification, so it is wise not to rely upon it today.

Maintenance was given a lot of thought so that the signatures of the TPM would not be compromised by someone doing maintenance. Basic digital signatures are at the root of much of the capabilities offered by the TPM.

## Secure Signatures

With the signing of the digital commerce act, digital signatures can now be legally used to sign contracts. They can actually be used in the same way that a handwritten signature is used. As such, it is important that a digital signature not be exposed to an attacker.

## Avoiding Exposure

It is very difficult to hide a private key from exposure purely in software. In most common client operating systems, there is very little security built into the kernel, and it is possible to read values in the RAM of a system from other applications. Thus, if a signature is being performed by one application (and hence, it would need to have the key in the clear), another application (such as a Trojan horse) could read the key. This attack was recently made more onerous by search techniques pioneered by Adi Shamir (the S in RSA) and called a "lunchtime attack." This attack can easily extract private keys if they are in memory when a person goes to lunch, leaving his computer unattended and unlocked.

The basic problem is that to use a key, it has to be in the clear, and if it is in the clear, a Trojan horse can usually extract it. Another problem for software is that the passwords used to authorize an action have to be stored somewhere in the system. This is usually done hashed or with some other algorithm, but because all versions of the software on the CD-ROM are identical, it is hard to customize the hiding algorithm on a PC-by-PC basis. As a result, "hammering" techniques can be used to guess the password offline.

With the TCG design, the keys are kept in hardware, and signatures are done in hardware in private local storage of the hardware that is not accessible from the outside. As a result, the hardware that contains the key has to be involved in any signature. In addition, passwords are stored inside each password blob, in its header, encrypted uniquely on each system by different 2048-bit public keys and inside an OAEP wrapper. Not only is that infeasible to attack on a separate computer, the TPM itself notices when it is under attack by someone trying to guess an authorization value. It will increase the amount of time that is necessary to wait between attempts to negate the capability of software to initiate a hammering attack directly against the hardware.

## Privacy and Multiple Signatures

Once I know your signature, can't I use your public key to track where you are and what you do on the web? This would be true if you were limited to a single signature, but the design of the TPM is deliberately made so as to avoid that problem. There are virtually an unlimited number of keys that can be generated and used by a TPM. Thus, every web site you go to could use a different public/private key pair.

Further, you could have different key pairs that have different signatures. One key could say you are a senior citizen. One could say you are a Libertarian. One could say you are a newspaper reporter. One could give your actual name and address.

If you were getting a senior citizen discount, you would use the first. If you were applying for food stamps, you might use the last. If you were going into the Libertarian web site, perhaps you would use the second. If you were trying to report on a football game and needed a press pass, you would use the third. Thus, the amount of information stored in a certificate can vary according to the use to which it is going to be put.

## Summary

Understanding how the TCG actually implemented its design goals allows the programmer to design his programs more rapidly and understand the weakness of the design. The daisy chain design of key storage requires administrative backup in case the hard disk crashes, but allows a cheaper TPM design. The linking of the TPM (with Platform Configuration Registers) allows trusted reporting of the state a PC is in. Non-migratable and migratable keys allow for upgrading of systems and provides protection among different users on the same system. Authentication for use of keys can be tied both to pass phrases and to the system state (through PCRs). The random number generator can be used for key creation and for Monte Carlo routines, and secure TPM identities can be created that also retain anonymity.

# PART II

# Programming Interfaces to TCG

# CHAPTER 4

# Writing a TPM Device Driver

The Trusted Platform Module (TPM) is in essence a passive storage device that is hard mounted on the motherboard. The TPM is attached to the Low Pin Count (LPC) bus, a low-pin count bus, which is also used for attaching the system BIOS Flash memory. This ensures that the TPM device is available during the early system bootstrap before any other device is initialized.

Communication with the TPM is typically handled by the TCG device driver library (TDDL), and its interface is defined by the TSS (TCG Software Stack) specification. This library typically communicates with a device driver inside the kernel, and this device driver communicates with the actual TPM device.

There are currently two different TPM device programming interfaces. The TPM 1.1b-compliant devices use a device interface that is vendor specific. Because of the lack of a standardized device interface, each vendor is forced to define its own interface. This interface is typically very simple because the TPM 1.1b specification places only modest requirement on the device interface. To curtail the myriad of incompatible device interfaces, TCG decided to standardize the PC client interface as part of its 1.2 TPM specification. This device interface supports dynamic root of trust and consequently requires a more sophisticated interface that supports locality and special LPC bus cycles.

In this chapter, we will examine how to write a TPM device driver. We start with the TDDL interface and illustrate how to program the TPM 1.1b and 1.2 low-level device interfaces to implement part of the TDDL interface. The code examples have been developed on Linux, but in the interest of staying operating system-neutral, we have removed all the Linux-specific device driver boilerplates. Instead we focused on the core device driver functions that are similar for any operating system.

In particular, this chapter covers the following:

- The TCG device driver library
- The 1.1 device driver interface
- The 1.2 device driver interface
- The device programming interface (both 1.1 and 1.2)

## TCG Device Driver Library

The TDDL interface is the standard interface that applications use for communicating directly with the TPM. This interface is part of the TSS library and is in fact used by the TSS stack to talk to the TPM. Although this interface is available for use by applications, its direct use is typically best avoided. The TDDL interface is a single-threaded synchronous interface, and it assumes that all TPM commands are serialized by the caller of the interface. If this interface is used together with TSS library calls, then the results may be undefined.

For those applications that do need direct device access, the TDDL interface specification is listed next:

```
TSS_RESULT Tddli_Open( );
TSS_RESULT Tddli_Close( );
TSS_RESULT Tddli_Cancel( );
TSS_RESULT Tddli_GetCapability(UINT32 CapArea, UINT32 SubCap,
                    BYTE* pCapBuf,  UINT32* pCapBufLen);
TSS_RESULT Tddli_SetCapability(UINT32 CapArea, UINT32 SubCap,
                    BYTE* pSetCapBuf, UINT32
                    SetCapBufLen);
TSS_RESULT Tddli_GetStatus(UINT32 ReqStatusType, UINT32*
                    pStatus);
TSS_RESULT Tddli_TransmitData(BYTE* pTransmitBuf, UINT32
                    TransmitBufLen,
                    BYTE *pReceiveBuf, UINT32*
                    pReceiveBufLen);
```

The TDDL interface is straightforward. It includes calls to open and close access to the TPM device, cancel any outstanding commands, get and set vendor-specific device capabilities, get the device status, and transmit a command blob to the TPM and receive a response. Unlike the actual device interfaces that are discussed later in the chapter, the TDDL interface is the same for TPMs that follow the 1.1b or the 1.2 specification.

In the next sections, we are going to examine how to implement the device driver equivalent of the Tddli_TransmitData function with a TPM 1.1b- and a TPM 1.2-compliant device.

# TPM 1.1b Specification Device Interface

The TCG 1.1b specification was the first TCG TPM standard that was widely available, and many vendors have developed products around that standard. Unfortunately, that standard did not define a mechanism by which to communicate with the actual TPM device. Consequently, each vendor was forced to define a low-level communication interface that was unique to that vendor.

In the following example, we describe the interface to the Atmel 1.1b TPM chip. This TPM device was one of the earliest available and is often used in desktop and notebook computers.

## Technical Details

The Atmel 1.1b TPM uses port I/O for communication and does not support interrupts. The port I/O addresses that the device uses are 0x4E, 0x4F, 0x400, and 0x401. The first two ports, 0x4E and 0x4F, are used to query the chip for details such as version number and manufacturer. They are used in an index/data pair configuration and are read as:

```
int rdx(int index)
{
        outb(index, 0x4E);
        return inb(0x4F) & 0xFF;
}
```

When read, port address 0x401 acts as the TPM status register. It signals that the TPM is busy (bit 1), or when data is available to be read (bit 2). Writing a value to port 0x401 with the first bit set will cause the TPM to abort the current command that it is executing. Port 0x400 is the data port; it is used to read and write TPM commands from and to the device.

A typical sequence for a TPM device driver is to send a command to the device, wait for a response, and then read the response. Because the Atmel TPM device does not support interrupts, the device driver has to poll the status register to determine whether a response is available. This is a rather inefficient way to wait for a device since, when done incorrectly, it can make the host system unresponsive for a long period of time. This is especially true for a TPM device. The wait time between a send command and a receive response may literally take 60 seconds or more for some operations, such as key generation.

For convenience, we use the following definitions in the code to make it easier to follow:

```
#define ATMEL_DATA_PORT           0x400   /* PIO data port */
#define ATMEL_STATUS_PORT         0x401   /* PIO status port */

#define ATMEL_STATUS_ABORT        0x01    /* ABORT command (W) */
#define ATMEL_STATUS_BUSY         0x01    /* device BUSY (R) */
#define ATMEL_STATUS_DATA_AVAIL   0x02    /* Data available (R) */
```

These definitions provide specifics for a particular Atmel TPM. Having that settled, we can now write cleaner code.

## Device Programming Interface

The Atmel TPM requires no special initialization for it to work correctly. The LPC bus, on which it resides, is typically already initialized and set up by the system BIOS. To check for the presence of the Atmel TPM, the following check suffices:

```
int init(void)
{
        /* verify that it is an Atmel part */
        if (rdx(4) != 'A' || rdx(5) != 'T' ||
            rdx(6) != 'M' || rdx(7) != 'L')
                return 0;
        return 1;

}
```

The Atmel TPM uses the signature "ATML" to signal that the device is present and operating correctly.

The `Tddli_TransmitData` function consists of two major components: a function to send a command to the TPM device and a function to receive the response from the device. The send command is illustrated next:

```
int send(unsigned char *buf, int count)
{
        int i;

        /* send abort and check for busy bit to go away */
        outb(ATMEL_STATUS_ABORT, ATMEL_STATUS_PORT);
        if (!wait_for_status(ATMEL_STATUS_BUSY, 0))
                return 0;

        /* write n bytes */
        for (i = 0; i < count; i++)
                outb(buf[i], ATMEL_DATA_PORT);

        /* wait for TPM to go BUSY or have data available */
        if (!wait_for_not_status(ATMEL_STATUS_BUSY|
                                 ATMEL_STATUS_DATA_AVAIL, 0))
                return 0;

        return count;

}
```

The first step of the send function is to ensure that the TPM device is in a well-defined state where it is ready to accept a command. This is achieved by aborting any outstanding command

and waiting for the device to become ready. The `wait_for_status` function does exactly that: It checks the status register for a state change using the condition `(status & mask) == value`, and if it did not evaluate to true, then it waits for a brief period and tries again. After a while, the function times out and will return 0. If the wait for condition is met, then the function returns 1. In this particular instance, `wait_for_status` waits for the busy bit to turn off.

Once the TPM device is ready to accept a command, it is simply written to the data port one byte at a time. The command is a TPM blob as defined by the TCG TPM specification. As soon as the command is written, we need to check for either of two conditions: 1) the TPM is processing the command, or 2) the command has already finished and the response is available. We check for these conditions by calling the `wait_for_not_status` function and test for the busy and available bits. This function is analogous to `wait_for_status` except that the test condition tests for inequality: `(status & mask) != value`.

The receive function follows similar concepts but is more complicated because it needs to handle more conditions:

```
int recv(unsigned char *buf, int count)
{
        unsigned char *hdr = buf;
        unsigned long size;
        int i;
        /* wait while the TPM to respond */
        if(!wait_for_status(ATMEL_STATUS_DATA_AVAIL|
                        ATMEL_STATUS_BUSY,
                        ATMEL_STATUS_DATA_AVAIL))
                return 0;
        /* start reading header */
        for (i = 0; i < 6; i++) {
                if ((inb(ATMEL_STATUS_PORT) &
                    ATMEL_STATUS_DATA_AVAIL)
                                                    == 0)
                        return 0;
                *buf++ = inb(ATMEL_DATA_PORT);
        }
        /* size of the data received */
        size = decode_u32(hdr + 2);
        if (count < size)
                return 0;
        /* read all the data available */
        for ( ; i < size; i++) {
                if ((inb(ATMEL_STATUS_PORT) &
                    ATMEL_STATUS_DATA_AVAIL)
                                                    == 0)
```

```
                          return 0;
                *buf++ = inb(ATMEL_DATA_PORT);
        }


        /* sanity check: make sure data available is gone */
        if (inb(ATMEL_STATUS_PORT) & ATMEL_STATUS_DATA_AVAIL)
                return 0;


        return size;

    }
```

Before calling the preceding receive function, you need to make sure that the device is not still busy working on the command itself. You can check this by examining the busy bit in the status command and schedule another task if it is still busy. Some commands can take up to more than a minute to process, so spinning on the busy bit may lead to an unresponsive system.

The first step in the receive function is to ensure that there is a response available and that the TPM is no longer busy processing a request. The next step is to read the response buffer.

Like most 1.1b TPMs, the Atmel TPM does not allow you to query the length of the response without reading the actual data. For this reason, receiving a response from the TPM consists of two parts. During the first part, we read the TPM blob header from the device. This header is always 6 bytes long and contains the total length of the response in a big endian byte order. After the length has been converted to native byte order, we use it in the second part to read the remainder of the response packet.

Although the device interface we described in this section is specific to the Atmel TPM implementation, the concepts and the way to interact with the device are similar for other 1.1b TPMs. Still, each 1.1b TPM requires its own device driver, which is quite a burden for firmware and operating system developers. To eliminate the need for multiple device drivers, TCG defined a single device interface standard for TPMs that follow the TPM 1.2 specification. We will discuss that next.

## TPM 1.2 Specification Device Interface

To reduce the myriad of TPM device interfaces and device drivers, TCG decided to standardize the device interface as part of its TPM 1.2 specification. This standard is called the *TCG PC Client Specific TPM Interface Specification*, or TIS for short.

As a result of this standard, firmware and operating system vendors need to implement only one device driver to support all the available TIS-compliant devices. It is exactly for this reason that Microsoft decided to only support TPM 1.2-compliant devices in its Microsoft Vista operating system, even though Vista currently uses only TPM 1.1b features.

The TIS defines two different kinds of device interfaces. The first is the legacy port I/O interface and the second is the memory mapped interface. Because the port I/O interface is similar to the one discussed in the previous section, we will only concentrate on the memory mapped interface in the next section.

## Technical Details

A TPM 1.2-compliant device uses memory mapped I/O. It reserves a range of physical memory that the host operating system can map into its virtual address range. Instead of executing explicit I/O instructions to communicate to the device, it is sufficient to use traditional memory accesses.

The memory mapped interface for the TPM is shown in Figure 4.1. It consists of five 4KB pages that each presents an approximately similar register set. Each page corresponds to a locality—that is, commands that are sent to the TPM through the register set at address FED4.0000 are implicitly associated with locality 0. Similarly, commands sent using the register set at FED4.2000 use locality 2. The reason for the duplication of register sets and the alignment on page boundaries is to enable the host operating system to assign different localities to different levels of the system and regulate their access by controlling their virtual memory mappings. For example, a security kernel would typically only have access to the register set associated with locality 1, while the applications would be associated with the register set belonging to locality 3. Locality 0 is considered legacy and is used by systems that use the static root of trust measurements.

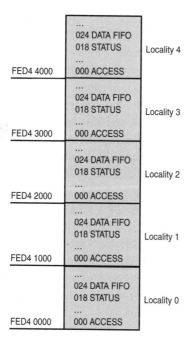

**Figure 4.1** TPM memory map

Locality 4 is special in the sense that it is used by the processor to store the measurement of a secure loader that was started as part of the dynamic root of trust mechanism. The secure loader measurement is stored in PCR17 and can only be set by using special LPC bus cycles that cannot be generated by software. This ensures that the secure loader measurement originated from the processor itself.

Unlike most devices that follow the TPM 1.1b specification, the TIS standard specifies that a TPM device should be able to generate interrupts. That is, whenever data becomes available or the device is ready for its next command, it generates an interrupt. However, sometimes interrupt-driven device drivers are inappropriate, especially during early bootstrap. In these cases, the TPM device can still be used in polled I/O mode.

An interesting aspect of the memory mapped interface is that multiple consumers can access the TPM device at the same time, leading to potential concurrency issues. For example, a trusted operating system and an application can concurrently issue commands to the TPM to update a particular PCR. To ensure the consistency of the internal TPM state, the TIS designers developed a locking protocol. Before a consumer at a certain locality can use the TPM, it needs to request access to the TPM by setting the RequestUse bit in the access register. If no locality is currently using the TPM, then access is granted. If the TPM is being used, then the access request remains pending until the owning locality relinquishes control. The highest-level locality is then given access first. If a locality has crashed or is malicious and does not relinquish control, a higher-level locality can take over the TPM by setting the Seize bit.

In the next section, we will describe how to implement a function that is similar to the `Tddli_TransmitData` function. Because the TIS interface is a lot more complicated than the TPM 1.1b driver, we will focus on a simplified driver that uses the memory mapped interface and only uses the legacy locality 0. A driver with these restrictions uses only a core set of the TIS interface, which we will describe later in the chapter.

Among the set of registers the TPM provides are the access, status, and data FIFO registers. These registers reside at offsets 000, 018, and 024 (hexadecimal), respectively. The access register is used to gain access to a particular locality and is used by the locking protocol described previously. When written, bit 2 signals a request to use and bit 6 relinquishes control. When reading the access register, bit 6 signals that this locality is currently active.

The status register indicates that the device is ready for a command (bit 6), has a response available (bit 5), or is expecting more data (bit 4). The high-order bit of the status byte (bit 8) indicates that the status is valid, and this bit can be used by a driver that uses polled I/O to wait for a particular status to occur. When writing the status register, bit 6 indicates that the recently written command blob should be executed. The status register is an 8-bit register. The remaining bytes of the status word (byte 1 and 2) form a burst count. That is essentially the size of the data FIFO and specifies the number of bytes that can be written or read consecutively. The TPM's data FIFO is available through the register at offset 024.

Some register sets, such as the set for locality 0, contain additional registers. An example of that is the device and vendor ID register at offset F00. This register is typically used to determine the presence of the TPM and, if one is present, the vendor. The assigned vendor IDs currently follow the PCI-Express vendor designations.

In the following code examples, we use this shorthand to read and write memory locations: The address argument is relative to the base of the memory range where physical address FED4.0000 is mapped and is only used to read and write the TPM register sets. The routines also include the necessary memory barrier operations to ensure coherency.

```
unsigned char read8(unsigned long addr);
void write8(unsigned char val, unsigned long addr);
unsigned long read32(unsigned long addr);
void write32(unsigned long val, unsigned long addr);
```

For convenience, we use the following definitions in the code to make it easier to follow:

```
/* macros to access registers at locality ''l'' */
#define ACCESS(l)                   (0x0000 | ((l) << 12))
#define STS(l)                      (0x0018 | ((l) << 12))
#define DATA_FIFO(l)                (0x0024 | ((l) << 12))
#define DID_VID(l)                  (0x0F00 | ((l) << 12))
/* access bits */
#define ACCESS_ACTIVE_LOCALITY      0x20 /* (R)*/
#define ACCESS_RELINQUISH_LOCALITY  0x20 /* (W) */
#define ACCESS_REQUEST_USE          0x02 /* (W) */
/* status bits */
#define STS_VALID                   0x80 /* (R) */
#define STS_COMMAND_READY           0x40 /* (R) */
#define STS_DATA_AVAIL              0x10 /* (R) */
#define STS_DATA_EXPECT             0x08 /* (R) */
#define STS_GO                      0x20 /* (W) */
```

## Device Programming Interface

Before we can use the TPM, we need to initialize the device. The following routine performs a trivial initialization and presence check:

```
int init(void)
{
        unsigned vendor;
        int i;

        for (i = 0 ; i < 5 ; i++)
                write8(ACCESS_RELINQUISH_LOCALITY, ACCESS(i));
```

```
    if (request_locality(0) < 0)
            return 0;

    vendor = read32(DID_VID(0));
    if ((vendor & 0xFFFF) == 0xFFFF)
            return 0;

    return 1;
}
```

The initialization routine is executed only once when the driver is instantiated. It first forces all localities to relinquish their access and then requests the use of the legacy locality 0. When access is granted, it checks for the presence of a valid vendor ID. When this check succeeds, the TPM is ready to accept commands. If you were writing a driver that uses interrupts, this would be the place where you would check for the supported interrupts and enable them.

```
int request_locality(int l)
{
    write8(ACCESS_RELINQUISH_LOCALITY, ACCESS(locality));

    write8(ACCESS_REQUEST_USE, ACCESS(l));
    /* wait for locality to be granted */
    if (read8(ACCESS(l) & ACCESS_ACTIVE_LOCALITY))
            return locality = l;

    return -1;
}
```

To request a locality that is specified by parameter l, we relinquish the current locality (stored in the global variable locality) and request the use of the specified locality. For a TPM driver that only provides access to the legacy 0 locality, this access should be granted immediately with the locality active bit set in the status register. If this routine is used for the non-legacy localities, it would have to wait until the access is granted. This wait can be done by either polling the active bit or by waiting for the locality changed interrupt.

To send a command to the TPM, we use the following function:

```
int send(unsigned char *buf, int len)
{
    int status, burstcnt = 0;
    int count = 0;

    if (request_locality(locality) == -1)
            return -1;
```

```
write8(STS_COMMAND_READY, STS(locality));

while (count < len - 1) {
        burstcnt = read8(STS(locality) + 1);
        burstcnt += read8(STS(locality) + 2) << 8;

        if (burstcnt == 0){
                delay(); /* wait for FIFO to drain */
        } else {
                for (; burstcnt > 0 && count < len - 1;
                                        burstcnt -) {
                        write8(buf[count],
                                DATA_FIFO(locality));
                        count++;
                }

                /* check for overflow */
                for (status = 0; (status & STS_VALID)
                                == 0; )
                        status = read8(STS(locality));
                if ((status & STS_DATA_EXPECT) == 0)
                        return -1;
        }
}

/* write last byte */
write8(buf[count], DATA_FIFO(locality));

/* make sure it stuck */
for (status = 0; (status & STS_VALID) == 0; )
        status = read8(STS(locality));
if ((status & STS_DATA_EXPECT) != 0)
        return -1;

/* go and do it */
write8(STS_GO, STS(locality));

return len;
}
```

In order for us to send a command to the TPM, we first have to ensure that the appropriate locality has access to the device. This is especially important when the driver supports multiple localities with concurrent access. Once we get access to the requested locality, we tell the TPM that we are ready to send a command and then proceed to write the command into the DATA FIFO at burst count chunks at the time. After each chunk, we check the status register for an overflow condition to make sure the TPM kept up with us filling the FIFO. As an added safety measure, we write the last byte separately and check whether the TPM is no longer expecting more data bytes. If it is not, then the TPM is ready to execute the command blob we just transferred to it. This is done by setting the status to GO.

Receiving a response from the TPM is slightly more complicated, and its code is divided into two parts: a helper function to get the data from the TPM and a receiver function to reconstruct the response.

The helper function is listed next:

```
int recv_data(unsigned char *buf, int count)
{
        int size = 0, burstcnt = 0, status;

        status = read8(STS(locality));
        while ((status & (STS_DATA_AVAIL | STS_VALID))
                        == (STS_DATA_AVAIL | STS_VALID)
                        && size < count) {
            if (burstcnt == 0){
                    burstcnt = read8(STS(locality) + 1);
                    burstcnt += read8(STS(locality) + 2) << 8;
            }

            if (burstcnt == 0) {
                    delay(); /* wait for the FIFO to fill */
            } else {
                    for (; burstcnt > 0 && size < count;
                                            burstcnt -) {
                            buf[size] = read8(DATA_FIFO
                            (locality));
                            size++;
                    }
            }
            status = read8(STS(locality));
        }

        return size;
}
```

Receiving a response from the TPM follows the same principles as writing a command to it. As long as there is data available from the TPM and the buffer count has not yet been exhausted, we continue to read up to burst count bytes from the DATA FIFO.

It is up to the following receive function to reconstruct and validate the actual TPM response:

```
int recv(unsigned char *buf, int count)
{
        int expected, status;
        int size = 0;

        if (count < 6)
                return 0;

        /* ensure that there is data available */
        status = read8(STS(locality));
        if ((status & (STS_DATA_AVAIL | STS_VALID))
                            != (STS_DATA_AVAIL | STS_VALID))
                return 0;

        /* read first 6 bytes, including tag and paramsize */
        if ((size = recv_data(buf, 6)) < 6)
                return -1;
        expected = be32_to_cpu(*(unsigned *) (buf + 2));

        if (expected > count)
                return -1;

        /* read all data, except last byte */
        if ((size += recv_data(&buf[6], expected - 6 - 1))
                                                < expected - 1)
                return -1;

        /* check for receive underflow */
        status = read8(STS(locality));
        if ((status & (STS_DATA_AVAIL | STS_VALID))
                            != (STS_DATA_AVAIL | STS_VALID))
                return -1;

        /* read last byte */
        if ((size += recv_data(&buf[size], 1)) != expected)
                return -1;
```

```
        /* make sure we read everything */
        status = read8(STS(locality));
        if ((status & (STS_DATA_AVAIL | STS_VALID))
                        == (STS_DATA_AVAIL | STS_VALID)) {
                return -1;
        }

        write8(STS_COMMAND_READY, STS(locality));

        return expected;
}
```

The receive function is called either after a data available interrupt occurs or, when the driver uses polling, the status bits valid and data available were set. The first step for the receive function is to ensure that the TPM has a response that is ready to be read. It then continues to read the first 6 bytes of the response. This corresponds to the TPM blob header and contains the length of the total response in big endian byte order. After converting the response size to native byte order, we continue to read the rest of the response. As with the send function, we treat the last byte separately so that we can detect FIFO underflow conditions. Once the entire response is read, the TPM is ready to accept its next command. This is achieved by setting the command ready bit in the status register.

## Summary

In this chapter, we have demonstrated how to talk to a TPM (both 1.1 and 1.2) at the lowest level. This will be useful for programmers who want to talk to the TPM directly—either in BIOS or a device driver. When developing new hardware that will make use of a TPM, this will be useful for determining if the TPM is working as designed. Although all commands can talk to the TPM directly, application-level programs should use the TCG Software Stack (TSS) application programming interface.

# CHAPTER 5

# Low-Level Software: Using BIOS and TDDL Directly

Most of this book discusses programming to high-level interfaces to the TPM. But in order to take advantage of the log recording and trusted boot capabilities of a TPM, it is necessary to talk directly to the chip before even a device driver interface is available, or before the full TSS services are available. In this case, the programmer must talk to the chip either through the BIOS or the TDDL. This chapter shows how to do that.

## Talking to the TPM Through BIOS

After an operating system is loaded, a device driver handles communication with the TPM. During the boot of the operating system, however, the boot loader program, such as *grub*, must measure all bootstrap and operating system code before each stage is executed; at this boot time, there is not yet a device driver to use. To facilitate communication with the TPM during boot, the PC-specific TCG specification defines a minimal set of BIOS interrupt calls that the boot loader can use; this provides an easy-to-use interface that is chip and vendor independent.

This interface is intentionally lightweight, since the anticipated users of this interface are in the space-restricted pre-boot "space"—for example, option ROM and boot-record code. As a result, an INT 1Ah interface is defined, which allows the caller of the interface to have direct access to a limited set of TSS functions and a pass-through to the TPM.

The main TPM functions that a bootstrap loader must perform are taking measurements of all subsequent code and configuration files about to be executed, before control is transferred to them. The PC-specific specification (see Table 5.1) defines standard usage of the PCRs during this boot process.

59

**Table 5.1**    The Standard Meaning of PCRs

| PCR Index | PCR Usage |
|-----------|-----------|
| 0 | CRTM, BIOS, and embedded option ROMs. |
| 1 | Motherboard configuration. |
| 2 | Option ROM code. |
| 3 | Option ROM configuration and data. |
| 4 | IPL code (usually the MBR). |
| 5 | IPL code configuration and data (for use by the IPL code). |
| 6 | State transition. |
| 7 | Reserved for future usage. Do not use. |

Thus, the bootstrap loader is normally going to extend PCR 4 with measurements of its own subsequent stage executables, PCR 5 with its own configuration files, and PCR 8 with measurements of the operating system, such as the kernel and initial ramdisk images. An example of a modified linux bootloader (grub) is available at the Trousers site:

http://sourceforge.net/projects/trousers

The BIOS calls for TPM use during bootstrap are the following:

- **TCG_StatusCheck:** Verify existence and version of TCG BIOS.
- **TCG_HashLogExtendEvent:** Hash data and log and extend a PCR.
- **TCG_PassThroughToTPM:** Send arbitrary TPM commands to TPM.

TCG_StatusCheck is used to verify that the BIOS supports the TPM calls, and must be called before attempting either of the other BIOS TCG functions. The TCG_HashLogExtend Event call does all the work needed to hash the data, extend the specified PCR, and log the extension event. If necessary, any arbitrary TPM request packet can be sent to the TPM with the TCG_PassThroughToTPM call. This is more complex, however, as the bootstrap code would need to do all the request and response packet handling, unlike the TCG_HashLogExtendEvent call, which does all that handling for the bootstrap program.

Let's look at the BIOS calls in more detail:

```
TCG_StatusCheck
    INT 1Ah (AH)=BBh, (AL)=00h
```

This function call verifies the presence of the TCG BIOS interface and provides the caller with the version of TCG BIOS specification to which the implementation complies.

```
On entry:
    (AH)   =    BBh
    (AL)   =    00h
On return:
    (EAX)  =    Return code. Set to 00000000h if the
                system supports the TCPA BIOS calls.
    (EBX)  =    'TCPA' (41504354h)
    (CH)   =    TCG BIOS Major Version (01h for version 1.0)
    (CL)   =    TCG BIOS Minor Version (00h for version 1.0)
    (EDX)  =    BIOS TCG Feature Flags
    (ESI)  =    Pointer to the Event Log
```

TCG_HashLogExtendEvent
    INT 1Ah (AH)=BBh, (AL)=01h

This function performs the functions of the TSS_HashAll, TPM_Extend, and TSS_LogEvent operation for the data region specified by the caller.

```
On entry:
    (AH)   =    BBh
    (AL)   =    01h
    (ES)   =    Segment portion of the pointer to the
                HashLogExtendEvent input parameter block
    (DI)   =    Offset portion of the pointer to the
                HashLogExtendEvent input parameter block
    (DS)   =    Segment portion of the pointer to the
                HashLogExtendEvent output parameter block
    (SI)   =    Offset portion of the pointer to the
                HashLogExtendEvent output parameter block
    (EBX)  =    41504354h
    (ECX)  =    0
    (EDX)  =    0
On return:
    (EAX)   =    Return Code as defined in Return Codes 8.1.2
    (DS:SI) =    Referenced buffer with return results.
```

TCG_PassThroughToTPM
    INT 1Ah, (AH)=BBh, (AL)=02h

This function provides a pass-through capability from the caller to the system's TPM. Refer to the TPM implementation appendix of the main TCG specification for input/output parameter block formats.

```
On entry:
    (AH) =    BBh
    (AL) =    02h
    (ES) =    Segment portion of the pointer to the TPM
              input parameter block
    (DI) =    Offset portion of the pointer to the TPM
              input parameter block
    (DS) =    Segment portion of the pointer to the TPM
              output parameter block
    (SI) =    Offset portion of the pointer to the TPM
              output parameter block
    (EBX)=    'TCPA'  (41504354h)
    (ECX)=    0
    (EDX)=    0
On return:
    (EAX)=    Return Code
    (DS:SI)= Referenced buffer updated to provide results.
```

## Talking to the TPM Through TDDL

After the device driver is loaded, there will typically be a short time during operating system initialization before the full TSS services are available. For example, during Linux boot, the initial ramdisk normally takes control, loads any needed device drivers, mounts the root filesystem, and transfers control to the init system, which in turn starts up services, such as TSS. During this operating system initialization, the TDDL interface is used to perform any necessary TPM operations, such as loading and unsealing keys in support of trusted boot. A small TDDL-based library provides any needed TPM operations during this process, as the full TSS is not yet available.

### The IBM libtpm Package

The IBM libtpm package, available as part of the "Trusted Computing for Linux" support package at http://www.research.ibm.com/gsal/tcpa, provides source code for an example TDDL library and example utility programs that demonstrate the use of the library functions. The libtpm code provides easy-to-use C interfaces for 14 of the commonly needed low-level TPM packet commands. The example programs demonstrate how to use libtpm to do common actions, including taking ownership, creating keys, loading keys, signing, sealing, and unsealing. This package is useful not only as a low-level library for boot-time use, it also provides an excellent introduction to the low-level TPM command packets. The following sections will include source code examples from the libtpm package.

## Enabling and Clearing the TPM

Before looking at specific TPM commands, we should cover one of the more mystifying aspects of the TPM—how to get it started. Fortunately, the BIOS is responsible for starting up and clearing the TPM, so this really is not as complex as it looks to be in the TPM specification. At power-on, the TPM is activated but not started. The BIOS then must issue a TPM_Startup command. This command can do one of three things: deactivate the TPM, start up the TPM with a reset of the PCR registers, or start up the TPM with a restore of PCR values from their saved states (as with a resume). If the BIOS deactivates the TPM, it remains deactivated until the next power cycle; for privacy reasons, no software command can reactivate it. A startup with clearing of the PCRs is done at boot time, so all PCR values are calculated correctly during boot. The TPM device driver is responsible for making a TPM_SaveState request at suspend time to ensure that valid PCR values are available at resume time.

The BIOS also is responsible for performing a TPM_ForceClear if desired. The clear command is a complete reset of the TPM, and it unloads all keys and handles and clears the SRK and owner authorization secret. TPM_ForceClear requires proof of physical presence, which on Thinkpads systems normally is given by holding down the Fn key (the blue key at the bottom left) when powering on the system.

The control of TPM deactivation and clearing by the BIOS is set in the BIOS setup mode. To get started with the TPM on IBM/Lenovo systems, hold down the Fn key and press the Power-On button. When the BIOS screen appears, release Fn, and press F1 to enter BIOS setup mode. Next, select Config?Security System, then select Enable and Clear entries. These steps enable operation of the TPM and clear the chip, so it is ready for us to take ownership.

## Talking to the TPM

On Linux, the TPM device driver is a pair of loadable kernel modules that provides a character device interface to the TPM chip. tpm.ko is the general driver, and there are chip-specific drivers, such as tpm_atmel.ko, which handle the chip-specific work. Normally, the modules are loaded automatically during boot. The device driver is a character device registered officially as Linux major number 10, minor number 224. Applications normally access it through the special file /dev/tpm0.

To send a command to the TPM, /dev/tpm0 is opened for read/write, a command packet is written, and the response packet is read. The TPM can process only one command at a time, so the entire request must be sent and the entire response must be read before another request can be made.

All 16- and 32-bit values are in network byte order (big endian) and must be converted to and from host byte order. When writing to the TPM, write exactly the number of bytes in the packet, as indicated in the packet's total length field. When reading the response, you should attempt to read 4,096 bytes (the defined maximum TPM packet size), and the return value of the read indicates how many bytes are in the returned packet. This should match the returned packet's length field exactly. The return code is zero for a successful command, and a positive value is a specific error code.

A function for sending/receiving TPM packets can look something like the following (error handling omitted for clarity):

```
#define TPMMAX 4096
uint32_t TPM_Transmit(unsigned char *blob)
{
    int tpmfp, len;
    uint32_t size;

    tpmfp = open("/dev/tpm0", O_RDWR);
    size = ntohl(*(uint32_t *)&blob[2]);
    len = write(tpmfp, blob, size);
    len = read(tpmfp, blob, TPMMAX);
    close(tpmfp);
    return(ntohl(*(uint32_t *)&blob[6]));
}
```

## Getting Started with Some Simple TPM Commands

Once the TPM is enabled and cleared through the BIOS setup and the TPM device driver is loaded, we can try some simple TPM commands. The TCPA main specification details some 73 TPM commands. Fortunately, we can demonstrate the desired signing and sealing functionality in this tutorial with only 14 of these commands.

The simplest command is **TPM_Reset**, a request to flush any existing authorization handles. TPM_Reset is a nice command to test a driver and library, as it is short, fixed, and should always succeed, returning a result code of zero. Here is the example code for TPM_Reset:

```
uint32_t TPM_Reset()
{
    unsigned char blob[TPMMAX] = {
        0,193,      /*TPM_TAG_RQU_COMMAND*/
        0,0,0,10,   /* blob length, bytes */
        0,0,0,90};  /*TPM_ORD_Reset */
    return(TPM_Transmit(blob));
}
```

The **TPM_GetCapability** command is another simple function that can return several items of information about a given TPM. It can return the version of the current TPM, the total number of key slots in the TPM (typically ten), the number of loaded keys and their handles, and the number of PCR registers (typically 16). Here is the example code for using TPM_GetCapability to read the TPM version:

```
uint32_t TPM_GetCapability_Version()
{
    unsigned char blob[TPMMAX] = {
        0,193,      /* TPM_TAG_RQU_COMMAND */
        0,0,0,18,   /* blob length, bytes */
        0,0,0,101,  /* TPM_ORD_GetCapability */
        0,0,0,6,    /* TCPA_CAP_VERSION */
        0,0,0,0};   /* no sub capability */
    return(TPM_Transmit(blob));
}
```

**TPM_PcrRead** returns the 20 bytes (160 bits) of a specified PCR register. It is useful to check that any desired TPM measurements are being made by the modified GRUB loader.

Although some of the TPM command packets can easily be constructed directly as shown previously, others are more complex. libtpm uses `TSS_buildbuff()`, a function similar to `sprintf()`, which uses a simple format string and arguments to build the packet in a more readable way. For example, the simplified code from `TPM_PcrRead`, using `TSS_buildbuff`, looks like the following:

```
uint32_t TPM_PcrRead(uint32_t pcrindex, unsigned char
                    *pcrvalue)
{
    unsigned char pcrread_fmt[] = "00 c1 T 00 00 00 15 L";
    uint32_t ret;
    unsigned char tpmdata[TPMMAX];

    TSS_buildbuff(pcrread_fmt, tpmdata, pcrindex);
    ret = TPM_Transmit(tpmdata, "PCRRead");
    memcpy(pcrvalue, tpmdata + TPM_DATA_OFFSET, TPM_HASH_SIZE);
    return ret;
}
```

In this code, the format string includes the literal "00 c1" for the request tag, the "T" is a format character for inserting the length of the resultant packet (32 bits in network byte order), and the "L" format character means translate a native 32-bit long to network order and insert it in the packet. The resultant packet is returned in the specified buffer (tpmdata).

For the remaining TPM descriptions, the example code gets too complex for review here. Please see libtpm to examine the full code.

**TPM_ReadPubek** is used to read the TPM's fixed public endorsement key (Pubek). Pubek initially must be read so it can be used by the owner to encrypt sensitive data in the TPM_Take-Ownership command. Once ownership is established, the owner typically disables reading of the Pubek for privacy reasons; after that, this command fails.

Using the TPM authorization protocols are TPM commands requiring authorization. Owner-related commands normally require authorization based on knowledge of the owner authorization 160-bit secret. Similarly, the use of keys may require authorization based on the key's authorization secret. Normally, this is done in the form of a hash of a password, or PIN, applied to the key when it is created.

The TPM supports two protocols for this authorization: Object Independent Authorization Protocol (OIAP) and Object Specific Authorization Protocol (OSAP). Both protocols are similar in that they create an authorization context with a handle returned to the user, and they both use rolling nonces. The main difference is OIAP creates a long-term session with a new session secret key, and it can be used across multiple objects within a session. OSAP relates to a single object, such as a given key. In the case of TPM_TakeOwnership, OIAP must be used because the objects and secrets have not yet been established. In most other cases, either authorization protocol may be used.

**TPM_OIAP** and **TPM_OSAP** both create authorization handles that should be terminated (freed) when finished. This is done with the **TPM_Terminate_Handle** command.

## Taking Ownership

We are ready to perform the essential **TPM_TakeOwnership**. This command executes four critical functions: It installs the owner-supplied owner authorization secret, creates the SRK, applies the owner-supplied SRK authorization secret, and, optionally, returns the public SRK portion to the owner. With the SRK available, we now have a functional TPM and are able to create and use signature and encryption keys.

## Creating and Using Keys

**TPM_CreateWrapKey** generates a new RSA key on the chip, using the hardware RNG. A key must be typed as being either for signing or for encryption/decryption. The TPM does not allow a signature key to encrypt or an encryption key to sign, as this can lead to attacks. A key optionally may be given a secret that it is required to produce to use the key in the future. In addition, keys can be wrapped to specified PCR values. If this is done, both the authorization data and specified PCR data must match to use the key. All keys must have a parent key—it may be the SRK—that is used to encrypt the private part of the key, before the key structure is returned to the user. The returned key data must be stored by the user for future loading.

**TPM_LoadKey** is used to load a key into one of the volatile key storage slots in the TPM. This command requires the authorization password for the parent key; once loaded, the TPM uses the parent key to decrypt the loaded key's private data for use. If the key has an authorization secret, it is not needed to load the key, but it is required for any subsequent command that tries to use the key for encryption or signing.

Because a limited number of key slots are available in the TPM, when a key is no longer needed, it must be evicted with **TPM_EvictKey** to make the slot available for other keys.

The **TPM_Sign** command uses a loaded key to sign presented data, normally the hash of the actual data. **TPM_Seal** is used to perform RSA encryption of data; it requires a loaded encryption key and any authorization secret for that key. TPM_Seal also may specify PCR values to be used in the seal. If a future unseal is attempted without matching PCR values, the unseal fails. TPM_Seal also applies a used-supplied data authorization value (password) to the sealed data. Thus, to unseal the data, the user may require the password for the sealing key and for the data, and the PCR values may have to match. **TPM_Unseal** performs the corresponding unseal operation.

## Checking the TPM Configuration

The TPM does not have commands to test for existence of an owner, or to test for correct passwords, so other commands have to be run, and the return codes inspected to infer status. The ability to open /dev/tpm0 can be used to determine if the tpm device driver is loaded. The TPM_Reset command should always succeed, even if the TPM is disabled, so it can be used to test the presence of a TPM. The TPM_PcrRead command should always succeed, so long as the TPM is enabled, so it can be used to check if the TPM is enabled. The owner and password can be inferred by trying a TPM_CreateWrapKey command and checking the failure codes. If there is not already an owner, TPM_CreateWrapKey will return TPM_NOSRK. If there is an owner with an unknown password, it will return TPM_AUTHFAIL. To avoid potentially long delays should the command succeed (there is an owner, and the password used is correct), the key parameters are deliberately invalid.

```
                /* check /dev/tpm0 */
    if ((tpmfp = open("/dev/tpm0", O_RDWR)) < 0) {
                        printf("Unable to open /dev/tpm0\n");
                exit(-1);
    }
        close(tpmfp);

    /* try a TPM_Reset (should work even if TPM disabled) */
            if((ret=TPM_Reset())){
                    printf("TPM_Reset failed, error %s\n",
                TPM_GetErrMsg(ret));
                    exit(-2);
            }

        /* check if TPM enabled with TPM_PcrRead */
        if((ret=TPM_PcrRead(0L,pcrvalue))){
                    printf("TPM_PcrRead failed, error%s\n",
                    TPM_GetErrMsg(ret));
                            exit(-3);
            }
```

## Summary

In this section, we described how a developer can talk to the TPM at boot time, before the standard TSS services are available. This includes talking to the chip using BIOS calls in assembly language, and using TPM commands directly through the TDDL interface. We then looked at examples of typical commands used for initialization of the chip, and for basic key operations.

# Trusted Boot

As described in Chapter 1, "Introduction to Trusted Computing," one of the goals of TCG is to establish at boot time that the booted operating system has not been compromised. This "trusted boot" has to establish that the entire boot chain, including master boot record, boot loader, kernel, drivers, and all files referenced or executed during boot, have not changed in any way. There are two ways that TGC defines to establish this trust during boot: static root of trust and dynamic root of trust. This chapter discusses how you create a trusted boot state using the following:

- The static root of trust
- Trust chains
- The dynamic root of trust
- Localities

## Trusted Boot with Static Root of Trust

In the static root of trust method, all trust starts with a fixed or immutable piece of trusted code in the BIOS. This trusted piece of code measures the next piece of code that is going to be executed, and extends a Platform Configuration Register (PCR) based on the measurement, before control is transferred to the next piece. If each new piece of code in turn measures the next before transferring control, a chain of trust is established. If this measurement chain continues through the entire boot sequence, the resultant PCR values reflect the measurement of all files used.

If an attacker successfully compromises one of the pieces of software in the boot chain, then the next time the system is booted, this compromised piece of code will be measured *before* it is executed. It cannot avoid being measured if it is part of the boot chain, and once it is executed, it cannot "take back" its own measurement, as the PCR extension operation can only hash in additional measurements. After the malicious code is executed, it is free to fake all the subsequent measurements, but there is no way for the malicious code to reset or "fix" the PCR back to the value it would have been in an uncompromised boot. Because the PCR extend operation is based on SHA-1 hash, which is cryptographically strong, it is computationally infeasible for the malicious code to calculate an extension value that would "fix" the PCR values.

The only assumption in the static root of trust chain model is that the first piece of software itself has not been compromised. Since most PC systems have reflashable BIOS software, which could allow an attacker to modify the BIOS and destroy the root of trust, TCG-compliant systems must have immutable initial BIOS code. This can be a small, fixed piece of BIOS, which can then measure the flashable bulk of the BIOS, but the initial part must be fixed.

Given an immutable static root of trust, after boot, the PCR values will reflect all measurements given to the chip. Any deviation of these values from the prior or expected values indicates that something has been changed. The question then is, how can the TPM enforce a trusted boot? Well, it can't—at least not directly. The TPM cannot control the operation of the main processor. It's just a character device that responds to any submitted request packets. So while the TPM's PCR values can indicate that the software is or is not trusted, there has to be some way to act on this knowledge.

One thing that the TPM *can* enforce is the use of keys, which are wrapped under a specific set of PCR values, or the unsealing of data that was sealed under a specific set of PCR values. If some part of the software has been compromised, the PCR values will be different, and the TPM will refuse to unwrap keys or unseal data for the "trusted" PCR values. If the boot can be made to depend at least in part on wrapped keys or sealed data, then the TPM can enforce that the boot is trusted.

There are several ways to create this dependency on wrapped keys or sealed data. One simple way is to encrypt the root filesystem under a symmetric key, which is sealed under the PCR values of a trusted kernel and trusted init ramdisk images. When control reaches the init ramdisk startup script, it can attempt to unseal the symmetric encryption key, which will succeed only if the kernel and init ramdisk images are trusted. If the unsealing is successful, then the startup script can mount the encrypted root filesystem and continue the boot. If the unsealing is unsuccessful, then some software in the boot sequence must have been compromised; no matter how hard the malicious code tries, it will not be able to trick the TPM into unsealing the key for the encrypted root filesystem, and thus will not be able to access its files.

Note that this technique does not prevent the malicious code from booting; it simply prevents it from being able to access any TPM-protected keys or data. Going back to the original threat analysis, however, we can see that this is exactly what we wanted the TPM to do—to protect our sensitive private keys from being stolen, and to protect them from being used by malicious software.

There is one more step needed to more fully protect any wrapped keys or sealed data used in the trusted boot. So far, in a trusted boot, the key use or data unsealing was possible because the

PCR values matched. If we leave the PCR values unchanged, then after the trusted boot, malicious code could be introduced that could continue to use the TPM to use the trusted boot keys or unseal the trusted boot data. For this reason, it is good practice to extend one or more of the PCRs used in the trusted boot with a random value. This "locks" the keys or sealed data against any further use until they are needed during the next trusted boot.

If any code or data that is measured into PCRs needs to change, it is necessary for the administrative action that takes this action to also unseal all the data values while in the old state and then reseal those values to what will become the new trusted state, so they will continue to be accessible.

## Dynamic Root of Trust Measurements

The original TCG 1.1b specification outlined an authenticated bootstrap processor, known as static root of trust measurement. It essentially assumes that a machine is in a secure state and starts in an immutable environment (ROM BIOS) when it is booted. This trust is then maintained by measuring the next layer and storing the measurement inside a TPM before executing that next layer. The process is then repeated. This *measure before you execute* paradigm leads to a chain of trust that can be evaluated by a remote party to assess the trustworthiness of a system.

Although conceptually simple, this static root of trust measurement approach has some considerable challenges, as follows:

- **Scalability:** A large chain of trust does not scale. In order for a recipient to determine the trustworthiness of a system, it needs to know the trustworthiness of all executable components that make up the chain. When you consider that a typical machine has some revision of a ROM BIOS and VGA BIOS, a number of extension ROMs, and some revision of an operating system with a set of patches applied, combined with the fact that some measurements are hashed into a single PCR and are thus dependent on the measurement order, it is easy to see that this problem can become intractable very quickly.

- **Time of measurement:** A lot can happen between the time when a machine was started securely and when its trustworthiness is determined. For example, attackers could have exploited a buffer overflow and replaced the running executable. It is important to realize that a static root of trust gives you a load-time guarantee, not a run-time guarantee—that is, it guarantees what program is loaded, not necessarily what is running.

- **Inclusivity:** For a static root of trust to be meaningful to a remote verifier, all executable content within the trusted computing base (TCB) needs to be measured. Many systems—for example, Linux and Windows—have an ill-defined TCB and therefore require all executable content to be measured (executables, libraries, shell scripts, and perl scripts) because all of them are security sensitive.

These shortcomings were identified by TCG, and as part of the TCG 1.2 specification, they defined a new mechanism for authenticated boot: *dynamic root of trust measurement*, or DRTM for short. Unlike static root of trust, with DRTM the root of trust can start at any moment in time and can be repeated as often as necessary.

DRTM is the underlying trust mechanism for Intel's Lagrande Technology (LT) and AMD's Presidio secure platform technology and requires processor as well as chipset changes. Although LT and Presidio include much more than just DRTM technology, DRTM does provide the core trust foundation for these systems.

The key concept behind DRTM is the introduction of a new CPU instruction that creates a controlled and attested execution environment. This environment cannot be influenced by any component in the system and therefore guarantees untampered execution of the *secure loader* that is typically started as a result of this new instruction. Intel calls this new instruction SEN-TER, and AMD calls it SKINIT. Although both DRTM mechanisms are functionally similar, they differ quite a bit when it comes to the details.

At the time of writing this book, only AMD has released a public specification on their *Secure Virtual Machine* CPU extensions (formerly known under the development name *Pacifica*), which includes support for hardware virtualization and DRTM instructions. In the following section, we examine this architecture more closely.

## AMD's Secure Virtual Machine

In 2005, AMD released a specification that describes their virtual machine and security extensions that are going to be part of their next-generation CPUs. Among the extensions is a new instruction, SKINIT, which is the basis for dynamic root of trust measurement support.

The SKINIT instruction reinitializes the processor and establishes a secure execution environment for the secure loader. That is an environment where the interrupts are disabled, virtual memory is turned off, DMA is inhibited, and all processors are quiesced except for the processor executing the SKINIT instruction. The secure loader of the virtual machine manager is wrapped inside a secure loader block, and before the CPU jumps into the secure loader, the secure loader block is measured and its measurement is stored in PCR17 inside the TPM. This PCR can be written only using special LPC bus cycles, which cannot be emulated in software. This ensures that only the CPU could have written the PCR17 value. It is this value that forms the dynamic root of trust measurement. To prevent any tampering with the SKINIT procedure, all the steps and conditions described previously are performed atomically.

The following function illustrates how to invoke the SKINIT instruction from C using the GNU compiler assembly extensions:

```
#define EFER_SVME (1 << 12)
#define MSR_EFER 0xc0000080          /* extended feature
                                      * register */


int skinit(struct slb *slb)
{
    unsigned long eax, edx;
```

```
            rdmsr(MSR_EFER, eax, edx);
            if (eax & EFER_SVME) {
                /* movl $slb, %eax; skinit */
                __asm__ __volatile__(
                        " .byte 0x0F, 0x01, 0xDE"
                        : : "a" (slb)
                );
            }
            return 0; /* failed */
    }
```

The skinit C function is called with the physical address of the secure loader block. After making
sure the processor supports the SVM extensions (identified by bit 12 in the EFER model specific
register), it stores the address of the secure loader block in the EAX register and then executes the
SKINIT instruction. Unless SKINIT fails, it is guaranteed not to return to the caller.

The secure loader block consists of a header that specifies an entry point where the secure
loader starts as well as the size of the block in bytes. The secure loader block should be aligned on
a 64KB boundary, and its total size is limited to 64KB. The secure loader is invoked with the
physical base address of the secure loader block in register EAX, the CPU model/family/stepping
information is stored in register EDX, and the stack pointer ESP is initialized with the value of
secure loader base address + 64KB. As far as the segment registers are concerned, CS and SS
point to a 4GB 32-bit segment and the remaining segment registers are initialized with 16-bit
descriptors.

Listing 6.1 is the skeleton for a secure loader in the GNU assembly file format.

**Listing 6.1**  Secure Loader in GNU Assembly Format

```
/* secure loader CS and DS descriptors */
#define SL_CS            0x08
#define SL_DS            0x10


        .text


sl_start:
        /* Secure loader block header */
        .word   sl_entry-sl_start       /* entry point offset */
        .word   sl_end-sl_start         /* size of SL */


        /* Secure loader runtime startoff */
        .align  4
        .globl  sl_entry
```

```
sl_entry:
        lgdt    %cs:sl_gdtr             /* only %cs and %ss are valid */

        movw    $SL_DS, %bx             /* secure loader data segment */
        movw    %bx, %ds
        movw    %bx, %ss
        movw    %bx, %es
        movw    %bx, %fs
        movw    %bx, %gs

        ljmp    $SL_CS, $1f             /* secure loader code segment */
1:

        pushl   %edx                    /* model/family/stepping */
                pushl   %eax            /* secure loader base */

                /* ... REMAINDER OF THE SECURE LOADER CODE ... */

                jmp     .                           /* just in case */


                .align 32
                .global sl_gdt_start
        sl_gdt_start:
                .quad 0x0000000000000000        /* reserved */
                .quad 0x00cf9a000000ffff        /* secure loader CS */
                .quad 0x00cf92000000ffff        /* secure loader DS */
        sl_gdt_end:

        sl_gdtr:
                .word sl_gdt_end - sl_gdt_start - 1 /* limit for gdt*/
                .long sl_gdt_start                      /* gdt base */

sl_end:
```

The secure loader code is located right after the header. Part of the calling guarantee of this code is that interrupts are disabled, virtual memory is disabled, DMA is inhibited, and only one processor is executing. The first order of business for the secure loader is to reinitialize the segment registers to flat 32-bit descriptors that allow the secure loader to access all of the 4GB address space (see Intel Architecture manuals for more details). Once the secure loader is initialized, it should prepare the system for the execution of a trusted operating system.

# Proof of Locality

The key idea behind the dynamic root of trust is that once the secure loader has bootstrapped a trusted operating system (OS), this OS will create multiple isolated security domains in which it can run guest OS or applications. A problem arises when the trusted OS, the guest OS, and the applications all use the TPM. How can you distinguish between measurements originating from the trusted OS, the guest OS, or the application?

To solve this dilemma, TCG introduced as part of their 1.2 specification the notion of a *locality*. A locality authenticates the originator of a TPM request. The specification defines five different localities. Locality 0 is intended for legacy support and behaves similar to a 1.1b TPM. The use of localities 1 to 3 are not specified, but they are typically associated with a trusted OS, guest OS, and the application. Locality 4 is special in that it authenticates the CPU, and it is used to authenticate the SKINIT instruction that is the basis for the dynamic root of trust.

Access to the localities 1–3 is controlled by the trusted OS. Each locality has its own interface to the TPM, and it is up to the trusted OS to assign the interfaces to the guest OS and application (see Chapter 4, "Writing a TPM Device Driver," for more details).

Attestation in a Trusted Computing Group sense is done by having the TPM use a special type of signing key (called an AIK) to sign (attest) to data values stored internal to the TPM, and thus to provide evidence of the state of the machine on which the TPM was placed.

To assist in the attestation process, the 1.2 specification introduced new PCRs whose access is controlled by the current locality. For example, PCR17 can be written only as part of the SKINIT instruction (locality 4). It cannot be written from any other software locality and thus ensures that the PCR17 value came directly from the CPU. The same is true for PCR20, where only requests from locality 1 can write it. Table 6.1 lists all the PCRs that are part of the 1.2 specification and their usage.

**Table 6.1**    Listing of PCRs for the 1.2 Specification

| Index | Usage | Reset | PCR Reset for Locality 4, 3, 2, 1, 0 |
|-------|-------|-------|--------------------------------------|
| 0 – 15 | Static RTM | 0 | 0,0,0,0,0 |
| 16 | Debug | 1 | 1,1,1,1,1 |
| 17 | Locality 4 | 1 | 1,0,0,0,0 |
| 18 | Locality 3 | 1 | 1,0,0,0,0 |
| 19 | Locality 2 | 1 | 1,0,0,0,0 |
| 20 | Locality 1 | 1 | 1,0,1,0,0 |
| 21 | Trusted OS controlled | 1 | 0,0,1,0,0 |
| 22 | Trusted OS controlled | 1 | 0,0,1,0,0 |
| 23 | Application | 1 | 1,1,1,1,1 |

Another feature that was introduced as part of the dynamic root of trust mechanism was the ability to reset certain PCRs. Only when the trusted OS is in control as a result of a SKINIT instruction can PCRs be reset according to the access control matrix listed in Table 6.1. Only PCRs that play a role in the DRTM mechanism can be reset.

## Summary

This chapter has covered how the TPM can be used to launch an OS, which can later attest to its "trusted" state in several ways. The static root of trust (available in 1.1 TPMs) and the dynamic root of trust (available in both 1.1 and 1.2) are covered, and a specific implementation for the AMD Secure Virtual Machine is given. Understanding the dynamic root of trust also provides the added value of motivating the "locality" attributes of the TPM. With these understood, the reader should be able to understand how to handle machine state attestation as provided by a TPM.

# CHAPTER 7

# The TCG Software Stack

The entry point for any programmer writing a trusted computing-enabled application is the Trusted Computing Group Software Stack (TSS). The TSS specifications define an architecture that makes accessing the TPM simple and direct, while exposing all the functionality that the TPM provides in a vendor-neutral way. The TSS also provides APIs for functionality on top of that provided by the TPM, such as

- The ability to store key objects persistently on disk
- Connecting with TPMs on both local and remote machines
- Conversion of data blobs between portable formats (TSS 1.2 only)

In this chapter, we cover the following topics:

- The overall design and architecture of the TSS
- TSS API conventions
- TSS object types and their uses
- Simple TSS programming examples
- TSS 1.2 additions and programming concerns

## TSS Design Overview

The TSS is composed of three logical components: the TCG device driver library (TDDL), the TCG core service (TCS), and the TCG service provider (TSP). See Figure 7.1 for an architectural overview of the TSS.

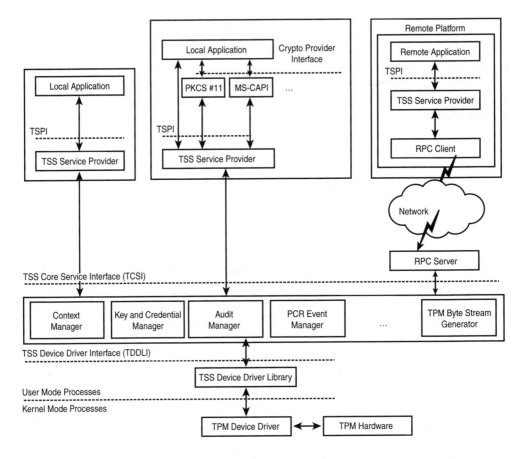

**Figure 7.1**    Architectural overview of the TSS

The TDDL is a library that provides an API to interface with the TPM device driver. Generally, TPM vendors will ship a TDDL library along with their TPM device driver so that TSS implementers can easily interface with it. The TDDL offers a small set of APIs to open and close the device driver, send and receive data blobs, query the device driver's properties, and cancel a submitted TPM command. For embedded applications where a full TSS doesn't exist and only a small subset of TPM commands will be used, the TDDL may be the best choice for interfacing with the TPM. In most cases, however, the TCS is the sole user of the TDDL.

The TCS layer has several jobs. It provides management of the TPM's resources, such as authorization session and key context swapping. It also provides a TPM command blob generator, which converts TCS API requests into the necessary byte streams that a TPM understands. It provides a system-wide key storage facility and synchronizes application access from the TSP layer. If the operating system supports it, the TCS layer must be implemented as a system service and should be the sole user of the TDDL. For more information on the TCS layer, see Chapter 10, "The TSS Core Service (TCS)."

The TSP layer is called directly by the application and is implemented as a shared object, or dynamic linked library. The TSP interface (referred to as the "Tspi") exposes all the TPM's capabilities and some of its own, such as key storage and pop-up dialog boxes for authorization data. In this chapter, we'll focus on the practicalities of programming to the Tspi and also its theory of operation.

## The TCG Service Provider Interface (Tspi)

The Tspi is designed such that each API is associated with an object type. There are seven object types defined by the 1.1 TSS spec: context, data, TPM, policy, PCR composite, hash, and key objects. The TSS 1.2 specification adds object types for certified migratable key data, non-volatile data, Direct Anonymous Attestation, and delegation families. Each Tspi API is named so that the programmer knows which object type it is operating on. For example, the simplest possible TSS application is shown in Listing 7.1, where both APIs shown operate on the TSP's context object. `Tspi_Context_Create` tells the TSP to generate a new context handle for the application to use and return it to the application. All other APIs in the TSP require an object that is associated with some TSP context; therefore, every TSS application must first call `Tspi_Context_Create`. `Tspi_Context_Close` frees all resources associated with a context.

**Listing 7.1**   The Simplest Possible TSS Application. A Context Handle Is Opened with the TSP Library and Then Closed.

```
TSS_HCONTEXT hContext;

Tspi_Context_Create(&hContext);

Tspi_Context_Close(hContext);
```

APIs that operate on data objects will begin with `Tspi_Data_`, those that operate on key objects will begin with `Tspi_Key_`, and so on. Support functions to get and set attributes of objects are prefixed only by `Tspi_`, such as `Tspi_SetAttribData` and `Tspi_GetAttribUint32`.

## TSP Object Types

Each of the TSP object types plays a role in the function of the TSP library. Let's walk through the roles of each of the different types of objects and how to use them. See Table 7.1 for the list of object types and the C language data type used to represent them in the Tspi.

**Table 7.1**   TSP Object Types

| Object Type | C Data Type | Available in TSS Version |
|---|---|---|
| Context | TSS_HCONTEXT | 1.1 and 1.2 |
| Data | TSS_HENCDATA | 1.1 and 1.2 |
| Key | TSS_HKEY | 1.1 and 1.2 |
| Hash | TSS_HHASH | 1.1 and 1.2 |
| PCR Composite | TSS_HPCRS | 1.1 and 1.2 |
| Policy | TSS_HPOLICY | 1.1 and 1.2 |
| TPM | TSS_HTPM | 1.1 and 1.2 |
| Non-Volatile Data | TSS_HNVSTORE | 1.2 |
| Migratable Data Object | TSS_HMIGDATA | 1.2 |
| Delegation Family | TSS_HDELFAMILY | 1.2 |
| DAA Credential | TSS_HDAA_CREDENTIAL | 1.2 |
| DAA Issuer Key | TSS_HDAA_ISSUER_KEY | 1.2 |
| DAA Anonymity Revocation Authority Key | TSS_HDAA_ARA_KEY | 1.2 |

In this section, the code fragments used to demonstrate the usage of each object type will contain some references to objects that are not defined. These examples are meant to be illustrative only—you should see the latest TSS specification for information on the use of each API.[1]

## Context Objects

The context object is used to maintain a handle to the current TSP library, connect to local and remote TCS providers, load keys, store and retrieve key objects from disk, and create new working objects. Each newly created object becomes associated with the context that it was created by. To create a new context object, use `Tspi_Context_Create`, and to close the context, use `Tspi_Context_Close`. See Listing 7.1 for an example. When `Tspi_Context_Create` is called, two things happen: A new context object is generated by the TSP, and a policy object is created and associated with the context. This policy object becomes the default policy for all authorized objects created in the context. When a new authorized object is created using `Tspi_Context_CreateObject`, it is associated with the context's default policy by default. If the use of that object requires authorization, the context's default policy is queried by the TSP for the authorization data.

---

1. See http://www.trustedcomputinggroup.org/specs/TSS for the latest public version of the TSS specification.

In order to send commands to a TPM, a TSP's context must connect to a TCS provider. This is done using the `Tspi_Context_Connect` API. `Tspi_Context_Connect` takes a context handle and the UTF-16–encoded hostname or IP address of the destination system. To connect to the TCS on the local machine, a NULL pointer is used as the destination address. If a connection to the TCS provider is successful, a TPM object is implicitly created by the TSP and associated with the context.

Any number of contexts may be created by an application and connected to any number of TCS providers. In a 1.2 TSS, there is a notion of the context's *connection version*, which is used to control the type of objects created using the context. By default, the context's connection version is 1.1, meaning that regardless of the version of TPM that you connect to using `Tspi_Context_Connect`, objects created by the context will be compatible with a 1.1 TPM. See Table 7.2 for the type of objects created when the connection version changes. To set the TSP context so that it will always create TSS 1.2 compatible objects, do the following:

```
Tspi_SetAttribUint32(hContext,
                     TSS_TSPATTRIB_CONTEXT_VERSION_MODE, 0,
                     TSS_TSPATTRIB_CONTEXT_VERSION_V1_2);
```

Or to tell the TSP to auto detect and create objects based on the version of TPM it is connected to, do the following:

```
Tspi_SetAttribUint32(hContext,
                     TSS_TSPATTRIB_CONTEXT_VERSION_MODE, 0,
                     TSS_TSPATTRIB_CONTEXT_VERSION_AUTO);
```

You may need to select which types of objects are created by your context depending on whether you need compatibility with migration of keys to different versions of TPMs. For instance, you may want to continue to create TPM 1.1 keys on 1.2 TPMs as new machines are rolled out so that you can guarantee migration between them.

**Table 7.2** The Types of Objects Created by `Tspi_Context_CreateObject` Based on the TSP Context's Connection Version

|  | Context Version 1.1 | Context Version 1.2 |
| --- | --- | --- |
| Key objects | TCPA_KEY | TPM_KEY12 |
| PCR objects | TCPA_PCR_INFO | TPM_PCR_INFO_LONG |

## TPM Objects

A TPM object is created implicitly when a TSP context is connected to a TCS provider. To retrieve a handle to the TPM object after a TCS connection is made, use `Tspi_Context_GetTPMObject`. When the TPM object is created, it also gets its own policy object, which is typically used to hold the authorization data for the TPM owner. Listing 7.2 shows the set of Tspi calls necessary to set up an owner-authorized command.

**Listing 7.2**    TSP API Calls Necessary to Set Up an Owner-Authorized Command

```
TSS_HCONTEXT hContext;
TSS_HTPM     hTPM;
TSS_HPOLICY  hOwnerPolicy;

Tspi_Context_Create(&hContext);

/* Connect to the local TCS provider */
Tspi_Context_Connect(hContext, NULL);

/* Get the handle to the implicitly created TPM object */
Tspi_Context_GetTPMObject(hContext, &hTPM);

Tspi_GetPolicyObject(hTPM, TSS_POLICY_USAGE, &hOwnerPolicy);

/* See listing 7.3 for the details of setting secrets */
Tspi_Policy_SetSecret(hOwnerPolicy, ...);

/* Put your owner-authorized commands here... */
```

## Policy Objects

Policy objects hold authorization data for use in commands that require it. Authorization data is needed to load keys, migrate keys, encrypt and decrypt data, take ownership of a TPM, and get and set sensitive properties of the TPM. Policies come in three types: usage, migration, and operator. Migration policies are used only when creating migratable keys. The operator policy is used to hold authorization data for the TSS 1.2's `Tspi_TPM_SetTempDeactivated` API. All other policies are considered usage policies.

The method a policy uses for getting its authorization data is called its *secret mode*. By default, all policies are created with secret mode `TSS_SECRET_MODE_POPUP`, which means that when it's used, the TSP will provide a graphical pop-up dialog box to retrieve the authorization data from the user. After retrieving the authorization data through the pop-up dialog the first time, the authorization data is saved and used whenever that policy is accessed. Unless `Tspi_Policy_FlushSecret` is called on the policy to flush the secret data, the pop-up will not be triggered again. Table 7.3 shows all the possible secret modes for a policy.

**Table 7.3**   Secret Modes for a Policy

| Secret Mode | Description |
|---|---|
| TSS_SECRET_MODE_NONE | No secret is associated with this policy. If an authorized command references a policy with this secret mode, expect an error return code of TSS_E_POLICY_NO_SECRET. The ulSecretLength and rgbSecret parameters to Tspi_Policy_SetSecret will be ignored. |
| TSS_SECRET_MODE_PLAIN | The data passed into Tspi_Policy_SetSecret will be hashed using the SHA-1 algorithm, resulting in the policy's secret. Zero-length data strings are allowed. |
| TSS_SECRET_MODE_SHA1 | The data passed into Tspi_Policy_SetSecret should be a 20-byte SHA-1 hash and will be set as the policy's secret. |
| TSS_SECRET_MODE_POPUP | The TSS will issue a dialog box to retrieve the secret data from the user. The ulSecretLength and rgbSecret parameters to Tspi_Policy_SetSecret will be ignored. This is the default secret mode for any new policy. |
| TSS_SECRET_MODE_CALLBACK | Use a callback function to request the secret from the application. Use Tspi_SetAttribUint32 (TSS 1.1) or Tspi_SetAttribData (TSS 1.2) on the policy object to set the address of the callback function. The ulSecretLength and rgbSecret parameters to Tspi_Policy_SetSecret will be ignored. |

The context object and TPM object each have their own policies created implicitly by the TSP. All newly created TSP objects that use policies (keys and data) then get a reference to the context object's policy. This means that for each object that needs a unique password, a new policy must be created and assigned to it. Listing 7.3 shows the process of creating a new key with a unique password.

**Listing 7.3**   Creating a Key with a Password Set to "Secret"

```
TSS_HCONTEXT hContext;
TSS_HKEY     hSRK, hKey;
TSS_HPOLICY  hPolicy;
BYTE         *secret = "secret";

Tspi_Context_Create(&hContext);

/* Connect to the local TCS provider */
Tspi_Context_Connect(hContext, NULL);
```

```
/* Load the new key's parent key, the Storage Root Key */
Tspi_Context_LoadKeyByUUID(hContext, TSS_PS_TYPE_SYSTEM,
                           SRK_UUID, &hSRK);

/* Create the software key object */
Tspi_Context_CreateObject(hContext, TSS_OBJECT_TYPE_RSAKEY,
                          TSS_KEY_SIZE_2048 |
                          TSS_KEY_TYPE_SIGNING |
                          TSS_KEY_AUTHORIZATION,
                          &hKey);

/* Create the usage policy object for the key */
Tspi_Context_CreateObject(hContext, TSS_OBJECT_TYPE_POLICY,
                          TSS_POLICY_USAGE, &hPolicy);

/* Set the secret in the policy */
Tspi_Policy_SetSecret(hPolicy, TSS_SECRET_MODE_PLAIN,
                      strlen(secret), secret);

/* Assign the policy object to the key */
Tspi_Policy_AssignToObject(hPolicy, hKey);

/* Call down to the TPM to generate the key */
Tspi_Key_CreateKey(hKey, hSRK, 0);
```

Policy object secrets can also be set to expire based on the number of times used or a number of seconds. For example, to create a policy that expires in 10 seconds, call:

```
Tspi_SetAttribUint32(hPolicy,
                     TSS_TSPATTRIB_POLICY_SECRET_LIFETIME,
                     TSS_TSPATTRIB_POLSECRET_LIFETIME_TIMER, 10);
```

And to create a policy that expires after one use, call:

```
Tspi_SetAttribUint32(hPolicy,
                     TSS_TSPATTRIB_POLICY_SECRET_LIFETIME,
                     TSS_TSPATTRIB_POLSECRET_LIFETIME_COUNTER,1);
```

Secrets are processed in different ways depending on their type, but they all end up as a SHA-1 hash internally in the TSP library. This SHA-1 hash is used in an HMAC calculation to establish an authorization session with the TPM. Unfortunately, the difference in processing for each secret type can lead to an incorrect hash being created and the authorization session failing. Table 7.4 documents the hash creation process for each secret type.

**Table 7.4**   Hash Creation Process for Each Secret Type

| Secret Mode | Secret Creation Process | |
| --- | --- | --- |
| | **TSS 1.1** | **TSS 1.2** |
| TSS_SECRET_MODE_NONE | None | |
| TSS_SECRET_MODE_PLAIN | Secret = SHA1(secret data as passed to Tspi_Policy_SetSecret) | |
| TSS_SECRET_MODE_SHA1 | Secret = secret data as passed to Tspi_Policy_SetSecret | |
| TSS_SECRET_MODE_POPUP | Secret = SHA1(UTF16-LE encoded secret data from dialog box + \0\0)* | Secret = SHA1(UTF16-LE encoded secret data from dialog box) |
| TSS_SECRET_MODE_CALLBACK | None | |

\*   Two zero bytes will be included in the hashed data due to the fact that the string is represented in UTF-16, which uses two-byte wide (16 bit) characters.

If your TSS application needs to operate in an environment with mixed user interaction (sometimes using pop-up policies, and other times not), it is prudent to convert your plain-text secrets to UTF-16LE before setting them in their policies. Also, in mixed TSS 1.1 and 1.2 environments, pay close attention to whether the NULL termination characters are included with your secrets. In the TSS version 1.2, an attribute of the context object, TSS_TSPATTRIB_SECRET_HASH_MODE, can be used to control whether the NULL terminating characters are included in secrets received from pop-up dialogs. To force the TSS 1.2 stack to include NULL terminating characters for compatibility with TSS 1.1, call:

```
Tspi_SetAttribUint32(hContext, TSS_TSPATTRIB_SECRET_HASH_MODE,
                TSS_TSPATTRIB_SECRET_HASH_MODE_POPUP,
                TSS_TSPATTRIB_HASH_MODE_NULL);
```

After making this call, all policies created explicitly or implicitly by the context hContext will include the terminating NULL characters in the pop-up secret data they hash.

## Key Objects

Key objects are used to represent TPM keys, which are actually RSA public/private key pairs. For a description of the different key types, see Chapter 3, "An Overview of the Trusted Platform Module Capabilities."

Key objects can be created like other objects, by calling Tspi_Context_CreateObject, or using calls to the TSS's persistent storage functions, such as Tspi_Context_GetRegisteredKeyByUUID. To have a new 1024-bit binding key pair created by the TPM, at least two calls are necessary:

```
TSS_HKEY hKey;

Tspi_Context_CreateObject(hContext, TSS_OBJECT_TYPE_RSAKEY,

TSS_KEY_SIZE_1024|TSS_KEY_TYPE_BIND|TSS_KEY_NO_AUTHORIZATION,
                          &hKey);

/* Create hKey, with hParentKey as its parent key (which must
 * already be loaded into the TPM) and 0 for the PCR composite
 * object handle in order to keep the key from being bound to
 * any PCRs */
Tspi_Key_CreateKey(hKey, hParentKey, 0);
```

The call to `Tspi_Context_CreateObject` creates a skeleton software key object inside the TSP library with the properties requested. The call to `Tspi_Key_CreateKey` will send that skeleton key to the TPM. The TPM will generate the key pair based on the properties of the software key and return the generated pair to the TSP. The TSP will then add the generated key pair data to its software object. Note that `hParentKey` must be loaded into the TPM prior to the `Tspi_Key_CreateKey` call.

Key objects are exported from the TSS in "blob" form—that is, the byte stream format used by the TPM. To retrieve a key in its blob form, use `Tspi_GetAttribData`:

```
BYTE   *keyBlob;
UINT32 keyBlobLen;

Tspi_GetAttribData(hKey, TSS_TSPATTRIB_KEY_BLOB,
                   TSS_TSPATTRIB_KEYBLOB_BLOB,
                   &keyBlobLen, &keyBlob);
```

After the call successfully returns, `keyBlob` will point to an allocated memory area of size `keyBlobLen` holding a serialized `TCPA_KEY` structure. There are other flags for `Tspi_GetAttribData` to get only the public key portion (a `TCPA_PUBKEY` blob) of the key:

```
BYTE   *pubkeyBlob;
UINT32 pubkeyBlobLen;

Tspi_GetAttribData(hKey, TSS_TSPATTRIB_KEY_BLOB,
                   TSS_TSPATTRIB_KEYBLOB_PUBLIC_KEY,
                   &pubkeyBlobLen, &pubkeyBlob);
```

And only the RSA modulus:

```
BYTE    *modulus;
UINT32 modulusLen;


Tspi_GetAttribData(hKey, TSS_TSPATTRIB_RSAKEY_INFO,
                   TSS_TSPATTRIB_KEYINFO_RSA_MODULUS,
                   &modulusLen, &modulus);
```

The difference between the `TCPA_PUBKEY` structure and the RSA modulus is that the `TCPA_PUBKEY` structure contains a `TCPA_KEY_PARMS` structure, which holds the encryption and signature schemes for the key as well as other properties of the key.

## Encrypted Data Objects

Data objects are used to hold sealed and bound data blobs during a seal or bind operation. Data can be inserted or extracted from them using `Tspi_SetAttribData` and `Tspi_GetAttribData`, respectively. During a bind or seal operation, the data encrypted will automatically be inserted into the encrypted data object by the TSS:

```
TSS_HENCDATA hEncData;
BYTE         *blob, *data = "data";
UINT32       blobLen;



Tspi_Context_CreateObject(hContext, TSS_OBJECT_TYPE_ENCDATA,
                          TSS_ENCDATA_BIND, &hEncData);


/* Call the TSS to bind the data, storing the encrypted data
 * blob in hEncData */
Tspi_Data_Bind(hEncData, hKey, strlen(data), data);


/* Retrieve the encrypted data blob to store elsewhere */
Tspi_GetAttribData(hEncData, TSS_TSPATTRIB_ENCDATA_BLOB,
                   TSS_TSPATTRIB_ENCDATABLOB_BLOB,
                   &blobLen, &blob);
```

The preceding example is simplified, not showing the creation of the key or context. Creating and using encrypted data objects is very straightforward, but there is one thing to remember—always free the data returned by `Tspi_GetAttribData` using `Tspi_Context_FreeMemory`. See the "TSS Memory Management" section of this chapter for more information.

## Hash Objects

Hash objects are used to hold hash values, compute the hash of data, and sign and verify hashes using keys. Natively, the TSS supports hashing data using the SHA1 algorithm only, although it can sign and verify hashes of any type. To create a SHA1 hash of some data, use `Tspi_Hash_UpdateHashValue`:

```
TSS_HHASH hHash;
BYTE      *digest, *data = "data to hash";
UINT32    digestLen;

/* Create the hash object */
Tspi_Context_CreateObject(hContext, TSS_OBJECT_TYPE_HASH,
                          TSS_HASH_SHA1, &hHash);

/* Hash the data.  The TSS knows to use SHA1 as the algorithm
 * because the object is of type TSS_HASH_SHA1 */
Tspi_Hash_UpdateHashValue(hHash, strlen(data), data);

/* Retrieve the digest from the hash object */
Tspi_Hash_GetHashValue(hHash, &digestLen, &digest);
```

Although the TPM supports it, the SHA1 hashing in the TSP is done by the TSS, not the TPM. The TPM's SHA1 hashing routines are provided mainly for use before a full operating system environment is available, such as during BIOS load, since adding an implementation of the SHA1 algorithm would be too expensive in those environments. Note that calling `Tspi_Hash_UpdateHashValue` implies that the TSS knows how to calculate the hash value for the hash algorithm associated with the TSP hash object. Because the SHA1 algorithm is the only supported algorithm in TSS 1.1 and 1.2, calling `Tspi_Hash_UpdateHashValue` on a hash object of any other type will return `TSS_E_INTERNAL_ERROR`.

If you need to sign or verify a hash value made using another hashing algorithm such as md5 or SHA256, you cannot use the TSS to create the hash value. You will need an external library that supports hashing using your required algorithm. Once the hash value is created using your required algorithm, use `TSS_HASH_OTHER` and `Tspi_Hash_SetHashValue` to set the hash value in the TSS object:

```
TSS_HHASH hHash;
BYTE      *digest = /* hash value */;
UINT32    digestLen = /* hash len */;

/* Create the hash object as some type other than SHA1 */
Tspi_Context_CreateObject(hContext, TSS_OBJECT_TYPE_HASH,
                          TSS_HASH_OTHER, &hHash);
```

```
/* Set the digest in the hash object */
Tspi_Hash_SetHashValue(hHash, digestLen, digest);
```

Note that once a hash object is created as type TSS_HASH_OTHER, Tspi_Hash_UpdateHashValue cannot be called on it, since Tspi_Hash_UpdateHashValue only operates on SHA1 hash objects.

For information on signing and verifying hashes and data using the TSS, see the section later in the chapter, "Signing and Verifying."

## PCR Composite Objects

PCR composite objects represent an array of hashes and their composite digest value. Creating a PCR composite object is done for one of two possible operations: those that need only a selection of PCR indices, such as Tspi_TPM_Quote, and those that require a selection of indices and a set of values, such as Tspi_Data_Seal. In the case of doing a quote operation, where the TPM signs a set of PCR values using a specified key, all the TPM needs to know is which PCRs to sign. In this case, use Tspi_PcrComposite_SelectPcrIndex:

```
TSS_HPCRS        hPcrs;
TSS_VALIDATION validationData; /* initialization not shown */
UINT32           i, pcrsToSelect[3] = { 7, 8, 9 };

/* Create a PCR composite object. */
Tspi_Context_CreateObject(hContext, TSS_OBJECT_TYPE_PCRS, 0,
                          &hPcrs);

/* Select PCR indices 7, 8 and 9 */
for (i = 0; i < 3; i++)
    Tspi_PcrComposite_SelectPcrIndex(hPcrs, pcrsToSelect[i]);

/* Quote on PCRs 7, 8 and 9.  See the section below for info
 * on validation data */
Tspi_TPM_Quote(hTPM, hKey, hPcrs, &validationData);
```

Selecting an index of a PCR composite object merely flips a bit in the object, indicating that the PCR index should be considered by the TPM in any operation that uses it. For operations that require specific PCR values to be set in an object, see Listing 7.4.

**Listing 7.4** Setting Up a PCR Composite Object for Use in Sealing Data

```
TSS_HPCRS    hPcrs;
TCPA_DIGEST digestValues[3] = { ..., ..., ... };
UINT32       i, pcrsToSelect[3] = { 7, 8, 9 };
```

```
/* Create the PCR composite object */
Tspi_Context_CreateObject(hContext, TSS_OBJECT_TYPE_PCRS, 0,
                          &hPcrs);


/* Select PCR indices 7, 8 and 9 and set their values in the
 * object */
for (i = 0; i < 3; i++) {
    Tspi_PcrComposite_SelectPcrIndex(hPcrs, pcrsToSelect[i]);

    Tspi_PcrComposite_SetPcrValues(hPcrs, pcrsToSelect[i],
                                   sizeof(TCPA_DIGEST),
                                   digestValues[i]);
}


/* Seal some data to the PCR values in the digestValues
 * array on PCRs 7, 8 and 9 */
Tspi_Data_Seal(hEncData, hKey, ulDataLength, rgbDataToSeal,
               hPcrs);
```

In Listing 7.4, the `digestValues` array contains three 20-byte SHA-1 hash values. These three hash values are passed to `Tspi_PcrComposite_SetPcrValue`, which then sets them as values for PCR registers 7, 8, and 9 inside the PCR composite object. You might notice that no initialization flags were passed to `Tspi_Context_CreateObject` when creating the PCRs object. In the 1.1 TSS, there were no valid flags for a PCRs object. In version 1.2 of the TSS, there are three flags to control which type of structure is associated with the PCRs object. To create a `TCPA_PCR_INFO` structure, either pass 0 for the initialization flags as you did in TSS 1.1, or use `TSS_PCRS_STRUCT_INFO`:

```
        Tspi_Context_CreateObject(hContext, TSS_OBJECT_TYPE_PCRS,
                                  TSS_PCRS_STRUCT_INFO, &hPcrs);
```

To create a `TPM_PCR_INFO_LONG` structure, use `TSS_PCRS_STRUCT_INFO_LONG`:

```
        Tspi_Context_CreateObject(hContext, TSS_OBJECT_TYPE_PCRS,
                                  TSS_PCRS_STRUCT_INFO_LONG, &hPcrs);
```

To default to the type of object that should be created based on the context's connection version, use `TSS_PCR_STRUCT_DEFAULT`:

```
        Tspi_Context_CreateObject(hContext, TSS_OBJECT_TYPE_PCRS,
                                  TSS_PCRS_STRUCT_DEFAULT, &hPcrs);
```

See the earlier "Context Objects" section for more information on setting the context's connection version.

## Non-Volatile Data Objects (TSS 1.2)

Non-volatile data objects represent areas of flash storage (NVRAM) inside the TPM itself. NVRAM storage is a feature of 1.2 TPMs that's meant to replace the less-flexible Data Integrity Register (DIR) functionality found in 1.1 TPMs. DIRs were 160-bit areas of flash inside the TPM that could be written to and read from using owner authorization and the TSS's `Tspi_TPM_DirRead` and `Tspi_TPM_DirWrite` APIs. NVRAM objects have expanded this functionality to allow predefined areas of flash inside the TPM for storing certificates and data as well as unused areas that can be defined by the TSS. Unlike DIRs, NVRAM areas can also be associated with PCR values, so that the TPM can enforce reading or writing based on its PCR state.

You might notice that although the TPM command to define a new NVRAM space in the TPM is owner authorized, there is no TPM object associated with the NV Tspi APIs to receive the owner's authorization. This was a slight oversight by the TSS working group of the TCG, but to work around it, `Tspi_NV_DefineSpace` will transparently look up the context object associated with the `TSS_HNVSTORE` object passed in, find the TPM object associated with that context, and use the owner's authorization data from its policy to authorize the command. If you'd like to define NVRAM space that requires authorization, set the secret for the space in the NVRAM object's policy before calling `Tspi_NV_DefineSpace`.

To create an NVRAM object and use it to store data that requires no authorization to read, do the following:

```
TSS_HCONTEXT hContext;
TSS_HTPM     hTPM;
TSS_HPOLICY  hOwnerPolicy;
TSS_HNVSTORE hNvStore;
BYTE         *data = /* some data */;
UINT32       dataLen = /* length of the data */;

Tspi_Context_Create(&hContext);

/* Connect to the local TCS provider */
Tspi_Context_Connect(hContext, NULL);

/* Get the handle to the implicitly created TPM object */
Tspi_Context_GetTPMObject(hContext, &hTPM);

Tspi_GetPolicyObject(hTPM, TSS_POLICY_USAGE, &hOwnerPolicy);

/* See listing 7.3 for the details of setting secrets */
Tspi_Policy_SetSecret(hOwnerPolicy, …);

/* Create the NVRAM object */
Tspi_Context_CreateObject(hContext, TSS_OBJECT_TYPE_NV, 0,
                          &hNvStore);
```

```
/* Set the attribute in the NVRAM object so that NV index 1 is
 * used. Selecting index 1 is essentially an arbitrary choice.
 * If you choose an index that already exists,
 * Tspi_NV_DefineSpace will return an error */
Tspi_SetAttribUint32(hNvStore, TSS_TSPATTRIB_NV_INDEX, 0, 1);

/* Set the permissions to require authorization to write to the
 * NVRAM area.  This may require a policy object to be
 * associated with the hNvStore object to hold the secret data */
Tspi_SetAttribUint32(hNvStore, TSS_TSPATTRIB_NV_PERMISSIONS, 0,
                       TPM_NV_PER_AUTHWRITE);

/* Set the size of the area we're about to define */
Tspi_SetAttribUint32(hNvStore, TSS_TSPATTRIB_NV_DATASIZE, 0,
                       dataLen);

/* Call down to the TPM to define the space.  Pass in zeroes
 * for the handles to PCR objects - we aren't associating this
 * NVRAM space with any PCR values */
Tspi_NV_DefineSpace(hNvStore, 0, 0);

/* Write the data into the defined flash area */
Tspi_NV_WriteValue(hNvStore, 0, dataLen, data);
```

## Migratable Data Objects (TSS 1.2)

Migratable data objects are used with Certified Migratable Keys (CMKs) to hold properties and migratable data blobs when passing them between APIs. Attributes of migratable data objects are set and retrieved using `Tspi_SetAttribData` and `Tspi_GetAttribData` in the same way as other objects. Refer to the TSS specification for information on the various attributes of migratable data objects.

## Delegation Family Objects (TSS 1.2)

Delegation family objects are used to manage the delegation tables used by the TPM. Attributes of delegation family objects are set and retrieved using `Tspi_SetAttribData` and `Tspi_GetAttribData` in the same way as other objects. See Chapter 16 for detailed information and example code for use in delegating TPM ordinals and authorizations.

## Direct Anonymous Attestation (DAA) Objects (TSS 1.2)

There are three different types of objects used to represent the keys and certificates used in the DAA protocols: `TSS_HDAA_CREDENTIAL`, `TSS_HDAA_ISSUER_KEY`, and `TSS_HDAA_ARA_KEY`. The key data types used with DAA key and certificate objects are set and retrieved from their TSP objects using `Tspi_SetAttribData` and `Tspi_GetAttribData` in the same way as key objects. See the "Key Objects" section for some examples.

## TSS Return Codes

The values returned from Tspi APIs are unsigned 32-bit integers, represented by the `TSS_RESULT` type. These values contain encoded data indicating which TSS layer produced the error, the error value itself, and some operating system-specific data. Due to this packing of data into one value, some care needs to be taken when checking for specific error codes to prevent mistakes. Figure 7.2 shows the layout of a `TSS_RESULT`.

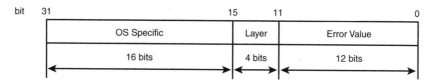

**Figure 7.2**   Layout of a TSS_RESULT

The upper 16 bits of a `TSS_RESULT` store the operating system-specific information. The next 4 bits are used to define the TSS layer that the error occurred in (TSP, TCS, TDDL, or TPM) and the lowest 12 bits represent the actual error code. In the TSS 1.1 and 1.2 specifications, only MS Windows® has defined use of the operating system-specific space. All other operating systems are advised to set this area to 0. See the latest TSS specification for more information on use of the OS-specific section.

In the TSS 1.2 header files, some preprocessor macros have been defined to make error code processing easier. `ERROR_CODE` and `ERROR_LAYER` are bit masks that strip away all but the indicated information. So, for example, a TSS application writer who wants to check for `TSS_E_PS_KEY_NOTFOUND`, which can occur at the TSP or TCS level, might naively write this segment of code:

```
result = Tspi_Context_GetRegisteredKeyByUUID(...);
if (result == TSS_E_PS_KEY_NOTFOUND) {
    /* This code cannot be reached! */
}
```

The preceding code would never pass into the error-handling section, since there will always be error layer information included in the return value. The following modification to the previous code will fix the problem:

```
result = Tspi_Context_GetRegisteredKeyByUUID(...);
if (ERROR_CODE(result) == TSS_E_PS_KEY_NOTFOUND) {
    /* process the error */
}
```

Adding the ERROR_CODE wrapper around the result strips off the error layer information and the operating system-specific information and the comparison to the return value is made correctly.

## TSS Memory Management

Many Tspi APIs return data to the application that has been allocated internally by the TSP. This data is tracked by the TSP's internal memory management routines and must be freed using the Tspi_Context_FreeMemory API. Calling the system's free routine on memory allocated by the TSP will likely cause double-free errors and corrupt your application's memory space when the TSS closes.

## Portable Data

When passing data in between TSSs on different platforms, it may be necessary to encode the data in some platform-neutral way so that the data can be consumed by both TSSs. The TSS 1.2 specification provides just such a mechanism in the Tspi_EncodeDER_TssBlob and Tspi_DecodeBER_TssBlob APIs. By default, TSS APIs will return data in blob form according to the "Portable Data" section of the TSS specification. For instance, when Tspi_SetAttribData is called to retrieve a TCPA_PUBKEY blob from a TSP key object, the TSS specification states that the data returned should be in the same form as the TPM would output:

```
BYTE   *pubKeyBlob;
UINT32 pubKeyBlobLen;

/* Pull the TCPA_PUBKEY blob out of the key object */
Tspi_GetAttribData(hKey, TSS_TSPATTRIB_KEY_BLOB,
                   TSS_TSPATTRIB_KEYBLOB_PUBLIC_KEY,
                   &pubKeyBlobLen, &pubKeyBlob);
```

Using this public key blob in the same application will be straightforward, since the current application will know what the data blob represents, but how will another TSS know what's in it? The other TSS could try parsing it to determine what it is, but that approach can be difficult. Instead of exporting the blob directly, the application should call Tspi_EncodeDER_TssBlob to encode the data:

```
BYTE   *pubKeyBlob, encodedBlob[512];
UINT32 pubKeyBlobLen, encodedBlobLen = 512;

/* Pull the TCPA_PUBKEY blob out of the key object */
Tspi_GetAttribData(hKey, TSS_TSPATTRIB_KEY_BLOB,
                   TSS_TSPATTRIB_KEYBLOB_PUBLIC_KEY,
                   &pubKeyBlobLen, &pubKeyBlob);
```

```
/* Call the blob encoding API to produce a platform neutral
 * encoding of the data */
Tspi_EncodeDER_TssBlob(pubKeyBlobLen, pubKeyBlob,
                       TSS_BLOB_TYPE_PUBKEY, &encodedBlobLen,
                       encodedBlob);
```

Data produced by `Tspi_EncodeDER_TssBlob` can be passed to another TSS without any description of the data being necessary. To determine what data you've received from another TSS, use `Tspi_DecodeBER_TssBlob`:

```
BYTE   rawBlob[512];
UINT32 blobType, rawBlobLen = 512;

Tspi_DecodeBER_TssBlob(encodedBlobLen, encodedBlob, &blobType,
                       &rawBlobLen, rawBlob);

switch (blobType) {
    case TSS_BLOB_TYPE_PUBKEY:
        /* handle the TCPA_PUBKEY blob */
        break;

    /* ... */
}
```

Use of the blob-encoding routines will enable your TSS application to interact with other TSS applications regardless of their platform type or endianess. Unfortunately, these routines are only specified by the TSS 1.2 specification. If you're targeting a TSS 1.1 implementation for your app, you'll need to create your own mechanism for passing data around safely.

## Persistent Key Storage

One service that the TSS offers independent of a TPM is key storage. At the TCS level, keys are stored (or *registered*) persistently on disk in what is called *system* persistent storage. The system persistent key store can be accessed by any application without restriction, due to the fact that the TPM is not involved in the operation of key registration to make any enforcement decisions. Because a rogue application could unregister any key in the system persistent store, it is generally of limited usefulness. The *user* persistent store, however, is managed by the TSP library and is private to the user of the application accessing it. Although its location is TSS specific, the user persistent key store is generally kept in a location accessible to the owner of the process that the TSP is operating as, such as that user's home directory.

Both user and system key stores use the `TSS_UUID` structure to address keys in the store. Each key in persistent storage has a UUID that is unique to that key store. If an application

attempts to store a key using a UUID that already exists, the API will return `TSS_E_KEY_`
`ALREADY_REGISTERED`. The TCG has predefined several UUID values to address well-known
keys, such as the TPM's storage root key. To load the storage root key, call `Tspi_Context_`
`LoadKeyByUUID`:

```
TSS_HKEY hSRK;
/* TSS_UUID_SRK is a well-known UUID defined in the TSS header
 * files */
TSS_UUID SRK_UUID = TSS_UUID_SRK;

/* Create an application handle to the SRK */
Tspi_Context_LoadKeyByUUID(hContext, TSS_PS_TYPE_SYSTEM,
                           SRK_UUID, &hSRK);
```

To store a key in system persistent storage, use `Tspi_Context_RegisterKey`. The application must pass in UUID information for the key it wants to store, as well as that key's parent
key. So, to store a child of the storage root key in user persistent storage, do the following:

```
TSS_UUID SRK_UUID = TSS_UUID_SRK;
TSS_UUID keyUUID = /* Unique UUID value */;

Tspi_Context_RegisterKey(hContext, hKey, TSS_PS_TYPE_USER,
                         keyUUID, TSS_PS_TYPE_SYSTEM,
SRK_UUID);
```

Then to load the key from storage:

```
TSS_HKEY hKey;
TSS_UUID keyUUID = /* UUID value */;
/* Create an application handle to the key and load it into
 * the TPM */
Tspi_Context_LoadKeyByUUID(hContext, TSS_PS_TYPE_USER,
                           keyUUID, &hKey);
```

Using the TSS's persistent storage functionality is a handy way to save and load keys for
any application. Managing a large store of keys is made easier by other TSS functions that can
query and return description information on the entire TSS key hierarchy, such as `Tspi_`
`Context_GetRegisteredKeysByUUID`:

```
TSS_KM_KEYINFO *info;
UINT32          infoLen;

Tspi_Context_GetRegisteredKeysByUUID(hContext,
                             TSS_PS_TYPE_SYSTEM, NULL,
                             &infoLen, &info);
```

Making the preceding call will return an array of `TSS_KM_KEYINFO` structures that describe every key stored in the system persistent key store. The key info structure contains the UUID of each key and its parent, whether the key requires authorization, whether the key is loaded or not, and optional vendor data that can be set by the TSS. The preceding code examples will work for a TSS 1.1 or 1.2 application. In addition, the TSS 1.2 specification offers a `TSS_KM_KEYINFO2` structure, which contains all the information as the `TSS_KM_KEYINFO` structure, but additionally includes the persistent storage type flag (`TSS_PS_TYPE_SYSTEM` or `TSS_PS_TYPE_USER`) that each key is stored in. To retrieve a `TSS_KM_KEYINFO2` structure, use `Tspi_Context_GetRegisteredKeysByUUID2`.

## Signing and Verifying

The process of signing and verifying data is made slightly more complex when using the TSS due to the fact that there are different behaviors, depending on the signature scheme associated with the key you use. Because the TPM cannot know all possible hash algorithms, it only provides support for signing SHA1 hashes and leaves support for all others up to the TSS and application. The general process for creating the digital signature of a hash value is the following:[2]

1. Create H1, the hash value to sign.
2. Create D1 by concatenating the Object Identifier (OID) for the hash algorithm used to generate H1 with H1 itself.
3. Create P1 by padding D1 using PKCS#1 v1.5 padding.
4. Create the signature by encrypting P1 with the private key.

When signing using the TSS, this process is kept intact. For signatures on hash values other than SHA1, however, the TSS must execute step 2 manually, since the TPM doesn't know which hash algorithm it's signing. Here's some sample code to demonstrate signing a SHA1 hash:

```
TSS_HHASH  hHash;
BYTE       *sig, *digest = /* hash value */;
UINT32     sigLen, digestLen = 20;

/* Create the hash object as type SHA1 */
Tspi_Context_CreateObject(hContext, TSS_OBJECT_TYPE_HASH,
                          TSS_HASH_SHA1, &hHash);

/* Set the digest in the hash object */
Tspi_Hash_SetHashValue(hHash, digestLen, digest);
```

---

2. For more information on creating digital signatures, see Public Key Cryptography Standard #1 at https://www.rsa.com/rsalabs/node.asp?id=2133.

```
/* Sign the hash using hKey, a signing key with signature
 * scheme TSS_SS_RSASSAPKCS1V15_SHA1 */
Tspi_Hash_Sign(hHash, hKey, &sigLen, &sig);
```

In this example, the data flow between the application, TSS, and TPM looks like Figure 7.3.

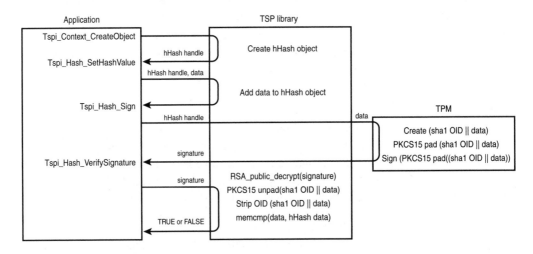

**Figure 7.3**   Signature flow of a SHA1 hash between the application and TPM

As you can see, the hash data is passed down to the TPM, which adds the SHA1 OID and padding and then does the encryption. To sign data other than a SHA1 hash, the signature scheme for the key used should be TSS_SS_RSASSAPKCS1V15_DER and the OID for the algorithm should be added manually by the application:

```
TSS_HHASH hHash;
BYTE      *sig, *digestAndOID = /* hash value || OID */;
UINT32    sigLen, digestLen = /* Length of digestAndOID */;

/* Create the hash object as some type other than SHA1 */
Tspi_Context_CreateObject(hContext, TSS_OBJECT_TYPE_HASH,
                          TSS_HASH_OTHER, &hHash);

/* Set the digest in the hash object */
Tspi_Hash_SetHashValue(hHash, digestLen, digestAndOID);

/* Sign the hash using hKey, a signing key with signature
 * scheme TSS_SS_RSASSAPKCS1V15_DER */
Tspi_Hash_Sign(hHash, hKey, &sigLen, &sig);
```

In this example, the TPM pads and signs only the data it receives; therefore, this process can be used to sign arbitrary data. Figure 7.4 shows the data flow between the application, TSP library, and TPM when using the _DER signature scheme.

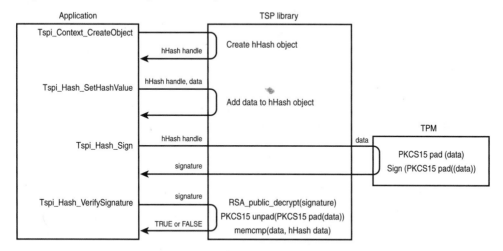

**Figure 7.4**   Signature flow of a non-SHA1 hash between the application and TPM

The two code examples shown previously are compatible with both TSS 1.1 and 1.2, but the TSS 1.2 specification has added an attribute of the hash object to aid in adding the OID. To have the TSS automatically add an OID to the hash value you set using `Tspi_Hash_SetHashValue`, use `TSS_TSPATTRIB_ALG_IDENTIFIER`:

```
BYTE    *oid = /* Your hash algorithm's OID */;
UINT32 oidLen = /* Length of oid */;

Tspi_SetAttribData(hHash, TSS_TSPATTRIB_ALG_IDENTIFIER, 0,
                   oidLen, oid);
```

If the algorithm identifier attribute of the hash object has been set, the TSS will add that data to the hash value before sending it to the TPM for signing. Otherwise, the TSS assumes that you added the OID data in the `Tspi_Hash_SetHashValue` call.

## Setting Callback Functions

The Tspi allows applications to use callbacks for several different operations, such as the authorization process and the identity key creation process. Callbacks are available to keep the application from having to reveal secret data to the TSS. In the TSS version 1.1, all callbacks were set using `Tspi_SetAttribUint32` on the appropriate object. Unfortunately, this did not allow applications compiled on platforms with 64-bit pointer types to use callbacks. The problem was solved in the TSS 1.2 specification by introducing the TSS_CALLBACK structure:

```
typedef struct tdTSS_CALLBACK
{
    PVOID               callback;
    PVOID               appData;
    TSS_ALGORITHM_ID alg;
} TSS_CALLBACK;
```

For applications written for the TSS 1.2 specification, create a TSS_CALLBACK structure and set it in the TSP object using Tspi_SetAttribData:

```
TSS_CALLBACK cb;

cb.callback = my_callback_func;
cb.appData = my_data;
cb.alg = TSS_ALG_3DES;

Tspi_SetAttribData(hPolicy, TSS_TSPATTRIB_POLICY_CALLBACK_HMAC,
                   0, sizeof(TSS_CALLBACK), &cb);
```

Since the TSS 1.2 interface is more portable, it should be used wherever possible by applications. If your application must be compatible with TSS 1.1, use the deprecated TSS 1.1 interface, Tspi_SetAttribUint32:

```
/* This will not work on 64-bit platforms! */
Tspi_SetAttribUint32(hPolicy,
                     TSS_TSPATTRIB_POLICY_CALLBACK_HMAC,
                     my_data, my_callback_func);
```

To clear a callback function you've already set, pass NULL (or 0) as the address of the callback using either Tspi_SetAttribData or Tspi_SetAttribUint32:

```
Tspi_SetAttribData(hPolicy, TSS_TSPATTRIB_POLICY_CALLBACK_HMAC,
                   0, 0, NULL);
```

or

```
Tspi_SetAttribUint32(hPolicy,
                     TSS_TSPATTRIB_POLICY_CALLBACK_HMAC,
                     0, 0);
```

After clearing the callback address in the preceding examples, the policy's type will still be set to TSS_SECRET_MODE_CALLBACK. If the policy is used by the TSS, an error will occur. To keep this from happening, set the policy's secret mode to something else after clearing the callback address.

# The TSS Validation Data Structure

The Tspi needed a way to allow applications to provide data to some APIs for use in their operations. For instance, when `Tspi_TPM_GetPubEndorsementKey` is called, the TSS passes a 20-byte nonce to the TPM so that the TPM can include it in a hash. The TPM calculates

```
checksum = SHA1(TSS_Nonce || TCPA_PUBKEY(EK))
```

and returns the calculated checksum data to the TSS. When the TSS receives that data back from the TCS, it computes the same hash value using the returned EK's `TCPA_PUBKEY` structure and compares it with the checksum returned by the TPM. This allows the TSS to verify the integrity of the data returned from the TPM, but what if the application cannot trust the TSS? To allow the application to pass data into the TSS for uses such as this, use the `TSS_VALIDATION` structure:

```
typedef struct tdTSS_VALIDATION
{
    TSS_VERSION versionInfo;
    UINT32      ulExternalDataLength;
    BYTE*       rgbExternalData;
    UINT32      ulDataLength;
    BYTE*       rgbData;
    UINT32      ulValidationDataLength;
    BYTE*       rgbValidationData;
} TSS_VALIDATION;
```

To have the TSS pass a nonce of your choosing to the TPM, set up a `TSS_VALIDATION` structure by setting the external (application provided) data parameters and pass it to `Tspi_TPM_GetPubEndorsementKey`:

```
TSS_VALIDATION vData;

vData.rgbExternalData = /* 20 byte nonce */;
vData.ulExternalDataLength = 20;

Tspi_TPM_GetPubEndorsementKey(hTPM, FALSE, &vData, &hPubEK);
```

After the API is called, the data and validation data fields of the structure will have been filled in by the TSS. The `rgbData` field will contain the provided nonce and the data returned from the TPM. The `rgbValidationData` field will contain the checksum value returned from the TPM. It's then the application's responsibility to verify that:

```
vData.rgbValidationData = SHA1(vData.rgbData)
```

The validation structure has different uses depending on which API it is passed to. For instance, when passing it to the `Tspi_TPM_Quote` operation, the external data is included in the signature made by the TPM over the selected PCRs. Upon returning, the validation data structure will contain the external data, the PCR data that was signed, and the signature itself. It's then up to the application to use the public part of the signing key to verify that the signature matches. See the TSS specification for more information on each API's use of the validation structure.

## Summary

The TCG Software Stack is a vendor-neutral API that provides the entry point for an application's use of TPM hardware. Its high-level interface abstracts away the details of authorization handling, TPM byte stream generation, and many other aspects that would be difficult for an application to manage. In this chapter, we discussed the architecture of the TSS, common errors, and misconceptions, as well as many of the concepts you might encounter when programming to the TSS API, such as the following:

- TSP object types
- TSS return codes
- TSS memory management
- Persistent key storage
- Signing and verifying data using the TSS
- Use of the TSS_VALIDATION structure

# CHAPTER 8

# Using TPM Keys

This chapter will walk you through creating a key hierarchy using TPM-generated keys. Depending on the environment (corporate, home, and so on), the code provided will most likely not be appropriate as is to suit your needs. However, this chapter will give an example of one way to implement each of the many types of operations you might like to do to create your own TPM key hierarchy.

The code in this chapter and the chapters that follow will make liberal use of external libraries to simplify tasks that the TSS doesn't provide APIs for natively. This will include symmetric encryption, creating software keys, loading and writing keys to disk, and so on. Two choices for these external libraries are OpenSSL's libcrypto and libgcrypt, each of which are released under different open source licenses. The examples that follow will use OpenSSL library calls. Before writing your own code, make sure you review the license for each available library and choose the one that suits you best.

## Creating a Key Hierarchy

Creating a key hierarchy using TPM keys will usually involve creating a new tree structure under the SRK for use by an individual user. The structure of the tree should be such that each user has separate keys to sign and encrypt with, keys that are migratable and not migratable, and an identity key. The following code will implement just such a hierarchy, and in addition, show how to wrap an external software key with a TPM key, migrate a key using an external migration authority, and create a TPM maintenance archive. The code will show you how to do the following:

- Seed the TPM's random number generator.
- Wrap an external software key with a TPM parent key.

- Register keys in system and user persistent storage.
- Create an Attestation Identity Key.
- Lock keys to PCR values.
- Sign keys with other keys.
- Do TPM maintenance.
- Migrate a key using a migration authority's key.

## Utility Functions

There are a few functions used through the sample code that are simple, but would be too lengthy to usefully be listed here. These functions will hopefully prove to be useful in building more complex trusted computing applications. First, we'll walk through these functions, and then introduce the functions that build on them.

```
char *strresult(TSS_RESULT);
```

strresult() takes a TSS_RESULT code and converts it to a character string. This function is most useful in providing informative error messages to the user.

```
TSS_FLAG get_tss_key_size(unsigned int size);
```

get_tss_key_size() takes an RSA key size in bits and converts it to a TSS key size flag for passing to a Tspi_Context_CreateObject() call.

MyFunc_CreatePubKey() simplifies the multiple calls to the TSS needed to create a software TSS key object from an OpenSSL public key object. It takes an OpenSSL RSA key object handle and a padding type and returns the newly created TSS key handle. Keep in mind that the TPM is not involved in this function at all and that the manipulations of the hKey object are done entirely in software in the TSP library.

**Listing 8.1**   MyFunc_CreatePubKey

```
#include <stdio.h>

#include <openssl/rsa.h>
#include <openssl/err.h>

#include <tss/tss_error.h>
#include <tss/tss_defines.h>
#include <tss/tss_typedef.h>
#include <tss/tss_structs.h>
#include <tss/tspi.h>
```

```
TSS_RESULT
MyFunc_CreatePubKey(RSA *rsa, int padding, TSS_HKEY *hKey)
{
    TSS_RESULT result;
    UINT32 encScheme, sizeN, keySize;
    BYTE n[2048];

    switch (padding) {
        case RSA_PKCS1_PADDING:
            encScheme = TSS_ES_RSAESPKCSV15;
            break;
        case RSA_PKCS1_OAEP_PADDING:
            encScheme = TSS_ES_RSAESOAEP_SHA1_MGF1;
            break;
        case RSA_NO_PADDING:
            encScheme = TSS_ES_NONE;
            break;
        default:
            return TSS_E_INTERNAL_ERROR;
            break;
    }

    if ((keySize = get_tss_key_size(RSA_size(rsa) * 8)) == 0)
        return TSS_E_BAD_PARAMETER;

    /* Create the TSS key object */
    result = Tspi_Context_CreateObject(hContext,
                                  TSS_OBJECT_TYPE_RSAKEY,
                                  TSS_KEY_TYPE_LEGACY | keySize,
                                  hKey);
    if (result != TSS_SUCCESS) {
        LogError("Tspi_Context_CreateObject failed: %s",
                strresult(result));
        return result;
    }

    /* Get the public 'n' value from the openssl key */
    if ((sizeN = BN_bn2bin(rsa->n, n)) <= 0) {
        LogError("BN_bn2bin failed");
        ERR_print_errors_fp(stdout); // Call OpenSSL's error function
```

```
        Tspi_Context_CloseObject(hContext, *hKey);
        return TSS_E_FAIL;
}


/* Set the public key data in the TSS object */
result = Tspi_SetAttribData(*hKey, TSS_TSPATTRIB_KEY_BLOB,
                            TSS_TSPATTRIB_KEYBLOB_PUBLIC_KEY,
                            sizeN,n);
if (result != TSS_SUCCESS) {
    LogError("Tspi_SetAttribData failed: %s", strresult(result));
    Tspi_Context_CloseObject(hContext, *hKey);
    return result;
}


/* Set the key's algorithm */
result = Tspi_SetAttribUint32(*hKey, TSS_TSPATTRIB_KEY_INFO,
                              TSS_TSPATTRIB_KEYINFO_ALGORITHM,
                              TSS_ALG_RSA);
if (result != TSS_SUCCESS) {
    LogError("Tspi_SetAttribUint32 failed: %s", strresult(result));
    Tspi_Context_CloseObject(hContext, *hKey);
    return result;
}


/* set the key's number of primes */
result = Tspi_SetAttribUint32(*hKey, TSS_TSPATTRIB_RSAKEY_INFO,
                              TSS_TSPATTRIB_KEYINFO_RSA_PRIMES, 2);
if (result != TSS_SUCCESS) {
    LogError("Tspi_SetAttribUint32 failed: %s", strresult(result));
    Tspi_Context_CloseObject(hContext, *hKey);
    return result;
}


/* Set the key's encryption scheme */
result = Tspi_SetAttribUint32(*hKey, TSS_TSPATTRIB_KEY_INFO,
                              TSS_TSPATTRIB_KEYINFO_ENCSCHEME,
                              encScheme);
if (result != TSS_SUCCESS) {
```

```
        LogError("Tspi_SetAttribUint32 failed: %s", strresult(result));
        Tspi_Context_CloseObject(hContext, *hKey);
        return result;
    }


    return TSS_SUCCESS;
}
```

MyFunc_CreateTPMKey() makes all the calls to the TSS needed to create a new key. It takes a TSS handle to the new key's parent key, a set of initialization flags that describe the new key, and a handle to a PCRs object that the new key will optionally be bound to. If the new key will require a password, the TSS will prompt the user for it using a GUI pop-up. This function relies on the default mode of operation to pop up a dialog box to prompt a user for a password when the new key's creation requires one.

**Listing 8.2**   MyFunc_CreateTPMKey

```c
#include <stdio.h>

#include <tss/tss_error.h>
#include <tss/tss_defines.h>
#include <tss/tss_typedef.h>
#include <tss/tss_structs.h>
#include <tss/tspi.h>

TSS_RESULT
MyFunc_CreateTPMKey(TSS_HKEY hParentKey,
                    TSS_FLAG initFlags,
                    TSS_HPCRS hPcrs,
                    TSS_HKEY *hKey)
{
    TSS_RESULT result;
    TSS_HPOLICY hPolicy;

    /* create the key object */
    result = Tspi_Context_CreateObject(hContext,TSS_OBJECT_TYPE_RSAKEY,
                                        initFlags, hKey);
    if (result) {
        LogError("Tspi_Context_CreateObject failed: %s",
```

```
                        strresult(result));
        return result;
    }


    /* Get the policy object, implicitly created when we created the
     * key object */
    result = Tspi_GetPolicyObject(*hKey, TSS_POLICY_USAGE, &hPolicy);
    if (result) {
        LogError("Tspi_GetPolicyObject failed: %s", strresult(result));
        Tspi_Context_CloseObject(hContext, *hKey);
        return result;
    }


    /* If we're creating this key with no password, set the secret
     * mode so that the popup will be supressed */
    if (!(initFlags & TSS_KEY_AUTHORIZATION)) {
        result = Tspi_Policy_SetSecret(hPolicy, TSS_SECRET_MODE_NONE,
                                       0, NULL);
    }


    /* Make the call to the TPM to create the key */
    result = Tspi_Key_CreateKey(*hKey, hParentKey, hPcrs);
    if (result) {
        LogError("Tspi_Key_CreateKey failed: %s", strresult(result));
        Tspi_Context_CloseObject(hContext, *hKey);
        return result;
    }


    return TSS_SUCCESS;
}
```

MyFunc_WrapKey() provides a convenient interface to wrapping an OpenSSL-generated key with a TPM key. It takes a path to the OpenSSL key on disk, a TSS handle to the new key's parent key, a set of initialization flags that describe the new key, and a handle to a PCRs object that the new key will optionally be bound to. If the new key will require a password, the TSS will prompt the user for it using a GUI pop-up. This function relies on the default mode of operation to pop up a dialog box to prompt a user for a password when the new key's creation requires one.

**Listing 8.3** MyFunc_WrapKey

```c
#include <stdio.h>

#include <openssl/rsa.h>
#include <openssl/err.h>

#include <tss/tss_error.h>
#include <tss/tss_defines.h>
#include <tss/tss_typedef.h>
#include <tss/tss_structs.h>
#include <tss/tspi.h>

TSS_RESULT
MyFunc_WrapKey(char *path,
               TSS_HKEY hParentKey,
               TSS_FLAG initFlags,
               TSS_HPCRS hPcrs,
               TSS_HKEY *hKey)
{
    RSA             *rsa;
    UINT32          pubKeyLen;
    BYTE            *pubKey;
    TSS_RESULT      result;
    unsigned char   n[2048], p[2048];
    int             sizeN, sizeP;
    UINT32          keySize;

    /* Read in the plaintext key from disk. */
    if ((rsa = openssl_read_key(path)) == NULL) {
        LogError("Failed opening OpenSSL key file!");
        return TSS_E_FAIL;
    }

    /* Pull the SRK's pub key into the hSRK object. Note that this is
     * not necessary for any key but the SRK. The SRK's pub key is not
     * stored in system persistent storage as other keys are. This
     * protects it from being loaded by unauthorized users who could
     * then use it to identify the machine from across the Internet. */
    result = Tspi_Key_GetPubKey(hSRK, &pubKeyLen, &pubKey);
```

```
if (result) {
    LogError("Tspi_Key_GetPubKey failed: %s", strresult(result));
    RSA_free(rsa);
    return result;
}


/* Free here since the pubKey data is stored internally to the
 * hSRK object in addition to being returned above */
Tspi_Context_FreeMemory(hContext, pubKey);


/* convert the OpenSSL key's size in bits to a TSS key size flag
 * suitable for including in initFlags. */
if ((keySize = get_tss_key_size(RSA_size(rsa) * 8)) == 0)
    return TSS_E_BAD_PARAMETER;


/* create the TSS key object */
result = Tspi_Context_CreateObject(hContext, TSS_OBJECT_TYPE_RSAKEY,
                                   keySize | initFlags, hKey);
if (result != TSS_SUCCESS) {
    LogError("Tspi_Context_CreateObject failed: %s",
             strresult(result));
    return result;
}


/* This function handles the OpenSSL calls to extract the public N
 * and private P, parts of the software RSA key. Both of these
 * components will be put into the wrapped TSS key object. */
if (openssl_get_modulus_and_prime(rsa, &sizeN, n, &sizeP, p) != 0) {
    Tspi_Context_CloseObject(hContext, *hKey);
    *hKey = 0;
    return result;
}


/* set the public key data in the TSS object */
result = Tspi_SetAttribData(*hKey, TSS_TSPATTRIB_KEY_BLOB,
                            TSS_TSPATTRIB_KEYBLOB_PUBLIC_KEY,
                            sizeN, n);
if (result != TSS_SUCCESS) {
    LogError("Tspi_SetAttribData failed: %s", strresult(result));
    Tspi_Context_CloseObject(hContext, *hKey);
```

```
        *hKey = 0;
        return result;
    }

    /* set the private key data in the TSS object */
    result = Tspi_SetAttribData(*hKey, TSS_TSPATTRIB_KEY_BLOB,
                                TSS_TSPATTRIB_KEYBLOB_PRIVATE_KEY,
                                sizeP, p);
    if (result != TSS_SUCCESS) {
        LogError("Tspi_SetAttribData failed: %s", strresult(result));
        Tspi_Context_CloseObject(hContext, *hKey);
        *hKey = 0;
        return result;
    }

    /* Call the TSS to do the key wrapping */
    result = Tspi_Key_WrapKey(*hKey, hParentKey, hPcrs);
    if (result != TSS_SUCCESS) {
        LogError("Tspi_Key_WrapKey failed: %s", strresult(result));
        Tspi_Context_CloseObject(hContext, *hKey);
        *hKey = 0;
    }

    RSA_free(rsa);

    return result;
}
```

MyFunc_CreateAIK() creates an Attestation Identity Key. It takes a handle to the OpenSSL public key object of the Privacy CA and an identity label to bind the AIK to and returns a TSS handle to the new AIK, the size of the newly issued credential, and the credential itself. If the new key will require a password, the TSS will prompt the user for it using a GUI pop-up. This function relies on the default mode of operation to pop up a dialog box to prompt a user for a password when the new key's creation requires one.

Given the complex process of creating an Attestation Identity Key, the interactions between the TSS application and the Privacy CA are presented here as function calls in the same process space as the application. At the time of this writing, no Privacy CA's yet exist to handle the issuing of certificates based on TPM AIKs, so the implementation of a Privacy CA's functionality in an application may prove to be useful in the short term.

**Listing 8.4**    MyFunc_CreateAIK

```
#include <stdio.h>

#include <openssl/rsa.h>
#include <openssl/err.h>

#include <tss/tss_error.h>
#include <tss/tss_defines.h>
#include <tss/tss_typedef.h>
#include <tss/tss_structs.h>
#include <tss/tspi.h>

TSS_RESULT
MyFunc_CreateAIK(RSA *PrivacyCA_rsa,
                 BYTE *label,
                 UINT32 labelLen,
                 TSS_HKEY *hAIKey,
                 UINT32 *credentialSize,
                 BYTE **credential)
{
    TSS_FLAG            initFlags;
    TSS_HKEY            hCAKey;
    TSS_RESULT          result;
    BYTE                *identityReqBlob;
    UINT32              ulIdentityReqBlobLen;
    UINT32              utilityBlobSize, credLen;
    UINT16              offset;
    TCPA_IDENTITY_REQ   identityReq;
    TCPA_IDENTITY_PROOF identityProof;
    TCPA_SYMMETRIC_KEY  symKey;
    BYTE                utilityBlob[2048], *cred;
    int                 padding = RSA_PKCS1_OAEP_PADDING;
    UINT32              asymBlobSize, symBlobSize;
    BYTE                *asymBlob, *symBlob;

    initFlags       = TSS_KEY_TYPE_IDENTITY | TSS_KEY_SIZE_2048  |
                      TSS_KEY_VOLATILE | TSS_KEY_NO_AUTHORIZATION |
                      TSS_KEY_NOT_MIGRATABLE;
```

```
/* Create Identity Key Object */
result = Tspi_Context_CreateObject(hContext,
                                   TSS_OBJECT_TYPE_RSAKEY,
                                   initFlags, hAIKey);
if (result != TSS_SUCCESS) {
   LogError("Tspi_Context_CreateObject failed: %s",
            strresult(result));
   return result;
}


/* Convert the CA's key from an OpenSSL to a TSS key object */
if ((result = MyFunc_CreatePubKey(PrivacyCA_rsa, RSA_PKCS1_PADDING,
                                  &hCAKey))) {
   LogError("MyFunc_CreatePubKey failed: %s", strresult(result));
   return result;
}


/* Create an Identity Request blob to send to the Privacy CA */
result = Tspi_TPM_CollateIdentityRequest(hTPM, hSRK, hCAKey,
                                         labelLen, label,
                                         *hAIKey, TSS_ALG_AES,
                                         &ulIdentityReqBlobLen,
                                         &identityReqBlob);
if (result != TSS_SUCCESS) {
   LogError("Tspi_TPM_CollateIdentityRequest failed: %s",
            strresult(result));
   return result;
}


/* Unload the TCPA_IDENTITY_REQ blobs created by the TPM. This
 * function will take a binary, flattened TPM_IDENTITY_REQ structure
 * and expand it into an unflattened version, calling malloc when
 * necessary. */
offset = 0;
if ((result = UnloadBlob_IDENTITY_REQ(&offset, identityReqBlob,
                                      &identityReq))) {
   LogError("UnloadBlob_IDENTITY_REQ failed: %s", strresult(result));
   return result;
}
```

```
/* Decrypt the asymmetric blob, which contains the symmetric key used
 * to encrypt the symmetric blob. */
if (RSA_private_decrypt(identityReq.asymSize, identityReq.asymBlob,
                        utilityBlob, PrivacyCA_rsa, padding) <= 0) {
    LogError("RSA_private_decrypt failed");
    ERR_print_errors_fp(stderr);
    return TSS_E_FAIL;
}

offset = 0;
if ((result = UnloadBlob_SYMMETRIC_KEY(&offset, utilityBlob,
                                       &symKey))) {
    LogError("UnloadBlob_SYMMETRIC_KEY failed: %s",
             strresult(result));
    return result;
}

/* Verify that we're using the algorithm as specified by the TPM */
switch (symKey.algId) {
    case TCPA_ALG_AES:
        break;
    default:
        LogError("symmetric blob encrypted with an unknown cipher");
        return result;
        break;
}

utilityBlobSize = sizeof(utilityBlob);
if ((result = openssl_decrypt_ECB(TSS_ALG_AES, symKey.data,
                                  identityReq.symBlob,
                                  identityReq.symSize,
                                  utilityBlob,
                                  &utilityBlobSize))) {
    LogError("openssl_decrypt_ECB failed: %s", strresult(result));
    return result;
}

offset = 0;
if ((result = UnloadBlob_IDENTITY_PROOF(&offset, utilityBlob,
                                        &identityProof))) {
```

```
        LogError("UnloadBlob_IDENTITY_PROOF failed: %s",
                strresult(result));
        return result;
    }


    /* Allow the Privacy CA to verify the identity binding */
    if ((result = PrivacyCA_verify_identity_binding(hContext, hTPM,
                                            hCAKey, *hAIKey,
                                            &identityProof))) {
        LogError("Identity Binding signature doesn't match!");
        LogError("PrivacyCA_verify_identity_binding failed: %s",
                strresult(result));
        return result;
    }


    /* Binding is verified, load the identity key into the TPM */
    if ((result = Tspi_Key_LoadKey(*hAIKey, hSRK))) {
        LogError("Tspi_Key_LoadKey failed: %s", strresult(result));
        return result;
    }


    if ((result = PrivacyCA_create_credential(hContext, hTPM, *hAIKey,
                                            &asymBlobSize, &asymBlob,
                                            &symBlobSize, &symBlob))) {
        LogError("PrivacyCA_create_credential failed: %s",
                strresult(result));
        return result;
    }


    /* Activate the TPM identity, receiving back the decrypted credential,
     * which was issued by the Privacy CA. */
    result = Tspi_TPM_ActivateIdentity(hTPM, *hAIKey, asymBlobSize,
                                    asymBlob, symBlobSize,
                                    symBlob, &credLen, &cred);
    if (result) {
        LogError("Tspi_TPM_ActivateIdentity failed: %s",
                strresult(result));
        return result;
    }
```

```
    *credential = cred;
    *credentialSize = credLen;

    return TSS_SUCCESS;
}
```

MyFunc_GetRandom() reads data from the system's random device. It takes the numbers of bytes to read from the device and a buffer to write it to. This function is used to gather random data to feed to the TPM's random number generator for entropy.

**Listing 8.5**   MyFunc_GetRandom

```
TSS_RESULT
MyFunc_GetRandom(UINT32 size, BYTE *data)
{
    FILE *f = NULL;

    f = fopen(RANDOM_DEVICE, "r");
    if (f == NULL) {
        LogError("open of %s failed: %s", RANDOM_DEVICE,
                strerror(errno));
        return TSS_E_INTERNAL_ERROR;
    }

    if (fread(data, size, 1, f) == 0) {
        LogError("fread of %s failed: %s", RANDOM_DEVICE,
                strerror(errno));
        fclose(f);
        return TSS_E_INTERNAL_ERROR;
    }

    fclose(f);

    return TSS_SUCCESS;
}
```

MyFunc_CreateKeyHierarchy() builds on the previous utility functions to give an example of how to create a full-featured TPM key hierarchy. Where appropriate, software keys are read from disk using an OpenSSL interface. Additional features of the TSS are used as examples, such as binding one of the keys to a current PCR value and signing two keys using the created AIK. In some cases, the result of the operation (such as the returned key signature) is discarded, where in an actual implementation, the result would be stored somewhere. The use of this additional data is left as an exercise for the reader. Please note that error checking has been left out of the code to save space.

**Listing 8.6** MyFunc_CreateKeyHierarchy

```
int
MyFunc_CreateKeyHierarchy()
{
    TSS_HPOLICY     hSRKPolicy;
    BYTE            entropyData[ENTROPY_SIZE];
    BYTE            secretData[] = TSS_WELL_KNOWN_SECRET;
    TSS_FLAG        initFlags;
    TSS_UUID        swMigKeyUuid, systemMigKeyUuid;
    TSS_HKEY        hUserSWMigKey, hSystemMigKey, hKeyPcrs;
    TSS_HKEY        hMigKeyBind, hSealingKey, hMAKey;
    TSS_HKEY        hAIKey, hMtncKey;
    TSS_HPOLICY     hUserSWMigKeyPolicy;
    TSS_HPCRS       hPcrs;

    UINT32          pcrLen;
    BYTE            *pcrValue;

    TSS_RESULT      result;
    TSS_BOOL        tpmState;

    BYTE            userPass[MAX_PASS_LEN];
    BYTE            *random;

    UINT32          aik_label_len, credSize;
    BYTE            *aik_label, *cred;
    TSS_UUID        AIKUuid;

    TSS_VALIDATION validationData;

    BYTE            *ticket;
    UINT32          ticketLen;
```

```
BYTE              *mtncBlob, *migBlob;
UINT32            mtncBlobLen, migBlobLen;

/* OpenSSL objects */
RSA *ca_rsa, *migration_pub_rsa, *maintenance_pub_rsa;

/* Make any necessary setup calls to OpenSSL */
init_external_libraries();

Tspi_Context_Create(&hContext);

Tspi_Context_Connect(hContext, NULL);

Tspi_Context_GetTpmObject(hContext, &hTPM);


/* Add entropy to the TPM's random number generator from the
 * system's random device */
MyFunc_GetRandom(ENTROPY_SIZE, entropyData);

Tspi_TPM_StirRandom(hTPM, ENTROPY_SIZE, entropyData);


/* Load the SRK from storage in the System Persistent Store */
Tspi_Context_LoadKeyByUUID(hContext, TSS_PS_TYPE_SYSTEM, SRK_UUID,
                          &hSRK);

/* Set the SRK's password since it will be referenced below */
Tspi_GetPolicyObject(hContext, TSS_POLICY_USAGE, &hSRKPolicy);

Tspi_Policy_SetSecret(hSRKPolicy, TSS_SECRET_MODE_SHA1,
                      sizeof(secretData) + 1, secretData);


/* Wrap the software generated key with the SRK's public key.
 * initFlags is set to make this key a migratable storage key
 * that requires a password. */
```

```
initFlags = TSS_KEY_TYPE_STORAGE | TSS_KEY_MIGRATABLE |
            TSS_KEY_AUTHORIZATION;

MyFunc_WrapKey(SOFTWARE_KEY_FILE_PATH, hSRK, initFlags, 0,
            &hUserSWMigKey)));


/* Register the wrapped key in user persistent storage */
Tspi_Context_RegisterKey(hContext, hUserSWMigKey,
                         TSS_PS_TYPE_USER, swMigKeyUuid,
                         TSS_PS_TYPE_SYSTEM, SRK_UUID);

Tspi_GetPolicyObject(hUserSWMigKey, TSS_POLICY_USAGE,
                     &hUserSWMigKeyPolicy);


/* Call an OpenSSL routine to get a password from the user for the
 * wrapped key. This approach will be useful when a GUI environment
 * isn't available to receive a password from the user */

EVP_read_pw_string(userPass, MAX_PASS_LEN, "Password: ", 0);

Tspi_Policy_SetSecret(hUserSWMigKeyPolicy, TSS_SECRET_MODE_PLAIN,
                      strlen(userPass), userPass);

/* Zero-out the password entered, keeping it in memory for the
 * smallest amount of time possible */
memset(userPass, 0, MAX_PASS_LEN);


/* create a non-migratable signing key not bound to any PCRs */
initFlags = TSS_KEY_TYPE_SIGNING | TSS_KEY_SIZE_2048 |
            TSS_KEY_NOT_MIGRATABLE;

/* Pass '0' as the handle to the PCRs object, to keep the TSS from
 * binding this key to any PCRs */
MyFunc_CreateTPMKey(hSRK, initFlags, 0, &hSystemMigKey);
```

```
/* Register the key in system persistent storage */
Tspi_Context_RegisterKey(hContext, hSystemMigKey, TSS_PS_TYPE_SYSTEM,
                         systemMigKeyUuid, TSS_PS_TYPE_SYSTEM,
                         SRK_UUID);


/* Create a PCR composite object with the current values of PCRs
 * 4 and 5 */
Tspi_Context_CreateObject(hContext, TSS_OBJECT_TYPE_PCRS, 0, &hPcrs);

Tspi_TPM_PcrRead(hTPM, 4, &pcrLen, &pcrValue);

Tspi_PcrComposite_SetPcrValue(hPcrs, 4, pcrLen, pcrValue);

/* Free the pcrValue data returned from the Tspi_TPM_PcrRead()
 * function.  At this point, the value of the PCR register has been
 * copied into the PCR object hPcrs by the TSS. */
Tspi_Context_FreeMemory(hContext, pcrValue);

Tspi_TPM_PcrRead(hTPM, 5, &pcrLen, &pcrValue);

Tspi_PcrComposite_SetPcrValue(hPcrs, 5, pcrLen, pcrValue);

Tspi_Context_FreeMemory(hContext, pcrValue);


/* Create a non-migratable signing key bound to PCRs 4 and 5 */
initFlags = TSS_KEY_TYPE_SIGNING | TSS_KEY_SIZE_2048 |
            TSS_KEY_NOT_MIGRATABLE;

/* Passing the hPcrs handle here ensures the new key is bound to
 * PCRs 4 and 5.  If the value of those PCRs changes, the key will
 * become unusable until a platform reset can return them to their
 * present state */

MyFunc_CreateTPMKey(hSRK, initFlags, hPcrs, &hKeyPcrs);
```

```
/* Create an Attestation Identity Key */

/* Read in the Privacy CA's key from disk */
ca_rsa = openssl_read_key(CA_KEY_FILE_PATH);

aik_label = "My Identity Label";
aik_label_len = strlen(aik_label) + 1;

/* Create the AIK */
MyFunc_CreateAIK(ca_rsa, aik_label, aik_label_len, &hAIKey,
                 &credSize, &cred);

/* Write the credential to disk here. Storing this credential should
 * be part of maintaining an individual user's TPM-based key
 * hierarchy */

Tspi_Context_FreeMemory(hContext, cred);

/* Register the AIK in system persistent storage */
Tspi_Context_RegisterKey(hContext, hAIKey, TSS_PS_TYPE_SYSTEM,
                         AIKUuid, TSS_PS_TYPE_SYSTEM, SRK_UUID);


/* Sign a key with the AIK. Initialize the validation data parameter
 * to Tspi_Key_CertifyKey in order to verify it later. */
Tspi_TPM_GetRandom(hTPM, sizeof(TCPA_NONCE), &random);

memcpy(&validationData.ExternalData, random, sizeof(TCPA_NONCE));
Tspi_Context_FreeMemory(hContext, random);

/* Sign hSystemMigKey with the AIK */
Tspi_Key_CertifyKey(hSystemMigKey, hAIKey, &validationData);

/* Here, use the data returned in validationData to verify that the
 * returned key signature is correct.  Then, store the signature in
 * a place of your choosing */
```

```
Tspi_Context_FreeMemory(hContext, validationData.ValidationData);
Tspi_Context_FreeMemory(hContext, validationData.Data);


/* Sign another key with the AIK */
Tspi_TPM_GetRandom(hTPM, sizeof(TCPA_NONCE), &random);

memcpy(&validationData.ExternalData, random, sizeof(TCPA_NONCE));
Tspi_Context_FreeMemory(hContext, random);

/* Sign hKeyPcrs with the AIK */
Tspi_Key_CertifyKey(hKeyPcrs, hAIKey, &validationData);

/* Here, use the data returned in validationData to verify that the
 * returned key signature is correct.  Then, store the signature in
 * a place of your choosing */

Tspi_Context_FreeMemory(hContext, validationData.ValidationData);
Tspi_Context_FreeMemory(hContext, validationData.Data);


/* Create a binding key underneath the migratable storage key we
 * wrapped above. Note that this key *must* be migratable, since
 * its parent is migratable. */
initFlags = TSS_KEY_TYPE_BIND | TSS_KEY_SIZE_2048 |
            TSS_KEY_MIGRATABLE;

MyFunc_CreateTPMKey(hUserSWMigKey, initFlags, 0, &hMigKeyBind);


/* Create a storage (sealing) key under the SRK */
initFlags = TSS_KEY_TYPE_STORAGE | TSS_KEY_SIZE_2048 |
            TSS_KEY_NOT_MIGRATABLE;

MyFunc_CreateTPMKey(hSRK, initFlags, 0, &hSealingKey);


/* Migrate a key using a migration authority */
```

```
/* Read in the migration authority's public key from a file */
migration_pub_rsa = openssl_read_key(MIGRATION_KEY_FILE_PATH);

MyFunc_CreatePubKey(migration_pub_rsa, RSA_PKCS1_PADDING, &hMAKey);

RSA_free(migration_pub_rsa);

/* Create a migration ticket using the MA's key */
Tspi_TPM_AuthorizeMigrationTicket(hTPM, hMAKey, TSS_MS_REWRAP,
                                  &ticketLen, &ticket);

/* Use the migration ticket to migrate hSystemMigKey into a migration
 * blob. */
Tspi_Key_CreateMigrationBlob(hSystemMigKey, hSRK, ticketLen, ticket,
                             0, NULL, &migBlobLen, &migBlob);

/* migBlob can now be migrated to another TPM */

Tspi_Context_FreeMemory(hContext, ticket);
Tspi_Context_FreeMemory(hContext, migBlob);


/* Can this TPM do maintenance? */
Tspi_TPM_GetStatus(hTPM, TSS_TPMSTATUS_ALLOWMAINTENANCE, &tpmState);
if (result != TSS_SUCCESS) {
    LogError("Tspi_TPM_GetStatus failed: %s", strresult(result));
    return result;
} else if (tpmState == TRUE) {

    /* This TPM can do maintenance, let's create a maintenance
     * archive */

    /* Read in the migration authority's public key from file */
    maintenance_pub_rsa =
                openssl_read_key(MAINTENANCE_KEY_FILE_PATH);

    MyFunc_CreatePubKey(maintenance_pub_rsa, RSA_PKCS1_PADDING,
                &hMtncKey);
```

```
        /* Load the manufacturer's maintenance pub key into the TPM */
        Tspi_TPM_LoadMaintenancePubKey(hTPM, hMtncKey, NULL);

        Tspi_TPM_CreateMaintenanceArchive(hTPM, FALSE, 0, NULL,
                                          &mtncBlobLen, &mtncBlob);


        /* Keep even the owner from doing maintenance until the TPM
         * changes ownership */
        Tspi_TPM_KillMaintenanceFeature(hTPM);

        Tspi_Context_FreeMemory(hContext, mtncBlob);
        RSA_free(maintenance_pub_rsa);
    }


    /* Flush secrets associated with this policy. This can be called
     * for any policy that may contain secret data, including the TPM
     * object's policy to clear the owner secret. */
    Tspi_Policy_FlushSecret(hUserSWMigKeyPolicy);


    Tspi_Context_CloseObject(hContext, hUserSWMigKey);

    /* Free all memory associated with the context */
    Tspi_Context_FreeMemory(hContext, NULL);

    Tspi_Context_Close(hContext);

    return TSS_SUCCESS;
}
```

## Summary

This chapter contained example code to perform many of the tasks needed to create a TPM key hierarchy using TSS calls and helper functions. You can use the example code to do the following:

- Seed the TPM's random number generator.
- Wrap an external software key with a TPM parent key.

- Register keys in system and user persistent storage.
- Create an Attestation Identity Key.
- Lock keys to PCR values.
- Sign keys with other keys.
- Do TPM maintenance.
- Migrate a key using a migration authority's key.

# CHAPTER 9

# Using Symmetric Keys

The TPM provides an excellent facility to create, store, and manage asymmetric keys, but when it comes time to encrypt large amounts of data, using the TPM may not be as obvious. Due to the speed of operations for asymmetric cryptography, it is not well suited for this task. This is where symmetric cryptography steps in to handle the load. Symmetric algorithms such as Triple-DES, AES, and Blowfish are many times faster for encryption and decryption, making them ideal to provide confidentiality for large amounts of data.

Although the TPM has no native support for symmetric encryption, it can play an important role in providing a secure way to store, use, and transport symmetric keys. Binding or sealing symmetric keys can prevent unauthorized access to keys, as well as providing a convenient way to store them securely while not in use. This chapter will lay out many of the issues surrounding use of TPM asymmetric keys to wrap symmetric keys and hopefully make use of the TPM for this purpose easier. In this chapter, we're given examples of how to do this, including the following:

- How to use the random number generator to create a symmetric key
- How to use a binding key to lock the symmetric key to a pass phrase
- How to use a sealing key to lock the symmetric key to a platform state

## Data Binding

Using the TPM to bind, or to encrypt by using an asymmetric key, is the simplest use of the TPM in asymmetric cryptography. The TSS APIs involved are `Tspi_Data_Bind` and `Tspi_Data_Unbind`. When using a TSS binding key, `Tspi_Data_Bind` will create a `TPM_BOUND_DATA` structure (called `TCPA_BOUND_DATA` in the 1.1 specification), copy the data into the structure, and encrypt the structure using the public key. The `TPM_BOUND_DATA` structure will be expected by the TPM at unbind time when the TPM detects that you're using a binding key. This is not the case with legacy keys, however. Data bound by a legacy key is simply decrypted by the TPM during an Unbind operation based on the padding type of the key. No bound data structure is checked for by the TPM.

There are a few things to be aware of when using asymmetric TPM keys to bind your symmetric keys using the TSS:

- The size of your TPM key
- The size of your symmetric key
- The size of the `TPM_BOUND_DATA` structure
- The type of TPM key
- The padding type of your TPM key

Current TPMs support RSA key sizes from 512 bits up to and including 2048 bits. Natively, this would allow symmetric keys from 64 bytes to 256 bytes to be encrypted. However, there are several factors to take into account even when not using a TPM. The first is RSA padding type. There are two main RSA padding types in use today: PKCS#1 version 1.5 and Optimal Asymmetric Encryption Padding, or OAEP.[1] Each of these types use different algorithms to pad the data to be encrypted in such a way that the possibility of the RSA key used to encrypt being exposed is minimized. Both of these types are supported by current TPMs, and the type of padding must be specified before creating your TPM key in the TPM if it is different from the default. The TPM uses the SHA-1 digest as its Message Generation Function, or MGF. Table 9.1 shows the default padding types when creating a TPM key.

**Table 9.1**   Default Encryption Schemes Set by the TSS for Each of the TSS Key Types

|                       | PKCS#1 v1.5 | OAEP SHA-1 |
|-----------------------|-------------|------------|
| `TSS_KEY_TYPE_BIND`   |             | X          |
| `TSS_KEY_TYPE_LEGACY` |             | X          |

Each padding type will use a different amount of data to pad the data to be encrypted. Table 9.2 shows the padding amount used for PKCS#1 v1.5 and OAEP.

**Table 9.2**   Padding Amounts in Bytes for Each of the TPM-Supported RSA Padding Types

|                | PKCS#1 v1.5 | OAEP SHA-1 |
|----------------|-------------|------------|
| Padding amount | 11 bytes    | $64 - (2 * 20) - 2 = 22$ bytes |

---

1. Please see "Optimal Asymmetric Encryption—How to Encrypt with RSA" at http://www.cdc.informatik.tu-darmstadt.de/TI/Lehre/WS02_03/Vorlesung/Kryptographie_I/oae.pdf for more information on OAEP.

In Table 9.2, 20 bytes is the size of a SHA-1 hash, which is the MGF used by the TPM in OAEP padding the data to be encrypted.

As you can see, OAEP padding incurs more of a cost in padding; however, OAEP is considered more secure and all newly implemented applications should be using it.

In addition to having to take into account the padding used for asymmetric encryption, you should be aware of how a TPM expects to receive data in an Unbind command. The TPM expects data to be unbound to be inside a TPM_BOUND_DATA structure when the key used is a binding key. Here's the definition of the TPM_BOUND_DATA structure:

```
typedef struct tdTPM_BOUND_DATA {
        TPM_VERSION ver;
        TPM_PAYLOAD_TYPE payload;
        BYTE *payloadData;
} TPM_BOUND_DATA;
```

TPM_VERSION is a 4-byte field and TPM_PAYLOAD_TYPE is a 1-byte field, reducing the number of bytes you're able to encrypt even further. As an example, let's say that you're using a 512-bit TPM binding key to encrypt your symmetric key. A 512-bit RSA key can encrypt 64 bytes, minus 5 bytes to take into account the TPM_BOUND_DATA structure, minus 38 bytes to take into account the OAEP padding, leaving a total of 21 bytes available to encrypt your key! This may not be acceptable, depending on the symmetric algorithm you choose to use. For instance, a Triple-DES key is 24 bytes long and an AES-256 key is 32 bytes long, making them impossible to encrypt using a 512-bit TPM binding key (in one operation). However, we do have options. Table 9.3 lays out the maximum amount of data encryptable with several different combinations of keys and encryption schemes.

**Table 9.3**    Showing the Maximum Size of Data Encryptable by Keys of Varying Sizes and Types

|  | **RSA 512 bit** | **RSA 1024 bit** | **RSA 2048 bit** |
|---|---|---|---|
| Legacy Key, PKCS#1v1.5 | 53 bytes | 117 bytes | 245 bytes |
| Legacy Key, OAEP | 21 bytes | 85 bytes | 213 bytes |
| Binding Key, OAEP | 21 bytes | 85 bytes | 213 bytes |

So, after all that, which type of key should you choose? In short, any currently strong symmetric key can be bound by a TPM key of at least 1024 bits, regardless of padding type. This includes the largest key size for AES, Triple-DES, Serpent, and Blowfish. Most modern software is now using AES, the Advanced Encryption Algorithm, chosen for use by NIST and the NSA.

## Sample Code

Let's create a TPM key that we'd like to use for binding a symmetric key (see Listing 9.1). We'd like to use a 512-bit key and give ourselves a little extra room for data to encrypt by using PKCS#1v1.5 padding. The key will be a child of the SRK.

**Listing 9.1**   Creating a TPM Key

```
TSS_HCONTEXT   hContext;
TSS_HTPM       hTPM = 0;
TSS_FLAGS      initFlags;
TSS_HKEY       hSRK = 0;
TSS_HKEY       hKey;
TSS_UUID       SRK_UUID = TSS_UUID_SRK;

Tspi_Context_Create(&hContext);
Tspi_Context_Connect(hContext, NULL);
Tspi_Context_GetTpmObject(hContext,&hTPM);

Tspi_Context_LoadKeyByUUID(hContext, TSS_PS_TYPE_SYSTEM, SRK_UUID,
                           &hSRK );

initFlags = TSS_KEY_TYPE_BIND | TSS_KEY_SIZE_512 |
            TSS_KEY_NO_AUTHORIZATION | TSS_KEY_NOT_MIGRATABLE;

Tspi_Context_CreateObject(hContext, TSS_OBJECT_TYPE_RSAKEY,
                          initFlags, &hKey);

/* Set the padding type before calling the TPM to create the key. This
 * is a requirement, since the key padding type is set at key creation
 * time and cannot be changed afterwards. */
Tspi_SetAttribUint32(hKey, TSS_TSPATTRIB_KEY_INFO,
                     TSS_TSPATTRIB_KEYINFO_ENCSCHEME,
                     TSS_ES_RSAESPKCSV15);

/* Create the key, not bound to any PCRs */
Tspi_Key_CreateKey(hKey, hSRK, 0);
```

Now let's use our binding key to bind some data. This function will take a binding key and some data and return the data bound using the key. This function assumes that the key is a binding key already loaded into the TPM and that hContext refers to a global TSP handle.

```
int
MyFunc_BindData(TSS_HKEY hKey, UINT32 in_size, BYTE *in,
                    UINT32 *out_size, BYTE *out)
{
        TSS_HENCDATA hEncData;
        UINT32 keySize, tmp_out_size;
        BYTE *tmp_out;

        /* Create the encrypted data object in the TSP */
        Tspi_Context_CreateObject( hContext,
                            TSS_OBJECT_TYPE_ENCDATA,
                            TSS_ENCDATA_BIND, &hEncData );

        Tspi_GetAttribUint32( hKey, TSS_TSPATTRIB_KEY_INFO,
                        TSS_TSPATTRIB_KEYINFO_SIZE, &keySize );

        /* Make sure the data is small enough to be bound by
         * this key, taking into account the PKCS#1v1.
         * padding size (11) and the size of the TPM_BOUND_DATA
         * structure (5) */
        if (in_size > keySize - 16) {
                LogError("Data to be encrypted is too big!");
                return -1;
        }

        Tspi_Data_Bind( hEncData, hKey, in_size, in);

        /* Now hEncData contains an encrypted blob, lets
         * extract it */
        Tspi_GetAttribData( hEncData,
                        TSS_TSPATTRIB_ENCDATA_BLOB,
                        TSS_TSPATTRIB_ENCDATABLOB_BLOB,
                        &tmp_out_size,&tmp_out);

        if (tmp_out_size > *out_size) {
                LogError("Encrypted data blob is too big!");
                return -1;
        }
```

```
            /* Copy the encrypted data blob to the user's buffer */
            memcpy(out, tmp_out, tmp_out_size);
            *out_size = tmp_out_size;

            /* Free the blob returned by the TSP */
            Tspi_Context_FreeMemory( hContext, tmp_out);

            /* Close the encrypted data object, it will no longer
             * be used */
            Tspi_Context_CloseObject( hContext, hEncData);

        return 0;
    }
```

## Data Sealing

Data sealing suffers from the same type of problems that binding does when using a TPM, but is even less flexible. Although you can use a legacy key or binding key to bind your data, only storage keys can be used to seal data. This means that the length requirements for using sealing keys are more restrictive. In addition, the size of a TPM_SEALED_DATA structure, which is used to wrap data before sealing by the TPM, is larger than the TPM_BOUND_DATA structure. Here's the layout of a TPM_SEALED_DATA structure:

```
        typedef struct tdTPM_SEALED_DATA
        {
                TPM_PAYLOAD_TYPE        payload;
                TPM_SECRET        authData;
                TPM_NONCE         tpmProof;
                TPM_DIGEST        storedDigest;
                UINT32            dataSize;
                BYTE              *data;
        } TPM_SEALED_DATA;
```

The total size of the additional elements of the TPM_SEALED_DATA structure is 65 bytes. Compare that to the 5 byte size of the TPM_BOUND_DATA structure, and you may be feeling the pinch when it comes times to seal your symmetric key. Table 9.4 illustrates the amount of data that can be sealed using each RSA key size.

**Table 9.4** Showing the Maximum Amount of Data Sealable by Keys of Various Sizes

|  | RSA 512 bit | RSA 1024 bit | RSA 2048 bit |
|---|---|---|---|
| Sealing Key, OAEP | N/A | N/A | 153 bytes |

Here, a 2048-bit key will suffice for any current symmetric key size; however, due to the size of the TPM_SEALED_DATA structure, no other key sizes can be used. Despite the size restrictions, though, data sealing is considerably more powerful than binding, allowing you to seal individual data blobs to any number of PCRs regardless of whether the key itself is bound to any PCRs.

## Sample Code

Let's create a TPM key that we'd like to use for sealing a symmetric key. We'd like to use a 2048-bit key, which must be a storage key. The key will be a child of the SRK.

```
TSS_HCONTEXT   hContext;
TSS_HTPM       hTPM = 0;
TSS_FLAGS      initFlags;
TSS_HKEY       hSRK = 0;
TSS_HKEY       hKey;
TSS_UUID       SRK_UUID = TSS_UUID_SRK;

Tspi_Context_Create(&hContext);
Tspi_Context_Connect(hContext, NULL);
Tspi_Context_GetTpmObject(hContext,&hTPM);

Tspi_Context_LoadKeyByUUID (hContext, TSS_PS_TYPE_SYSTEM,
                            SRK_UUID, &hSRK );

initFlags = TSS_KEY_TYPE_STORAGE | TSS_KEY_SIZE_2048 |
            TSS_KEY_NO_AUTHORIZATION |
            TSS_KEY_NOT_MIGRATABLE;

Tspi_Context_CreateObject (hContext, TSS_OBJECT_TYPE_RSAKEY,
                           initFlags, &hKey );

/* Create the key, not bound to any PCRs.  That can be done on
 * a blob by blob basis */
Tspi_Key_CreateKey (hKey, hSRK, 0 );
```

Now let's use our sealing key to seal some data. This function will take a sealing key, a PCRs object, and some data and return the data sealed using the key. This function assumes that the key is a sealing key already loaded into the TPM and that `hContext` refers to a global TSP handle.

```
int
MyFunc_SealData(TSS_HKEY hKey,
                TSS_HPCRS hPcrs,
                UINT32 in_size,
                BYTE *in,
                UINT32 *out_size,
                BYTE *out)
{
    TSS_HENCDATA hEncData;
    UINT32 keySize, tmp_out_size;
    BYTE *tmp_out;

    /* Create the encrypted data object in the TSP */
    Tspi_Context_CreateObject(hContext,
                    TSS_OBJECT_TYPE_ENCDATA,
                    TSS_ENCDATA_SEAL, &hEncData );

    Tspi_GetAttribUint32(hKey, TSS_TSPATTRIB_KEY_INFO,
                    TSS_TSPATTRIB_KEYINFO_SIZE,
                    &keySize);

    /* Make sure the data is small enough to be bound by this
     * key,taking into account the OAEP padding size (38) and
     * the size of the TPM_SEALED_DATA structure (65) */
    if (in_size > keySize - 103) {
        LogError("Data to be encrypted is too big!");
        return -1;
    }

    Tspi_Data_Seal(hEncData, hKey, in_size, in, hPcrs);

    /* Now hEncData contains an encrypted blob, let's extract
     * it */
    Tspi_GetAttribData(hEncData, TSS_TSPATTRIB_ENCDATA_BLOB,
                    TSS_TSPATTRIB_ENCDATABLOB_BLOB,
                    &tmp_out_size, &tmp_out);
```

```
        if (tmp_out_size > *out_size) {
            LogError("Encrypted data blob is too big!");
            return -1;
        }

        /* Copy the encrypted data blob to the user's buffer */
        memcpy(out, tmp_out, tmp_out_size);
        *out_size = tmp_out_size;

        /* Free the blob returned by the TSP */
        Tspi_Context_FreeMemory( hContext, tmp_out);

        /* Close the encrypted data object, it will no longer
         * be used */
        Tspi_Context_CloseObject( hContext, hEncData);

        return 0;
    }
```

Sealing a symmetric key to a set of TPM PCRs is nearly as straightforward as binding. The two main differences are that there's less flexibility in the types of key you can use, and a PCR composite object must be created to use in sealing. We've covered key creation before; now let's create a handy way to set up a PCR composite object.

MyFunc_CreatePcrs takes an array of UINT32s, which represent the indices of PCR registers to set in the created PCR composite object. The PCR composite object is then created by querying all the PCR indices specified and setting those values in the object. This function will again assume a global hContext already created and a global handle to the TPM object hTPM.

```
    int
    MyFunc_CreatePcrs(UINT32 num_pcrs,
                      UINT32 *pcrs,
                      TSS_HPCRS *hPcrs)
    {
        UINT32  numPcrs, subCap, i;
        UINT32  ulPcrValueLength;
        BYTE    *rgbPcrValue, *rgbNumPcrs;

        Tspi_Context_CreateObject(hContext, TSS_OBJECT_TYPE_PCRS,
                                  0, hPcrs);
```

```
// Retrieve number of PCRs from the TPM
subCap = TSS_TPMCAP_PROP_PCR;
Tspi_TPM_GetCapability(hTPM, TSS_TPMCAP_PROPERTY,
                       sizeof(UINT32), (BYTE *)&subCap,
                       &ulPcrValueLength, &rgbNumPcrs);


numPcrs = *(UINT32 *)rgbNumPcrs;

Tspi_Context_FreeMemory( hContext, rgbNumPcrs );

for (i = 0; i < num; i++) {
    if (pcrs[i] >= numPcrs) {
        LogError("PCR value %u is too big!", pcrs[i]);
        Tspi_Context_CloseObject(hContext, *hPcrs);
        return -1;
    }

    Tspi_TPM_PcrRead(hTPM, pcrs[i], &ulPcrValueLength,
                     &rgbPcrValue);

    Tspi_PcrComposite_SetPcrValue(*hPcrs, pcrs[i],
                                  ulPcrValueLength,
                                  rgbPcrValue);

    Tspi_Context_FreeMemory( hContext, rgbPcrValue );
}

return 0;
}
```

## Encrypting Files

Now let's pull together all the code that we've written so far and do something useful with it. What we'd like to do is have a function that takes a path to a file and a TPM key handle and creates a new symmetric key, encrypts that file using the symmetric key, and seals the symmetric key with the TPM key. We'd like to invoke the function like this:

```
MyFunc_SealFile(FILE_PATH, hKey, NULL, 0);
```

or to seal the symmetric key to PCRs 8, 9, and 10:

```
UINT32 pcrs[] = { 8, 9, 10 };
UINT32 num_pcrs = 3;


MyFunc_SealFile(FILE_PATH, hKey, pcrs, num_pcrs);
```

For this example, we'll just write the encrypted file out to FILE_PATH.enc, and we'll write the encrypted symmetric key blob to FILE_PATH.key. Also, we'll use a dummy function to do the symmetric encryption, since that will have to be provided by an external library.

```
int
MyFunc_SealFile(char *file, TSS_HKEY hKey, UINT32 *pcrs,
                UINT32 num_pcrs)
{
    FILE *fin, *fout;
    UINT32 inSize, outSize, encSymKeySize = SYM_KEY_SIZE;
    BYTE *symKey, in[BUF_SIZE], out[BUF_SIZE],
                encSymKey[SYM_KEY_SIZE];
    TSS_HPCRS hPcrs;
    char *outFileName;

    inSize = outSize = BUF_SIZE;

    outFileName = malloc(strlen(file) + 5);

    sprintf(outFileName, "%s.enc", file);

    fin = fopen( file, "r" );
    fout = fopen( outFileName, "w" );

    Tspi_TPM_GetRandom( hTPM, SYM_KEY_SIZE, &symKey );

    /* Note: depending on the symmetric algorithm you choose
     * to use, you should check the returned random number
     * against a database of known weak keys for that
     * algorithm. It's possible that data encrypted with a
     * weak key could allow an attacker to discover the key
     * by analyzing the encrypted text */

    while ((inSize = read(fileno(fin), in, inSize) ==
            BUF_SIZE)) {
```

```
        /* Call our external library to do the bulk encryption
         * using the symmetric key */
        symmetric_encrypt(symKey, in, inSize, out, outSize);

        /* Write the encrypted file back out */
        write(fileno(fout), out, outSize);
    }

    fclose(fin);
    fclose(fout);

    /* Create the PCR composite object to seal the symmetric
       key with */
    MyFunc_CreatePcrs(num_pcrs, pcrs, &hPcrs);

    /* Now seal the symmetric key using our TPM key */
    MyFunc_SealData(hKey, hPcrs, SYM_KEY_SIZE, symKey,
                    &encSymKeySize, &encSymKey);

    /* Write out the encrypted symmetric key blob */
    sprintf(outFileName, "%s.key", file);
    fout = fopen( outFileName, "w" );
    write(fileno(fout), encSymKey, encSymKeySize);
    fclose(fout);

    return 0;
}
```

Protecting a file using symmetric keys sealed to the TPM couldn't be much easier. Some simple scripts or further wrapping of MyFunc_SealFile could add support for piping data between other programs or even across a network via a socket.

## Summary

Despite lacking support for doing symmetric encryption itself, the TPM can be very useful for securing symmetric keys and thereby securing your symmetrically encrypted data. The most important issues to be aware of when selecting TPM keys to seal or bind your symmetric keys are the following:

- The size of your TPM key
- The size of your symmetric key
- The size of the structure used to house your key (TPM_BOUND_DATA or TPM_SEALED_ DATA)
- The type of TPM key
- The padding type of your TPM key

# CHAPTER 10

# The TSS Core Service (TCS)

The primary goal of this book is to assist application developers in using TCG-related services via the TSS. Some readers may be looking to implement a TSS themselves or may want to have a better understanding of what's really happening and how actual hardware resources are being handled. This chapter describes the TCS—the TSS Core Service—at a basic level and give some introduction into this part of the stack.

This chapter addresses the following:

- A TSS Core Service is much like a software TPM.
- A TSS Core Service provides abstraction to finite resources.
- TCSs can provide further virtualization.
- TCSs can be used by both local and remote service providers in the same way.

## Overview of a TCS

A TSS Core Service has only a few real purposes. Its intent was to be as simple as possible while providing a single point of resource management to both local and remote requests.

One way to explain a TCS is to liken it to a software TPM. Some of the drawbacks of a hardware-based TPM include the following:

- Only one operation can be performed at a time.
- It is really slow.
- It has a finite number of resources, including key slots, auth slots, and so on.
- Communication to it is serial and via a driver.
- Communication to it is limited to local software.

A software abstraction can address each drawback in various ways. By owning the interface to the hardware, the TCS can queue operations that are pending to the TPM. The actual operations in the TPM cannot be quickened, but the order can be optimized to improve performance—and in some rare cases, the TCS can respond to commands without the TPM. The finite resources can be made seemingly infinite by shuffling state information in and out of the actual TPM. C-like functions implemented at the TCS interface can be parsed into parameter blocks that are needed by the TPM and from byte streams back into C-like parameters to the caller. The TCS can run as a service to expose both local and remote requests to the resource.

The TCS has a few other capabilities, such as a local key storage, management configuration, and some pure software queries. One should recognize that the TCS is meant to be as lean as possible and as simple as possible. The TCS does not have any cryptographic capability, nor does it manage any sensitive information. It is important to realize that the interface to the TCS is not sensitive and does not need protection for these reasons. Any data that has reached this layer is either protected by the TSP or is public. Shared secrets between the TPM and the TSP or the application are used whenever sensitive information crosses this layer, and so the TCS need not implement anything to protect or ensure the integrity of the data. This becomes a real benefit to implementers because design and development is much more simple, and there is less opportunity for poorly written code to be a security problem. It's also philosophically consistent with the goal of the TSS to not be secure and trusted, but rather rely on the security built into the TPM itself.

So, with the idea that a TCS is much like a software abstraction of a TPM, it makes sense then why so many of the TPM functions are almost directly translated to the TCS interface described by the TSS specification. The TCS must have its own handles for each resource type as it must maintain what resources are actually in the TPM and relay to the TPM what resources are intended to be used with each command. The TSP does all of the important work to get the data ready for the command, and then passes it to what looks like a TPM, and receives the reply back when it has completed.

## How the TCS Manages Finite Resources

When someone calling the TCS wants to perform a protected command, typically a TSS Service Provider, the authentication data calculated from the command itself and a shared secret is already included. The calculated digest intentionally does not include the resources handles themselves for two main reasons:

1. The TCS needs to be able to manipulate the handle value.
2. The TSP is not aware of the hardware handle, which is really a side effect of #1.

If the TCS were to confuse the resources and use the wrong handle, or the TSP were to specify the wrong handle, the worst case is that the protected command would fail. So, with this mechanism in place, the TCS is able to translate hardware resources based on software handles and provide protected command digests with no trouble.

A TCS will typically have a cache of all resources that are not loaded in the TPM. When a request comes to create a new instance—for example, a key—the TCS will create a new TCS handle for this key that maps to a TPM handle. Note that the creation of a key handle translates to a key being loaded and not the actual creation of a key by the TPM. Actual TPM key creation does not load the key in TPM 1.1.

While the key is loaded in the TPM, the TCS key handle will be mapped to a TPM key handle for any commands that require it. If the TCS needs to make room for another key, it can offload the key. When it offloads the key, the state information of the key is protected by the TPM and exported as an encrypted blob only decryptable by that TPM and in a state enforced by the TPM. More on this can be found in the TPM specification, and later in this chapter. An offloaded key is now tracked by the TCS, and later requests for this key will simply mean the TCS has to reload the key. Because the TCS key handle will never change, it does not matter if the key ends up in a different hardware slot.

Other resources can be a little more complex to manage, but the idea is still as simple. The TCS abstracts the resources to the TSP, and depending on how many resources are actually available in the TPM and how intelligent the TCS is at managing them, performance can be greatly influenced by the combination of the TCS and TPM implementations.

Naturally, there is a required minimum to a TPM's resources. Since a single operation can require at most two keys, two key slots is the minimum a TPM can implement. All other resources have similar restrictions.

So, the next question one may ask is how a TCS can really offload information and not compromise the security. The TPM maintains a symmetric key internally that cannot be used for anything else, cannot be exported, and changes every clean startup of the TPM. When a TPM resource is offloaded, the blob is protected by this ephemeral key. This ensures that a resource cannot be used in other boot cycles.

When a TCS offloads a key, the exported information is called the key context. When the TCS removes a key, including its cached contents, it is called key eviction. Key eviction allows both the TPM and the TCS to release resources used by the key.

When a key is loaded, it may also contain optional PCR information that tells the TPM that the key may be used only when the TPM is in a valid state. Since loading a key implies usage of the parent key to unwrap it, the parent key's PCR info must match up with the TPM state to allow the child key to be unwrapped. Similarly, a signing key must match PCR info to be used to sign. For this reason, there is a distinction between loading a key and loading a key context. Loading a key is creating a new key instance in the TPM, but loading a key context means the actual load operation was already verified. So, the PCR state of the TPM may have changed, but the key was removed for space considerations, not because of an eviction.

With this scheme in place, the TCS should be able to allow an infinite number of any resource that can be managed in this way. One exception to this, however, is authorization sessions. Due to the nature and usage of authorization sessions, it's required that the TPM maintain some state information about the session even when the resource is offloaded. Essentially, the

TPM must ensure not only that the session is valid, but also that it is not a stale session so that it can't be reused. Because of this, again there is a hardware limitation in place, and the real number of open sessions becomes finite.

## Further Abstracting the TCS Abstraction

To enhance your understanding of the TCS abstraction, this section explores the theoretical possibility of "stacking" TCSs. An abstraction layer that is designed to be independent of its callers or callees should really be able to handle changes to the expected model. The TCS is no exception.

If there were a module underneath the TCS that appeared to be a TPM, one would expect that the TCS would not know the difference as long as the entity acted like a TPM does. Because a TCS in many ways looks like a TPM, if it were to implement a driver layer that a higher TCS could use to talk to it, then stacking should work.

This works because the TCS is aware of its own resource handles and the resource handles of what it thinks is hardware. The lower TCS, or TCSlow, allocates handles for its own resources that in turn correspond to TPM resources. The TCS on top, or TCShigh, does not know that these are not hardware resources. As long as TCSlow gives the appearance of full and independent control of its resources to TCShigh, it should all work.

A couple of use cases present themselves for this type of stacking. One obvious example is a rogue TCS fooling another into thinking it's using a TPM. Fortunately, since the TSS offers no claims of security or trust, the protection is entirely enforced by the TPM mechanisms, and this will not give the attack any real gain other than to deny service. Of course, if an attack could slide a layer into the TSS, denial of service is likely imminent. A positive use case for this could be virtualization. One could use a real TCS to manage the real TPM, but this TCS in turn implements virtual TPM interfaces to various software layers. As long as the resources are kept separate and independent, this scheme should work.

## Why a TCS Is Exposed Locally and Remotely

Providing a TCS core service to local service providers, or TSPs, will be the primary goal to ensure that several concurrent applications can all use local TPM resources at the same time. However, there are benefits to providing this type of service to applications on other systems. Exposing a service in this way typically raises concern about privacy and security. As we've already discussed, security is not an issue since the TCS neither manages nor requires its own security to perform correctly. Privacy, on the other hand, is indeed a concern and will be addressed later in the section.

Historically, one of the primary appeals of the TPM that separates it from other security devices is attestation. *Attestation* allows many interesting things to happen with software validation and the ability to control what things a TPM can do in certain states. Because software on one system can communicate with software on another system, there was great interest in ensuring that attestation could be done from one computer to another. So, this is one of the main reasons the TCS started out as a local and remote service. Although attestation was one of the primary reasons, other functions could provide software vendors with other capabilities, and the TSS goals to give this flexibility is desired.

The next question one may ask, then, is why expose the TCS, when remote communication can be done by applications to other applications in a secure fashion. First, applications that use software-based security can indeed secure the line between them. But without knowing the state of the software on the other system, local software cannot know if it can trust the remote software with its secrets or to do the work it requests after the data has been transmitted over. Because the interface to a TCS is not sensitive and since the local TSP can manage any sensitive information in-process, the local TSP can communicate with a remote TCS (or remote TPM, if you prefer that model) with the same functionality it does locally. Also, the TSP is already designed to talk with a TCS, and no extra work is required by the application to talk remotely versus locally. This makes the remote interface at the TCS layer very desirable.

## Utilizing and Implementing a TCS

With a better understanding of what a TCS is and what it does for a TSS, it is a little easier to start writing code to interact as a TCS or with a TCS. This next section covers how to get started in that area and what resources are available to make it easier. Once you have the basic idea and get the communication or service working, the rest is as simple as completing the implementation for each function.

### Getting Started

Getting started with either writing your own TCS or writing code to talk to an existing TCS are the same. As explained earlier, there is a C interface to the TCS defined by the TSS, but it doesn't actually exist anywhere. This C interface is purely theoretical and is meant to give some baseline for discussion, but the real definition of the TCS interface lies in the .wsdl file published by the TSS. This file is a Web Services Description Language file. You can find entire books that deal with XML, Web Services, SOAP, and HTTP in great detail. This book is not intended to explain or even augment those discussions. You can get along just fine without understanding the inner workings of these technologies unless you find you need to write your own conversion tools to use the .wsdl file. If you are content with using existing tools to exploit the .wsdl file, then the explanations in this chapter are sufficient.

The high-level goal of the .wsdl file published by the TSS is to provide a generic and agnostic definition of the TCS interface usable by as many developers on as many platforms as possible while also being compatible with as many tools as possible. There will always be exceptions, but the TSS working group tried its best to provide developers with the most flexible and generic starting point that it could.

## Why WSDL Was Chosen

To understand some of the benefits and abilities that the WSDL format provides, it is useful to also understand why the working group chose this as the format to publish. TSS 1.1 defined a core service that was local and remote accessible and dictated that a Windows implementation be implemented using DCOM. The flaw here is obvious, and TSS 1.2 sought to correct this flaw. Technologies and software were emerging on non-Windows platforms that needed to be able to interact with other platforms, and there was even a desire by some to have a TSS that could be compiled on several OS types. The 1.2 working group had to publish something that met the needs of all.

When we talk about remote capabilities, what we really mean is Remote Procedure Calls, or RPC. RPC has taken on a more specific meaning to some, as there are tools that do a very specific means of RPC; but in a general sense it simply means a way to do function-like calls over a socket.

There were several goals that needed to be addressed when determining how the TCS interface should really be defined, some of which included the following:

- Platform agnostic
- Fair tool support
- Industry accepted
- TCP/IP based
- Backward compatible to 1.1

Although any sensible remote capability of this kind is TCP/IP based, it was important to keep it in mind since it offered both local/remote support via the same protocol, and embedded systems could theoretically create very bare-bones implementations if they needed it. Platform-agnostic support was obvious. It was important to choose some method that other people in the industry have accepted as viable. Though not a requirement, publishing something that could be back-ported to 1.1 was a good idea because some people wanted a non-Windows implementation of 1.1 to work with upcoming 1.2 implementations with little or no update required.

The answer was to use Web Services and SOAP and transport it over HTTP. The port number assigned to this service is yet to be defined by the TSS working group, although the last decision was to choose something in the lower range where typical services like FTP, HTTP, and other known services exist. This would require registration and special privileges on some platforms.

Typically, a Web Services service exports a file in .wsdl format, which has its own specification. More information about this can be found at http://www.w3.org/TR/wsdl.

One well-known example is Google.com. Google exports a .wsdl file that can be used by a developer to send and receive queries to their service. In a similar way, the TSS WG has chosen to publish a .wsdl file that accompanies the normal header files.

# Brief Breakdown of the .wsdl File

This section covers a little bit about what is going on internally to the .wsdl syntax. Keep in mind that the explanations here are intentionally somewhat vague and are not perfectly accurate, especially to someone with experience in Web Services and SOAP. However, that doesn't detract from the educational factor of these explanations to the intended audience of this book. The intent is to quickly and briefly explain a little bit about what the .wsdl file provides at a very base level. To understand it further, you should research SOAP and Web Services specifically.

It's good to keep in mind that many of the analogies made in this section are meant to illustrate the correlation between the WSDL syntax when used specifically for this purpose and how it translates to the C interface for the purposes of RPC. You should understand that these analogies may not apply for all .wsdl files.

If you inspect the .wsdl file, you'll see that it is nothing more than an XML file with some special tagging and format. This WSDL format attempts to define the way in which the data will be organized and parsed as it is passed from the TSP to the TCS and back. There are various ways to set up the data and set up the structuring in a .wsdl file, and the organization chosen in this file, though not optimal, is meant to provide something that works with a broad range of tools and is easily readable by a human. Many of the authoring decisions of this file were made because it was validated against several common tools.

## The Header

At the top, you'll find a block of text that is pretty simple, and as a programmer, you should understand its purpose, even if you don't understand exactly what it does:

```
<?xml version="1.0" encoding="UTF-8"?>
<definitions name="Service"
        xmlns="http://schemas.xmlsoap.org/wsdl/"
        targetNamespace="urn:TCG-TSS"
        xmlns:tns="urn:TCG-TSS"
        xmlns:SOAP-ENV="http://schemas.xmlsoap.org/
                                soap/envelope/"
        xmlns:SOAP-ENC="http://schemas.xmlsoap.org/
                                soap/encoding/"
        xmlns:xsd="http://www.w3.org/2001/XMLSchema"
        xmlns:tcs="urn:TCG-TSS"
        xmlns:SOAP="http://schemas.xmlsoap.org/wsdl/soap/"
        xmlns:WSDL="http://schemas.xmlsoap.org/wsdl/">
```

The "definitions" tag spans the file, and so everything is contained in this element. The attributes here more or less give some explanation as to the namespace and encoding type and other things that the parser will need to do its job.

## The <types> Section

The first major section you'll find in this file is the `<types>` element. This section can be viewed similar to a `typedef` section of a C header file where an author would place his `struct`'s. This section describes some complex types derived from more primitive types. One example is a break-down of something that is meant to relate to TPM_AUTH. The C structure used in the C interface is as follows:

```
typedef struct tdTPM_AUTH
{
    TCS_AUTHHANDLE    AuthHandle;
    TPM_NONCE         NonceOdd;    // system
    TPM_NONCE         NonceEven;   // TPM
    TSS_BOOL          fContinueAuthSession;
    TPM_AUTHDATA      HMAC;
} TPM_AUTH;
```

The WSDL description of this data type is the following:

```
<complexType name="tdRPC-TPM-AUTH">
  <sequence>
    <element name="hSession" type="xsd:unsignedInt"
            minOccurs="1" maxOccurs="1"/>
    <element name="szN0" type="xsd:string" minOccurs="0"
            maxOccurs="1" nillable="true"/>
    <element name="szN1" type="xsd:string" minOccurs="0"
            maxOccurs="1" nillable="true"/>
    <element name="bContinueAuthSession" type="xsd:byte"
            minOccurs="1" maxOccurs="1"/>
    <element name="szDigest" type="xsd:string" minOccurs="0"
            maxOccurs="1" nillable="true"/>
  </sequence>
</complexType>
```

The relationship between the two is fairly easy to see. The `hSession` of the `tdRPC-TPM-AUTH` is the `AuthHandle` of the `TPM_AUTH` and so on. The `minOccurs` and `maxOccurs` describe how many of the items could exist. For example, in the C world, a TSS coder knows that both `NonceOdd` and `NonceEven` cannot have meaning at the same time in the `TPM_AUTH` structure. Similarly, the `szN0` and `szN1` fields of the `tdRPC-TPM-AUTH` structure will not exist simultaneously. The `minOccurs="1"` tells the parser that this element will always be there, but the `minOccurs="0"` tells the parser that, in some cases, it may not be there. Similarly, `maxOccurs` may be `"unbounded"` to indicate an array of unknown size.

All of the primitive types here may make sense except for the `xsd:string` type. Why is a null-terminated string used for a C byte array? The answer lies in the conventions of HTTP and

XML. Note that XML is meant to be a fully human-readable way of representing information. If the binary data were written directly, it would be unreadable. HTTP, the transport over which our data will be transmitted, is also text based. One industry convention for writing binary data as a string of readable text is to use base64 conversion. Without the details of this conversion, it can be viewed simply as a way to convert 8-bit data into 6-bit data. 3 bytes of binary data, 24 bits, are broken down into four pieces of 6-bits each. 6 bits requires 64 different characters to write to a string-readable string. Using lowercase, uppercase, and a handful of other characters, these 4 bytes of 6-bit data can be written as a string that is completely readable. Note that the value of "A" in the C language is not the same as an "A" in base64 encoding. The result is that any blob of variable or fixed length data can be written as a null-terminated base64 encoded string and both the data and the size can be derived from this string.

The other derived types in the `<types>` section follow in the same way.

## InParms and OutParms in the Complex Types

Also in the `<types>` section, you may find an "InParms" and "OutParms" for every method that the C interface describes. You may wonder why a type would need to wrap the parameters for each *in* parameter and *out* parameter of each method. Ideally, this would not be necessary. We define what types are passed in and out of each method later in the file. So, what is the purpose of wrapping our primitive and newly defined complex types into *in* and *out* wrappers for each function? The reason lies in ensuring that the file will be usable by a broader range of toolsets. Many tools available have limitations as to the number of *in* parameters or *out* parameters of a function or operation. Of course, a tool would be useless if it didn't allow at least one of each, so to ensure that these tools will work, each function or operation will be defined to have at most one *in* and one *out* parameter. Really, all functions will have exactly one, with the exception of `Tcsi_Open-Context()`, which has no parameters.

One example is for `Tcsi_GetCapability()`:

```
<complexType name="GetCapability-InParms">
  <sequence>
    <element name="hContext" type="xsd:unsignedInt"
             minOccurs="1" maxOccurs="1"/>
    <element name="cap" type="xsd:unsignedInt" minOccurs="1"
             maxOccurs="1"/>
    <element name="szSubCap" type="xsd:string" minOccurs="0"
             maxOccurs="1" nillable="true"/>
  </sequence>
</complexType>

<complexType name="GetCapability-OutParms">
  <sequence>
```

```
<element name="szResponse" type="xsd:string" minOccurs="0"
        maxOccurs="1" nillable="true"/>
<element name="result" type="xsd:unsignedInt"
        minOccurs="1" maxOccurs="1"/>
</sequence>
</complexType>
```

Note that the *out* parameters are all optional—that is `minOccurs="0"`—for every element except the result. This is to mimic the C interface. If the result is not 0, then the other parameters have no meaning and so populating them is nonsense.

With these wrapper types, now each operation or function will have at most one *in* parameter and one *out* parameter.

## The Messages

After the *types*, you'll find a bunch of messages. For each function, there is a `Request` and a `Response`. For each `Request`, there will be a corresponding InParms and for each `Response`, there will be a corresponding OutParms, except for `OpenContext`, of course. This section exists to bundle the InParms and OutParms into the messages that will then be used to define the "prototypes" of the functions:

```
<message name="GetCapabilityRequest">
  <part name="inParms" type="tcs:GetCapability-InParms"/>
</message>

<message name="GetCapabilityResponse">
  <part name="outParms" type="tcs:GetCapability-OutParms"/>
</message>
```

Legally, it would be OK to put multiple parameters into these messages, but as noted earlier, for compatibility with some tools, each message is limited to at most one parameter.

## The Operations in portType

You may have noticed some interchange with the use of the word *function* or *prototype* and the use of the word *operation*. The interchange is meant to illustrate the correlation between the two in this context. Essentially, we are trying to define a WSDL file to break down into a header file or something similar. The next section can be viewed as a way to create C function prototypes.

Our example uses the `Tcsi_GetCapability()` function:

```
<operation name="GetCapability">
  <documentation>Service definition of function
GetCapability</documentation>
  <input message="tns:GetCapabilityRequest"/>
```

```
<output message="tns:GetCapabilityResponse"/>
</operation>
```

Note here that the single input message is the `GetCapabilityRequest`, which we know uses the `GetCapability-InParms`, which in turn contains the various C parameters we are hoping to pass in. Similar to the output message is the `GetCapabilityResponse`, which contains the C output parameters and the C return code.

## The Operations in the Binding

To define the functions further, we need to describe how the data will be interpreted for each operation. This `<binding>` section describes this. For each operation, namespace and encoding is described. The further details are not important.

## The Service

The final element of the WSDL is the `<service>` section. This section pulls the name of the service and the binding information together. It also has an entry that acts as a placeholder for some tools:

```
<port name="TSSCoreService"
binding="tns:TSSCoreServiceBinding">

<!-- Although we may not be talking always to localhost, some
tools may require this field to exist. It doesn't hurt
anything to have it around has a placeholder -->
  <SOAP:address location="http://localhost"/>
</port>
```

This was added because some tools require this to exist, though the `http://localhost` acts more as a guideline since most stub compiles will allow you to manually set what the destination address really is.

## Summary of the WSDL File

So, that is the simple and somewhat smoky explanation of the internal structure of this .wsdl file. Again, it will likely not be important for you to know the ins and outs of this file explicitly, but it is good to know what is happening underneath. For more detailed and likely accurate explanation, you should research SOAP and WSDL formatting separately.

## Using the WSDL File

The previous section gave some insight as to what the text in the .wsdl file intends to describe. So, how can this insight be used by a programmer to either talk to a TCS, write a TCS, or both? The intent, though not a requirement, of authoring a .wsdl file and publishing it was to provide a generic file that was both human readable and machine readable that could be used by a broad range of toolsets to aid a programmer in development. This section will describe the intended use of the file, although you are free to do whatever you want as long as the end result works.

## The Ideal Situation

The ideal situation for a programmer would be some seamless way to take existing, or currently developing, C-based TSP code and have it talk to something that looked like the C-based interface of the TCS and not care what is going on underneath. Lucky for you, the programmer, this is pretty close to what a .wsdl file can do for you with the right tool. A TSP doesn't care how data gets to a TCS, just as long as it can call some C function that looks like a TCS function and it gets to a TCS that also expects function calls on a C interface. A good toolset will make this model the reality.

The intent was that a .wsdl file could be used with a toolset that would parse the .wsdl file. It would then generate some helper code that would give the sender, a TSP, a C interface to send the data and give the receiver some stub service. This stub service would expect a C interface to be defined by the TCS programmer to receive the various function calls. This is the basic model of most toolsets that will handle .wsdl files.

If you are familiar with IDL files, you may notice a similarity. Though IDL is meant to be generic, many programmers find that it is really only useful when programming in Microsoft-specific technology. The model is similar, however. The Description Language file describes the interface in some language, and some interpreter converts it to another language source code.

## Example Using gSOAP

There are several tools, public and private, that can be used to convert a .wsdl file. Both C/C++ and Java™ have tools with this capability. In fact, there is nothing prohibiting someone from writing a TSP in Java and having it work with a C-based TCS. Did the TSS authors consider this when deciding to use WSDL? The answer is "yes," it was part of the decision, though obviously not the primary reason. Anyway, the point is that you should be able to find a toolset that meets your needs. Unfortunately, Microsoft's .NET tools will support a .wsdl conversion but generate C# stubs, so this will not be used in this example.

One very useful tool, which is also free, is a toolset called gSOAP. This can be downloaded from http://gsoap2.sourceforge.net. Of course, you should consider all license restrictions if you want to put this into a product, but for a programmer wishing to play around, this is a great toolset. The following examples will explain the conversion using this toolset in particular, though every toolset should be very similar. Consulting the documentation of your toolset should help you relate the examples to your work.

gSOAP breaks down a header file into source files, which in turn are compiled and linked into your sender and/or receiver code. First, you must convert the .wsdl file into a header file.

Other toolsets can convert directly from .wsdl to source, C/C++, or Java, but this toolset needs an intermediate conversion first. To do this conversion, execute the following:

```
[prompt]# wsdl2h tcs.wsdl -o tcs.h
```

Of course, this assumes that your .wsdl file is named tcs.wsdl and you wish to dump the results into tcs.h. If it passes, and it should, it will indicate the next required step. Execute the following command, replacing <gsoap_dir> with the location of your gSOAP installation:

```
[prompt]# soapcpp2 tcs.h -I<gsoap_dir>/import
```

This will generate C++-based source and header files, as well as a whole bunch of XML files. If you want pure C-based source files, you will need to use the -c option. Explore some of the other switches of this tool for more flexibility.

The C/C++ sources files and header files make sense, but what are the XML files for? Actually, they are not necessary for the development, and you may choose to suppress their creation using -x for your build process. They are very interesting, though, and lead to this illustration. Up until now, we've discussed the fact that we are using Web Services and SOAP and somehow these get passed to the TCS, but we haven't discussed what the data on the "wire" looks like. Well, it's an .xml file and nothing else. Take a peek at the file TSSCoreServiceBinding.GetCapability. req.xml. You'll see a bunch of overhead text and then some text that seems to have some meaning to the actual function we intend to call:

```
<ns1:GetCapability>
 <inParms>
  <hContext>0</hContext>
  <cap>0</cap>
  <szSubCap></szSubCap>
 </inParms>
</ns1:GetCapability>
```

Note the ns1. This is a namespace thing and doesn't really mean anything except to gSOAP. This is a request file, which corresponds to the `GetCapabilityRequest` described earlier. Within the `<inParms>` of the request, you'll find the simpler types of the complex type. The values here are not populated, but the file offers a very nice look into what will actually be passed to and from a TCS. What's to stop you from writing a simple socketing program that opens a port to a TCS and pushing a static request to a TCS to open a context? Nothing. It will work, or at least respond.

## Using the gSOAP Stubs

You now have some source and headers that were converted from the .wsdl file. How can you use them? For each toolset, you can read documentation on how to use your stubs, including how to compile and link them into your programs. gSOAP requires you to include some of their header files that come with the toolset, some of the generated files, and some of their source files from the toolset as well as the generated ones to link.

Read the documentation and the samples of your toolset to determine what files are needed for the client side and the server side and to know how to compile and link.

The gSOAP-generated files will have many support functions that include resource management and prototypes to the functions you must use on the sender side or the functions you must implement on the receiver side. For the sender, the TSP side, you'll find a prototype to the functions in soapStub.h. One example will be something that resembles `soap_call_ns1__GetCapability`. Of course, this function name is arbitrary and specific to the toolset, and even the version you are using. This is the generated stub call for soapcpp2 version 2.7.6e. The server side will generate a prototype that you must implement that resembles `ns1__GetCapability`. Note that for each, you'll see the InParms and OutParms among other context parameters for gSOAP, which are better described in the documentation of that tool.

Again, all toolsets will differ in their output and usage, but the sequence is more or less the same. You should strive to find a toolset that you can use for your product that gives you the flexibility you need and provides the support functions you need to simply program your TSS and not worry about TCP/IP, HTTP, SOAP, or Web Services.

## Privacy Concerns with the TCS

The TSS working group does not want to overlook privacy in regard to the remote capabilities of the TSS. Privacy has been an important part of the design philosophy of the hardware, and the software is no different. Anyone in the field knows that security and usability have an interest-inverse relationship. Many people also know that security and privacy unfortunately get lumped as the same thing, though they are not. Despite this fact, privacy also seems to be inversely proportional to usability. So the TSS WG weighed the need to be flexible and usable with the concerns many system administrators have, or at least should have, about the privacy of their system.

### Addressing Privacy

Though the specification is not complete on this subject, there seems to be a consensus as to how it will be addressed. The TCS cannot enforce any security on its interface, as that would be a contradiction to its design philosophy—it would imply some level of trust in the software when the whole point is that not even the TSS can be trusted, which is why we use a TPM. This does not, however, prohibit system administration in a common way by some local means. The section describes some of the ideas that the specification will likely implement at a high level. Please be aware that this section was written prior to the formal release of the 1.2 specification.

### Grouping Desirable Functions

The TSS has always known that there are a finite set of macro functions for which someone will want to use a TPM remotely. However true that may be, the TSS also knows it does not want to prohibit a system administrator and/or a software vendor from extending this since it does not prohibit extensions to the software itself to be compliant. The thought then is that the TCG would define a set of macro functions that it knew would be desirable, and this functionality would be imported via a configuration file to the TCS. The format of this file would essentially be state information representing a state diagram that defined what functions would be allowed within a TCS context at any given state of that context. For example, there is no reason to allow queries to keys if the desired key operation has already happened. The administration file would be some XML file that would tell the TCS what it could allow to remote contexts. The file would even allow administration based on source IP and could be extended to allow or disallow any or all functionality based on the way the data was organized. This implementation gives the system administrator and software vendors all the flexibility they need to use the TSS as is and to get the function they need. Naturally, remote function would be disabled by default.

One use of this is for classic attestation. A system administrator may designate that a subset of IP addresses can do attestation and the administration file would reflect that wish. It would limit what could be done to only those operations in some logical order for any TSP to do the work of performing a quote and then terminating the context.

This model works very well with the current 1.1/1.2 architecture with one exception. The remote TSP must somehow convey to the TCS what its intentions are, which is a small change to the TCS interface, some small changes to the TSP interface, and perhaps a few extra TCS functions to allow query capabilities. These are yet undefined by the working group.

Again, the proposed implementation here does not in any way assure security or even that someone cannot do something he shouldn't do. What it does do, however, is provide administration configuration abilities so that a system admin can decide how much or how little information can be obtained via a TCS interface. A server would likely expose some function, while a workstation would likely not expose anything. This is pretty typical, as a server public key used for SSL is unique information in the same way an SRK public key is unique information.

## Summary

This chapter gave you an understanding of the means built into the TCS that allows remote access to a TPM across a network. This is done by using a TSS stack on one system to talk to the TCS stack on a different system. The interface has been standardized on SOAP.

# CHAPTER 11

# Public Key Cryptography Standard #11

Public Key Cryptography Standard number 11 (PKCS#11) is an industry standard API for accessing cryptographic hardware. It presents a common interface to the application, abstracting away the details of the hardware it's interfacing with. This allows applications to be more portable, maintainable, and easier to write. It's precisely for these reasons that a PKCS#11 interface to the TPM is beneficial. Existing PKCS#11 applications could immediately begin using the TPM, without having to be ported to use the TSS API. Despite its name, PKCS#11 provides interfaces to do symmetric cryptography as well as asymmetric for a laundry list of different algorithms.

This chapter discusses the issues surrounding implementing a PKCS#11 interface to the TSS. Specifically, we'll look at the PKCS#11 implementation openCryptoki, which is a freely available, open-source implementation with TPM support. Learning the details of the PKCS#11 specification is outside the scope of this chapter, so it will be left as an exercise to the reader, except when relevant to implementing a TSS PKCS#11 interface, which is covered later. For more information on PKCS#11, see http://www.rsasecurity.com/rsalabs/node.asp?id=2133.

In this chapter, we discuss the following:

- Administration of a PKCS#11 token and the TPM
- RSA key restrictions when using TPM keys through the PKCS#11 API
- Design requirements for a PKCS#11 TPM token
- Example code from a PKCS#11 TPM token implementation, openCryptoki

## PKCS#11 Overview

PKCS#11 can provide access to all the cryptographic devices, or "tokens," on a machine. This could potentially be a large number of devices, including TPMs, smart cards, cryptographic accelerators, or even native CPU instructions for cryptography. PKCS#11 provides access to a device on the machine through a "slot," or a logical view of a hardware token. Each slot can potentially contain a hardware token, which may or may not be present at application run time. Each hardware token on your machine would be accessible through a PKCS#11 slot, which would then provide a set of "mechanisms," or algorithms to the application. When a PKCS#11 application starts, it generally first would query which slots are available. From the list of available slots, the application would then query which mechanisms are available from each slot.

In PKCS#11, two passwords (called PINs in PKCS#11) are used to provide access to cryptographic tokens. The Security Officer (SO) PIN is used to administrate a token, and the User PIN is used to provide access to the token's data.

Much like the TSS, PKCS#11 provides a data storage facility that can be used to store certificates, data, keys, and any other objects you might create. According to the PKCS#11 spec, providing the User PIN should give access to all the objects stored in the PKCS#11 data store.

To gain access to objects in a PKCS#11 data store, an application first must open a session with a token and optionally log in. Depending on the type of session and the login state the application creates, only a subset of objects may be visible to the user. There are two types of PKCS#11 objects: public objects and private objects. Public objects are readable by anyone who opens a session with the token, whereas private objects are visible to a user only after he logs in to the token using the User PIN. For a more detailed description of access control to the data store, please see the PKCS#11 specification.

## A PKCS#11 TPM Token

Translating one high-level API to another is bound to lead to some problems, and these APIs are no exception. Some of the potential bumps in the road that we'll touch on are the following:

- RSA key types and padding
- Administration
- Migration

### RSA Key Types

Not all TPM keys can be used for all purposes, so attention must be paid at key creation time to best match a key's type to the wishes of the PKCS#11 application. For example, if the PKCS#11 key attributes used to create the key are set as

```
CK_ATTRIBUTE key_attrs[] = {
        {CKA_SIGN, true, sizeof(true)},
        {CKA_ENCRYPT, true, sizeof(true)},
        ...
};
```

then the user would like a key that has the ability to sign and encrypt data. The only type of TPM key that can do both is a legacy key, created in the TSS using TSS_KEY_TYPE_LEGACY. If, however, the key attributes specified are merely

```
CK_ATTRIBUTE key_attrs[] = {
        {CKA_ENCRYPT, true, sizeof(true)},
        ...
};
```

then a binding key would be sufficient for the purpose, since the created key doesn't need the ability to sign data. Creating the right type of key through the TSS is important, then, to restrict its use to be as minimal as is needed.

## RSA Key Restrictions

Because the RSA padding type for a TPM-generated key is defined at key creation time, the flexibility that PKCS#11 offers becomes somewhat restricted. In most uses of RSA keys, the type of padding used on data encrypted by the keys can be specified at signing or encryption time and can differ on a key operation-by-operation basis. This is not true for TPM keys, and so the padding type of the key must be checked at the time of the operation, as a sanity check. Since padding type is not typically an attribute of the key in the same way it is for TPM keys, the PKCS#11 TPM code must make some assumptions about the key at the time it's created. Many RSA keys will have "legacy" type uses, where encrypting data using PKCS#1 v1.5 padding will be a requirement. This virtually mandates that all RSA keys generated through the PKCS#11 interface will be set to the TSS_ES_RSAESPKCSV15 encryption scheme and the TSS_SS_RSASSAP-KCS1V15_DER signature scheme, to avoid these problems.

Creating TPM keys with encryption and signature schemes that allow for the largest amount of data to be encrypted or signed will prevent unexpected surprises when using them through a PKCS#11 interface. As discussed in Chapter 8, "Using TPM Keys," depending on the type of key, a TPM_BOUND_DATA structure may be used to house data encrypted by a TPM. This reduces the effective size of data to be encrypted (refer to Table 9.3 for more information). Knowing little about how the TPM works, a PKCS#11 user may be surprised to find that his new 1024-bit key can encrypt only up to 81 bytes!

To work around these restrictions, a PKCS#11 TPM implementation can set the encryption and signature schemes manually and use the legacy type for all keys created. See Listing 11.1 for the key generation function in openCryptoki.

**Listing 11.1**   tss_generate_key: A Function for Generating TPM Keys Inside a PKCS#11
Implementation

```
TSS_RESULT
tss_generate_key(TSS_FLAG initFlags,
                 BYTE     *passHash,
                 TSS_HKEY hParentKey,
                 TSS_HKEY *phKey)
{
    TSS_HPOLICY hPolicy;

    Tspi_Context_CreateObject(hContext, TSS_OBJECT_TYPE_RSAKEY,
                              initFlags, phKey);

    Tspi_Context_CreateObject(hContext, TSS_OBJECT_TYPE_POLICY,
                              TSS_POLICY_USAGE, &hPolicy);

    if (passHash == NULL) {
        Tspi_Policy_SetSecret(hPolicy, TSS_SECRET_MODE_NONE, 0, NULL);
    } else {
        Tspi_Policy_SetSecret(hPolicy, TSS_SECRET_MODE_SHA1, 20,
                              passHash);
    }

    Tspi_Policy_AssignToObject(hPolicy, *phKey);

    if (TSS_KEY_TYPE(initFlags) == TSS_KEY_TYPE_LEGACY) {
        Tspi_SetAttribUint32(*phKey, TSS_TSPATTRIB_KEY_INFO,
                             TSS_TSPATTRIB_KEYINFO_ENCSCHEME,
                             TSS_ES_RSAESPKCSV15);

        Tspi_SetAttribUint32(*phKey, TSS_TSPATTRIB_KEY_INFO,
                             TSS_TSPATTRIB_KEYINFO_SIGSCHEME,
                             TSS_SS_RSASSAPKCS1V15_DER);
    }

    Tspi_Key_CreateKey(*phKey, hParentKey, 0);

    return TSS_SUCCESS;
}
```

In openCryptoki, this function is used to generate all TPM-based keys. If the request is for a legacy key, set the signature and encryption schemes so that PKCS#11 software can make full use of the key.

Because there's no way to specify a padding type at key creation time through PKCS#11, this problem will not go away. Unfortunately, PKCS#11 users of a TPM interface will have to familiarize themselves with the TPM in order to understand these seemingly arbitrary restrictions.

## Administration

Because PKCS#11 was designed as a truly generic interface to cryptographic hardware, it lacks specific functions to do some of the things that the TSS API provides. Administration of the TPM chip, for instance, cannot be done through the PKCS#11 API. A sample set of instructions for administration of a TPM chip may be as follows:

- Enable the TPM chip in your machine's BIOS.
- Enable operating system support for the TPM (device driver or configuring a TSS).
- Take ownership of the TPM, setting SRK and owner passwords.

Setting up your PKCS#11 system requires similar steps, as follows:

- Set up and configure all tokens you want to use.
- Set a PKCS#11 Security Officer (SO) password.
- Set the PKCS#11 User password.

The preceding six steps are mutually exclusive—that is, no one step in either list substitutes for an item in the other. This becomes a problem when the setup of the TPM must be known by PKCS#11 without a way to communicate it through the API. Such is the case with the SRK password. In order to load keys into the TPM, PKCS#11 must know the SRK password. Although the TSS supports GUI pop-up dialog boxes to receive password information, a PKCS#11 user may not be savvy enough with both standards to know what to enter, especially if the interface has been set up for him by an administrator. What's this dialog box for? My PKCS#11 User password? My PKCS#11 SO password? A new password for the key I've just created? It can potentially be very confusing.

There are a few ways to solve this problem, although none are without drawbacks. First, you can set the SRK's usage policy to pop up a dialog box, providing descriptive text to hopefully ensure that a user isn't confused. You can accomplish this by setting the pop-up string in the SRK's usage policy object.

Another method of solving the problem is setting the SRK password to a known value. This may or may not be desirable, depending on whether your machine will allow remote access to its

TCS daemon. If an easy-to-guess password such as TSS_WELL_KNOWN_SECRET is used for the SRK, rogue users across the Internet may be able to load your SRK public key from your system persistent store and use it as a unique identifier for your machine. This would allow them to track your Internet usage from any point on the Internet. If you do choose to use a well-known or weak password for your SRK, consider disabling remote access to your TCS daemon. Note that if your TSS is compliant with the specification, remote access to it will be disabled by default.

## Design Requirements

A PKCS#11 user will typically create many keys for many different uses. What the uses of each of these keys will be in the future may be impossible to know, even by the user. This makes deciding how to protect each key in the user's hierarchy a difficult task. Restricting access to every generated key becomes vital, because we have no idea how sensitive it may be, or may become in the future. Therefore, every key created by a user through the PKCS#11 interface must be protected by a password.

First, as was discussed earlier, the PKCS#11 API doesn't offer a mechanism for providing password data on a key-by-key basis. If we were to set the policy for all keys to pop up a dialog prompting the user, he would quickly become irritated by being repeatedly prompted by the TSS. After all, he's already entered his PKCS#11 User password to gain access to the TPM token. He shouldn't have to enter any other password to gain access to his entire PKCS#11 data store according to the PKCS#11 spec.

In addition to this requirement of one password for many objects, there's also a requirement for migration of the PKCS#11 data store should your TPM hardware fail. If your TPM dies and the result is that you cannot recover any of your keys, few people would embrace the TPM as a useful tool long term. Users need to be able to migrate their entire PKCS#11 data store to a new machine, should that ever be desired.

In order to satisfy these requirements, a PKCS#11 data store should have the following properties:

- The root of the key hierarchy in the data store should be migratable, so that all data can be moved to a new TPM.
- Each key in the store should require authentication data.
- PKCS#11 public objects kept in the data store should not require a password to access, but all private data should be accessible using the User PIN.

## openCryptoki's Design

In order to accomplish these design points, openCryptoki uses two key hierarchies: one for PKCS#11 objects stored as private and one for public. The keys that make up the roots of these two trees are referred to as the Public Root key and the Private Root key (see Figure 11.1). Both are software-generated keys that are wrapped by the SRK. After these keys are created in software, copies of them are saved to disk, outside the PKCS#11 data store, and encrypted by the User (for the Private Root key) and Security Officer (for the Public Root key) PINs. These backup copies will be accessed whenever the PINs are changed (to keep them updated with the current PIN, not because they're used during the login process) and during migration.

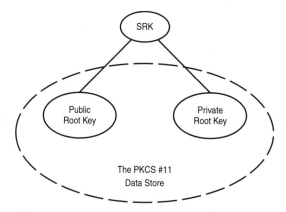

**Figure 11.1**   The root keys of the PKCS#11 data store

The Private Root key is the parent of all private PKCS#11 keys, and the Public Root key is the parent of all public PKCS#11 keys. Both are software generated and wrapped by the SRK so that they can be migrated to another platform. This is the same technique in the key hierarchy creation example in Listing 8.6.

Now that we have a parent key for public and private PKCS#11 objects, we need a way to tie the loading of these keys to the User and Security Officer PINs. To accomplish this, a child key is created for both of the root keys. These child keys are referred to as the Public Leaf key and Private Leaf key and are generated in the TPM as binding keys with authorization. When the User wants to log in, PKCS#11 does the following:

1. Loads the SRK.

2. Loads the Private Root key.

3. Loads the Private Leaf key, using the User PIN as a password.

4. Attempts to bind some data using the Private Leaf key.

If the bind of the data succeeds, we know the application supplied the correct User PIN and we can return success. The same process happens when the Security Officer logs in using the Public Root key and Public Leaf key. Figure 11.2 shows the two leaf keys in the hierarchy.

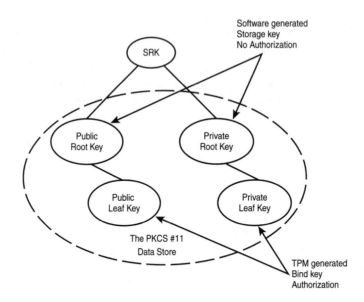

**Figure 11.2**   The root and leaf keys of the PKCS#11 key hierarchy

All keys shown are created as PKCS#11 hidden objects since they're used only for management of the PKCS#11 data store. A PKCS#11 application that searches for objects on the TPM token will not see these objects.

Now that we've successfully tied the authorization for the leaf keys to the PKCS#11 User and SO PINs, we need to define the process for creating a new key. When a PKCS#11 `C_GenerateKeyPair` call is made, three new objects are created in the data store. First, the new key is generated as a child of either the Public or Private Root key, depending on how the user is logged in. Random authorization data is created for the new key and stored encrypted by the appropriate leaf key in a hidden symmetric key object in the data store. Then, the PKCS#11 public key and private key objects are created from the generated TPM key. The private key object is linked to the encrypted authorization data object by a PKCS#11 attribute. Figure 11.3 shows the PKCS#11 data store after one new key has been created by an application logged in as User.

Since the authorization data for the new key is encrypted by the Private Leaf key, the user must be able to load the Private Leaf key to load the new key. This in effect will allow a PKCS#11 application to create any number of keys protected by authorization data without having to provide more than one password to access them all.

Let's take a look at the code in Listings 11.2 and 11.3 for creating the Security Officer's public data hierarchy.

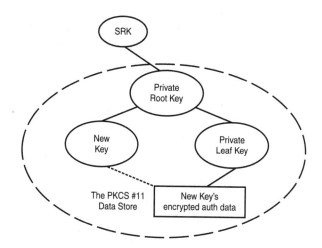

**Figure 11.3** Objects in the PKCS#11 data store after the first key is created

**Listing 11.2** token_create_public_tree: A Function to Create the Public Half of the Key Hierarchy That Supports a PKCS#11 Implementation's Key Store

```
CK_RV
token_create_public_tree(CK_BYTE *pinHash,
                         CK_BYTE *pPin)
{
    RSA            *rsa;
    unsigned int   size_n, size_p;
    unsigned char  n[256], p[128];

    /* Generate the public root key in software. */
    rsa = openssl_gen_key();

    openssl_get_modulus_and_prime(rsa, &size_n, n, &size_p, p);

    /* Wrap the software key using the Storage Root Key. */
    token_wrap_sw_key(size_n, n, size_p, p, hSRK,
                      TSS_KEY_NO_AUTHORIZATION | TSS_KEY_TYPE_STORAGE,
                      &hPublicRootKey);

    /* Write out the software key to disk, encrypted using the
     * PKCS#11 SO's PIN. This key could be read back in under two
```

```
 * circumstances: if the PKCS#11 SO PIN changes, or if we
 * have to migrate the public root key to a new platform,
 * it will be read in and re-wrapped. */
openssl_write_key(rsa, TPMTOK_PUB_ROOT_KEY_FILE, pPin);

/* Free the software key from memory */
RSA_free(rsa);

Tspi_Key_LoadKey(hPublicRootKey, hSRK);

/* Store the newly created root key in the PKCS#11 data store,
 * and create a new PKCS#11 object at the same time. The
 * PKCS#11 object handle for the root key is a global handle
 * that will never be returned to an application, but will be
 * used internally when needed. */
token_store_tss_key(hPublicRootKey, TPMTOK_PUBLIC_ROOT_KEY,
                    &ckPublicRootKey);

/* Create the SO's leaf key.  See listing 11.3. */
token_generate_leaf_key(TPMTOK_PUBLIC_LEAF_KEY, pinHash,
                        &hPublicLeafKey);

Tspi_Key_LoadKey(hPublicLeafKey, hPublicRootKey);

return TSS_SUCCESS;
}
```

**Listing 11.3**   token_generate_leaf_key: A Function Used to Generate Either the Public or Private Leaf Key

```
CK_RV
token_generate_leaf_key(int        key_type,
                        CK_CHAR_PTR passHash,
                        TSS_HKEY    *phKey)
{
    TSS_HKEY        hParentKey;
    CK_OBJECT_HANDLE *ckKey;
    TSS_FLAG        initFlags = TSS_KEY_MIGRATABLE |
                                TSS_KEY_TYPE_BIND |
                                TSS_KEY_SIZE_2048 |
                                TSS_KEY_AUTHORIZATION;
```

```
    /* The handles assigned here are kept in global space inside
     * the PKCS#11 code for easy access, since they're loaded and
     * used for any RSA key operation. */
    switch (key_type) {
        case TPMTOK_PUBLIC_LEAF_KEY:
            hParentKey = hPublicRootKey;
            ckKey = &ckPublicRootKey;
            break;
        case TPMTOK_PRIVATE_LEAF_KEY:
            hParentKey = hPrivateRootKey;
            ckKey = &ckPrivateRootKey;
            break;
        default:
            return ERROR;
            break;
    }


    /* The leaf key is a TPM-generated key, so call
     * tss_generate_key() to generate it. See listing 11.1 for its
     * definition. */
    tss_generate_key(initFlags, passHash, hParentKey, phKey);

    /* Store the leaf key internally */
    token_store_tss_key(*phKey, key_type, ckKey);

    return CKR_OK;
}
```

The code to create the user's private key hierarchy is nearly identical.

Let's look at the PKCS#11 code used to test when the Security Officer's PIN is correct. After a PKCS#11 token is initialized before its first use, the SO PIN is set to a default value. We know that the token is in this state if we can't find the Public Root key object in the data store. In this case, we just compare the supplied SO PIN to the default. After the SO sets his/her PIN, we follow the steps you might expect, loading the key hierarchy (see Listing 11.4).

**Listing 11.4**   PIN Verification Routines

```
CK_RV
token_verify_so_pin(CK_CHAR_PTR pPin,
                    CK_ULONG ulPinLen)
{
```

```
CK_BYTE hash_sha[SHA1_HASH_SIZE];
CK_RV rc;

compute_sha(pPin, ulPinLen, hash_sha);

/* Find, load the migratable root key.  If this is the first
 * time that the SO is attempting to log in, his key hierarchy
 * will not exist. In this case, just compare the default PIN
 * hash with the hash of the SO's PIN. */
if ((rc = token_find_key(TPMTOK_PUBLIC_ROOT_KEY,
                         CKO_PRIVATE_KEY, &ckPublicRootKey))) {
        /* The SO hasn't set his PIN yet, compare the login pin
         * with the hard-coded value */
        if (memcmp(default_so_pin_sha, hash_sha,
                SHA1_HASH_SIZE))
                return CKR_PIN_INCORRECT;

        return CKR_OK;
}

token_load_srk();

/* We found the root key, so load it into the TPM. This will
 * allow us to load the leaf key below, in order to do the bind
 * test in token_verify_pin(). */
token_load_key(ckPublicRootKey, hSRK, NULL, &hPublicRootKey);

/* Find, load the public leaf key */
token_find_key(TPMTOK_PUBLIC_LEAF_KEY, CKO_PRIVATE_KEY,
                &ckPublicLeafKey);

token_load_key(ckPublicLeafKey, hPublicRootKey, hash_sha,
                &hPublicLeafKey);

if ((rc = token_verify_pin(hPublicLeafKey)))
        return rc;

return CKR_OK;
}
```

```
CK_RV
token_verify_pin(TSS_HKEY hKey)
{
        TSS_RESULT result;
        TSS_HENCDATA hEncData;
        UINT32 ulUnboundDataLen;
        BYTE *rgbUnboundData;
        char *rgbData = "ARBITRARY_DATA";

        Tspi_Context_CreateObject(hContext, TSS_OBJECT_TYPE_ENCDATA,
                            TSS_ENCDATA_BIND, &hEncData);

        Tspi_Data_Bind(hEncData, hKey, strlen(rgbData), rgbData);

        /* Unbind the data to test the key's auth data. Remember that
         * the unbind operation is done by the TPM itself (bind is done
         * in software inside the TSS), so the password check is
         * enforced by the hardware. */
        result = Tspi_Data_Unbind(hEncData, hKey, &ulUnboundDataLen,
                            &rgbUnboundData);
        if (result == TCPA_E_AUTHFAIL)
                return CKR_PIN_INCORRECT;

        return CKR_OK;
}
```

The operation of verifying the PKCS#11 Security Officer's PIN is done by loading the SO's key hierarchy and attempting to bind and unbind some data using the leaf key. If the supplied pPin is incorrect, an error will occur and the SO will not be allowed to log in to the token.

## Migration

So now we have a way to securely create an arbitrary number of keys in the data store and test the login credentials of a PKCS#11 user, but how will migration be handled? Since PKCS#11 has no notion of migration, there are no commands in the PKCS#11 API to help us migrate. This would appear to be a problem, but openCryptoki is implemented in such a way that migration is completely seamless to the user and requires no interaction.

To understand how this is possible, we need to think about the state of the PKCS#11 store after the user has transferred it to a new system. Because the token has already been initialized on the old TPM, the Public and Private Root keys would be available; however, trying to load either of them would fail, since they've been wrapped to a different SRK. This is the key event that allows migration to happen transparently. When an application tries to log in as either User or SO and the appropriate Root key is found, but its load fails, we can take a migration path, look for the backup copies of the software Root keys, and automatically rewrap them to the new SRK. At this point, we can continue to login as normal, without the application having to know what happened. Let's look at Listing 11.5, openCryptoki's login function.

**Listing 11.5** token_specific_login: A Function to Handle Logging in Either by the PKCS#11 User or Security Officer

```
CK_RV
token_specific_login(CK_USER_TYPE userType,
                     CK_CHAR_PTR  pPin,
                     CK_ULONG     ulPinLen)
{
    CK_RV rc;
    CK_BYTE hash_sha[SHA1_HASH_SIZE];
    TSS_RESULT result;

    token_load_srk();

    compute_sha( pPin, ulPinLen, hash_sha );

    if (userType == CKU_USER) {
        /* Find, load the private root key, which is the
         * PKCS#11 user's side of the key hierarchy. */
        if (token_find_key(TPMTOK_PRIVATE_ROOT_KEY,
                           CKO_PRIVATE_KEY,
                           &ckPrivateRootKey)) {
            /* user's key chain not found, this must be the
             * initial login */
            if (memcmp(hash_sha, default_user_pin_sha,
                   SHA1_HASH_SIZE))
                return CKR_PIN_INCORRECT;

            return CKR_OK;
        }

        if (token_load_key(ckPrivateRootKey, hSRK, NULL,
                           &hPrivateRootKey)) {
            /* Here, we've found the private root key, but
             * its load failed. This should only happen in a
             * migration path, where we have the PKCS#11 key
```

```
            * store available, but the SRK is now
            * different. So, we will try to decrypt the PEM
            * backup file for the private root key using
            * the given password. If that succeeds, we will
            * assume that we're in a migration path and
            * re-wrap the private root key to the new SRK.
            */
           token_migrate(TPMTOK_PRIVATE_ROOT_KEY, pPin);

           /* At this point, the public root key has been
            * successfully read from backup, re-wrapped to
            * the new SRK, loaded and the PKCS#11 objects
            * have been updated. Proceed with login as
            * normal. */
        }

        /* Find, load the user leaf key */
        token_find_key(TPMTOK_PRIVATE_LEAF_KEY, CKO_PRIVATE_KEY,
                    &ckPrivateLeafKey);

        token_load_key(ckPrivateLeafKey, hPrivateRootKey,
                    hash_sha, &hPrivateLeafKey);

        /* See listing 11.4 for a definition of
         * token_verify_pin() */
        return token_verify_pin(hPrivateLeafKey);
    } else {
        /* SO path -
         *
         * Find, load the public root key */
        if (token_find_key(TPMTOK_PUBLIC_ROOT_KEY,
                        CKO_PRIVATE_KEY,
                        &ckPublicRootKey)) {
            /* The SO hasn't set his PIN yet, compare the
             * login pin with the default value */
            if (memcmp(default_so_pin_sha, hash_sha,
                    SHA1_HASH_SIZE))
                return CKR_PIN_INCORRECT;

            return CKR_OK;
        }
```

```
        /* Load the key hierarchy and verify the pin using the
         * TPM. */
        if (token_load_key(ckPublicRootKey, hSRK, NULL,
                        &hPublicRootKey)) {
            /* Here, we've found the public root key, but
             * its load failed. This should only happen in
             * a migration path, where we have the PKCS#11
             * key store available, but the SRK is now
             * different. So, we will try to decrypt the
             * PEM backup file for the public root key
             * using the given password. If that succeeds,
             * we will assume that we're in a migration
             * path and re-wrap the public root key to the
             * new SRK. */
            token_migrate(TPMTOK_PUBLIC_ROOT_KEY, pPin);

            /* At this point, the public root key has been
             * successfully read from backup, re-wrapped to
             * the new SRK, loaded and the PKCS#11 objects
             * have been updated. Proceed with login as
             * normal. */
        }

        /* Find, load the public leaf key */
        token_find_key(TPMTOK_PUBLIC_LEAF_KEY, CKO_PRIVATE_KEY,
                    &ckPublicLeafKey);

        token_load_key(ckPublicLeafKey, hPublicRootKey, hash_sha,
                    &hPublicLeafKey);

        /* See listing 11.4 for a definition of
         * token_verify_pin() */
        return token_verify_pin(hPublicLeafKey);
    }

    return CKR_OK;
}
```

Notice the migration path, which is shown in Listing 11.6.

The `token_migrate` function handles the loading of the backup key, deleting the old Root keys from the PKCS#11 data store and storing the new keys in their place (see Listing 11.6).

**Listing 11.6** token_migrate: A Function to Handle Rewrapping a Root Key (Either Public or Private) to a New SRK, Based on Software Backup Copies

```
CK_RV
token_migrate(int      key_type,
              CK_BYTE *pin)
{
    RSA                *rsa;
    char               *backup_loc;
    unsigned int       size_n, size_p;
    unsigned char      n[256], p[128];
    TSS_HKEY           *phKey;
    CK_OBJECT_HANDLE   *ckHandle;

    /* key_type controls whether we're attempting to migrate the
     * public root key for the SO or the private root key for the
     * user */
    if (key_type == TPMTOK_PUBLIC_ROOT_KEY) {
        backup_loc = TPMTOK_PUB_ROOT_KEY_FILE;
        phKey = &hPublicRootKey;
        ckHandle = &ckPublicRootKey;
    } else if (key_type == TPMTOK_PRIVATE_ROOT_KEY) {
        backup_loc = TPMTOK_PRIV_ROOT_KEY_FILE;
        phKey = &hPrivateRootKey;
        ckHandle = &ckPrivateRootKey;
    }

    /* Read the software backup key with the provided pin */
    openssl_read_key(backup_loc, pin, &rsa);

    /* Reading the backup openssl key off disk succeeded with the
     * SO's PIN. We will now try to re-wrap that key with the
     * current SRK */
    openssl_get_modulus_and_prime(rsa, &size_n, n, &size_p, p);

    /* Re-wrap the same root key using the new SRK */
    token_wrap_sw_key(size_n, n, size_p, p, hSRK,
                      TSS_KEY_TYPE_STORAGE |
```

```
                    TSS_KEY_NO_AUTHORIZATION,
                    phKey);

    Tspi_Key_LoadKey(*phKey, hSRK);

    /* Loading succeeded, so we need to get rid of the old PKCS#11
     * object and store a new one. */
    token_find_key(key_type, ckHandle);

    object_mgr_destroy_object(*ckHandle);

    token_store_tss_key(*phKey, key_type, ckHandle);

    return CKR_OK;
}
```

Maintaining a hierarchy of TPM keys inside PKCS#11 isn't easy, but PKCS#11 users are rewarded by needing few (or possibly no) application changes to start using the TPM. As a comparison between the two APIs, Listings 11.7 and 11.8 are example functions that each create a key, store it persistently, and then encrypt and decrypt some data using it. Listing 11.7 uses the TSS API and Listing 11.8 uses PKCS#11.

**Listing 11.7**   TSS_Encrypt: Create a New Key, Store It Persistently, and Use It to Encrypt a String of Data Using the Supplied Password to Authorize Loading the TPM's Storage Root Key

```
void
TSS_Encrypt(char *pass, char *data)
{
    TSS_HCONTEXT hContext;
    TSS_HKEY     hSRK, hKey;
    TSS_HPOLICY  hSrkPolicy;
    TSS_HENCDATA hEncData;
    TSS_UUID     SRK_UUID = TSS_UUID_SRK;
    UINT32       out_len;
    BYTE         *out;
    TSS_UUID     key_uuid = { 0, 0, 0, 0, 0, { "my key" } };


    Tspi_Context_Create(&hContext);
```

```
Tspi_Context_Connect(hContext, NULL);

Tspi_Context_CreateObject(hContext, TSS_OBJECT_TYPE_RSAKEY,
                          TSS_KEY_TYPE_BIND | TSS_KEY_SIZE_1024,
                          &hKey);

Tspi_Context_CreateObject(hContext, TSS_OBJECT_TYPE_ENCDATA,
                          TSS_ENCDATA_BIND, &hEncData);

Tspi_Context_LoadKeyByUUID(hContext, TSS_PS_TYPE_SYSTEM,
                          SRK_UUID, &hSRK);

Tspi_GetPolicyObject(hSRK, TSS_POLICY_USAGE, &hSrkPolicy);

Tspi_Policy_SetSecret(hSrkPolicy, TSS_SECRET_MODE_PLAIN,
                      strlen(pass), pass);

/* Force the key to use PKCSv1.5 padding by setting its
 * encryption scheme here */
Tspi_SetAttribUint32(hKey, TSS_TSPATTRIB_KEY_INFO,
                     TSS_TSPATTRIB_KEYINFO_ENCSCHEME,
                     TSS_ES_RSAESPKCSV15 );

Tspi_Key_CreateKey(hKey, hSRK, 0);

Tspi_Context_RegisterKey(hContext, hKey, TSS_PS_TYPE_SYSTEM,
                         key_uuid, TSS_PS_TYPE_SYSTEM, SRK_UUID);

/* Encrypt the data, storing it internally to the hEncData
 * object */
Tspi_Data_Bind(hEncData, hKey, strlen(data), data);

/* Decrypt the data stored inside hEncData, returning it in
 * a newly allocated memory space, which 'out' points to */
Tspi_Data_Unbind(hEncData, hKey, &out_len, &out);

Tspi_Context_Close(hContext);
}
```

**Listing 11.8**  PKCS11_Encrypt: Create a New Key, Store It Persistently, and Use It to Encrypt a String of Data Using the Supplied Password to Authorize Logging into the Token

```
void
PKCS11_Encrypt(char *pass, char *data)
{
    CK_SLOT_ID          slot_id = 0;
    CK_SESSION_HANDLE   session;
    CK_MECHANISM        mech;
    CK_OBJECT_HANDLE    publ_key, priv_key;
    CK_FLAGS            flags;
    CK_ULONG            user_pin_len, bits = 1024;
    CK_BYTE             pub_exp[] = { 0x1, 0x0, 0x1 };
    CK_BYTE             cipher[1024/8], out[64];
    CK_ULONG            cipher_len, out_len = 64;
    CK_BBOOL            true = 1;
    CK_BYTE             *label = "my key";
    CK_ATTRIBUTE        pubkey_tmpl[] =
    {
        { CKA_TOKEN,            &true,    sizeof(true)      },
        { CKA_LABEL,            label,    strlen(label)+1 },
        { CKA_MODULUS_BITS,     &bits,    sizeof(bits)      },
        { CKA_PUBLIC_EXPONENT,  &pub_exp, sizeof(pub_exp) }
    };
    CK_ATTRIBUTE        priv_tmpl[] =
    {
        { CKA_TOKEN, &true, sizeof(true)    },
        { CKA_LABEL, label, strlen(label)+1 }
    };


    user_pin_len = (CK_ULONG)strlen(pass);

    /* Open a session and log in as the user. Some tokens may
     * require a R/W session to do some operations. See the
     * PKCS#11 specification for details */
    flags = CKF_SERIAL_SESSION | CKF_RW_SESSION;
    C_OpenSession(slot_id, flags, NULL, NULL, &session);
```

```
C_Login(session, CKU_USER, pass, user_pin_len);

/* In PKCS#11, two object are created, one for the public key
 * and one for the private key. In the TSS, there is one object
 * handle representing both */
mech.mechanism      = CKM_RSA_PKCS_KEY_PAIR_GEN;
mech.ulParameterLen = 0;
mech.pParameter     = NULL;

C_GenerateKeyPair(session, &mech, pubkey_tmpl, 4, priv_tmpl, 2,
                  &publ_key, &priv_key );

/* mech is set up so that C_EncryptInit initializes the encrypt
 * operation for RSA using PKCSv1.5 padding */
mech.mechanism      = CKM_RSA_PKCS;
mech.ulParameterLen = 0;
mech.pParameter     = NULL;

/* Encrypt the data */
C_EncryptInit(session, &mech, publ_key);

C_Encrypt(session, data, strlen(data), cipher, &cipher_len);

/* Decrypt the data */
C_DecryptInit(session, &mech, priv_key);

C_Decrypt(session, cipher, cipher_len, out, &out_len);

C_CloseSession(session);
}
```

Let's compare the two APIs. As you can see, both APIs offer nearly equivalent function in almost the exact same number of lines of source code. In PKCS#11, objects are created using arrays of attributes. In order to tell PKCS#11 to store your key persistently, the CKA_TOKEN attribute should be set to true in the template used to create the key, indicating that the object should exist on the token. The TSS treats all newly created objects as temporary, so in order to store a key persistently, an explicit call to Tspi_Context_RegisterKey is made. After registering the key using the TSS, the UUID structure identifies the key in the persistent store. PKCS#11's mechanism is slightly more flexible, in that any attribute of the key may be used in searching for it. In the preceding example, a CKA_LABEL attribute is used to identify the key.

Another difference in the APIs is that during the encrypt operation, PKCS#11 requires that you allocate space to store the encrypted data. In Listing 11.8, the output of the `C_Encrypt` command is written to the `cipher` buffer. In the TSS API, `Tspi_Data_Bind` stores the encrypted data inside the encrypted data object, keeping the application from having to handle it during the operation. To retrieve the encrypted data from inside the encrypted data object, use `Tspi_GetAttribData`.

## Summary

Creating a PKCS#11 interface to the TSS poses some design challenges but offers the huge gain of allowing current PKCS#11 applications to immediately begin using the TPM. Keeping in mind issues such as data padding and signature schemes, token migration and authorization will allow you to implement your own PKCS#11 interface smoothly. Also, writing your next crypto-enabled application to the PKCS#11 standard will allow you to easily transition it to the next generation of cryptographic hardware.

# PART III

# Architectures

# Trusted Computing and Secure Storage

In a world of government regulations, such as Sarbanes-Oxley, the Health Insurance Portability and Accountability Act (HIPAA), and overall sensitivity to privacy, it is important that people be able to secure data. However, when a hard disk is available to an attacker (such as when a laptop is stolen), software cannot easily hide the keys necessary to provide security. This is particularly the case since the things a person needs to authenticate to a machine have to be remembered easily. The software is unable to defend itself against a dictionary attack, and although a removable device may be a good solution to this problem, in practice these devices get lost or broken. Often this happens when the end user is away from the office, causing a major problem. Fortunately, a chip that enables secure storage was a major design point of the TPM specification. This chapter considers how the TPM can be used to provide security to the keys used for secure storage, while still providing security in case of theft or improper read access to hard disk storage.

## Linking to Symmetric Algorithms

When the TPM was designed, it was important to the designers that it not lock the developer into a particular symmetric algorithm. The TPM is used to store symmetric keys, not to determine the algorithm used to encrypt. However, when developing a secure storage system, you must remember that the first rule of thumb in symmetric algorithms is to use one that has been tested successfully by large numbers of people. There is no reason to make up your own algorithm when there are plenty of free, fast, and highly secure algorithms available. You may think that hiding the algorithm is a means of security—security through obscurity—but this is false for a number of reasons:

- The algorithm is exposed anyway if it is running on a computer not in your possession. (If it is not running on such a computer, then you won't sell very many copies of your software.)

- You create a weak security environment by claiming to have highly secure algorithms, but not submitting them to public scrutiny for rigorous testing. (Of course, there are exceptions, such as the National Security Agency [NSA] and similar organizations who didn't want competitors using their routines.)

- Even a good algorithm can be compromised by poor implementation.

However, if the best minds in cryptoanalysis have been working on breaking a code or cipher for years and have come up with nothing better than brute force, then the cipher is likely to be very secure (if the key is long enough).

To help you in creating a secure system that uses a vetted symmetric algorithm, the NIST site, www.nist.gov, provides the source code for all of the advanced encryption standard (AES) contenders, including the one finally selected as the standard known as "Rijndael." One big caveat on using any symmetric algorithm: *Make sure you check with lawyers about the exportability/importability of the final product. Although the laws on export from the U.S. have been considerably weakened over the last few years, this can still be a minefield. And importing into some countries like France, Russia, and China can also cause problems*. See the site http://csrc.nist.gov/encryption/aes/rijndael/ containing the Rijndael source code.

After you have chosen a symmetric algorithm, you can do a number of things to design encryption software. For the rest of this chapter, I will assume you have chosen Rijndael with a 256-bit key. This is one of the strongest symmetric algorithms available, and it is also both fast and free. A 128-bit key is probably more secure than is necessary, but there is a tendency for customers to demand more security than is necessary in key length, so 256 is a good bet. On the other hand, getting a 128-bit key out of a passphrase is easy—merely use SHA-1 to hash the passphrase to get 160 bits, and drop off the first 32 bits. Getting a 256-bit key out of a passphrase is harder, but now that SHA-256 is available, it is easier—merely apply SHA-256 to the passphrase, and it spits out 256 bits.

If you are really paranoid about security, then you can use techniques such as Mars, Serpent, or a one-time pad. The first two techniques are located on the www.nist.gov site. One-time pads are very difficult to generate, but are still used by governments. One-time pads pose a problem: If the structure of the information XORed with the one-time pad is known, then it is possible that certain bits have known values, which can be easily changed in an intercepted message. As a result, integrity checks are important especially if a one time pad is used.

There are a large number of kinds of encryption software you might want to write using the TPM chip, such as the following:

- Encrypting files to send to someone else on the net without a public key

- Encrypting files to send to someone else on the net with a public key

- Encrypting files for storage on your hard disk

- Encrypting files for storage on a group hard disk for group access only
- Encrypting files for storage in a backup facility
- Locking data to specific PCs

We examine each of these in turn.

## Encrypting Files to Send to Someone Else on the Net Without a Public Key

Encrypting files to send to someone else on the net who does not have a public key can be accomplished easily as long as there is another covert channel that can be used to exchange a key. For example, a phone call might be made to transfer a passphrase. This type of program can be written to either use the TPM or not. Two specific ways that the TPM could be used to increase the security of the application are mentioned next.

First, the TPM's capability to produce a random number is used to generate a number that is transferred securely between the two parties. This number is not the actual key to be used, but rather a "salt," which will be used to reduce hammering potential. This salt will stick around for a while. To make it easy to transfer over the phone, the number should be alphanumeric. Twelve case-sensitive alphanumerics (yields $62^{\wedge}12 = 3E+21$, or about 71 bits of randomness) ought to be more than enough, but the extra paranoid may want to use more. Sprinkling randomness into a password is known as "salting" the password. The purpose of this "salt" is to prevent someone from guessing the passphrase used by hashing many passphrases together into a dictionary and then doing a comparison to the hashed passphrase in the sent file. This number is sent to both parties and put in a file on their hard disk. Call it salt.txt.

Next, the program will ask the user for the file he wishes to encrypt as well as a passphrase. This passphrase is concatenated with the salt, and then the TPM is asked to hash the result. This only provides 160 bits for use as the key, so some means needs to be used to get another 96 bits. There are many options. For example, another passphrase can provide another 160 bits when salted and hashed, from which 96 bits can be extracted (for example, the first 96 bits). This is called P.

Another way to encrypt uses the mask generation function 1(MGF1) of optimal asymmetric encryption padding (OAEP) to create 256 bits from a passphrase. Yet another would be to use one of the extensions to SHA-1, such as SHA-256, which produces 256 bits of hash out of the passphrase. (See http://csrc.nist.gov/encryption/shs/sha256-384-512.pdf for a description of this algorithm.) Recent weakness exposed in SHA-1 does not affect its use in this solution, but some governments are now asking that people move away from SHA-1 to SHA-256—so you may want to use SHA-256 for that reason.

We are still not done. Now we use the TPM to generate a random number, R, of 256 bits. P is used as a key to encrypt R, forming D. R will be the encryption key, but D will travel with the encrypted file. An easy way to encrypt R with P is to simply XOR them.

The reason the random number is generated and used to encrypt the file is to prevent over-use of a passphrase leaking data. For example, if the same message were to be sent several times with the same key, an observer might not be able to read the message, but he would be able to know that the messages were the same. This is known as traffic analysis. (As a side note, when the Gulf War began in 1991, the pizza delivery services in Washington D.C. were among the first to know it. The number of pizzas being delivered late at night to the Pentagon and the White House went way up. See http://home.xnet.com/~warinner/pizzacites.html.) One solution to this problem is to use Cipher Block Chaining (CBC) mode of encryption, where each new block is encrypted partly based on the results of encrypting the previous block. Even if chaining is used, it is possible that if the first portions of the messages are the same, then the beginning of the encrypted value of the messages will be the same. (If the sender compresses the message first, that would tend to reduce the probability of this happening.) Sometimes an initialization vector (IV), a random number, is inserted at the beginning of the encrypted file to prevent this. The IV can be discarded after the file is decrypted.

However, by using a random number each time the file is encrypted, a message would be encrypted differently each time it is sent. Of course, the size would still be the same. You could always pad messages or break them up so they are always the same size to avoid this type of traffic analysis.

When the recipient gets the file, he would detach D, and then re-create the salted hashes of the passphrase to re-create P. P is used to decrypt D to re-create R. R then would be used to decrypt the file.

There is one "gotcha" in this description. Of course, when creating your encryption program, it is important to make the structure reserved for this file size big enough to accommodate any files likely to be encrypted by the program. I would suggest 8 bytes, just to be on the safe side. Currently, the new Intel® chips are 64-bit, able to access 16,000,000,000 gigabytes. It seems unlikely, even at the current exponential rate at which storage is growing, that this number will be exceeded in a single file. Even a year-long video with 60 frames/second and using no compression, along with a window size of 4 megapixel and 4 bytes for every pixel for color, would contain less than 35,000,000 gigabytes. And to view it would require a data rate of 1 GB/second! That is why video is compressed so severely with MPEG. Clearly with a buffer large enough to accommodate a file this size, we need not worry about buffer overflow.

As written, this would require that both the sender and recipient have a file to do the encryption/decryption. But this is really not necessary. When creating the encrypted file, the encryption routine can also paste the decryption routine onto the beginning of the data. The decryption routine would then read itself into memory, extract the data, and then decrypt the data, returning the file. This is not particularly difficult. You merely need the decryption routine to know its own size and to read itself in, skip its own length down the file, and begin decrypting afterward.

However, if you are planning on doing this, it is important that the decrypting executable file also be signed. Otherwise, a nefarious attacker could intercept the message and change the executable so that it does nasty things on the recipient's machine—like send the key once it is exposed to the attacker, or install a backdoor, or a rootkit. Indeed, there have recently been reports on the net of people verifying that this is feasible, and there is speculation that the FBI's latest surveillance software works this way.

What about the file name itself? File names can actually contain a lot of information, so the file name should probably not remain with the file. Instead, it should probably become part of the data that is encrypted. Similar considerations affect other file access table (FAT) information such as the time the file was created. One additional problem that needs your attention: The size of the actual decrypted file also needs to be stored in the data, and recovered before the rest of the file is decrypted. This is because symmetric encryption algorithms are usually block algorithms, and require that the original data be an even multiple of some quantity. Since the file being encrypted isn't likely to be exactly that size, padding is added to the end of the file, and then it needs to be discarded after the file is recovered.

In this design, use of cipher block chaining is probably the best cipher mode to use. And you may want to also do integrity checking of the file—attaching a random number to the beginning and doing a hashed message authentication code (HMAC) against the file using the random number as the key. Doing this prevents an attack chopping off the end of a message, thus changing the meaning.

There are all sorts of enhancements that could be made to such a program. For instance, the file could be compressed before it is encrypted (never in the reverse order—after being encrypted, the result is pretty random, and hence not compressible).

Next, you could add a GUI, and allow the user to select a single or collection of files to encrypt.

And of course, you could add a signing function, to prove that the data came from the recipient and was unchanged in transit.

The basic steps of the design in pseudocode go like this:

1. Create a salt (once per pair of individuals):

```
BYTE*   salt;
FILE    *saltFile
uchar   alphaSalt[65]={0};


Tspi_TPM_GetRandom(hTPM,32,&salt);


    ConvertToAlphaNumerics(alphaSalt);
    saltFile=fopen("salt.txt","wb");
fprintf(saltFile,%s,alphaSalt);
fclose(saltFile);
```

2. Exchange alphaSalt (via phone, perhaps). It gets stored in a salt file: salt.txt.

3. Create a symmetric key:

```
BYTE*  symmetricKey;

Tspi_TPM_GetRandom(hTPM, 32, &symmetricKey);
```

4. Create a 256-bit mask from a salted passphrase (once per message) and XOR it with the symmetric key to form a `MaskedSymmetricKey`:

```
char SymmetricKey[33]={0};
char MaskedSymmetricKey[33]={0}
char alphaSalt[65]={0};
void getSymmetricKeys()
{
    struct SHAContext sha;
    char mask[33]={0};

    word8 hash[SHA_DIGESTSIZE];
    long i;
    word32 t;
    char message[5000]={0};
    char message1[5000]={0};
    File *saltFile;

    saltFile=fopen("salt.txt","rb");  //Read in the Salt
    fread(alphaSalt,1,64,saltFile);
    fclose(saltFile);



    strcpy(message,alphaSalt);  //Salt the message

    message1[0]=1;
    printf("Type in your passphrase and hit enter\n");
    gets(&message[strlen(alphaSalt)]);

shaInit(&sha);// Hash the result to get the first 20 bytes
             // of the mask
shaUpdate(&sha, (word8 *)message, strlen(message));
shaFinal(&sha, hash);

for(i=0;i<20;++i)sprintf(&mask[2*i],"%02x",hash[i]);
```

```
              strcat(message1,message); // Preprend a '1' and
                                        // rehash
          shaUpdate(&sha, (word8 *)message1, strlen(message1));
          shaFinal(&sha, hash);
       for(i=20;i<32;++i)sprintf(&mask[2*i],"%02x",hash[i-20]);
                              // Get last 12 bytes of mask

          for(i=0;i<32;++i) MaskedSymmetricKey[i]=
              SymmetricKey[i]^mask[i]
   }
```

5. Encrypt the file using the symmetric key. The encryption should follow these steps:

   a. Open up a new file for the encrypted file to be written to.

   b. Write decryption executable to the new file.

   c. Append the encrypted data to the new file.

   d. Append information about the file (for example, its length) to the new file.

   e. Append the masked symmetric key to the new file.

```
void encryptMARS(char *filename, char *selfname)
{
    BYTE instring[128]={0};
    int i;
    long lengthOfFile;

    keyInstance keyin;
    cipherInstance encipher;
    BYTE ctbuf[32], outbuf[32];

    int size=strlen(filename);
    char *encryptedname=(char *)malloc(size+5);
    strcpy(encryptedname,filename);
    strcat(encryptedname,".exe");
    FILE *infile,*encryptedfile;
    infile=fopen(filename,"rb");
    if(infile==NULL)
    {
       printf("I can't find that file\n");
       return;
    }
    lengthOfFile=filelength(fileno(infile));
```

```
    encryptedfile=fopen(encryptedname,"wb");
    free(encryptedname);

// The following is to write the decryption executable at the
// beginning of the output file, so that the file is
// self decryptable

    FILE *decryptexecutable;

// decryptexecutable=fopen("decmars.exe","rb"); - This is if
// the decrypt executable is in a separate file. If it is at
// the end of the encryption file, use the next line.
    decryptexecutable=fopen(selfname,"rb");
    fseek(decryptexecutable,78848,0);   // this assumes the
                                        // decryption executable
                                        // takes up the last 78848
                                        // bytes of the encryption
                                        // executable

    char buffer[64000];
    int numread;
    while(0<(numread=fread(buffer,1,64000,decryptexecutable)))
    {
        fwrite(buffer,1,numread,encryptedfile);
    }
// fclose(decryptexecutable);           This is used if the
//                                      decrypt executable is in
//                                      a separate file


// The following is used to write the size of the file
// encrypted in a position that the decrypt file can find and
// read, and thus only write out the portion of the decrypted
// file that is actually from the file, and not from padding.
    fwrite(&lengthOfFile,sizeof(long),1,encryptedfile);



//  Generate the expanded subkeys from the key. The expanded
//  keys are what mars uses.

    makeKey(&keyin,DIR_ENCRYPT,256,MARS256Key);

cipherInit(&encipher,MODE_CBC,"00000000000000000000000000000000");
```

```
        int sizeread=0;
        while(32==(sizeread=fread(instring,1,32,infile)))
        {
           blockEncrypt(&encipher, &keyin, instring,256, ctbuf);
           fwrite(ctbuf,1,32,encryptedfile);
        }
        if(sizeread!=0) for(i=32;i>sizeread; -i) instring[i-1]=0;

        blockEncrypt(&encipher, &keyin, instring,256, ctbuf);
        fwrite(ctbuf,1,32,encryptedfile);
        fwrite(ctbuf,1,32,MaskedSymmetricKey);

        fclose(infile);
        fclose(encryptedfile);
    }

    int main(int argc, char **argv)
    {
       int i;
       getMARS256Keys();
       encryptMARS(argv[1],argv[0]);
       return 0;
    }
```

6. Exchange the passphrase over the phone.

7. Send the executable to the recipient.

8. Recipient executes the executable:

   a. Asks the recipient to supply a passphrase.

   b. Salts the passphrase.

   c. Recovers the masked symmetric key from the executable.

   d. Recovers the symmetric key using the salt and passphrase.

   e. Recovers the size of the encrypted file from the executable.

   f. Recovers the encrypted file from the executable.

   g. Decrypts the encrypted file using the symmetric key.

   h. Writes out the recovered file to a new file with the correct name.

Now let's consider various attacks on this file.

- If someone overhears the passphrase, but does not know the salt, he has to try out 3E21 salts to exhaustively search the space.[1]
- If he knows the salt, he has to try out a dictionary of passphrases to break the message.
- If the user re-uses a passphrase again and again, then if it is ever recovered, the observer still has to regain the salt (3E21 possibilities). Once that is done, all the messages are available, so it is a good idea not to reuse a key.
- If the passphrase and salt are not recovered, then the next best attack is to attack the 256-bit Rijndael key. Good luck. There are only 1E77 possibilities to try.

## Encrypting Files to Send to Someone Else on the Net with a Known Public Key

If the recipient has a public/private key pair, and the public key is known, there is another solution that looks very similar to the preceding process, but it can be done with more security. The problem with the previous process is that if someone can obtain the salting value (which, after all, is in the clear on the recipient's machine) and then can guess the passphrase, they can decrypt the file. They might guess the passphrase by using a dictionary type attack—trying a large number of commonly used passphrases such as "Now is the time for all good men." In other words, the 256-bit mask might not be random enough.

When the recipient has a public key that you know, the 256-bit mask need not be used at all. Of course, it didn't need to be used in the first place, either. Instead of exchanging the passphrase, a 256-bit key could be exchanged. This has two problems, though. The first is that if the key is overheard, the message is now readable. The other is that it is hard to transmit a 256-bit key over the phone—and getting a single bit wrong makes the message unreadable.

A better solution would make the decryption automatic. This can be easily achieved by doing the following:

1. Use the TPM to generate a random 256-bit key.
   ```
   uchar symmetricKey[32];
   Tspi_TPM_GetRandom(hTPM,32,&symmetricKey);
   ```
2. Encrypt the message/file with the key. Use your own symmetric encryption executable.
3. Encrypt the key with the recipient's public key using the TSS.

---

[1]  Note that 6e16 possibilities have been searched with specialized hardware and a very large number of computers working in concert in about a day. It is likely that the NSA could crack 3e21 possibilities in less than a minute. If you have to protect your information from this kind of attack, then this is not the best approach. The NSA could probably read your data directly using Tempest technology, without bothering to crack the key.

```
BYTE* encryptedKeyBlob;
                    UINT32* encryptedKeyBlobSize;

                    Tspi_Data_Bind(encryptedKeyBlob,
   hRecipientsPubKey,
32,
symmetricKey);
```

4. Send the encrypted file and encrypted key to the recipient.

This solution does not offer perfect forward secrecy—that is, if anyone records the encrypted message and then later discovers the recipient's private key, he can then decrypt the recorded message. Still, it is a pretty good solution if the recipient's private key is kept safe inside a TPM. If the recipient's private key is not kept secure, this solution may not be as secure as the previous one.

If the recipient's machine is online, a session could be established with perfect forward secrecy. Both machines generate a random number. The numbers are exchanged encrypted with the public keys of each other, and then the two numbers are XORed to create a session key used for the exchange of data. In this case, both private keys would have to be recovered to decrypt an old encrypted message.

Signing of the messages going back and forth, especially using nonces to guarantee that the messages are "fresh" and not replayed, can enhance the security as well.

But there are standard protocols to do this exchange, and it would be better to use those protocols via drivers that in turn make use of the TPM. One example would be an SSL exchange with both client-side and server-side authentication.

The same enhancements could be made to this program as to the previous one. The decryption code could use PKCS#11 to automatically decrypt the key and then decode the file. Compression is always recommended, as it reduces redundancy, time to transfer the file, and statistical attacks that can be applied to the encrypted file.

An interesting variant of this solution involves using a public storage location on the web. Google is now offering large mail storage for free, and a hosted ftp server can be obtained for less than $50/year. In this environment, it is tempting to create a program that uses a secure email system to transfer keys, and then uses those keys to encrypt files that are transferred to a public storage site. A system that does all of this in a drag-and-drop environment would probably be very useful.

## Encrypting Files for Storage on Your Hard Disk

One of the most common ways a TPM is used is in encrypting data to be stored on a hard disk. This is especially true when very valuable data can be stored on a laptop or PDA, which can be easily stolen. Even data that is stored on special disks that will not spin up unless given a password are vulnerable to being sent to a data recovery business that will open up the hard disk in a clean room and read the discs inside directly.

If a customer has valuable data on a media that is placed in situations that make it vulnerable to theft, he definitely wants to make certain that the files are encrypted securely. In this case, one does know the public key of the recipient, because the sender and recipient are the same person! As a result, we can follow closely the last solution, but instead of sending the file to the recipient, it is simply stored on the hard file. This can be done automatically using `TSS_Data_Bind`. The public key used would be a storage key, which is locked to the TPM.

Again, you could get really fancy with this type of solution, as follows:

- You could designate a subdirectory (or partition) to be encrypted, so that everything that is stored in that directory is automatically encrypted.

- You could compress before encrypting. This reduces redundancy in the encrypted file, which further makes it difficult to decrypt. However, this is probably not necessary. It also reduces the amount of data being encrypted, garnering a time savings both in encryption and transmission, at the expense of increasing the amount of time being spent on compression. Older algorithms (such as 3DES) probably would benefit from compression because they were not designed to be fast in software, but it isn't clear that will be true with modern algorithms such as Rijndael.

- You could allow the user to select the type of key usage, where authentication is necessary every time a file is decrypted or just once after power up.

- You could store the storage key on separate storage, such as a memory smart card, so that even dissecting the TPM and hard disk together would not be sufficient to obtain the data.

- You could encrypt the file names so that they do not appear when an unauthorized person looks at the directory; but after authorization, they would appear as normal.

You probably should use a different key for every file that is being encrypted, but you could use the same storage key for storing the encryption keys. If multiple users were to use the same PC, they could all have different subdirectories tied to storage keys they own, and those subdirectories would only encrypt/decrypt if they have logged on.

The basic algorithm is as follows:

1. Obtain the name of the file to be encrypted.

2. Obtain a random number of the correct size for encryption (for example, 256 bits for high-strength AES). Use `Tspi_TPM_GetRandom`.

3. Encrypt the file using the random number as the symmetric key.

4. Hide the symmetric key (using `TSS_DATA_Bind`) to encrypt the symmetric key behind an asymmetric key whose authorization (password) is known to the user.

5. Attach the blob created by `Tspi_Data_Bind` to the end of the file.

A number of refinements can be made to this algorithm. For example, although it is the case that every file should be encrypted with a different symmetric key, it isn't necessarily the case that the end user wants to put in a passphrase every time he decrypts a key. A more likely use scenario would be that the end user would want to put in a passphrase once that would allow all of the files to be decrypted. This can be done via a daisy chain design, in which the key, K, which is used to store the symmetric keys, does not require a passphrase—but the key used to store K does require a passphrase to load K. In this way, the end user only has to enter the passphrase needed to load K once, and after that, every file can be decrypted without coming back to the user for more data.

Alternatively, a "helper program"—a file I/O subsystem—can be invoked that is given the passphrase needed to use K, and the helper program then decrypts/encrypts files as needed. This helper program can be specially designed to never cache the passphrase onto the disk. This then leads to another problem: How can we guarantee that the helper program is not really a Trojan horse, bent on stealing the passphrase and leaving all the files exposed to the cracker?

The best answer to the problem is based on getting inside the mind of the cracker. Is he intent on getting the asymmetric keys? No. He is intent on getting the clear text of the files that are decrypted. If the cracker has gotten so far into the system as to be able to replace the helper program with one of his own, the system has much worse problems than just having the helper program replaced. Nonetheless, there is an answer for even this problem, albeit a tricky one.

One particularly nice thing that a TCG-compliant system allows is more secure key management. A storage key could be stored and locked with both a user's passphrase and Platform Configuration Registers (PCRs) that are in the correct state only if that user has logged on. Utilizing this device during the logging on procedure, the helper program device will be able to retrieve a root symmetric storage key, given that both the PCRs contain the correct value and the correct passphrase are entered. In this case, one of the PCRs extended by the OS would record the value of the program being run to do file encryption I/O. Ideally, this would happen early in the boot sequence so that encrypted files would be available for privileged information during the rest of the boot sequence.

The file I/O subsystem keeps this value in its own local storage for use in decrypting file encryption keys. After the file I/O subsystem has retrieved the root symmetric storage key, though, it extends one of the PCR values, making that key unavailable to any further applications.

This solution is likely to first appear in a Linux® system, because it requires a change to the OS—specifically, having the OS extend a PCR to record the first program it launches or to record the file I/O subsystem being used for decryption.

One interesting thing to note about file system encryption: It is sometimes important that a random block in a file be decrypted without having to decrypt the entire file. This can be done if counter mode is used for the encryption. This mode starts with a unique number being generated for the file. A random number is generated—or the hash of the fully qualified file name could be used. This number is successively incremented for each block, and then the resultant number is encrypted. The resultant encrypted block is XORed with the file block. Note that this way, after reading the random number associated with the file, it is possible to decrypt any block without first decrypting all the previous blocks.

## Encrypting Files for Storage on a Group Hard Disk for Group Access

Sometimes a group of people are allowed access to data. For example, top-secret data might be available to anyone with top-secret clearance. Providing this kind of access can be solved in many ways using the TPM. One design starts with someone—for example, the group leader—creating a migratable storage key on his TPM by using TPM_CreateWrapKey to create a group key.

This key is then migrated to non-migratable storage keys on the machines of all the other members of the group by using TPM_AuthorizeMigrationKey for non-migratable keys from the machines of other members of the group.

Then the key is migrated using TPM_CreateMigrationBlob and the results sent to each member of the group. Separately, each member of the group has to be given the authorization data to use this group key.

Whenever a member of the group wants to encrypt a file, he uses TSS_Data_Bind to create a symmetric key, encrypt the file with it, and then bind the symmetric key to the migrated group key. The bound key and encrypted file are sent to the server, and every member of the group can access the file and decrypt the symmetric key so as to gain access to the clear text of the file.

This design allows the group leader to add people to those who have access to the file and keeps other users from granting access to people without his knowledge. It should be noted, though, that once a user has access to the decrypted document, he can share that document without restriction.

In order for this design to work well, the group leader needs to have a way of determining if a public key given to him is a non-migratable storage key. Fortunately, the TCG specification allows for this to be done. Each client system creates an identity key, I. This key, together with the endorsement certificate from the system manufacturer, is sent to a Certificate Authority (CA), who produces a certificate for I, encrypts the certificate with a symmetric key, and encrypts the public portion of I and the symmetric key with the public portion of the endorsement key. These two pieces—the encrypted symmetric key and the encrypted certificate—are then sent to the end user, who uses his TPM to decrypt the symmetric key (his TPM first checks that the public portion of I is correct). Then, using the symmetric key, the certificate is decrypted. This certificate then attests that the identity key (I), is a valid TPM identity key, as listed next:

```
TPM_MakeIdentity
Tspi_TPM_CollateIdentityRequest
Tspi_TPM_ActivateIdentity
```

The CA may have used any means to encrypt the certificate; you will have to use a utility from the CA to decrypt the certificate using the key recovered with TPM_ActivateIdentity.

This identity key can then be used to create certificates for any non-migratable key that the TPM generates.

```
    *   TPM_CertifyKey
```

This design makes it easy to add a new member to the list, but it has a problem if a member of the group ever leaves the group. There is no way to "un" migrate a key, so a new key has to be chosen for a group key. Also, all the files need to be re-encrypted using different symmetric keys—although in many cases, this is like locking the barn door after the horse is stolen.

One thing that can be done to remove a member from the group, though, is to retrieve the machine that he was using to decrypt the files. Once that machine is retrieved, his capability to access the files is also removed.

Another way to manage a member of a group leaving involves diffusing the control of the keys among the team so that whenever a file is encrypted, it is automatically encrypted in such a way that only members of the group are able to decrypt it. Also, it should allow for removal of access as soon as any member of the team departs. You can do this by using `TSS_Data_Bind` multiple times for each member of a group.

In this case, a list of public keys is given to each member of the group, endorsed by the administrator of the group with a signature. These public keys correspond to non-migratable keys owned by each member of the group. This list also includes an expiration date. And there is a revocation list posted by the administrator and signed by him (and probably sent to all members of the group periodically). Now when a file is to be encrypted, everything proceeds as follows.

1. The list and revocation list are referenced to find out the list of keys, S, to be used.

2. `Tspi_TPM_GetRandom` creates the symmetric key for the encryption, and then `TSS_Data_Bind` is used to bind that key multiple times, once for each public key on the list S.

3. Now the sequence of bound keys is attached to the file (in the same order as on the list) and the list attached as well.

4. When a request comes to decrypt a file, the encrypted file is downloaded and the different payloads detached. Each user finds the bound key that corresponds to his own private non-migratable key and uses his TPM to decrypt the bound key using `TSS_Data_Unbind`.

   Having the symmetric key, he is then able to decrypt the file.

Now, however, if a member of the group leaves the group, he is added to the revocation list, and a new list of group members is sent to the remaining group members. Further, the files on the server have their bound key corresponding to the old group member and the old file of public keys stripped and the new file of public keys (which is one key smaller) attached.

This design works for removing a member from the group, but does add some problems for adding a member to the group. In this case, the administrator adds a new member to the group, and a new bound key and new public key list needs to be added to every file on the server. This requires running `Tspi_Data_Unbind` and `TSpi_Data_Bind_Bind` for every file on the list to create a new bound key. It does NOT, however, require decrypting and re-encrypting every file.

This can be simplified by having the administrator keep a few extra migratable keys in his list that can be transferred to a new employee's machine as necessary. In this case, this cache of extra keys can be used to give immediate access to files to a new member of the group.

## Encrypting Files for Storage in a Backup Facility

Sometimes a person wants to back up his data for storage in a backup facility. This problem is inherently no different from encrypting files for storage on a hard disk. As long as the files cannot be decrypted without the active support of the TPM on the user's system and proof of knowledge of the user authentication data provided to that TPM by the user, the backup storage is safe. However, there is a subtlety in using a backup program together with a file encryption program. Most file encryption systems automatically decrypt data if an authorized user is logged on. Thus, a backup system would decrypt the data before it backs it up! This is clearly not what the user wants. In this particular case, the user wants the data to remain encrypted during backup.

Two solutions are available: Either the file encryption I/O driver makes an exception for the backup software, or the backup software encrypts data before it exports off the system. Actually, there is another solution sometimes used. This sophisticated technique, such as used by eCryptfs, solves the problem by stacking one file system on top of the base file system. The stacked file system is encrypted, and the base file system is backed up. As a result, backup products do not autodecrypt the files being backed up.

This provides a way for multiple users to use the same backup facility without allowing any user to view another user's files. Additionally, it provides a way for multiple groups to share a backup storage area without compromising security (although traffic analysis data might still be obtained this way).

There is an additional advantage to this type of solution that isn't immediately apparent. Because TPMs are tied to specific machines, and some specific machines can be tied down (literally) to specific secure locations, it is possible to encrypt data in a way that can be decrypted only by a machine that is in a specific secure location.

Let's consider, though, an extension of this to a backup service that exists on the Internet and that is going to be used by a group of devices, all owned by the same person. There are a number of security problems that need to be solved, as follows:

- No one should be able to snoop transmissions from the Internet storage company and the device.

- If a device is lost, it should not compromise the security of the data.

- New devices ought to be able to be easily added to the list of approved devices.

- The owner of the Internet storage should not be able to access the data (even if presented with a search warrant).

- It should be possible to manipulate data so that it is easily presentable by the device that is viewing it (for example, a PDA's display requires different formatting than a PC's display).

Let's consider ways in which this could be accomplished.

With only one device accessing the data, the solution is pretty easy. The data is encrypted with a symmetric key, and the key is encrypted with the user's public key. The user can retrieve the data and decrypt it easily. Assume for a moment that this device is a PC.

Now suppose another device with a different public/private key pair is to be added to the authorized user list. Assume that this device is a PDA. Two things need to be given to the PC: the new device's public key, and data on how to format data so that it can be read from the PDA. (The PC is more sophisticated than the PDA, so it is assumed it can handle the display of PDA originated data.) The next time the PC re-encrypts data, it will do the following:

- Provide information necessary for the PDA to display the information (perhaps translating the data to another format entirely).

- Encrypt the symmetric key twice: once with its own public key and once with the PDA's public key. Data is also signed as having originated with the PC.

When the PDA reads in the data, it decrypts the symmetric key, decrypts the data, and reads it in (and possibly modifies it). If modified, it writes out just its modifications, encrypted with a symmetric key. The symmetric key is encrypted both with its own and with the PC's public key.

Optionally, the PC may also go into other data on the Internet database and provide the changes necessary to allow the PDA to also read them.

When a third device is given access to the database—for example, a portable PC—the PC owner need only sign the PDA and portable PC's public keys and post them also on the database. Then when encrypting, it can include another copy of the symmetric key—this time encrypted with the public key of the portable PC. The portable PC also gets a copy of the PC's public key, and from that sees the PDA's public key is also "certified" by the PC to get data.

We now have a number of things that are stored on the Internet storage device:

- A table of public keys, signed and certified by one of those public keys. Any member of the group is able to certify another member to the group (or optionally, a single or a few of the members may be the only ones with that ability).

- Data encrypted with a symmetric key.

- Symmetric keys encrypted with public keys.

- A table of transforms necessary to put data into a format viewable by other members of the group.

How does this help solve the problems?

- No one can snoop transmissions between the Internet storage company and devices as the data is all encrypted.

- If a device is lost, it should not compromise the security of the data—a public key can be removed from the list of allowed ones, and the header files with symmetric keys encrypted with that public key can be erased.

- New devices can easily be added to the list of approved devices by having their public key signed by an existing administrator for the data.

- The owner of the Internet storage is not able to access the data (even if presented with a search warrant), as he does not have any of the private keys and cannot sign one for himself, not being an administrator.

- The data can be manipulated so that it is easily presentable by the device that is viewing it, because devices are given the information necessary to do that before encryption.

## Locking Data to Specific PCs

Many companies have expressed interest in locking data to specific PCs. It is a problem that is beginning to get more and more focus. Fortune 500 companies have their "crown jewels" of pricing and cost information used for bidding on systems. Government National Labs have nuclear secrets on systems. Both want to prevent an employee who has access to this data from copying that data and putting it on an insecure system—or, worse yet, deliberately transmitting it to the competition.

This is a difficult problem, but one that can be solved with a TCG-enabled system. The steps to achieve this are as follows:

1. Verify boot into a secure operating system (use PCRs).

2. The operating system hashes and extends a PCR for the first program it launches, before the operating system is launched.

3. Verify that the first program launched is the viewing program (use a PCR).

4. A viewing program decrypts the key it will use to view the data (stored behind the PCR values) in its own local memory, and then extends its own PCR, so it will not be available to any other application. All viewing of data by the viewing program is done in the application's local memory. The application does not allow for hard disk caching of this memory. Memory is scrubbed before it is released.

Let's consider this solution and the attacks it prevents, step by step.

## Step 1

One problem that comes up in this type of system is that an OS is able to go behind the back of an application and copy information once the application has decrypted it. This is usually in the form of doing something like a Ctrl-Print Screen (in Windows) to copy the contents of the video buffer into a bitmap. Clearly when using this type of program, you want to be sure that it isn't being run on an OS that permits such shenanigans.

A possible solution to this is to create a version of Linux that has known properties that do not allow for the OS to give away information from an application. Because device drivers also run in ring zero, it is important that any device drivers also be known, secure drivers. The PCR structure is designed specifically to allow a user to guarantee that the PCRs are in a specific state only if the system boots into a specified OS and device driver state such as this one. There are two ways that a TPM can use PCRs to verify the machine's state. The first one, TPM_Quote, is designed to be used remotely. The second one, TPM_Seal, can be used locally.

## Step 2

There are 16 PCR registers in a TPM, and only some of them have specified contents. One reason for not specifying contents was to allow other programs to use PCR values. In this case, we direct the OS to extend the selected PCR as the OS completes its boot and brings up its first user-initiated program. This is done so we can guarantee that the system has not been modified by any hacking program, Trojan horse, virus, or snooping program when we run the program that will be used to view the secure data. The best way to guarantee no other program is trying to crack the system is to guarantee that the only program running is the one that has been validated. So this PCR will be used to guarantee that the secure viewing program was the first program run (this happens in Step 3).

## Step 3

The viewing program will be able to decrypt the encryption key used to store the secure data at this point, because authorization to view the data is tied to the joint PCR values of the trusted OS and the first program being run. This is done with the TPM_Seal command. Authorization data in the form of a passphrase or biometrics (or both) probably will also be required. As soon as the viewing program obtains the decryption key, it extends the PCR corresponding to the first program launched. After this point, it is not possible for any other program to read in the encryption key, as the TPM will fail the attempt because the PCRs will not be in the correct state. At this point, the viewing program knows how to read the file, but no other program that is launched will be able to obtain the key.

## Step 4

At this point, the viewing program has all the information necessary to view the data in the clear. It is important that the viewing program not inadvertently make that information available to someone not authorized to view the data. This is accomplished by a combination of tweaks to the OS described in Step 1, and tweaks to the application itself. The application cannot cache out data to the hard disk, as it might include secrets. It must maintain the encryption key in RAM only. Together with the OS, it must not allow the starting of another program running concurrently with it if that program can have access to its private memory space.

Actually in this scenario, the only time a PCR check is really necessary is inside the Viewing program, and that happens automatically as the TPM will not release the key to the viewing program unless the PCRs check out.

The viewing program can be hobbled so that it doesn't allow printing of data. You can't prevent someone from taking a photograph of the screen this way, and possibly making bitmap images of the screens if the OS is set up to allow that; but it should prevent bulk transfer of confidential information from one PC to another.

## Content Protection

First, a caveat: The TPM was not designed for Digital Rights Management (DRM)—keeping content protected against the owner of the TPM—and as a result, is not terribly suitable for that. Hoops need to be jumped through, and specialized hardware and software designed around a TPM in order to provide a content protection solution. Nonetheless, the TPM does provide one piece that can be used in content protection solutions: It can contain keys that are unique to a system. It does this in a way that is privacy sensitive by abstracting the identify using either the Endorsement Key or the DAA protocol.

Content protection has been a long unsolved problem in the industry. Inexpensive specialized hardware could be created using a TCG-compliant miniature system that could help solve this problem. The problem is this: How can music or an e-book or other media distributed over the Internet be sold more than once? Once a digital copy of the media is distributed, it is easy to make a perfect copy of the bits and distribute it further.

Analog reproduction has been around with us for a long time. It is not of such a concern to the publishing houses, but digital copies are exact replicas, and as such are causing media giants real heartache.

One solution would be to create a device that would play content but that would not simultaneously expose that content. The previous section on locking content to a PC could easily be used in a smaller, single-purpose device. This device would have a TPM module perhaps of FIPS 140-2 level 3. This module would be integrated with a solid state boot into a reader/player of the media. Then the following would take place:

1. Before shipment, a PCR locked, non-migratable storage key is created by the TPM, called S.

2. The manufacturer provides a certificate for S with each system.

3. When purchasing media, the owner provides the certificate of S and its public key along with a credit card.

4. The media provider encrypts the media with a symmetric key, K (for example, a Rijndael key) and then encrypts the symmetric key with the public portion of S.

5. The two encrypted bundles are sent to the owner of the device.

6. The encrypted bundles can be saved anywhere or duplicated for backup.

7. When inserted into the device, and upon it being powered up, the device loads the reader/player software. The reader software, in its own memory, uses S to decrypt K and then uses K to decrypt the media. If music, the media is sent to an A/D converter and analog music is output. If an e-book, the book is displayed on the screen.

An ideal situation to avoid problems of "suits" in the event of someone breaking a device (and no matter how well-built a device, someone will break it) would be to have the industry group of media providers jointly own the certification agency.

It should be noted that a solution like this is not amenable to the PC for a number of reasons. PCR control is at too fine a level for PCRs to be used to lock content. PCRs are wonderful for applications when an owner wants to keep a bad guy from hacking the hardware, but are impractical for use to prevent an owner from hacking his own system. This type of content protection can be used only with single-purpose devices that are hardened against attack by the owner. There are ethical questions that come up in designing a solution of this type, though, as some people (myself included) believe that if a person buys a piece of hardware, he ought to be able to control it.

# Secure Printing

There are a couple of different ways that TPMs can be used to enhance the security of printing solutions. The problem is basically how to make sure that data is not able to be seen while it is being transferred between a system and the printer. This problem is particularly acute because standard formats (like Postscript) are used to transfer the data, and free programs, like Ghostscript, can be used to convert Postscript files back to readable files.

## Intranet

In a business, internal threats are as bad or worse than external threats. The intranet is available to anyone who wants to put their Ethernet card into promiscuous mode so that it can read all the packets on the shared media. If a printer is on that shared media, all the bits going to it are available to such an Ethernet card.

Email systems, such as Lotus Notes®, can compensate for the party-line aspect of the intranet by encrypting information that flows between users. IPSec cards can be set up to compensate for normal data exchange between systems.

However, printers are typically a different beast. Confidential information that is sent to a printer is usually sent "in the clear." If it is in Postscript, it can be imported into many word processor applications where it can be viewed or changed.

Communication that goes to a printer needs to be kept confidential and go to a printer located at a known (secure) location. Both of these requirements can be met with TCG. The printer's public key would be embedded in the printer driver residing on a client. A certificate could be generated by the IT organization and attached to the driver.

When the printer driver creates the data stream to be shipped to the driver, first it creates a key for either a stream cipher (like RC4) or another symmetric cipher, such as AES. Next, it would encrypt that key with the public printer key. Then it would attach the resultant bundle to the header of the print stream. The printer would, upon receipt of the header, detach the bundle, use its TPM to decrypt the symmetric or stream cipher key, and then use the key to decrypt the rest of the printing stream. Note that such a use of a TPM would require that the TPM be able to decrypt the bundle without a password.

For more safety, it would be possible to set up the printer so that it will not accept print jobs unless they were signed by private keys corresponding to a public key, which was in turn loaded into the printer. This would prevent a non-authorized person from using the printer and its supplies. Additionally, instead of loading in every authorized person, a certificate authority public key could be loaded into the printer. Anyone authorized by the CA would be authorized unless they were also on a de-listing list. Some printers require users to be present at the printer (and enter a password) before their output is actually printed. This provides further security.

## Internet

A number of companies have begun to offer a service wherein a user may print his documents directly to their printers. Special software is downloaded from their site onto the client's PC, and then the word processor can create a file compatible with the printing shop's system. This file is then either sent over the Internet to the printing shop, or brought on a floppy disk to the print shop for printing.

The problem with sending the file directly to the printing company over the Internet is that there is no privacy. Actually, there is another problem as well—this two-step process is much more difficult than a one-step process of simply printing to the printer. However, there are a number of ways of solving this problem.

### Solution 1

The file, once created, could be sent to the printing company using any one of a number of secure technologies, including SMIME, SSL, or IPSec. It could also be encrypted as a file into a self-decrypting file, locked behind a passphrase. The passphrase could be sent to the printing company over the phone.

### Solution 2

This solution is perhaps a bit more interesting. The printing company sets up its printer driver to match its paper/color options, and it is uploaded (signed) to their website. However, the driver is a secure driver, having a public key inside it, which in turn is used to encrypt the file encryption key. When the user installs it and then uses that driver to print, it uses TCG to create a random number for a stream file encryption key. It then encrypts the file with a stream cipher, encrypts the key with the public key of the printer, and sends the whole mess to the printing company.

The data that streamed to the printing company is either stored on a server until such time as a credit card is also received or it can be validated with standard PKI. In the latter case, the printing company certifies the public key of the end user via some side-band process, and then the printed stream is signed with the public key of the end user, and the certificate is also passed.

## Secure Faxing

Spam faxing has become a problem in the industry. People troll through telephone numbers until they get a fax number and then sell the aggregation of numbers to spam advertisers. These advertisers then fax large numbers of advertisements to their fax directory. They are using the machines and supplies of the recipients of their advertising without permission. Clearly this is a problem.

One way of solving this problem would be to simply turn off the fax machine when it is not in use, but this isn't terribly practical. Some businesses may have different groups in different locations faxing information back and forth at all times of day. What is needed is a means of determining if the sender of a fax is authorized to send the fax—before valuable resources are spent printing it out. A list of authorized phone numbers for senders could be created and loaded into each fax system, but this would be awkward as well.

## Super Secure Migratable Storage

TCG deliberately did not address the problem of someone being worried about his TPM (chip) being physically taken apart and analyzed by nefarious persons. This usually involves removing the plastic packaging, etching silicon, using specialized microscopes to determine where current is flowing, and so on. There is some protection documented in the common criteria certification, but for the most part, all bets are off if you are up against a concerted enemy that has physical means for attack. In the case that the attacker has physical access to the machine and has the means to determine which bits of the SRK are stored as 1's and which ones are stored as 0's, then all of the keys used on the system become exposed. Using the SRK, you can unwrap all the keys one step down, allowing you to view not only the keys but also their authorization and migration data. These keys, in turn, can be used to unwrap all the keys underneath them, so the whole structure of keys unzips, leaving everything potentially exposed.

There is, however, a way of blocking this exposure for migratable key stacks. Note that this is a bit of a different way of looking at things, as migratable keys typically don't have the same level of trust as non-migratable ones do. Consider the key chain shown in Figure 12.1.

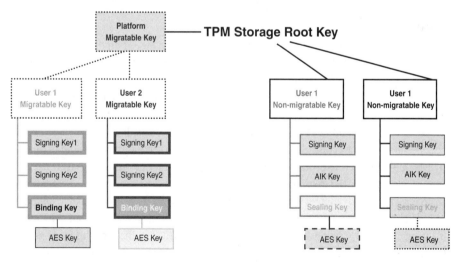

**Figure 12.1**   Example key chain

In this design, suppose the User1 Migrate key was never stored on the disk as a key blob, but instead is stored as a `migrationKeyBlob` wrapped with the Platform Public key.

In this situation, the User1 Migrate key could only be loaded into the system with the Platform Public key if the user loading the key knew the random string needed to load the `migrationKeyBlob`. Now suppose the TPM were to be de-layered and stripped and analyzed so that the SRK key was known. The attacker would be able to obtain the Platform Private key, but would not be able to obtain the User1 Migrate key. Now the attacker would not be able to obtain any of the keys stored below that key.

This, however, presents a usability problem: How does the key owner store the random string needed to load the key in such a way that the key can be easily loaded and yet not expose the random string to an attacker?

Although not an ideal solution, one way of doing this would be to XOR the random string with a pseudo-random string generated from a passphrase. For example, the program could take a passphrase generated by the key owner, run it through a hash algorithm, and use that to seed a mask-generating function (such as MGF1 used in PKCS#1 V2.0) and then XOR the result with the random string. This produces a random string that the user would store on the disk.

When the user wanted to load the key, he would enter the passphrase, which would be used to re-generate the pseudo-random string, which in turn would be XORed with the string stored on disk to produce the random string needed to load the User1 Migrate key.

Should an attacker unlayer the chip and determine the Platform key, he still would have to figure out the passphrase in order to get any further. This should be very time consuming (particularly if the mask-generating function was a time-consuming one—say, taking a second to perform on a fast computer).

Should an attacker obtain the `migrationBlob` and string stored on the hard disk, but not have access to the TPM, it would not be possible to determine if the passphrase were correct via an offline attack, and the TPM would prevent determining the string via guessing.

There are several things to note about this solution. This kind of "roadblock" that can be put in the way of an active attacker allows for an off-machine hammering attack—assuming that the attacker has already peeled the TPM. But it may be noted that if the hardware can be peeled, then there are no hardware controls that are going to work. A second thing to note is that a dual set of TPMs could be used to protect the key by having the first one sign the passphrase with a key to use as the seed for the mask-generating function.

This has an added advantage. It requires the attacker to peel two chips and also entails the attacker having to do a sign with a different key for every machine attacked. Thus, no database of random strings created by first hashing and then applying MFG1 to the result of large numbers of passphrases could be created—the first step would be different for every public/private key pair.

Actually, this technique could be used even in the case where only one TPM resides on the machine, by signing the passphrase with another key. The fact that the key will be available to the attacker is almost beside the point—it isn't being used to hide the key, but rather used to prevent the attacker from using a dictionary "look up" attack against the random string. This increases the amount of time it will take the attacker to crack the passphrase in an offline attack.

The interesting thing about this system is that it allows for storing a migratable key on a migratable stack controlled by someone else without abandoning control of the migratable key. Earlier we showed how storing the migratable key to a non-migratable stack achieves the same end. However, that solution entails giving up a certain amount of manageability of the stack and is vulnerable to chip peeling.

If a migratable key is stored onto a migratable stack not controlled by the end user, though, the owner of the migratable key stack does not have to peel the TPM to obtain the storage key. This leads to the owner of the migratable key stack being able to perform an offline attack against the passphrase, should he obtain the XORed random string stored on the hard disk.

Most secure would be a combination of storing the migratable key to a non-migratable key using the `migrationBlob`.

## Summary

It can be seen from the examples in this chapter that securing files and data has enormous utility in the industry. Files need to be encrypted when at rest or when being moved. The only time they don't need to be encrypted is when they are in use. TPMs provide capabilities that make developing such solutions much easier. Specific examples of architectures for keeping files encrypted when being sent to users with or without public keys, storing them on a hard disk, or for group use have been given. New use cases of locking data to machines or providing a means of securely sending data to be printed (or faxed) have also been presented. Additionally, a technique of enhancing the security of normal keys even in the event that a TPM is cracked has been provided. Even if none of these particular architectures solve your problem, they may provide techniques that can be used to create the architecture you need.

# CHAPTER 13

# Trusted Computing and Secure Identification

One of the main purposes envisioned for the TPM was identification. Passwords have multiplied at an alarming rate, including phone voicemail passwords, Windows logon, hard disk passwords, power-on passwords, email passwords, intranet passwords, bank pins, Amazon passwords, Paypal passwords, eBay passwords…the list seems endless. They cost enterprises on average $50 for each call used to reset a forgotten password, and have become notorious for being insecure. A public private key is secure—as long as the private key is secure—and tokens such as smart cards or USB keys are harder to manage than passwords. The TPM provides a basic capability to help alleviate all of these problems.

First, we examine how to make legacy systems that use passwords more secure. Then we look at using a key for a VPN interface. Because this may require a key to be delegated, this problem is examined as well. A host of other problems are then considered in rapid succession, including credit cards, multiple users on a single system, multiple users on multiple systems, Public Key Infrastructure (PKI) creation, biometrics, smartcards, dongles, and machine authentication. We also consider HIPAA architecture enhancements, as well as uses of noncomputer system architectures—such as voice over IP (VOIP), IPSec, service meters, and network switches. All of the designs focus on what the TPM can bring to enhance the solution of identification, specifically in the case of the following:

- Client-centric local-based authentication, to enhance ease of use of the person at the keyboard and reduce the cost of password reset.

- Machine-based authentication, to prove which machine is trying to connect and what state it is in.

- Server-based authentication, where most of the work happens on the back end.

- Peer-to-peer authentication, where there is a balance between the two.

## Logon Password Storage

Although it is not the ideal way to use the TCG capabilities, an initial use of the TPM may provide better storage of passwords than a pure hash (or even a salted hash). This technique may graft onto existing solutions more easily than some of the more sophisticated solutions described later in the chapter, which use public key authentication instead of passwords.

In particular, a number of OSs use a standard hash (MD5 or SHA-1) of passwords and store the hash, ready to compare to the hash of a password that is entered. This is certainly better than storing the passwords for comparison in the clear, but it still falls prey to dictionary attacks, and particularly offline dictionary attacks if the list of hashed passwords can be obtained. Even worse, a large list of the most frequently used passwords can be run through the hash algorithm and then sorted into a look-up table that provides the hacker with a quick way of cracking passwords. If there is a large list of password hashes, the likelihood of one of them being weak, given that the end user has to remember them, is quite high.

There are a number of solutions to this problem: using random data as a salt, using the password to generate a key that encrypts salted known data, and then seeing if the password can decrypt the data, and so on.

However, all of these methods tend to give the attacker all the information necessary to break a key. Hopefully the attacker does not have enough time to determine the key using that information by accessing a faster system.

Suppose each user creates a 2048-bit RSA key on the TPM, and uses that key to sign a standard hash phrase. Because the `passphrase` associated with the key, known as the `Use_Auth`, is not presented each time—but rather proof of its knowledge is presented to the TPM to authorize a signing operation—the signature used for authentication can be done remotely. Because there is a large amount of entropy in 2048-bit RSA keys, and they are generated on chip by a random number generator, it should not be possible to take the resulting list of signed values and use it to break a key. Since the TPM is hardware, it will notice if too many attempts are made to guess the key, and shut off the attacker. Because the TPM must be involved in doing the signature, this provides a means of shutting off any hammering or dictionary attacks. Contrast this with a list of hashes that can be copied onto another system and then hammered away at by a bad guy without any interaction of the user's system.

## VPN Endpoints

An obvious use of a TPM would be for VPN (virtual private network) endpoint identification. A machine that has a TPM could identify itself to a firewall using PKI. This could work in a number of ways, but we illustrate one in the following example.

An administrator creates a large number of migratable public/private key pairs on his own system. The public portion of those key pairs is stored on the VPN server. The private portion is stored on the administrator's site as a set of blobs.

When a new client is added to the VPN, an administrator migrates the private portion of one of the unused keys to one of the client's non-migratable storage keys.

When the client wants to go through the VPN, his machine sends a message to the VPN with a request, his public key, and a random number encrypted with the server's public key. The server then checks the public key against his database. If it is in the database, it creates a random number (GetRandom), encrypts the random number with the public key, and sends it back to the client.

The client and the server then decrypt the random numbers they were sent and XOR them with the random number they sent to each other. This becomes the ephemeral symmetric key they use for their temporary tunnel through the firewall.

If the VPN that is currently in use uses SecureID, then a subroutine process could be done as follows as a patch. Secure ID works based on a time and the seed of a pseudo-random number generator. Both a pocket device and a server are given a base seed, and they generate random numbers in synch based on the time. A second process in the server could be running that generates those same pseudo-random numbers with the base seed. It gets the seed to use from the ephemeral symmetric key in the previous setup. Here the second process acts as a "trusted man in the middle," sort of an impedance match between the two systems.

The problem with this particular solution is that it requires the server end point of the VPN to have multiple keys stored in the database. There is a much easier way to accomplish the same thing: Instead of having multiple keys for authentication, only one (or a few), owned by the IT administrator, is necessary for the server to have.

In this case, when a user wants to get in through the VPN, he can do one of the following:

- Generate a signing key and ask the IT administrator to give him a certificate for that key, certifying he is allowed to use the key to get through the VPN. An IT administrator may want to verify that such a key is non-migratable before signing it, because that will in turn verify that the key is kept securely stored by a TPM. This has an added problem: If the user wants to get in through the VPN from multiple machines, it requires multiple keys. Although generating and certifying multiple keys is not that big a deal, it also means that if the end user should ever lose authorization to get into the VPN, all his public keys have to be revoked. The plus side of this solution is that the administrator never has access to anyone's private keys, and thus if he leaves the company, he cannot take those secrets with him.

- Generate a non-migratable storage key and send it to the IT administrator. The IT administrator now generates a public/private key pair, migrates it to the user's non-migratable storage key, and sends both it and a certificate back to the user. Because this key is migratable, the IT administrator can migrate it to all of the end user's different computers. But because it is stored with a non-migratable storage key on the user's computer (and presumably the IT administrator does not give the end user the migration authorization data), the user is unable to migrate the key any further. However, the down-side is that the administrator has potential access to everyone's private key pair that they use to enter the VPN, and if he should leave the company in the future, that is a potential security exposure.

In either of these cases, the certificate can be verified by the server, because it has the public IT administrator key. The certificate then attests that the key pair the end user uses to get into the VPN is valid.

There is another interesting way of solving the same problem—remote authentication to a server assumes that there is a TPM on the server itself—but not necessarily on the client. Today most servers authenticate using a password list. A long time ago, the passwords were in the clear, but that quickly was shown to be insecure. Next, the table became a table of hashes—but that fell victim to dictionary attacks, where attackers would have large dictionaries of the hashes of passwords and simply look up the results. Now entropy is added to the list using encryption instead of hashing, and the list is shadowed elsewhere on the disk to try to make it hard to obtain. Although this is much better than previous solutions, if an attacker is able to get the key and the password table, he can use a brute force attack and probably gain access to the server.

The TPM can be used to solve this problem. When a user registers for access with the server, he generates a key on the server's TPM. This key is associated with him, and he is the only one who knows its `password`. The results of signing the word "Password" with the key are stored in the table. Now when the user logs into the system, he uses the standard HMAC method of authenticating himself to the server's TPM, and uses that TPM to sign the word "Password." The OS does a comparison of the result with the signature in the table, and if it matches, lets him in. In this way, the entropy of the signing key (approximately 112 bits) becomes part of the stored password, but the entropy itself is never in the clear on the system.

## Delegation of Authority

Delegation of authority is sort of like a power of attorney. When a power of attorney is established, it can be either a limited power of attorney (for example, to make decisions on a house) or it can be unlimited power of attorney (for example, when a person is ruled incompetent).

Either type of delegation of authority to use a key can be granted using a TPM. We examine a number of ways this could be done using the 1.1b TPM. The 1.2 TPM explicitly allows delegation directly.

The first and most straightforward means of delegating authority is to migrate the root migratable storage key from one machine to another. In this case, both machines have the same capability to sign things with migratable keys. Someone might do this type of delegation if he has two systems that he uses interchangeably.

Migrating only certain keys (and their children) from one system to another is another type of delegation of authority. In this case, the authority given to certain keys might be different from that given to other keys. One set of keys might enable a secretary to read the mail of her principal, whereas another set of keys might be used to sign contracts. If the secretary changes, the key still remains with the system. One problem with this system is that if a secretary supports multiple principals, and one of them leaves, it is difficult to delete a single key from her system and show proof of it. This can be done by doing the following:

- Creating migration blobs for the executives still supported.
- Resetting the TPM.
- Migrating the supported keys back to the system.

However, this solution might be impractical as it requires the executive who is not being migrated to periodically re-authorize his secretary to view his mail.

Yet another type of delegation of authority is very similar to a power of attorney. A secretary would generate his own keys, and then the principal would create a certificate for that key, specifying what authority he is delegating to the key. The principal's own certificate would also be attached to the key. In this way, the principal becomes a miniature certificate authority through a chain of certifications. These certificates could either periodically expire, as most certificates do, or they could point to an additional list of expired certificates, signed and dated by the principal.

## Delegation Without Allowing Further Migration

When a key is migrated to another person's control, a decision has to be made: Should the person who owns the system to which the key has been migrated be allowed the right to further delegate a key? In the case of a power of attorney, this right is not conferred. However, if the key being migrated is stored under a migratable key, then that capability has been implicitly given. Migrating a migratable storage key also migrates the keys it stores.

There is a solution if the owner of the key wants to make certain that a key that has been migrated is not further migrated by the recipient. This solution migrates to a non-migratable storage key. Migration is then controlled jointly between the owner of the new TPM and the original owner of the key. This is because the design of the blob separates the passphrase needed to use the key (the Use_Auth) and the passphrase used to migrate the key (the migration_auth). Clearly the Use_Auth has to go with the migrated key (otherwise, the recipient could not use it), but the migration_auth does not have to be given to the recipient.

Without the latter, the key cannot be further migrated.

## Credit Card Endpoints

Smart cards are like a more secure kind of credit card, especially for use on the Internet. They look like credit cards, but have an electrical interface on them, so they can be used to provide a token for authentication. Usually a PIN needs to be entered into the smart card in order for it to function. Smart cards are used today for physical access to buildings, for logical access to computer systems, and as credit cards. The main drawbacks of this technology center on cost of use and the portability of a smart card. The cost is mostly driven by the cost of the smart card reader, which is beginning to drop. There are strengths and weaknesses of the portability of a smart card. On the pro side, it can be used in as many places as have a smart card reader that can accept it. Additionally, it can be much stronger cryptographically than magnetic stripe cards. On the con side, it is possible for it to leave the control of the owner of the card. At that point, there are people who can do destructive analysis of the chip on the card and often recover the information stored on the card. It is also bad because you can't know that the reader into which the smart card is placed has not been gimmicked to record the pin being entered. Readers can also be built to use power usage analysis to determine the keys stored in a smart card (unless the cards have been specifically designed to obviate that attack).

In the credit card industry, there are basically two types of purchases: card present purchases and card absent purchases. The fraud rate for the latter is quite a bit higher than that for the former. Internet purchases are obvious card absent purchases, and so it makes sense for additional security to be used for these types of purchases. Mobility of the security solution is not a help but rather a hindrance. Here a TCG solution is ideal. It provides a mechanism to lock a smart card-like function to a specific machine whose location is known and can be protected.

There are a number of mechanisms to use a TCG-compliant system, such as a credit card machine. The first would entail using a TCG system hooked to the Secure Electronic Transaction (SET) protocol directly. This has an advantage of using an existing standard that has been thoroughly vetted by the security community. It also has the disadvantage of being a standard that is not in widespread use. Another standard that is already in widespread use and that could be easily hooked into TCG systems is the Verified by VISA protocol. This protocol requires a purchaser to prove to his bank that he is who he says he is each time he purchases something online.

In any case, it is necessary that the client system have a public/private key pair that the credit card company trusts. There are two ways of doing this. The first is as follows:

1. The client asks the TPM to generate a public/private signing key pair.
2. The client asks the TPM to endorse the key pair with an identity to show it is a non-migratable TPM key pair.
3. The client goes to the credit card company and establishes an SSL session with the company.
4. The client sends the public key and certificate to the credit card company.
5. The credit card company verifies the client's credit worthiness.
6. The credit card company verifies the client's address.
7. The credit card company creates a certificate for the key.
8. The credit card company sends the certificate (by mail).

This first way of doing this is still susceptible to someone impersonating the client and then stealing his mail, but that risk is no different from today's present card solution.

There are a number of problems with this solution. The first is that the key is not migratable, so that if a client uses the credit card from multiple systems, he has to register multiple times. Secondly, the credit card company has to keep track of multiple public keys for that client. Further, if a machine dies, its key dies with it.

There is a second solution to this scenario that avoids some of these problems:

1. The client establishes an SSL session with the credit card company.

2. The client requests a credit card.

3. The client provides a non-migratable storage public key to the credit card company with a certificate showing that it is a non-migratable TPM storage key.

4. The credit card company checks the client's credit worthiness.

5. The credit card company creates a migratable public/private key and wraps it with the client's non-migratable storage public key.

6. The credit card company creates a certificate for the newly generated public key and sends it to the client.

7. The credit card company sends the "blob" to the end user via snail mail (to verify address).

Because this key is migratable, the credit card company can wrap it for several machines at once and also act as a migration authority for the key in case of a machine being damaged.

One downside is that the credit card company obtains enough information to sign things with the private key itself. However, that is no different from today's usage in a card present situation. Another problem is that if I am in a situation where I share a number of computers with a large number of users, I may not have my keys present at the system I am using on any given day. This situation is considered in the next section.

## Multiple Users on a Single System

There might be situations where several users will share a PC. In the extreme case, where hundreds (or more) users want to share a system, this is referred to as "hoteling" or "free seating," which is addressed in the next chapter. However, in other cases, such as for home use, there may also be a reason to keep different records separate. For example, parents may want to keep their credit card authorization, income tax records, and so on encrypted and unavailable to their children.

This situation is easily solved by the daisy chain structure that is recommended in the description of the TPM. To be most secure (and since only a few users are involved), it probably makes the most sense to have each end user (family member) generate their own root storage key directly beneath the SRK, in the place where the platform migration key is often put.

The disadvantage of this solution is that it requires each member of the family to independently create backups of their root migratable keys and store their random string. Another option would be for each family member to have their own root migratable key stored under the platform migratable key, in which case only the platform migratable key needs to have a backup migration blob created. However, this does theoretically expose the individual family members' keys to an attack by the collusion of the owner of the TPM and the owner of the platform migratable key (who are likely to be the same person).

In the case of a family, the latter solution is probably sufficient. In the case of a small business, the second solution may also work, since the manager may need to recover migratable keys in the case of the death or firing of an employee. When an employee sits down at a PC, he would copy his root migration key directly onto the hard disk of the machine. Since the base migratable key is already on the system, he can then use this key. All of his other keys would be loaded through it. Because there are only a few computers, he only has to do this a few times, and then he never has to copy his key again.

One difficulty with this first solution is that it does not scale. If more computers are bought, then the root keys of all the end users have to be migrated to the new systems. If a new employee is hired, his key needs to be migrated to all the existing systems.

The second solution scales well—only the root key needs to be migrated to a new system, and then if the machines are networked, all the other keys can be brought down to function underneath that root key. However, in the case of an enterprise or large business, neither of these solutions is a good fit. In those cases, one needs to move to secure hoteling.

## Secure Hoteling

Hoteling (or free seating) refers to a new practice in many corporations, where an end user is not associated with a specific machine, but rather is associated with an identity that is kept on a server. At such time, as an end user wants to use a computer, he sits down at any terminal that exists in the office space, connects with the server, and downloads his system image.

This is an extreme form of a security structure that is enabled with smart cards. In this case, an end user has a smart card, which he uses for identification. He places it in a machine and types in a pin to identify himself. The mobility of the smart card enables it to be used in multiple systems. However, the mobility of the smart card is also a problem, because the reader turns out to be a very important part of the security system. Readers that have been compromised can be used to obtain the secrets stored in many cards by monitoring, for example, the power usage of the card as it is used to sign something. It can also be used to grab the PIN and reuse the PIN while the smart card is inserted to do something other than what the user is authorizing.

How can we achieve the same user mobility with TCG? And further, does the solution scale?

First, we consider a situation where a corporation has 100 systems in a building and 200 users who are allowed to use those systems. When a user sits at a system, he wants to use that system as though it were his own, with the rights to use his own keys, but without exposing his keys, even to the system administrator.

The system admin creates a non-migratable key pair on his TCG-compliant server system(s), X. As each new machine is bought, the IT department takes ownership of the TPM and authorizes migration of keys by the system to X by creation of a migration ticket. IT also creates a non-migratable key on each client system (which can be the SRK) and authorizes X to migrate to the client system by creating a migration ticket on X that corresponds to the client.

Each of the 200 users, or any new user, sits down at a client system and uses its TPM to create a migratable key, and then migrates it to X using the migration ticket.

Now when one of the 200 users sits down at one of the 100 systems, he contacts the administrator's server, X, and performs a migration of his migratable key from the administrator's system to the system before which he sits. His key is still protected, even though he is doing a remote migration because migration authorization is done using an HMAC. His root migratable key is now on the system at which he is sitting, and hence all the keys he stored using that key are also available.

How well does this solution scale? For the medium-size business, it scales quite well. Adding a new system or a new user requires a minimal amount of work. However, if we are talking about a very large corporation with buildings in multiple locations (for example, the military), some modifications of this solution need to be made (but not many).

The first problem is one of simple size. If 4 million personnel are going to be hoteling, then it is not going to be possible for one TCG-compliant system to keep up with the demand for migration of keys. This can be solved by adding in multiple TCG-compliant servers, or by using a 4758 card instead of a TPM to do migration activities.

A second problem is one of locale. It is assumed that the normal duties of a soldier will cause him to be transferred to many locations. However, it would be infeasible to have copies of all 4 million soldiers' keys at all of the bases. The solution to this is to have the key travel from base to base with the soldier.

When a soldier is transferred from one base to another, his old administrator system will not recognize the machine he wants to use at the new base. Therefore, first his key is migrated to the new base server, which does recognize the machine he wants to use. Then his key is migrated to the system at the new base.

Because these migrations are taking place remotely, the migration has to be the one that is done in a single step, as opposed to the backup type migration that can be further migrated. If the two-step migration process is used, the intermediary migration blob produced could be migrated to another machine. The random number that is output by the function, which usually protects against decryption, is now available to the administrator because the process is being done remotely. The administrator looking after the server from which the key is being migrated also likely owns the administration of the server/machine to which the key is being migrated. This leaves the key vulnerable to attack.

Of course, there are a number of steps that have been glossed over: Each server needs to have a database of users and migratable blobs that are associated with them. There needs to be software at the server that will perform the correct functions for the user given the request. One way to implement this would be to have a web page on the server that is linked to the database. The user would log on to the web page and provide his user ID and the name of the client system he is sitting at. The server would load the user key and the public key of the client system into the server TPM. The server would contact the chip and ask to start a session, receiving a nonce in reply that would be transmitted to the client. A Java app running on the client would ask the user for his migration authorization password. (Java is a good choice in a mixed OS environment.)

The Java app would then use the nonce, the migration authorization password, and the public key of the machine the user is sitting at, to provide the correct command that is transmitted to the server. The server would transmit this command (which does not contain his authorization data, but rather an HMAC calculated from that data) to the server TPM.

The server TPM would then rewrap the user-key with the public portion of the client system key and transmit this key to the client system. At this point, the user has his key on the client system, and he can use his authorization data (different from his migration day) to utilize the key on that system's TPM.

In the case that the user or the client system's PC was not in the database of the server, the server could then check with other servers in the corporation (or other military bases), asking them to give it the requisite data. If another server is found with the user ID, the user could be asked to first migrate to the new server, and then as a second step migrate to his client system. If another server is found with the client system, the user would be asked to first migrate his user blob to the new server, and then control would be given to that server to walk the user through migrating the user blob to the client system.

## Creating a PKI with the Endorsement Key

One of the biggest problems faced by an enterprise today is the establishment of a PKI. If an organization has a large number of employees in diverse locations, this involves creating public/private key pairs and distributing them to users in secure containers. One technique for doing this is to use smart cards, recording the private portion of the smart card-generated key in a certificate, mailing the smart card to the employee, and mailing the PIN via a separate path. Sometimes the PIN is sent via a trusted email path that already exists in a bootstrap.

The endorsement key can make the process quite a bit easier with the following procedure. It is assumed that the enterprise knows the serial number of the machines that each employee uses. This is the case in the large majority of enterprises. From the serial number, they should be able to determine the public endorsement key of the TPM associated with that system. Keep in mind that knowing the public portion of the endorsement key would not help in tracing the movements of a person on the Internet as the endorsement key can be used only for distribution of certificates.

The IT administrator then remotely requests the TPM to do the following:

1. Self-generate a root key.

2. Self-generate an identity key.

3. Self-generate a non-migratable storage key and/or a non-migratable signing key.

4. Certify the non-migratable storage key with the identity key.

5. Send the public portion of the identity key to the IT administrator.

6. Send the public portion of the non-migratable storage key and its certificate to the IT administrator.

Next the IT administrator creates a certificate for the identity key and encrypts it with an AES key, wraps the AES key along with the public portion of the identity key with the public portion of the endorsement key, and sends it back to the TPM.

The IT administrator requests the TPM to use its endorsement key to decrypt the certificate and send it back. (The TPM will do this only if the public portion of the identity key matches an identity key that it has in memory.)

Upon successful completion of the last step, the IT administrator creates a certificate for the non-migratable storage key and/or signing key and sends that back to the system.

At this point, the system in question has a private key installed in it (with certificate) that can be used only by that system. The password/passphrase to use that key must still be sent to the end user.

Additional changes to this routine can be made to simplify this last part. For example, the end user can create the non-migratable storage/signing key himself, thus choosing the password. In this case, when the key is sent to the IT administrator, it has to come with something authenticating that it was generated by the user himself (for example, he could give it to his manager to send in, or he could establish an SSL connection with the server and use a previously existing password-based system to verify who he is). As every user will be required to have a private key, it should quickly become obvious if more than one private key is associated with a user. In that case, simply having each key sign a certificate for each of the others would provide proof that it was OK.

Now that the IT administrator knows a private key that the user has, IT can send further messages securely to the user, including passwords (bound with the storage key) or additional migratable keys (bound to the storage key). The user can then decrypt them using his own system.

Another addition to this system is a link directly to the previous section on secure hoteling. In that case, it is necessary for the IT administrator to know non-migratable storage keys on each system he owns, so he can identify them as target storage keys that can be targets of migration from a master server system in the sky. That is exactly what is provided by this PKI distribution system.

The astute reader will realize that there is one scenario absent: Letting a remote user create a key on the server and then migrate it to the machine he is on. There is a good reason that this is absent: A TCG-compliant server has no way of keeping the authorization data or the migration data (both of which are presented to the TPM upon key creation) from the server administrator. Although an SSL connection to the server from the client could keep this information away from eavesdroppers on the IP link, the TPM does not provide for a means of secure communication to the TPM during creation of a key. However, this scenario can be supported using the transport session of the 1.2 TPM.

In the meantime, it is interesting to note that a 4758 card from IBM® (which is rated at FIPS 140-1 level 4!) could provide this service, if software were written for it. The 4758's public key could be published and the 4758 could run an SSL server inside itself. Then upon request, it could create a migratable TCG-compliant key, which it could then migrate to authorized clients.

In any of these cases, the end user still has to remember passwords or passphrases, something that is loathed by most system administrators. The cost of changing passwords on systems is on the order of $50 per user-system per year! This leads many administrators toward biometrics.

## Links to Biometrics

Biometrics have become an increasingly interesting field, and of increasing interest to the public. Whenever possible, people would like to avoid remembering passwords, and a biometric identifier, such as a fingerprint, is one way of doing this. This is a good thing, because passwords are notoriously weak. People choose passwords so easy to remember that they are easy to crack, or they pick passwords that are so difficult to crack they are difficult to remember. So the user writes down the password, where it is susceptible to a different kind of attack.

There are a number of problems with a biometrics approach to security, though:

- The match is statistical rather than exact.
- The biometric being matched can often be easily obtained (copy of fingerprint, for example).
- There are a limited number of revocable biometric measurements.
- There are privacy concerns.
- There are hygienic concerns.

Additionally, people are always concerned about having their finger chopped off for a fingerprint reader, a concern exacerbated by films like *Never Say Never*, where an eye transplant is performed, and other spy movies. This has actually happened in Malaysia in order to obtain access to a $75,000 car (see http://news.bbc.co.uk/2/hi/asia-pacific/4396831.stm). In real life, this is not a concern, though. Most fingerprint readers claim they won't work with dead fingers.

The match being statistical rather than exact means that a key can't be generated easily from the fingerprint itself. If it could, then fingerprint "minutia" of each user would not have to be kept on a stand-alone system. Instead, the fingerprint-generated key itself could be used for either encryption or authentication data. However, such a system would not be terribly secure—the information available to the machine from a fingerprint could also likely be available to any other system given the image of a fingerprint. And the item that stores the data is likely to be covered with fingerprints of the user.

In addition, because of the statistical nature of the matching, fingerprint (or other biometric) systems are susceptible to both type 1 (false verification) and type 2 (false rejection) errors. Most modern fingerprint readers have fairly low error rates, and they can be made much lower by requiring two fingerprints to match.

Voice ID is susceptible to record/playback attack unless the phrase a person must speak changes each time. In this case, matching is done on a voice print basis, which is somewhat less accurate. Signature matching is usually done on the velocity/acceleration of the pen movement rather than the shape of the letters, but that can easily be captured as well (and most people have let their digital signature be captured at stores, such as Best Buy, when signing for credit cards).

The typical way this is solved is by using a trusted reader for the biometric. This reader has been hardened against some of these attacks. For example, a photostatic image of a fingerprint will not work on some of the more-sophisticated fingerprint readers. Neither will a dead finger. However, this begs the question somewhat. How does one know that a trusted reader has taken a fingerprint? One obvious solution is to have a TPM embedded in the reader and use the reader's TPM to report its status and to sign a fingerprint it takes or the results of a fingerprint match. Such data should be "nonced" so that the recipient can tell it is fresh. This means that the recipient TPM provides a random number, which is appended to the data sending the TPM signs. Another solution would be to have the fingerprint reader embedded in the device receiving the authentication. This does leave exposed some physical attacks on wires, though—if all the reader does is provide a Go/No Go signal on a wire, that wire can be directly stimulated to mimic a Go signal.

Privacy concerns in biometrics are, for the most part, easily handled. Even in the most restrictive environments, if the fingerprint matching is done on the local machine, and it is only used to replace a passphrase, the design should meet the local requirements. In some environments, doing matching remotely is specifically not allowed, as it requires a large database of fingerprint templates to exist on a server. In other environments, this is perfectly fine. Some governments use fingerprints to prove someone has the right to vote! However, since privacy organizations tend to be very vocal, it is important that you advertise how you have taken care of any local problems, so as not to get bad press over someone's bad assumption of how the system works. In general, to avoid problems, do as follows:

- Don't keep a database of images of fingerprints or other biometrics
- Don't keep information that can be reverse computed into such an image
- Matching information generally should not be accessible

One good client-based solution is for fingerprint templates used for matching (usually about 300 bytes for a fingerprint, and not sufficient information to reverse engineer a fingerprint from it) to be kept physically in the device that takes the fingerprint. In this case, after the matching is done, the results of the match are transmitted to the PC from the trusted reader. In this way, the biometric minutia are not even accessible to a hacker.

In the case of hoteling, this becomes more difficult. Clearly the fingerprint (or other biometric) minutia for every user cannot be stored on every system. So that minutia data must be stored on a server. However, this has the potential of causing a privacy problem. Therefore, in this case, the minutia stored on a server should be encrypted in such a way that only the owner will be able to access that data. For example, the minutia data can be encrypted into a blob sealed with a user's public key. The user can then retrieve the encrypted blob from a network and send the encrypted blob to the reader's TPM after he has installed his user migratable key.

Ideally, the minutia should be signed by a user and have a certificate attached testifying that the minutia belongs to the user. This way, the fingerprint reader, which uses the minutia for matching, can verify that the minutia belongs to the user. Note that in this case, the user has to have decrypted the minutia file before it is used the first time, so the fingerprint reader can't be used for that first verification.

Similar problems affect all the other biometric schemes, from handprints to voice to handwriting to retinal scans—the minutia data used to make a match should be kept stored securely in a way that requires a user's approval before they are released.

## Links to Smart Cards

Although it appears that a TPM module is a competitor to a smart card, there are a number of ways in which they could be used together. One of the major differences between a smart card and a TPM is in portability. One of the major disadvantages of a smart card is its small amount of storage space. Used in concert, both capabilities can be used to provide a stronger union.

Smart cards come in many varieties, from simple memory cards, which are very cheap, to sophisticated cards that can do full 2048-bit signatures. Any of these cards can be used in concert with a TPM.

### Smart Memory Cards and TPMs

A memory card could be used for PIN-protected storage of the random number, which is used for loading a migrated blob into a new system. It could also be used to store a blob so that even if a shoulder-surfing enemy was able to obtain a passphrase for the blob and unattended access to the computer on which the blob's TPM resides, he would still not have access to use the blob.

In the case of hoteling, a base storage key could be migrated to all the machines in a specified area, and then base user keys could be stored in blobs on smart cards. When a user wanted to use a specific machine, he could insert his smart card, load his blob into the TPM, and then use a secondary signing blob (also on the smart card) to request the rest of his (encrypted) data be downloaded on that system.

### Smart Signing Cards and TPMs

For highly secure operations, it might be nice to know not just that a particular machine was used by someone who knew the correct passphrase, but also that the person using the machine was in possession of a smart card. This could be done with a double signing, first by the machine, and then by the cardholder.

Another interesting model would be to put a TPM actually into a smart card or smart card reader, and use a non-sniffable keyboard entry to sign things with the smart card once the reader checked that the system TPM recorded it and had booted into a secure state. This is a two TPM design.

A smart card with a TPM in it could also store a migration blob, along with the random number needed to insert it into a new TPM. It could then be used to install a user's key into a hoteling system, which could in turn daisy chain the process that brings down all the user's data. This way the user could have total protected control on the migration of his migration key. One nice thing about this design is that it could allow the smart card-based TPM to be portable between systems, a requirement for some use cases such as virtual dongles.

## Virtual Dongles

Dongles are devices attached to a PC, usually to the parallel port, which are used by software to verify that the software is running on a registered machine. They are used for high-value software to prevent cloning of that software. Dongles can be a problem to use. Although they are designed to pass through printer commands, they still stick out of the back of the PC where they can be damaged, and if several packages are running on the same system, the dongles may be hooked into dongles, making a chain of dongles.

A TPM module can be used as a virtual dongle by software in a number of ways. If the software is an OS, the OS can check a registration number each time it boots by putting the registration number inside a PCR locked container. The PCR would be extended after it is checked. If the manufacturer loads the OS, this prevents the OS from being moved to another system by the buyer, as the buyer never is able to obtain the registration number.

For software that is loaded after the boot point, at registration time a non-migratable storage key would be sent to the software manufacturer. It would come signed and certified as a genuine TCG non-migratable storage key. The manufacturer can then migrate a private signing key to that non-migratable storage key. During execution, self-modifiable code would periodically sign sections of itself with the private signing key and XOR the results with other sections of the code to recover the working program. Although such a system could be broken, it is probably at least as secure as current dongles. New versions of the software could use different keys, so that breaking every new version would require a new effort that would have to be done on a valid copy of the code running on the correct system. Essentially, this design makes a system into a trusted endpoint for software instance. Trusted endpoints have broader uses, though.

## Trusted Endpoints

Identification is often thought about as pertaining to the user of a system rather than to the system itself. Systems of identification were designed for the identification of people rather than identification of machines. TCG allows for remote machine identification and also reporting on the status for a machine set up in a stand-alone mode.

In order to do this, it is important that an operator need not be present to accomplish its task. In the usage data of each key, when it is generated, it is possible to select "no user authentication necessary" as the usage model. If such a key is non-migratable, it is a key that can be used by the machine in stand-alone mode, but cannot be used by any other system. If such a key is also locked to PCRs, then the key can by used by the system in stand-alone mode, only when the machine has booted into a certain predefined state.

For example, the system might be set up to boot only from a hard disk, with no keyboard, video, or I/O other than a network card present. Upon being booted in that configuration, the PCRs will be in an appropriate state to allow the TPM to sign messages with a particular key. The mere fact that the machine is able to sign a random message then tells the remote user that the PCRs are in that predefined state.

If this system is being used as a remote monitor, it can sign data that it is monitoring with this key before sending it over the network. Such a system could be used as one of many in an electronic voting system, tabulating votes and returning the signed total. Such a design may help meet certification requirements that will be required for eVoting to be acceptable. Certification requirements are also required for other solutions, such as the Health Insurance Portability and Accountability Act (HIPAA).

## Medical Solutions for HIPAA Compliance

The HIPAA regulations make it a crime to expose a person's personal medical record to an unauthorized viewer. This places a burden on hospitals and insurance providers to keep data records private and at the same time easily accessible to authorized users.

In a hospital, a doctor may need to use a terminal to view a patient's records (or view it from his PDA). But if he is called away for an emergency, it is necessary that the terminal not provide unauthorized access to the patient's records to the next person who steps up to the terminal.

This provides a number of challenges. Data needs to be stored in a central location so that it is available via numerous connections that can attach to that central database. But doctors are only allowed to see the data on their own patients, so it is not the case that any doctor can see all the data in the database. Authorization has to be fine-grained enough to be user dependent.

One solution is to segregate patients' data into separate subdirectories and let doctors each have their own subdirectory. But that doesn't work, as it is possible for multiple doctors to have access to a single patient's data. And having an individual directory for each patient quickly becomes a management nightmare.

Authorization has to be tied to authentication, as well. Biometrics would be fine for this usage, as long as the biometric data doesn't get exposed to the general populace. A problem equally difficult to solve is the problem of un-authorization. Because ease of use precludes the possibility of requiring frequent re-authentication, there needs to be a way of removing authorization if the authenticated person leaves a terminal. Since a doctor may have to leave quickly on a code, it is not practical to require an overt action.

Fortunately, hardware radio badges exist to provide proximity information to a machine, so that when a radio transmitter is not near the PC, the PC knows this and can take appropriate steps to remove authorization.

It appears that all the technology necessary to provide a solution exists. Next, put it in a system. No doubt there are many ways of assembling such a system, but we will concentrate on only one of them.

First we choose a common criteria-evaluated back-end system, with a labeled security protection profile, and a level of at least EAL4+. Trusted Solaris, AIX®, and e zOS are all examples of OSs that have achieved this, and both Linux and Solaris 10 with trusted extensions are in the process of being evaluated. This provides auditing capability for the server, so it will be possible to see who has accessed a file.

> Note that while the choice of a back-end system is influenced by security, keep in mind that the data stored by the system needs to be secure from earthquake, fire, flood, and so on, and always available.

Files will be stored encrypted on this file server, as described in Chapter 12. Files will be encrypted with a secure algorithm with a large key (such as AES at 128 or 256 bits). This key will in turn be encrypted several times, with the public key of the owner of the data, the public keys of those authorized to view the data, and a backup authorization key, which will be split among $n$ administrators, any $m$ of which are sufficient to decrypt the file. The private key of the owner of the data is also used to certify the public keys of those authorized by him to view the data. In the case of emergency, an adminstrator can sign the public keys of an emergency practicitioner authorized to view the data. (Of course, this would be logged in any event.) Certificates could allow further access, as in a patient signing a doctor's key that would allow the doctor to consult with other doctors regarding his case. Then the doctor would be able to sign other public keys allowing access to the data.

The next time the file is accessed and changed, the accessor (who has the symmetric key) can generate a new symmetric key, and re-encrypt that symmetric key with all the signed/certified public keys associated with the earlier version of the file, thus allowing continuing access to the update file.

Now let's talk about the infrastructure. The wires in the hospital (or the wireless access points) will be considered insecure, so all traffic between access points and the server will use IPSec or similar protocol. This will encrypt all the traffic between the access points and the server. Public/private keys will be used to authenticate both the client and the server.

At this point, we have described a secure server, and the securing communications between the server and the clients. The last part, where TCG can help, is the interaction that takes place at the client.

Clients need to be secure. When the server gets a request to view data about a patient from a client, the server has to be able to determine that the request has come from an authorized user. Authorization is built upon authentication, so the authentication step has to be kept secure. Once authorization has been achieved and data is sent to the client, the data has to be kept secure. This requires that the client itself be in a trusted state. Client systems may be floating—there may be one at every center on every floor of a hospital. These sytems need to be used by authorized staff. These requirements can be summarized in the following list:

- The client machine must be in a secure state.
- The client system must be able to authenticate a user from any client.
- The client system must protect data from unauthorized users after it obtains the data

TCG-enabled systems have these capabilities.

To meet the first requirement, when a logon request from a user is completed, the server will request a signed PCR list from the client system. Analyzing this list will provide the server with information regarding the status of its boot, which can include such things as what level of virus protection has been installed and run.

There are a number of ways of authenticating a user, and a number of levels of authentication. Authentication in a variable environment (where a doctor may obtain information from any number of clients) is a bit more difficult than in an environment where each doctor has only a few machines from which he authenticates himself.

In the latter case, a TCG chip can be used for authentication. A passphrase can be used to log on to the device and also for accessing binding keys. These keys are used to decrypt the symmetric key used to decrypt a patient's file. Binding keys can be stored (without requiring a password) behind a storage key that does require a passphrase.

When the doctor passes beyond range where his radio badge can be heard by the machine, the machine will flush the binding keys out of the TPM's memory, thus requiring the doctor to re-authenticate to use them again. Software could be set to do this periodically as well. If there is a problem with storing enough keys in the TPM at once, a double indirection can be used: A storage key that requires authentication is used to load a storage key that does not require authentication, which is used to load binding keys that do not require authentication. As long as the second storage key is in the TPM, all the rest of the binding keys can be loaded in easily. Once the binding keys and the second storage key are evicted, however, re-authorization is necessary to access any of them.

Keeping the data private once it is loaded on a system is a bit tricky. The viewing program should not cache unencrypted data onto permanent storage. Data should be unencrypted only when it is in RAM, and that RAM should not be accessible by other concurrently running programs. When the doctor's radio badge leaves range, the RAM should be purged, too.

The only remaining question is this: How does the doctor's key get into the client device from which he is logging on? There are several possible answers to this question. The easiest is to have a single "doctor" storage key installed on each of the client systems, and each doctor then will have his own key (or keys) stored behind this doctor key. This doctor key will not require authorization in order to load keys, and so when a doctor logs on to the server, the server replies with a copy of his private key, encrypted with the doctor key. This key then can be decrypted on the client hardware and be password protected against hammering attacks by the hardware.

Another way of accomplishing the same task, but which is slightly more complicated, is to have the owner of the TPM on the server authorize migration *to* the root public keys of all of the various clients. Then each user could have their master key be a migratable private key stored under a non-migratable TCG storage key on the server. In order to log on to a new client, the user would then migrate his user root key onto that client from the server. But this would be possible because the owner of the key has the right to migrate it to any public key that is authorized by the owner of a TPM, and it does not require the owner of the TPM to be involved in each such transaction.

Once the key is migrated on to the new client, it could be used on any other client, but since the clients will be owned by the administrator, the keys will not be further migratable beyond the limits set by the administrator. HIPAA solutions are important for privacy reasons, but the military have even more stringent requirements for keeping their data secret.

## COTS Security Solutions for the Military

Secure military personal computers built from common off-the-shelf components has long been a dream of the NSA and the U.S. Military. It would save large amounts of money. It may now be possible to build such a system using a TPM module at its core.

Common requirements of such a system are as follows:

- Any data on the system must be wiped out both before and after it is used.
- The system must be able to securely identify itself.
- The user must be able to securely identify himself.
- Information passed to the system must not be visible during the transfer.
- Confidential information on the system must not be available to other processes running on the system.

All of these objectives could be accomplished as follows. A system is designed that has no hard disk, but *lots* of RAM. This is becoming more doable now that 64-bit architecture chips are shipping, but even 2 gigabytes of RAM is sufficient for most purposes—especially the fact that RAM is easier to erase than a hard disk. The machine boots to the network over an IPSec card, and a server at the other end loads a secure operating system into the RAM. This whole procedure is verified by extensions to the PCR values in the TPM.

After the OS is loaded, it hashes the first program it will execute, extends the appropriate PCR, and then executes that first program, which may have limited functionality and a protected memory space. This application can read a key locked to predetermined PCR values (which are now in the correct state) that have been wrapped with the public key of the SRK. Then, it can use this key by sending it to the TPM with a nonced request to sign the request. A correct signature coming back indicates that the PCR values are set as expected, thus showing that the boot was secure.

At this point, the server makes encrypted data available to the PC along with the blobs necessary to unlock those blobs. The encrypted blobs (or a single base encrypted blob) can be locked to the PC's PCRs so that they are only available to the first program running. They also will require authentication data from the end user.

The first program then decrypts the encrypted blobs to get the key (or keys) it will use for the session and immediately extends one of the PCRs so that the encrypted blobs cannot be decrypted again. As necessary, the first program will decrypt and display the data.

## Working with IP Telephony

IP telephony is becoming more and more popular since it eliminates one entire wiring infrastructure in a company by combining the Ethernet wiring with the PBX wiring. Not only does this generate huge savings, it also provides a means to add more services by running those services on servers already on the network. However, one thing about IP telephony is that it uses a partyline concept for transmission. As a result, IP telephony is about as private as a postcard, although people think it is as private as a normal phone conversation. Further, when an intermediary is used to shunt an IP telephony conversation onto the POTS (plain old telephone system), bills need to be directed to the correct person who placed a call. Because the whole process takes place unencrypted on the network, it's easy to make it appear that a call has been placed by someone other than the real caller.

The best design for this type of system is to use encryption to provide for both privacy and for billing information. Where should the encryption take place? Ideally, it would take place in the handset itself. Since power is at a premium, and the processor may not be particularly robust, Rijndael makes the most sense as the algorithm. However, it is necessary, for identification and authentication, that a public key also be available. Here a TPM (particularly one that has Rijndael as an added feature) is an ideal solution for handset.

Unfortunately, this may not be possible depending on the technology used. If the handset is cordless, a lot depends on the quality of the signal that can be transmitted to the base station. In this case, the base station may have to take over responsibility both for packetizing the voice and also for the encryption of the resultant data stream. Another solution is to simply encrypt all communication between the VOIP phone and the VOIP server, using IPSec.

## Working with IPSec

There are a number of IPSec network interface cards (NICs) that are now available. All of them accelerate the symmetric encryption of a stream. Some of them also will store an asymmetric key and use it for establishing the initial connection and exchanging the key.

Typically cards like these are used when there is a large amount of confidential information transiting the bus at high speed, so the CPU of the machine on either side of the pipe has trouble keeping up with the signal. This type of data can occur when a company has two intranets on either side of the country and wants to link them together into a single system. It can also occur when a video stream is being sent, either from a video conference or from video editing.

For those NICs that do not create and store their own private key (and most of them do not), a TPM is an ideal method of providing for that connection. A signing key that does not require Use_Auth can be set to provide for initial setup and key exchange. By using a TPM-protected key, the machines that are talking to one another will not be spoofed. IPSec is also used for Virtual Private Networks (VPNs). In this case, a user at a remote location is trying to log in to an intranet. He wants to make sure that the data stream he sends to the intranet and receives back is private, and that is typically done via encryption.

There are many ways this can be accomplished. One of the easiest would be to use the IPSec built in to Windows 2000 and XP. Unfortunately, at the time of this writing, Microsoft® has not opened the CAPI stack for this application to other CSPs. It only allows its own software version of the CSP for doing authentication. However, in the future, Microsoft may open up its CAPI stack to match its published architecture, and if it does, then hardware-based authentication will become much easier. Authentication usually requires some number of the following:

- Something the user knows (like a password)
- Something he has (a token such as a smart card or a SecureID fob)
- Something he is (a biometric such as a fingerprint)

In the case of a portable computer, the user already has something—the portable computer—and it is somewhat silly to require him to have something else. It has been necessary in the past because security tokens had not been integrated into the device. With the advent of security tokens being integrated into the device itself, the market for nonintegrated security tokens may disappear.

One place where you might think a security token would still be useful would be in the case of hoteling assets (see the section earlier in this chapter, "Secure Hoteling"). Another is in the case where the security token is going to be used in machines not under the control of the user at all. This latter might exist if hotels start installing machines hooked to the Internet in their rooms and a guest wants to use them for dialing back into his intranet. This latter case is somewhat problematic for security, though. Even if a token is used to prove that the user at the system is indeed entitled to get into the intranet, there is still a question as to the security of the computer at which the user is sitting. That computer needs to be trusted, which brings us back to TCG. And if the computer in the hotel is TCG compliant, it should be possible to use it without a token.

## Working with Service Meters

Electrical usage, natural gas usage, and water usage are all areas where local metering is necessary but require a person go to each meter periodically and read it. This is a problem for a large number of reasons:

- The meter is located outside, making it inconvenient for the end user to read.
- It costs a lot to send someone to make the rounds.
- Meter reading is subject to errors in reading/recording.
- Meter readers are subject to dogs, etc.
- Immediate feedback cannot be generated based on meter data.

Having a meter that reports back to base as to the value it is reading is a problem for several reasons, as follows:

- Cost of the additional hardware
- Cost of connection to a phone
- Meters can be tampered with, and need to be checked to avoid tampering

However, the Internet (with cable connections to it) can provide a quick way of providing constant communication to the meter, and integrated clients with embedded software can provide relatively cheap ways to connect to the utility. What is now possible with TCG is the capability to create an inexpensive device that will sign the meter values being sent back. This connected to standard tamper-evident bits can provide all the technology necessary to provide for secure remote metering.

So consider how this compares to the current situation. The meter today has a small lock put on it that is meant to show tampering if a homeowner opens it up to change the meter. A meter reader notices if this "lock" has been cut, and then can investigate the reason why. Once a month the homeowner is given a bill, which tells him how much of the utility he used during the last 30 days. Occasionally the bill will not be accurate, either due to a number being transposed or an average usage substituted for the actual usage.

Now if a meter is able to respond to queries as to its current value, a new service can be offered to the customer—the capability to see what the instantaneous usage rate is, and to get a graph of the usage rate by the hour for a month. This is particularly important to users who get differential pricing based on how much energy they use during peak periods.

If the meter case is opened, or other tampering is detected (such as an extreme magnetic field), a tamper evident bit can be set by the meter that would remove the meter's capability to sign the messages it sends. One way to do this would be to simply wipe the SRK of the meter's TPM, thus killing all its keys. This would in turn be a signal to send a person out to investigate why the meter has been tampered with. The monetary savings to the company of not having to send out meter readers to every house periodically to read meters has to be quite large, so this appears to be a reasonable place to make large savings.

Another place where large amounts of money are spent is in corporations cleaning up after a virus infection. Root cause analysis in a number of cases have shown that viruses that infected an intranet came not through the firewall, but rather from a client connected to the system that was not running a corporate image. Either a contractor or an employee had brought an infected machine into the building and hooked it up to the network.

## Working with Network Switches

Ethernet is basically a shared service that presents a problem. Anyone can put their NIC into promiscuous mode and listen to all of the traffic that is going by. They can also flood the lines with bogus data, causing a denial-of-service attack.

An IPSec connection can be set up between a client and a server. However, this requires an NIC in the client that can do heavy-duty encryption. When connection speeds increase, getting decryption on the fly becomes more and more difficult, even with an accelerator.

In a wired solution, using a switch instead of a hub can help with the situation, because it can essentially place each conversation on a separate wire so that packets don't collide. We propose a hardware change to the switch and an outline of a protocol that would increase the security associated with this solution.

First, we want only certain allowed clients connecting to the server. This is useful for defending against a denial-of-service attack, in which a server is flooded with messages from bogus clients.

Our design verifies which client is asking to talk to a server using public/private key technology, and then verifying that the connection from that client to that server is allowed before proceeding with the connection.

In the event that the organization is large, so that more than one switch is transited before reaching the server, the protocol also provides a means of securing the connection from client to server. There is flexibility where many trusted clients can share certain ports of a switch, or a port may be shared among many systems (for example, laptops), but only authorized systems can get from the port to the server.

We begin with a client making a request to a switch to connect to a server.

The switch obtains the public key of that server, or some other suitable certificate authority, either from a table or from the server in question.

The switch generates a random, or pseudo-random number (referred to as a nonce) and passes it back to the requesting client.

The client signs the nonce, and then passes the signed nonce and the client's public key, which the server has certified in question or the appropriate certificate authority back to the switch.

The switch verifies the client by checking the client's identity, and then checks to see if the client is allowed access to the server. This can be done either by table lookup or by asking the server. (Such tables can be signed, we note.)

Once the switch verifies the client is allowed to talk to the server, it establishes a virtual connection between the two, and the switch is not further involved.

In the event that there is more than one switch between the client and the server, once the authentication to the first switch is done, the client repeats its request to the second switch, and so on.

Note that in a distributed denial-of-service (DDOS) attack, such as was applied against eBay and others recently, the switch as described previously may or may not apply. On eBay, for the sections of the service that only registered clients can get to, this would reduce the amount of attack. However, for the public portions of the system, it is not reasonable to expect that all those allowed on the site would have certified public keys. However, it would still be possible to have a few of the switches reserved for certified clients, so that those clients would not be affected (or as affected) by a DDOS. And it would be possible to use those switches to connect from the inside out to the Internet to try and fix the DDOS attack.

Identification problems are getting increasingly severe, with the multiplication of Trojan horse programs, rootkits, keyloggers, and other nasty software. In such a world, it is nice to know that the TPM exists to provide the capabilities necessary to develop solutions to these problems.

## Summary

Through the numerous examples in this chapter, it should be clear that TPMs have a lot to offer in terms of identification. The design easily allows for an architecture that provides for users to securely identify themselves—architectures such as in HIPAA, VPN, VOIP, and IPSec. It also provides a means for a user to lock his own data so that it is only read by him and only when he is in a secure state. Additionally, it provides utilities that can be used by IT administrators to securely identify the machines that they are managing and reliably test that they are in a secure state. Last, it provides the capability to make hardware using standard components that will meet the increasingly severe needs of things attached to the Internet.

# CHAPTER 14

# Administration of Trusted Devices

With the advent of TCG-equipped personal computers, there is a need for management software to take care of situations that may arise. These include registering keys, backing up migratable key chains, and creating maintenance blobs. These administrative needs also provide the opportunity for third-party business models to be constructed (or added to existing ones). This chapter considers how TPM administration problems can be solved by making use of the architectural design of the TPM. We will discuss the following:

- Backup and maintenance of keys
- Creating a database of non-migratable system keys and their certificates
- Setting up a secure time reporting system

## Secure Backup/Maintenance

The TCG key architecture can recover from many different disaster scenarios. Looking at the architecture in Figure 14.1, the migratable key chain is designed so that only one key, the platform migratable storage key, needs to be migrated in order to take all the keys below it to a new TPM. In the case of upgrading a system, migration of a key is relatively easy, requiring only the following:

- The new public key
- The migration authorization for the system migratable storage key
- Owner authorization for the system being migrated from
- Temporarily receiving and then sending a random number

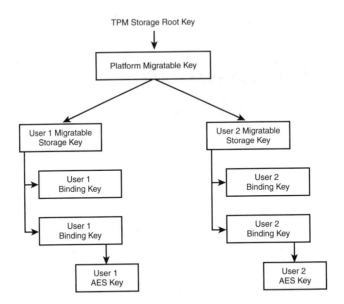

**Figure 14.1**    TCG key architecture

The migration authorization and the new public key can create a public backup key for the old TPM. The key being migrated is then loaded in the old TPM along with this public backup key and migration authorization for the key being migrated. The TPM will then output two things: the migration blob (which consists of the key encrypted twice—once using the public key of the target system, and once with a one-time pad) and a rather long random number, which was used for the one-time pad.

The migration blob and rather long random number are then taken to the new TPM and presented to it. The new TPM reads in the two and writes out a newly created key blob with the old key now wrapped with the new key's public key.

This works fine if the new system and the old system are both simultaneously working. However, what happens if the old system dies? In this case, it is important that you create the migration blob before the old system dies. But since the new system hasn't even been bought yet, how do you pick the public backup key?

The TCG spec has been designed to get around this problem. Instead of picking the new system's public key, a trusted second party, such as an administrator's public key, is chosen for the backup. When the old system dies, the migration blob without the random number is delivered to the administrator, together with the new public key of the new TPM of the new system. The administrator applies a `MigrateMigrationBlob` command to the migration blob and converts it into a migration blob for the new system.

The owner of the new system then takes the new migration blob, together with the random number, and inserts it into his new system.

The process that we just followed can be condensed to a numbered list, which represents the life cycle of a system key. It goes like this (as shown in Figures 14.2 and 14.3):

1. Obtain trusted second party's public key (possibly from a website).

2. Create a root migratable key for the base system.

3. Create migration blob for trusted second party's system.

4. Squirrel away migration blob and random number (back up a secure copy).

5. Machine dies.

6. Obtain new system.

7. Obtain new system's public key.

8. Send new system's public key and old system's migration blob to trusted second party.

9. Second party migrates migration blob, creating new migration blob.

10. New migration blob is sent to owner.

11. Owner takes new migration blob and random number and inserts key into new system.

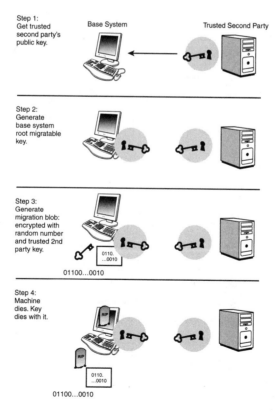

**Figure 14.2**    Initial setup until death of system

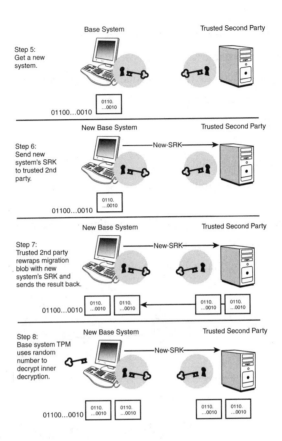

**Figure 14.3**    Recovery to a new system

The new system now can use all the old system's migratable keys.

Now you may ask: "How trusted does the trusted second party have to be?" The answer, surprisingly, is "Not very." The trusted second party has to be trusted so you don't lose the private key and to still be in business if the machine dies. If the trusted second party goes out of business, you can create a new migration blob for a new business. Without the random number, it is not possible for the trusted second party to insert the key into a new system or to read the key. The owner of the TPM gets to select the trusted second party. He must select one he trusts will not decrypt the migration blob and then send the results to the owner of the key. If the second party does this, the owner of the key would then be able to use his random number to decrypt the key. Similarly, the owner of the TPM trusts that the trusted second party will not migrate the key to the public key of a TPM the trusted second party does not own. (Both of these requirements assume that the owner of the TPM cares whether or not the owner of the key can read it.)

Two service opportunities emerge out of this discussion:

- A service to migrate migratable keys (to be the trusted second party)
- A service to securely store both the migration blob and the random number

The first service can be provided by anyone with TCG-compliant machines. Such a company would publish its certified non-migratable public keys on the web. A client would create migration blobs for several of those keys (several keys should be used for disaster recovery in case a machine no longer works). The company could then have RAID 5 storage with hierarchical backup (highly reliable storage) to store keys for clients. Upon a disaster occurring, the owner of the keys would be able to go to the local store of the chain and request his key be migrated to his new system. FedEx Kinkos would be an ideal store to do something like this. At the time of storing the key, the owner can decide what type of identification needs to be used to recover a key, who can authorize it, if it can be delivered over the web, and so on.

The second service is to store the random number itself. This is more problematic, because having both the random key and a migration blob could expose the key. However, the TCG system can solve this problem as well. A system can be built that boots off a floppy and has no hard drive or I/O ports. The random number can be brought to this system on a floppy, and locked to the PCR values and a password of the user. This blob would be written back to the OS floppy. The floppy (or multiple copies of the floppy) could be stored either by the user or by the company.

Upon the event of a disaster, the floppy could be used in the same system to recover the random number.

There are other ways of accomplishing the same thing. The client could use the same non-migratable storage keys that are published on the company's website and migrate one of his own migratable storage keys to those non-migratable storage keys. Full migration in a secure environment could be accomplished by being at the site, by using quoted PCR values, or by simply trusting the trusted second party. He could then use the migratable storage key to store his random number.

Additionally, the client could split his random number into two pieces. This is easily done by generating a new random number and XORing it with the first random number. The result is a third random number. Now the client can independently store the second and third random numbers. Upon recovery of both of them, he can XOR them together to re-create the first random number—the one he requires.

This has shown how you can back up client keys in case of disaster. However, one key to doing this securely is knowing when you are talking to a specific client. The next section describes how to do this.

## Assignment of Key Certificates

In the past, for most secure networks you could not assume that the clients were "trusted" in any sense. Instead, trust was rooted in a single server that was guarded in a single location. Cracking that one server was tantamount to cracking the entire network and everything on it, so it was important to have extremely good security for that server. Cracking a single client machine was easy, but that would crack only the account that was using that machine, an account that was usually not that valuable. This "all your security eggs in one basket" approach made the secrets on the one trusted server very valuable, as they represented the aggregate of the value of many client systems.

Today the security landscape is more distributed. Because of the security that is embedded in our trusted clients, and soon in our Intel e-servers, security can be rooted in each individual machine in a way that was not possible just a year ago. This now leads to the possibility of distributed security and distributed risk—such that cracking a single machine would not have the catastrophic consequences of cracking the root server in the past, and cracking any individual client becomes much more difficult.

Consider, for example, the idea of using a distributed structure for key certificates. A typical organization consists of employees who work for managers, who in turn work for other managers. This tree organization will be used to create a certificate list. A user will take his public key, for which he wants a certificate, and send it to a certificate server (one of many). This certificate server will check its copy of the management chain and create a certificate for the user and send it to the user's manager. The certificate would include the name of the manager of the user as per the server. The manager would sign the certificate and then send it to the user, if indeed the user worked for him. If not, the manager would send a note back to the server, telling it to update its organization list.

When the client wants to use his key, he attaches the certificate. The server to which it is sent checks to see if both certificates are valid, and checks his own list of who the employee works for. If the employee works for someone else, then he sends a note to both managers, to see which one claims the employee. In the case that both do, the server will not proceed further, other than to send an alert to the original server and to the administrator. If neither do, hopefully you will be able to tell the server the identity of the new manager or that the employee was terminated. This information would be broadcast to all the servers. In the case that the employee has a new manager, the original certificate would be invalidated, and a new certificate created by the new server would send a note to the new manager asking for a new certificate. And so on.

Much of the work could take place automatically, with a manager time stamping and signing a list of his employees whenever it is changed and the changes then propagating through the system in an automatic fashion.

In this manner, a Public Key Infrastructure (PKI) solution gets created without a single point of failure and without a single point of security failure. Each server is responsible only for its own services, each manager for his/her own employees, and so on. This distributes not just the overall security, but there is also a distribution of value, so that hacking a single server does not mean that the whole security of the system is compromised.

When the TPM is first turned on, it will generate an internal storage root key. At this point, if a maintenance blob is going to be created, it should be, using the `Tspi_TPM_CreateMaintenanceArchive` command. However, I recommend that it *not* be created. For those paranoid about the maintenance blob, directly after creation of the SRK, the maintenance feature should be turned off using the `Tspi_TPM_KillMaintenanceFeature` command. I recommend doing this. Then a signature key tied to the SRK needs to be created to be used to prove that a new SRK has not been created later and a maintenance blob made for it. (In 1.2, this is not necessary, as there is a flag in the TPM that can be queried as to whether a maintenance archive has been created. It is the `TSS_TPMSTATUS_MAINTENANCEUSED` flag.)

Aside from this minor issue, there is also the question of distribution of certificates to show that a given key belongs to a particular user. In a large enterprise environment, certificates used for enterprise-related tasks can be distributed in an efficient way by a top-down procedure. Each manager certifies the keys of his direct reports, and the certificates are sent back to a single point where the new certificates are then issued with a common CA. Automation of this process requires some software to be written.

This procedure is not as useful for environments where a person wants to make sure his identity is not stolen. For people to believe a certificate is really that of Bill Gates, or George W. Bush, it is important that the certificate is issued for a key that Bill Gates or George W. Bush is willing to sign for. Although it might be easy for someone to identify Bill Gates or George Bush, it is important that a high level of security be used to certify keys that are going to be used in place of credit cards. It must be at least as good as that which is already being used, and preferably quite a bit better. Use of public/private key technology for identification meets this standard.

Now that mailboxes are being raided for credit card application forms, and identity theft is growing, more focus will be placed on this problem in the future. An ideal CA (Certificate Authority) will have local branches in every neighborhood, deep pockets, will have been trusted for a long period of time in establishing identities, and will be in touch with nearly everyone. The Post Office seems to be about the only agency or business that satisfies all of these characteristics.

## Secure Time Reporting

A number of applications—such as ones that would like to "rent" the usage of software according to the time it is being used or which would like to time stamp messages—would like to have the use of a secure clock. As mentioned earlier in the description of the TPM, a secure timer was *not* one of the capabilities that was put in. This does not mean that the TPM cannot be used in an application that does provide this service.

First, consider the case of time stamping a message. There needs to be a service somewhere with a reliable clock that is going to provide the time stamping. Because this service is not likely to be under the control of the person who is sending the message, it is important that the message not be sent to the service. The time stamp that is sent is either done on a hash of the message (so there is no release of confidential information to the time stamp service), or the user merely includes verified time stamps in his message without even sending the hash of the message to the service. This provides a latest date at which the message could have been signed.

You also want to guarantee that the message was signed after a specific date. This can be accomplished by a timeserver that provides periodic (or upon demand) signed times.

Now the message can include in it a signed time from the server, and the signature be signed (and dated) by the time service. When the recipient receives the message, he can verify it was signed after the first time/date and before the second time/date.

Now let us consider the case of "renting" software. In this case, the owner of the software wants to know how long the software will be used and cut off usage after a certain time period has expired. There are a number of ways this could be done.

The first technique involves "tokens" that need to be received periodically from the owner of the software that are used to keep the software running. An easy way to do this would be to have the software periodically provide a random number (such as the current execution code and memory register contents) to the server, and delay continuing execution until a correctly signed version of that data is sent back to the user. The problems with this include the following:

- It requires the server to be connected to the client.
- It may delay execution of the program to the extent that it is noticeable to the user, thus reducing usability.
- It is subject (to some extent) to the whims of the network.

What would be nicer would be a single token that would contain a guaranteed usage time for the end user program, even when the machine is offline. In the past, this problem has been nearly insoluble. Programs that are locked to a specific key or dongle have been broken in the past by hackers who go into the code and code around the logical comparison that is done, or hard code the result to be true. Now that TCG can guarantee that the system is in a specified, trusted state, this can be accomplished in a way that is not susceptible to software attacks.

In this case, the token would be sealed behind PCRs that represent the system having been booted directly into the program that is to be executed, and one of the PCR values would represent a hash of the executing program. This provides assurance that the program has not been altered. The program would read the token when it boots and determine the amount of time it has to execute. At this time, it would call back (once) to the server to verify that the key is current. The TPM would generate a random number, and the application would attach it to the token and send it to the server. The server would verify that the token had not been used and then sign the packet and send it back. The software would then begin its execution, running for as long as it can. When it is done, it would create a packet sealed to the same PCRs as the machine started in (and the TPM will record if the PC is still in that same state). An extend will be done on the PCR representing the program immediately after the seal operation is done.

The next time the program is booted, it will unseal the "time left" token, which was clearly created by the program itself (since the PCR state at the time it was created is part of the program) and the procedure repeats itself.

If any such architecture is used, however, it is important that there is a means of recovery of keys so that if a machine dies before the tokens bought have been fully used, it is possible for the tokens to be moved to another system. This can be accomplished if one can recover the base key pairs.

# Key Recovery

Most of the work done in creating the specification was aimed specifically at making key recovery hard. However, in the case of migratable keys, if the owner of the key and the owner of the TPM that uses the key collaborate, it is possible to recover the key. There are two reasons for pointing this out. The first is that security through obscurity does not work. Knowing that the key recovery mechanism exists in certain cases may be sufficient reason for not using migratable keys in some areas or it may be a specifically very good reason for not storing a key under a migratable key owned by someone else. Further, there may be cases involving the death of an individual where it becomes necessary to recover data stored underneath a key, I, owned by that individual, and the authorization data is not available. We therefore describe how this can be done, as follows:

1. The first step is to create a public/private key pair, RSA 2048-bit, and keep a copy of the private key. We call this key B, for broken (the private portion is known).

2. The second step is to authorize migration to the public portion of B. The owner of the TPM can do this.

3. The third step is to load the key *or one of its ancestors* into the TPM and request migration of that key to B. Note that if the individual stored his key to a non-migratable key, and the migration authorization of I is not available, this step cannot be done. If I is wrapped to the platform migration key, the owner of the platform migration key can accomplish this. During the migration, a random string, R, is generated as well as the migration blob, M.

4. M is decrypted using the private portion of B, and then a reverse optimal asymmetric encryption padding (OAEP) is done to expose the insides.

5. The insides are then XORed with R to reveal an inner OAEP.

6. The inner OAEP is then undone to reveal the private portion of I, including its use authorization data.

If a migration blob and the random data that came with it are available, then the migration blob can be first migrated to an insecure public key, B, this time without requiring the owner of the TPM to authorize it.

If a migration blob is not available, it is also possible to do a one-step migration of I to B, and this would then only require decrypting with the private portion of B and doing a reverse OAEP to recover I.

If the migration authorization data of I is not available, but it is wrapped with a key P that is migratable and for which the migration authorization is known, then I can be determined as follows:

1. First, determine the private portion of P using one of the previous techniques.

2. Use P to unwrap the key blob that contains I. Do a reverse OAEP to recover I.

3. In a similar way, the whole stack of keys below P can be extracted, once P is known.

These programs do require more work than other programs in the book, because none of the steps after creation of the blob are represented by TCG functions, so they will have to be done by the programmer himself.

We referred to OAEP earlier. A quick description of OAEP follows. OAEP stands for Optimal Asymmetric Encryption Padding, and is a means of keeping data, D, secure against certain attacks when it has been encrypted with a public key. There is a function MGF1, the Mask Generation Function 1, that is used to produce a string of arbitrary size based on an input of arbitrary size. It is relatively slow, but it is considered a good stream cipher derived from SHA-1. The first thing that is done is to create a random number, R.

Now we take MGF1 (R) and XOR it with D, and MGF1 (MGF1(R) XOR D) and XOR it with R. (The MFG1 is used because R and D aren't usually the same size.) The results are then concatenated.

It is interesting to note that after OAEP is done, it can be reversed by first recovering R and then recovering D, but if a single bit of the OAEPed concatenated result is changed, the original data will be unrecoverable.

OAEP is also used in the standard before an XOR is done with a random number in one of the migration schemes for keys. This is done to provide a "double encryption" of the key so that there is a "division of power" between the owner of the chip and the owner of the key. The owner of the chip may want to restrict the public keys to which a key may be migrated (and he can do this), because he may not trust the owner of the key. The owner of the key may want to migrate his key (for backup) but not trust the owner of the chip. Using this migration scheme, neither has to trust the other. If a simple XOR of the data were used instead of an OAEP scheme, the owner of the chip could decrypt the outside shell. He would not then be able to decrypt the key itself, but he would be able to change values in known locations of the structure of the key—for example, changing it from requiring authorization to not requiring authorization. With the OAEP encoding, this is not possible—changing a single bit of the data in the key renders it unencryptable.

## TPM Tools

There are, of course, sets of tools available to handle user administrative jobs of a TPM, namely the following:

- Turning on the TPM
- Taking ownership of the TPM (creating an SRK)
- Changing the ownership authorization of the TPM
- Resetting a TPM
- Getting the public key of the TPM endorsement key
- Preventing non-owners from reading the public key of the TPM endorsement key
- Having the TPM perform a self test

- Finding out the version of the TPM
- Creating base migratable and non-migratable keys

As far as I am aware, every system that ships with a TPM can handle these chores. Additionally, you can find tools that do these things (and more) at http://trousers.sourceforge.net/.

## Summary

Along with the new capabilities the TPM provides, there are some attendant difficulties that need to be solved. Key management is the biggest problem. In spite of best efforts of the industry, machines die, are dropped, or are stolen. An IT organization needs a way to quickly get its employees to recover from these situations. This requires that an IT organization be able to help an employee get a new system that has the same keys and capabilities as his old one. The TPM was designed with an understanding that those problems would need to be solved, so capabilities were designed into it to help solve those problems. Using these capabilities can provide a robust enterprise solution for managing the keys that are used by a TPM.

# CHAPTER 15

# Ancillary Hardware

One of the key requirements of a TPM specification is that it be possible to make an inexpensive TPM. As a result, there are security problems that the TPM cannot address by itself. This chapter describes how you can add other hardware devices to a TPM in order to create solutions for problems not addressed by the TPM alone. In particular, this chapter looks at the following security problems:

- How to authenticate to a TPM in a secure way
- How to hook biometric readers to a TPM securely
- How to create a linkage between a TPM and a display

## Trusted Path

Problems have been pointed out by the Eurocard, Mastercard, and VISA specification for secure terminal usage of credit cards and smart cards, which will apply equally well to TCG hardware. In particular, two are the "trusted path" and "trusted display" problems, which affect usage of trusted hardware. In both of these cases, it is possible to create more secure machines if one adds ancillary hardware to the system. This hardware is designed to work well with a TPM, and provide solutions to these problems.

Although neither of these trusted problems is fixed directly by the TCG specification, there are design features of TCG that make it possible to fix these problems with additional hardware. Those design features are specifically the means that are used for authentication. Because authentication takes place using a hashed message authentication code (HMAC) instead of simply presenting a password to the TPM, it is possible to do the authentication step remotely from the TPM, in an isolated, controlled, secure environment. Because such an environment is not a general-purpose environment, it can be rigorously controlled so as not to be vulnerable to viruses and Trojan horses.

The trusted path problem refers to a problem in the process of giving authorization to trusted hardware. It is important that when such authorization (such as a password or pass phrase) is given to the hardware, that the authorization not be "overheard" and copied by an untrusted third party, such as a Trojan horse resident in the platform. If authorization is copied, and although the third party may not know the private key, he can still use it as if he knew the key, thus using the private key to spoof the user.

One example of such an attack is "shoulder surfing," where a person (or camera) watches a person as they type in their password. A more sophisticated attack (from the movie *National Treasure*) is to determine what keys were pressed by looking at physical residue left on the keyboard. Easier attacks are done by rootkits, which monitor the keyboard buffer to read keystrokes as they are entered. Recently a hypervisor-based keystroke logger was demonstrated at Black Hat, making a virtually undetectable means of stealing a password. Another attack is a simple device inserted between a keyboard and the PC that simply records all keystrokes made by the user. The FBI has used such devices, and they are easily found for sale on the web.

In the financial industry, the trusted path problem is usually solved with credit card readers that read the credit card and validate the pin in a separate piece of hardware. This creates a barrier from keylogger type attacks. However, ATMs have been attacked by people placing a hardware shell over the ATM, which acts as a middleman, reading the ATM card and recording the PIN as it is typed in.

PCs have a more difficult problem, because it is necessary for the main system to be able to read the keystrokes of a keyboard, so it is not possible to totally isolate the keyboard from the main memory. However, the problem can still be solved.

## Special Keyboards

In particular, a USB keyboard could be designed that has the following features:

- A macro that does HMAC and hashing of a message
- An indicator light that shows the keyboard is in secure mode
- A display that can show the message being signed

When a message is to be signed, software would send the message to the keyboard along with all the other data necessary to create the HMAC (other than the authentication data itself). This would also send a signal to the keyboard that lights up the indicator light and effectively disconnects the keyboard input from the USB interface. At this point, the keyboard becomes an isolated device, thus not subject to being read by rootkits and other malware. Keystrokes are not being put into a PC software readable keyboard buffer. The display on the keyboard is also a special purpose device—only displaying the message being signed.

Now the user can scroll through the message to make sure that he wants to sign it, and then provide his authentication data to the keyboard. The keyboard can then hash the message and create the appropriate HMAC to send to the TPM for signing.

In order to avoid having to remember large numbers of authentication data, it should be possible to have the keyboard use a single key to decrypt authentication data sent to it from the computer so that the keyboard becomes involved in every authentication.

This keyboard provides a solution to both the trusted path and the trusted display at the same time. For Fingerprint Readers, however, the display part would likely be an expensive add-on, and as a colleague points out, would only move the point of attack from the main CPU to the keyboard CPU.

Fingerprints by their very nature do not contain secrets. If someone were to steal a laptop, it is likely that the user's fingerprints would be plastered all over the machine—particularly the screen, if my system is typical. Although it is tempting to derive an encryption key from a fingerprint image, such a key would not be secure. Instead, use the fingerprint to authenticate to a TPM, which will then release a key.

A fingerprint-matching chip can be designed that will take the incoming fingerprint image (which can be directly attached to the matching chip to avoid software attacks), and upon matching provide the HMAC necessary to authenticate to a TPM. There are some subtleties, however.

One design would encrypt fingerprint templates together with authentication data, using an AES key known only to the fingerprint-matching chip. These encrypted blobs would be passed to the matching chip along with the TPM nonce (using the standard callback mechanism)—the command and parameters that are being requested to be executed. The chip would then decrypt the template and authentication data and match the incoming fingerprint to the template. If the template matched, it would then provide the correct HMAC to the callback function and the function would complete.

There are several things to be careful of when designing such a solution. First, the fingerprint image that is being compared needs to have some sort of proof of freshness to avoid replay attacks. This can be something as simple as an HMAC based on a secret that is shared between the reader and the matcher. This design would have the matcher passing a random number to the reader, and the reader passing both the image and an HMAC created out of the random number, the image, and the shared HMAC key. Another even easier solution is to have the reader and the matcher be hardwired together.

A second thing to worry about is the ease of "spoofing" the reader. There have been numerous spoofs of readers in the past decade. Initial readers could be spoofed by using fingerprint powder to "develop" a latent image on the reader from the last time it was used. The attacks got more sophisticated with the advent of latex fingers, which had a fingerprint pressed into them. Gelatin fingerprints were announced by a researcher in Japan most recently. However, this is a standard arms race—as the hackers get more sophisticated, so do the designers, and it is becoming more and more difficult (and expensive) to mount these kinds of attacks against modern readers.

The third thing to worry about is the quality of the matching software. One in ten-thousand false accept or false reject rates are now common. One can easily square that by requiring two matching fingerprints, but at the risk of reducing user ease of use. Although this number may seem high, it is important to remember that while a computer can try 10,000 passwords in the blink of an eye, trying 10,000 fingerprints is substantially more difficult.

Enhancements are mostly involved with ease of use. People don't want to provide their fingerprint to create a template more than once, and so a system should be made that would allow registration of a fingerprint a single time, and association with passwords at a later time.

Fingerprints (and all biometrics) have another problem that requires consideration: privacy. While fingerprint images are not used in doing fingerprint match, but rather fingerprint templates (of about 300 bytes), there are privacy advocates who are very concerned that no biometric data of a person should be easily harvested from applications or systems. This has particular implications in how a biometric reader/matcher should be designed.

An ideal design will do all fingerprint matching locally, and not on a remote server. This allows a person to control his own biometric data. Additionally, all biometric data should be encrypted when not in use, to prevent harvesting attacks. Fingerprint images that are captured for matching should not transit the machine's memory in the clear if at all possible. Finally, matching of the fresh fingerprint images should always be done in a protected memory environment so that there is no chance of data harvesting the image.

## Trusted Display

The trusted display problem is slightly more subtle. When a person is signing a document with a digital signature, typically he is signing something that is displayed on his display—or at least, he thinks he is. It is theoretically possible for rogue software to change the data that is signed on its way to the chip, or to change what is displayed to be different from what is being signed. In this way, a person might be signing a contract with a different value than the one that is being displayed.

There are two different kinds of trusted displays to consider. The first, being sure that what you sign is what you think you are signing, can be solved by techniques such as the trusted keyboard. The second is much more robust. It is a trusted display that allows a user to believe that everything he is typing into a computer and displaying on his screen remains on a trusted device. Given the ability of hardware to do direct memory access (DMA), this is not particularly easy. TPMs do not provide the means to lock a display to particular system access. Fortunately, both Intel and AMD have recently provided some solutions to that problem, by using memory controllers to partition access to memory. This in turn allows you to create a "secure state" of the system that can provide security function. Because of legacy apps, however, it is necessary that such a system be able to be put into two modes: a secure one and an insecure one.

Trusted display is a particularly hard problem to solve. Suppose you have a machine that can be in two modes—one of which is secure and one of which is not. There is software that can switch between the modes, but if one is in the insecure mode, a software command to switch into the secure mode may or may not work. In this case, how does the user know that the system has actually switched into a secure mode?

You might think that this is as easy as putting up a secure border around the screen—but software can easily spoof this design. Indeed, one of the earliest viruses made a screen appear to be upside down. Anything that can be done to a screen by trusted software can also be done by untrusted software as a spoof.

The next thing you might try is to do a read-out of PCR values to determine if the system is in a trusted state. But malicious software could easily report good PCR values.

You also can do a signed read of your PCR values in order to get an unspoofable verdict about the state of the platform. However, this doesn't work for a different reason—not that the signature obtained is spoofable. (It isn't.) But it isn't possible for a person to verify that the signature is correct without using the computer because verification requires doing large modular arithmetic. However, if the thing the signature is verifying is that the computer is trusted, you are left in a Catch 22! If the computer is trusted, you can trust the answer—but you are trying to find out if you can trust the computer.

So what do you do? The key does depend on the PCRs keeping track of the state of the computer. But instead of reporting PCR values, you do something that depends on the PCR values being in the correct state. During initialization, the user will select a song, background, or light flashing pattern on the keyboard that will indicate he is in secure mode. This selection is sealed to the PCR values that indicate a secure mode has been selected.

Later, when a secure mode is selected, and PCR values indicate that a boot is in a secure system, the OS can unseal the personalization data, and either play the background music, show a screen background, or flash lights on the keyboard in the way selected by the user. At this point, the user knows that the display can be trusted, so it is a secure display.

For secure commerce, it is important that a means be found for providing to the user both a secure means of authorizing a transaction (trusted path) and a secure means of knowing what transaction he is authorizing (trusted display). The Trusted Computing Group's TPM can be a component used in an overall system that enables this solution.

## Summary

It is clear that the TPM does not provide trusted path and trusted display capabilities, but it does provide facilities to create systems that do. These systems require ancillary hardware. In designing such facilities, though, it is important to be aware of privacy considerations that need to be met in order to avoid clashes with privacy groups.

# CHAPTER 16

# Moving from TSS 1.1 to TSS 1.2

For the most part, the move from 1.1 to 1.2 will be seamless. A lot of work was done in the 1.2 specification to make sure that programs written for the 1.1 stack would continue to work for the 1.2 stack. There is really only one exception. This has to do with the reading of the SRK public key. This now can be set to be possible only with the owner key, and by default this setting is selected on many implementations. Other changes to the TPM specification due to security holes were discovered early enough that the older broken functions never made it into the 1.1 TSS specification.

The biggest change going from 1.1 to 1.2 is the addition of a number of features to the TPM specification that are exposed in the 1.2 TSS specification. These features include a Certified Migratable Key (CMK), delegation, Direct Anonymous Authentication (DAA), locality, PCR-long, NVRAM, auditing functions, monotonic counter, tick counter, a SOAP interface for remote commands sent to the TCS, transport sessions, and some new administrative commands.

## Certified Migratable Keys

The CMK is a kind of key that is halfway between a non-migratable key and a migratable key. Migratable keys can be generated anywhere and, if they are migrated to an insecure key or from an insecure location, can be inherently insecure. The TPM cannot tell. Non-migratable keys are generated inside the TPM and never leave it, so they are inherently secure, but are not transportable between TPMs.

CMKs, on the other hand, are generated inside a TPM, but at the time they are generated, the creator has to pick a Migration Authority (MA) or a Migration Selection Authority (MSA), which will have the authority to migrate the key. All the normal controls on migration of a key continue to exist with a CMA—the owner of the chip must authorize MSAs and MAs with a "ticket," and the owner of the created key has to decide to migrate a key before the key is migrated. If an MA is selected at the time of key creation, that MA cannot ever be changed. If an MSA is selected at the time of key creation, that MSA cannot ever be changed, but the MSA can change the MAs that are allowed. Why do all this? A CMK can be certified by a TPM as being a CMK, and that certificate will list the MSA (or MAs) that are allowed to migrate the key. Thus, CMKs can both be migrated and also be considered secure (if you trust the MSA and MAs allowed to migrate the key).

## Commands

### Tspi_TPM_CMKSetRestrictions

**Purpose:** The CMK command is kind of dangerous in that control for migration is being given away from a user to another entity. As a result, an implied contract is being made at the time a key is created. If the MA or MSA decides later to charge an unreasonable price for the service of migrating a key, the end user has no options. As a result, the `Tspi_TPM_CMKSetRestriction-sCommand` was implemented. This command, which is one of few that cannot be delegated, allows the owner to decide which types of CMK keys a delegated authority can create on behalf of the owner.

**Usage:** `Tspi_CMKSetRestrictions ( TSS_HTPM          hTPM`
`                               TSS_CMK_DELEGATE   CmkDelegate`
`                               )`

Here `hTPM` is the handle of the TPM, and `CmkDelegate` is a bitmask, with each bit representing a type of key (storage, signing, and so on) that a delegated entity will be authorized to create on behalf of the owner.

**Returns:** `TSS_SUCCESS`   The command completed successfully.
`          TSS_E_INVALID HANDLE`      Can't find the TPM.
`          TSS_E_INTERNAL_ERROR`      The command failed.

**Context:** This command is used to allow delegated software to handle the details of using CMKs for backing up keys or for creating CMK keys in general. In so doing, the owner is allowing the delegated entity to create an implied contract with an MA or MSA.
`Tspi_TPM_CMKApproveMA`
`Tspi_TPM_CMKCreateTicket`

### Tspi_Key_CMKCreateBlob

**Purpose:** The first step after creating a CMK is probably to create the CMK blob. This is an encrypted set of data that can be used by the MA or MSA to migrate the key to a new TPM.

**Usage:** `Tspi_CMKCreateBlob ( TSS_HKEY      hKeyToMigrate`
`TSS_HKEY      hParentKey`
`TSS_HMIGDATA  hMigrationData`
`UINT32*       pRandomLength`
`BYTE**           pRandom`
`)`

Here `hKeyToMigrate` is the handle of the key being migrated, `hParentKey` is the parent of the key being migrated, and `hMigrationData` is the handle to an object in which the data is sent to the TPM and the encrypted blob is put. `pRandomLength` is a pointer to where the length of the random data (used to XOR the inside of the blob) is stored, and `pRandom` is a pointer to where the array of random bytes is stored.

**Returns:**

`TSS_SUCCESS`    The command completed successfully.

    `TSS_E_INVALID HANDLE`      Can't find the TPM.

    `TSS_E_INTERNAL_ERROR`      The command failed.

**Context:** This command is used to allow delegated software to handle the details of using CMKs for backing up keys or for creating CMK keys in general. In so doing, the owner is allowing the delegated entity to create an implied contract with an MA or MSA.

`Tspi_TPM_CMKApproveMA`
`Tspi_TPM_CMKCreateTicket`

## Tspi_Key_MigrateKey

**Purpose:** This command just re-wraps migration data so that a TPM can be used by an MA in migrating CMKs.

**Usage:** `Tspi_Key_MigrateKey ( TSS_HKey    hMaKey`
`TSS_HKey    hPublicKey`
`TSS_HMIGDATAhMigData`
`)`

Here `hMaKey` is the handle of the Migration Authority Private Key, `hPublicKey` is the public key to which the key is migrating, and `hMigData` contains the encrypted key data (doubly encrypted, once with the MA public key and once internally with the random number).

**Returns:**

`TSS_SUCCESS`    The command completed successfully.

    `TSS_E_INVALID HANDLE`      Can't find the TPM.

    `TSS_E_BAD_PARAMETER`      One of the passed parameters was wrong.

    `TSS_E_INTERNAL_ERROR`      The command failed.

**Context:** This command is used by an MA to perform migration.

## Tspi_TPM_CMKApproveMA

**Purpose:** In a way analogous to migratable keys, the owner of the TPM has to create a ticket authorizing the use of an MA before it can be used to create a CMK tied to that MA.

**Usage:** `Tspi_CMKSetRestrictions ( TSS_HTPM      hTPM`
`                                 TSS_HMIGDATA   hMaAuthData`
`                                 )`

Here `hTPM` is the handle of the TPM, and `hMaAuthData` contains the information about the MA in question.

**Returns:**

`TSS_SUCCESS`    The command completed successfully.

`     TSS_E_INVALID HANDLE`   Can't find the TPM.

`     TSS_E_INTERNAL_ERROR`   The command failed.

**Context:** This command must be used by the owner before a CMK is created. It creates a ticket necessary to authorize the target MA.

## Tspi_TPM_CMKCreateTicket

**Purpose:** This command is used to prove to a TPM that a signature over a digest was correctly created by a TPM.

**Usage:** `Tspi_CMKCreateTicket ( TSS_HTPM      hTPM`
`                               TSS_HKEY      hVerifyKey`
`                               TSS_HMIGDATA  hSigData`
`                               )`

Here `hTPM` is the handle of the TPM, and `hVerifyKey` contains the public key used to verify the signature contained in `hSigData`.

**Returns:**

`TSS_SUCCESS`    The command completed successfully.

`     TSS_E_INVALID HANDLE`   Can't find the TPM.

`     TSS_E_INTERNAL_ERROR`   The command failed.

**Context:** This command is used to verify a signature.

## Tspi_Key_CMKConvertMigration

**Purpose:** This command is the one used to install a migrated key into a new TPM.

**Usage:** `Tspi_CMKConvertMigration (` `TSS_HKEY`      `hKeyToMigrate`
                                    `TSS_HKEY`      `hParentKey`
                                    `TSS_HMIGDATA`  `hMigrationData`
                                    `UINT32`        `ulRandomLength`
                                    `BYTE*`         `rbgRandom`
                                    `)`

Here `hKey` is the handle of the key being migrated, `hParentKey` is the key it is wrapped with, `rgbRandom` is the random data needed to do the internal decryption, and `hMigrationData` is a handle to the structure in which the migration blob is input and the newly created key blob is returned. In order to be used, the keyblob has to be loaded with a normal LoadKey operation.

**Returns:**

`TSS_SUCCESS`   The command completed successfully.

`TSS_E_INVALID HANDLE`   Can't find the TPM.

`TSS_E_INTERNAL_ERROR`   The command failed.

**Context:** This command is only used after a data is given to the TSS from an MA with a particular parent key in mind. This data is then sent to the TPM, the random number input, and the TPM decrypts it externally with the parent private key and internally with the random number; the TPM then wraps the result with the parent public key and returns it in the structure that `hMigrationData` refers to.

# Delegation

In the TSS 1.1 specification, some keys and functions required knowledge of authorization data. In order to delegate use of a function or key, it was necessary to give that authorization data away. Once given away, it became difficult to remove the authorization to use those functions or keys. Authorization data could be changed, of course, but the authorization data itself was the gate to changing that data, so more authority was being given with the authorization data than just use authorization. This problem was particularly acute in the case of keys, because the blobs that contained the authorization data were stored outside the TPM, making it impossible for the TPM to be sure that all copies of the authorization data were changed. In this case, it wasn't possible to be entirely sure that even changing authorization data removed the ability for the delegatee to use the key. (The owner could migrate all non-suspect keys to a second key, change the SRK, and then migrate all non-suspect keys back to the new SRK, but this requires discarding all non-migratable keys, and is not ideal.)

Although convoluted means existed to use the 1.1 TPM to accomplish most of what the delegation function in 1.2 provides, Delegation is much more straightforward. Basically, it allows the TPM to keep track of a secondary authentication that can be used to provide authorization to use either a key or an owner-authorized function. This secondary authorization is "delegated" to either trusted software or a trusted user to provide them authorization to use a function or key. This authorization can also be revoked by the person who knows the primary authorization.

The TPM uses two internal tables to keep track of what functions/keys have been delegated, and what users have been associated with a group of delegations. The two tables are Delegation Tables and Family Tables. The Delegation Table is the easiest to understand. It contains a list of ordinals that are to be delegated, or a key that is being delegated, and the process that can use those ordinals (identified by PCR values), a new AuthData that can also be used (in addition to the owner auth) to authorize those ordinals, a delegation label, a family ID (to associate it with the user), and a verification count (used to invalidate a delegation row).

Before we can address what is in a Family Table, we need to describe what a family is. It is just a collection of delegated rows associated with a particular delegatee. It is collected so that there is a way to manage the delegation of a group of commands and keys without having to touch each one individually. So for example, I may delegate owner-authorized commands or keys to a piece of trusted software. A year later, my trusted software is found to have a security hole. I upgrade the software. I now want to delegate those same commands to the upgraded software—and delete the ability of my old software to use those commands. Or I may want to modify which commands my software has access to due to some new regulation or law that has been passed.

Another example is a group of keys that I delegate to my secretary. A year later, my secretary is changed. I now want to delete all delegations of keys to my old secretary, and re-delegate all those keys to my new secretary. By grouping the keys this way, it makes it easy to administrate them.

Another less-obvious property of delegation is that it allows you to associate particular PCR values to commands that used to be associated only to an owner—and it provides a means to associate the use of a migratable key with PCR values.

Delegated rows, like keys, can be stored either inside or outside the TPM. Enough room is required in a TPM to store at least two of them inside the TPM, for storage constrained situations. A new command has been created specifically to store (and evict) a row in non-volatile space.

In order to create a delegated row, one first creates a family row, so that one will have a familyID necessary for the creation of the delegated row. Delegated rows are similar to normal users in a Linux system, and the owner of the TPM or owner of a key are like super-users—able to add or delete users to a command or key, under limited circumstances.

A typical life cycle of delegation use would be as follows:

1. Create a family row (user).

   ```
   AddFamily
   GetFamily
   ```

2. Create a delegation of TPM owner-authorized commands to the user.

   ```
   CreateDelegation
   ```

3. Create a delegation of keys to the user.

   `CreateDelegation`

4. Cache one or more of those delegations into the TPM.

   `CacheOwnerDelegation`

5. Read out what delegations are stored in the TPM.

   `ReadTables`

6. Invalidate a delegation (by incrementing `VerificationCount`).

   `CreateDelegation` (with `ulFlags = incrementVerification`)

7. Reauthorize delegations killed by the invalidation of a particular delegation belonging to same user.

   `UpdateVerificationCount`

8. Invalidate a family (user).

   `InvalidateFamily`

## Tspi_TPM_Delegate_AddFamily

**Purpose:** This command is used to add a new row to the Family Table inside the TPM.

**Usage:** `Tspi_CMKCreateTicket ( TSS_HTPM          hTPM`
`                        BYTE             bLabel`
`                        TSS_HDELFAMILY*  phFamily`
`                        )`

Here `hTPM` is the handle of the TPM, and bLabel contains a label to be used by software to determine which family is being referred to. You can consider the `bLabel` to be the delegated user name, but software has to translate the user name into the correct BYTE. For ease of use, you may want the `bLabel` to be simply the first byte of the hash of the `user_name`.

**Returns:**

`TSS_SUCCESS`          The command completed successfully.

`TSS_E_INVALID HANDLE`   Can't find the TPM.

`TSS_E_INTERNAL_ERROR`   The command failed.

**Context:** This command should be run before you delegate a group of commands or a key to a user, so that you have a user to delegate them to.

## Tspi_TPM_Delegate_GetFamily

**Purpose:** This command is used to get a handle to a previously created row of the Family Table.

**Usage:** Tspi_TPM_Delegate_GetFamily ( TSS_HTPM          hTPM
                                         BYTE              ulFamilyID
                                         TSS_HDELFAMILY*   phFamily
                                         )

      Here hTPM is the handle of the TPM, and ulFamilyID contains a label to be used by software to determine which user is being referred to. phFamily returns a pointer to the handle of the family row.

**Returns:**

TSS_SUCCESS     The command completed successfully.

    TSS_E_INVALID HANDLE    Can't find the TPM.

    TSS_E_INTERNAL_ERROR    The command failed.

**Context**: This command is used for management of a group of delegation rows that all belong to the same user.

## Tspi_TPM_Delegate_InvalidateFamily

**Purpose:** This command is used to invalidate all delegations made to a particular user.

**Usage:** Tspi_DelegateInvalidateFamily( TSS_HTPM   hTPM
                                          TSS_HDELFAMILY   hFamily
                                          )

      Here hTPM is the handle of the TPM, and hFamily is the handle of the family member (user or trusted software) that is being invalidated.

**Returns:**

TSS_SUCCESS           The command completed successfully.

    TSS_E_INVALID HANDLE    Can't find the TPM.

    TSS_E_INTERNAL_ERROR    The command failed.

**Context:** In order to find out the hFamily to use, use the Tspi_TPM_Delegate_GetFamily command.

## Tspi_TPM_Delegate_CreateDelegation

**Purpose:** This command is used to create a new delegation made to a particular user or to invalidate all old delegations made to a user (by using `IncrementVerification` for the `ulFlags` parameter).

**Usage:** `Tspi_Delegate_CreateDelegation (TSS_HOBJECT    hObject`
`                                    BYTE           bLabel`
`                                    UINT32         ulFlags`
`                                    TSS_HPCRS      hPcr`
`                                    TSS_HDELFAMILY hFamily`
`                                    TSS_HPOLICY    hDelegation`
`                                    )`

Here `hObject` tells the story of what is being delegated. If `hObject` contains the TPM handle (`hTPM`) with an owner authorization policy attached, then this will delegate owner authorization. If it contains the handle of a key (`hKey`) along with a key use authorization policy, then a key is being delegated. `bLabel` is the BYTE that is used to determine the user to which the owner authorization or key is being delegated. `UlFlags` is NULL if a new delegation is happening and `IncrementVerification` if the command is being used to revoke all delegations made to a user. `hPcr` is a handle to a structure that defines what PCRs with which values are going to being delegated to, `hFamily` is the handle of the family member (user or trusted software), and `hDelegation` is an existing policy, in which the delegated authorization is stored.

**Returns:**

| | |
|---|---|
| `TSS_SUCCESS` | The command completed successfully. |
| `TSS_E_INVALID HANDLE` | Can't find the TPM. |
| `TSS_E_BAD_PARAMETER` | One of the parameters does not meet the requirements. |
| `TSS_E_INTERNAL_ERROR` | The command failed. |

**Context:** In order to use this function, one must first establish at least one family member (user) who is going to be the recipient of the delegation.

## Tspi_TPM_Delegate_CacheOwnerDelegation

**Purpose:** This command is used to store a particular delegation in NVRAM in the TPM. Each 1.2 TPM has to have room for at least two delegations stored internally (although more are allowed).

**Usage:** `Tspi_Delegate_CacheOwnerDelegation` (`TSS_HTPM      hTPM`
`TSS_HPOLICY   hDelegation`
`UINT32        ulIndex`
`UINT32        ulFlags`
`)`

Here `hTPM` of course refers to the TPM in which the delegation is to be stored. `HDelegation` is the delegation to be stored, `ulIndex` is the location in which it is to be stored, and `ulFlags` currently can only have a value of `OverwriteExisting`.

**Returns:**

`TSS_SUCCESS`          The command completed successfully.

`TSS_E_INVALID HANDLE`      Can't find the TPM.

`TSS_E_BAD_PARAMETER`       One of the parameters does not meet the requirements.

`TSS_E_NV_AREA_EXIST`       Index doesn't exist in this TPM.

`TSS_E_INTERNAL_ERROR`      The command failed.

**Context:** In order to use this function, one must first establish a delegation and find out how many indices one's TPM can store. It is also wise to read the Delegation Table and find out if you are about to overwrite an existing delegation.

## Tspi_TPM_Delegate_UpdateVerificationCount

**Purpose:** When a delegation is being revoked, an internal counter (called the verification counter) in the TPM is incremented, to make sure that an old delegation stored outside the TPM is no longer allowed to function. However, this means that *no* delegation outside the TPM can function any longer. The solution is to use this command to update the verification counter for delegation blobs. It needs to be done to all the blobs in a family if any are to survive one of them being deleted.

**Usage:** `Tspi_Delegate_UpdateVerificationCount` ( `TSS_HTPM      hTPM`
`TSS_HPOLICY   hDelegation`
`)`

Here `hTPM` is the TPM whose verification count has been incremented, and `hDelegation` is the delegation that needs to be re-set to the current verification counter of the TPM.

**Returns:**

`TSS_SUCCESS`          The command completed successfully.

`TSS_E_INVALID HANDLE`      Can't find the TPM.

`TSS_E_BAD_PARAMETER`       One of the parameters does not meet the requirements.

`TSS_E_INTERNAL_ERROR`      The command failed.

**Context:** This command is typically used after a delegation has been revoked, to keep other delegations from the same family authorized.

## Tspi_TPM_Delegate_VerifyDelegation

**Purpose:** This command is used to check if a delegation is currently active.

**Usage:** `Tspi_Delegate_VerifyDelegation (`

```
                              TSS_HPOLICY      hDelegation
                              )
```

Here `hDelegation` is an existing policy, and this command checks to see if it is currently active.

### Returns:

| | |
|---|---|
| `TSS_SUCCESS` | The command completed successfully. |
| `TSS_E_INVALID HANDLE` | Can't find the TPM. |
| `TSS_E_BAD_PARAMETER` | One of the parameters does not meet the requirements. |
| `TSS_E_INTERNAL_ERROR` | The command failed. |

**Context:** One, of course, has to have created a delegation to use this command.

## Tspi_TPM_Delegate_ReadTables

**Purpose:** This command is used to find out what delegations (and families) currently are stored on TPM. It does not (of course) reveal any private information of those delegations.

**Usage:** `Tspi_Delegate_CreateDelegation (`

```
                    TSS_HCONTEXT          hContext
                    UINT32*               pulFamilyTableSize
                    TSS_KM_KEYINFO**      ppFamilyTable
                    UINT32*               pulDelegateTableSize
                    TSS_KM_KEYINFO**      ppDelegateTable
                    )
```

Here `hContext` is the context set up with the TPM, and the `ppFamilyTable` and `ppDelegateTable` receive the information from the TPM.

**Returns:**

| | |
|---|---|
| TSS_SUCCESS | The command completed successfully. |
| TSS_E_INVALID HANDLE | Can't find the TPM. |
| TSS_E_BAD_PARAMETER | One of the parameters does not meet the requirements. |
| TSS_E_INTERNAL_ERROR | The command failed. |

**Context**: This command can be executed by anyone.

## Direct Anonymous Attestation

In the original 1.1 TPM, a lot of work was put into designing a system that would allow the owner of a TPM, together with a Certificate Authority (CA), to provide certificates to keys that could be proven to be non-migratable TPM keys, but which did not weaken privacy protections. The successful design incorporated the EK (Endorsement Key). However, for the protocol to work, it was necessary that there be CAs available. No CAs have shown up yet (probably due to a dearth of EK credentials—without which there are no privacy threats), so there was some skepticism voiced in the privacy community about the efficacy of the solution.

The solution to this problem was a new protocol built into the TPM based on research into group signatures. A group signature provides a means for a group of people to all have the ability to sign things as "members of the group" without having a global secret susceptible to a Break Once Run Everywhere (BORE) attack, and without allowing members of the group to tell which one of them signed a particular hash. Nevertheless, in spite of having these properties, if the individual secret used by a particular member of the group is revealed, it is possible to invalidate it without revealing or invalidating the secrets of the other members of the group. It is quite a trick mathematically.

The solution embedded into the TPM 1.2 is known as DAA, or Direct Anonymous Authentication. It provides a means for AIKs to be certified as being a member of the group of TPM AIKs, without requiring each AIK be individually certified by a CA. Instead, a DAA authority, one time, authenticates some TPM secrets as belonging to a TPM that is authentic. This authentication can be done before the TPM is shipped out to its final owner, though it need not be. Authentication in the field can be based on the EK and its certificate.

There are a number of things that should be noted about DAA. It is a very complicated protocol, based on group signatures. There are not, at the time of this writing, any DAA authorities that exist, to provide the DAA certificate necessary to run the protocol. It is only useful in the limited case that a remote end user with no direct access to the TPM wants to verify that it is talking to a genuine TPM, and the owner of the TPM wants to protect all information that might be used to identify him.

In the case of a business that is managing TPMs of systems owned by the business, it is not important to use DAA at all—the EK mechanism is perfectly fine, with the business acting the part of the third-party verifier. It is difficult to imagine how DAA (at least by itself) could provide the means to purchase something anonymously online. After all, money has to travel from the purchaser to the store. And if what is being bought is tangible, it has to travel from the store to the purchaser.

One might imagine that DAA would be used some time in the future to provide some sort of DRM management where a key is stored in the TPM to enable use of software or media, but as we have already pointed out, on a PC, a TPM does not provide ideal help for such things—clearly other special-purpose hardware would be used by such a solution. And if that is being done, there are much easier ways to enforce DRM.

The best scenario we can think of to illustrate the functions of DAA would be in providing a way to do anonymous Internet voting. First, one proves to a DAA authority that one is a member of the group eligible to vote. This amounts to "joining" the group. After this is done, a certificate is given to the owner of the TPM, which enables his TPM to vote. Next one signs one's vote using the DAA protocol, for each vote that is presented.

Votes are tallied, and though it is clear that no one voted more than once, and only eligible voters voted, no one can tell how anyone voted. If all the votes that were counted are displayed, it is possible for everyone to tell that their own vote was counted as well.

Revocation of a particular voter is difficult, however (unless their TPM has been disassembled and the keys become public on the web), and probably entails every member of the group who remains eligible re-joining the group.

Because these functions are not available in a 1.1 TPM or TSS, the first thing a programmer needs to know before using any of these functions is what level TPM and TSS stack he is talking to. This is done easily using the `GetCapability` command.

The basic life cycle of a DAA certificate goes like this:

**Get a DAA certificate, proving your TPM belongs to the group of TPMs.**

- DAA authority: Start the protocol.
  - `IssueSetup` (sets up the DAA authority's public and private key)—usually done once
  - `IssueInit` (Start the process of providing a certificate)
- TCG application: Check the pub key of the DAA authority; compute the TPM DAA pub key.
  - `JoinInit`
- TCG application: Create messages back to the DAA authority providing information to the certification.
  - `JoinCreateDaaPubKey`
- DAA authority: Issue a credential to the TPM.
  - `IssueCredential`
- TCG application: Finish up the creation of the DAA credential.
  - `JoinStoreCredential`

**Use an existing DAA certificate/key to sign a message (for example, a vote).**

- TCG application
  - Sign a message
  - Message recipient
- IssuerKeyVerification
  - VerifyInit
  - VerifySignature

**Revoke a DAA certificate.**

- DAA issuer
  - RevokeSetup

## Tspi_TPM_DAA_JoinInit

**Purpose:** This command is used in the protocol that establishes a DAA Credential.

**Usage:** Tspi_TPM_DAA_JoinInit (TSS_HDAA        hDAA
                                TSS_HTPM         hTPM
                                UINT32           daaCounter
                                TSS_HKEY         issuerPk
                                UINT32           issuerAuthPKsLength
                                TSS_HKEY*        issuerAuthPKs
                                UINT32           issuerAuthPK
                                                   SignaturesLength
                                BYTE**           issuerAuthPKSignatures
                                UINT32*          capitalUprimeLength
                                BYTE**           capitalUprime
                                TSS_DAA_IDENTITY_  identityProof
                                  PROOF*
                                TSS_DAA_JOIN_    joinSession
                                  SESSION*
                                )

Here hDAA is the handle of the DAA object, hTPM is the handle of the PTM, daaCounter is the daaCounter, issuerAuthPK is the public key of the DAA certificate issuer, issuerAuthPKSignatures is the signature of the authorizer, captialUprime is an intermediate variable, identityProof contains the endorsement, platform, and conformance credential, and joinSession contains some session information.

**Returns:**

TSS_SUCCESS            The command completed successfully.

    TSS_E_INVALID HANDLE    Can't find the TPM.

    TSS_E_BAD_PARAMETER     One of the parameters does not meet the requirements.

    TSS_E_INTERNAL_ERROR    The command failed.

**Context:** This is used as the first of three commands that are needed to establish a DAA credential for a TPM.

## Tspi_TPM_DAA_JoinCreateDaaPubKey

**Purpose:** This command is used to create a Daa key.

**Usage:** Tspi_TPM_DAA_JoinCreateDaaPubKey (

| | |
|---|---|
| TSS_HDAA | hDAA |
| TSS_HTPM | hTPM |
| UINT32 | authenticationChallengeLength |
| BYTE* | authenticationChallenge |
| UINT32 | nonceIssuerLength |
| BYTE* | nonceIssuer |
| UINT32 | attributesPlatformLength |
| BYTE** | attributesPlatform |
| TSS_DAA_JOIN_SESSION* | joinSession |
| TSS_DAA_CREDENTIAL_ REQUEST* | credentialRequest |

)

Here hDAA is the DAA object handle, hTPM is the TPM handle, the authentication Challenge is the second nonce the issuer sends (encrypted with the EK pub), nonceIssuer is the nonce of the DAA issuer, attributesPlatform are the attributes of the platform requesting a DAA certificate, joinSession is information of the current joining session, and credentialRequest is where the blinded DAA pub key goes for the platform for which the cert is being issued.

**Returns:**

TSS_SUCCESS            The command completed successfully.

    TSS_E_INVALID HANDLE    Can't find the TPM.

    TSS_E_BAD_PARAMETER     One of the parameters does not meet the requirements.

    TSS_E_INTERNAL_ERROR    The command failed.

**Context:** This is used as the second of the three commands to establish a DAA certificate.

## Tspi_TPM_DAA_JoinStoreCredential

**Purpose:** The last step in getting a DAA credential.

**Usage:** `Tspi_TPM_DAA_JoinStoreCredential (`

| | |
|---|---|
| `TSS_HDAA` | `hDAA` |
| `TSS_HTPM` | `hTPM` |
| `TSS_DAA_CRED_ISSUER` | `credIssuer` |
| `TSS_DAA_JOIN_SESSION` | `joinSession` |
| `TSS_HKEY*` | `hDaaCredential` |

`)`

Here `hDAA` is the handle of the DAA object, `hTPM` the handle of the TPM, and `credIssuer` is the credential issued, including its proof of correctness. `JoinSession` contains session information and `hDaaCredential` is the handle to the DAA credential.

**Returns:**

`TSS_SUCCESS`    The command completed successfully.

| | |
|---|---|
| `TSS_E_INVALID HANDLE` | Can't find the TPM. |
| `TSS_E_BAD_PARAMETER` | One of the parameters does not meet the requirements. |
| `TSS_E_INTERNAL_ERROR` | The command failed. |

**Context:** This is the last step in getting a DAA credential. The first are: `Tspi_DAA_JoinInit` and `Tspi_DAA_JoinCreateDaaPubKey`.

## Tspi_TPM_DAA_Sign

**Purpose:** This command is used to sign a message with a DAA key.

**Usage:** `Tspi_TPM_DAA_Sign  (`

`)`

**Returns:**

`TSS_SUCCESS`    The command completed successfully.

| | |
|---|---|
| `TSS_E_INVALID HANDLE` | Can't find the TPM. |
| `TSS_E_BAD_PARAMETER` | One of the parameters does not meet the requirements. |
| `TSS_E_INTERNAL_ERROR` | The command failed. |

**Context:** This is the command used to prove to prove ownership of a DAA credential, and which also allows that proof to be joined to a message via a signature. It cannot be used until a credential exists.

## Tspi_TPM_DAA_IssuerKeyVerification

**Purpose:** This command is used to create new delegations made to a particular user.

**Usage:** `Tspi_TPM_DAA_IssuerKeyVerification (`
     `)`

### Returns:

`TSS_SUCCESS`     The command completed successfully.

| `TSS_E_INVALID HANDLE` | Can't find the TPM. |
| `TSS_E_BAD_PARAMETER` | One of the parameters does not meet the requirements. |
| `TSS_E_INTERNAL_ERROR` | The command failed. |

**Context:** This command is used to verify that a DAA credential of a public key is correct. It is used by the recipient of a `DAA_signed` message.

## Tspi_DAA_IssueSetup

**Purpose:** This command is used by a DAA authority (certificate issuer) to create their public/private key pair, so that they are ready to become a DAA authority. It also creates a proof that the public keys were correctly chosen. It is interesting that this type of signature allows the platform to choose attributes (such as age, address, and marital status) that are not visible to the DAA issuer, but which can be made visible during a signature at the will of the signer.

**Usage:** `Tspi_TPM_DAA_IssueSetup ( TSS_HDAA        hDAA`
                    `UINT32          issuerBaseNameLength`
                    `BYTE*           issuerBaseName`
                    `UINT32          numberPlatformAttributes`
                    `UINT32          numberIssuerAttributes`
                    `TSS_HKEY*       keyPair`
                    `TSS_DAA_PK_     publicKeyProof`
                     `PROOF*`
                    `)`

Here `hDAA` is the handle to a DAA object, and `issuerBaseName` is, of course, the name of the DAA issuer. The next two parameters represent the number of attributes the platform can choose that will not be visible to the issuer, and the number of attributes that will be visible to both the platform and the issuer. The last parameter is the proof that the public keys were correctly selected.

**Returns:**

TSS_SUCCESS    The command completed successfully.

      TSS_E_INVALID HANDLECan't find the TPM.

      TSS_E_BAD_PARAMETER  One of the parameters does not meet the requirements.

      TSS_E_INTERNAL_ERRORThe command failed.

## Tspi_DAA_IssueInit

**Purpose:** When a DAA authority is set up, it can then start issuing certificates. It is a two-command process, as far as the DAA authority is concerned, and this is the first of the two commands he uses. Before he issues this command, he should check credentials that verify that the platform he is about to issue a certificate for are genuine. These could be EK credentials, or physical presence, or on a manufacturing line.

**Usage:** Tspi_TPM_DAA_IssueInit ( TSS_HDAA            hDAA
                                             TSS_HKEY            issuerAuthPK
                                           TSS_HKEY            issuerKeyPair
                                           TSS_DAA_IDENTITY_   identityProof
                                             PROOF
                                           UINT32              capitalUPrimeLength
                                           UINT32*             nonceIssuerLength
                                           BYTE**              nonceIssuer
                                           UINT32*             authentication
                                           ChallengeLength
                                           TSS_DAAA_JOIN_
                                           ISSUER_SESSION*     joinSession
                                           )

      hDAA is, of course, the DAA object. The issuerAuthPK is a public/private key pair of the DAA issuer, and issuerKeyPair comes from IssueSetup; so does the identityProof. The remaining variables are used in the protocol by sending them to the TSS application on the requesting platform, where they will be processed and then results returned to the DAA authority, which will use the result to perform the IssueCredential command.

**Returns:**

TSS_SUCCESS    The command completed successfully.

      TSS_E_INVALID HANDLE     The DAA handle is invalid.

      TSS_E_BAD_PARAMETER      One of the parameters does not meet the requirements.

      TSS_E_INTERNAL_ERROR     The command failed.

**Context:** This is the first of two commands the DAA authority performs to create a certificate for a TPM platform.

## Tspi_TPM_DAA_VerifyInit

**Purpose:** This command is used by the *receiver* of a DAA signed message. It is the first of a two-part command, as it creates a challenge (nonce) for the TPM to use to prove it is a correctly signed DAA message.

**Usage:**
```
Tspi_TPM_DAA_VerifyInit ( TSS_HDAA      hDAA
                          UINT32*       nonceVerifierLength
                          BYTE**        nonceVerifier
                        )
```

**Returns:**

`TSS_SUCCESS`   The command completed successfully.

| | |
|---|---|
| `TSS_E_INVALID HANDLE` | Incorrect DAA object handle. |
| `TSS_E_BAD_PARAMETER` | One of the parameters does not meet the requirements. |
| `TSS_E_INTERNAL_ERROR` | The command failed. |

**Context:** This is the first command used by the recipient of a DAA signature to verify it.

## Tspi_TPM_DAA_VerifySignature

**Purpose:** This command is the second (and final) command used by the *recipient* of a DAA signed message to verify a DAA signature.

**Usage:**
```
Tspi_TPM_DAA_VerifySignature (
                    TSS_HDAA            hDAA
                    TSS_DAA_SIGNATURE   daaSignature
                    TSS_HKEY            hPubKeyIssuer
                    UINT32              attributesLength
                    BYTE**              attributes
                    UINT32*             nonceVerifier
                                        Length
                    BYTE**              nonceVerifier
                    UINT32*             baseNameLength
                    BYTE**              baseName
                    TSS_BOOL*           isCorrect
                  )
```

hDDA is the handle of the DAA object, `daaSignature` is the `daaSignature` (returned from the TPM), hPubKeyIssuer is the handle of the public key of the DAA authority, attributes refers to the attributes exposed in the signature, `nonceVerifier` is the random challenge number produced by the recipient with the `VerifyInit` command, and baseName is the name that was chosen for the signature. Of course, `isCorrect` returns whether or not the signature verified correctly.

**Returns:**
`TSS_SUCCESS`    The command completed successfully.

      `TSS_E_INVALID HANDLE`    Can't find the TPM.

      `TSS_E_BAD_PARAMETER`    One of the parameters does not meet the requirements.

      `TSS_E_INTERNAL_ERROR`    The command failed.

**Context:** This is the second command used by the recipient of a DAA signature to verify it.

## Tspi_TPM_DAA_RevokeSetup

**Purpose:** This command is used by the DAA authority to revoke a DAA certificate if the base secrets (which are supposed to be held securely in a TPM) become known. This could happen if a chip were delayered, for example.

**Usage:** `Tspi_TPM_DAA_RevokeSetup ( TSS_HDAA     hDAA`
                                   `TSS_HKEY     daaPublicKey`
                                   `TSS_HKEY*    keyPair`
                                   `)`

**Returns:**
`TSS_SUCCESS`    The command completed successfully.

      `TSS_E_INVALID HANDLE`    Can't find the TPM.

      `TSS_E_BAD_PARAMETER`    One of the parameters does not meet the requirements.

      `TSS_E_INTERNAL_ERROR`    The command failed.

**Context:** This is used to revoke a DAA certificate if the private keys that are supposed to be held securely in the TPM become exposed. It returns a public/private key, which can be used to show a key has been revoked.

## Tspi_TPM_DAA_ARDecrypt

**Purpose:** This command is used to create new delegations made to a particular user.

**Usage:** `Tspi_TPM_DAA_ARDecrypt (`
                                   `)`

**Returns:**

`TSS_SUCCESS`   The command completed successfully.

`TSS_E_INVALID HANDLE`   Can't find the TPM,

`TSS_E_BAD_PARAMETER`   One of the parameters does not meet the requirements,

`TSS_E_INTERNAL_ERROR`   The command failed.

**Context:** This is used to revoke a DAA certificate if the private keys inside it have been compromised and become known (for example, by publishing them on the Internet).

## Locality

Locality is a new authorization mechanism in the TPM. In 1.1, the TPM could be authorized to perform a function based on an HMAC or based on PCRs being in a particular state. In 1.2, an additional function, called locality, can be used. There are six locality states: none, 0, 1, 2, 3, and 4. Locality is a state of the TPM that is based on special signals sent to the TPM. Locality is so called because the locality setting is supposed to be used to represent where a command is coming from. If a command is coming from a location that is trusted (for example, a special processor executing ROM code), then that command can be trusted in how it performs. In that case, the command may be running at locality 4. As the number increases in locality, so does the trust—so a process running in locality 4 is trusted more than a process running in locality 3, and so forth.

If the command, on the other hand, is running from Windows 95, it will run in either locality none or 0. "None" differs from 0 only in the bus used to talk with the chip, so that is irrelevant to software.

At key creation, or at sealing time, data or keys now can be "locked" to HMACs, PCR values, and/or locality.

Additional authentication techniques will likely be added in future revisions of the TPM.

Locality itself does not have any particular commands, but rather is a status that is maintained within the TPM. However, it is a property of the PCRlong structure.

## PCRs—New Behavior

As discussed earlier in the book, when data is sealed to a set of PCRs, the value of those PCRs at time of sealing is also recorded, and can be read out and verified at time of unsealing. However, the PCRs recorded were not independent of the PCRs used for unlocking the data. A new structure was put together, called PCRlong, which includes both the locality and two separate PCR structures: one for the historical data and one for the release data. Older commands were "overloaded" so that the TPM could receive either the older PCR data or the newer PCRlong data, and a 1.2 TPM will notice which is being input and do the appropriate thing with it. Older 1.1 TPMs will, of course, not be able to handle the data and will return an error.

Additionally some PCRs are given some new functionality, which is a bit complicated. Some PCRs can be reset! (In particular, PCR 16 can be generally reset to be all 0's.)

Some PCRs can be reset only by certain localities (for example, PCR 17 and 18 can only be reset by locality 4) and when reset, they are reset to all F's rather than all 0's.

The PCRlong structure is used in a number of existing commands, but also appears in some new commands: For the most part, differences in commands are hidden in the TCS layer.

**Commands:**

```
Tspi_Context_GetRegisteredKeysByUUID2
Tspi_TPM_PcrReset
Tspi_Data_SealX
Tspi_TPM_Quote2
Tspi_PcrComposite_SetPcrLocality
Tspi_PcrComposite_GetPcrLocality
Tspi_PcrComposite_GetCompositeHash
Tspi_PcrComposite_SelectPcrIndexEx
```

## NVRAM

In the 1.1 specification, the TPM had only 20 bytes of data that could be used to store things (in the DIR register). This space was not large enough to be considered useful for most purposes. Additionally, there were problems with the idea of a certificate for the EK—most PC OEMs had no place to put such a beast. If it were located on the hard drive, it would be easily lost, especially as many customers wipe the hard disk as soon as they get a new system and then put their own preload on it.

As a result of these considerations, the TPM was given its own variable-sized NVRAM (variable according to the TPM manufacturer), and special location handles were set aside to hold a certificate, if one were present, and other specific data.

The NVRAM was not merely stock NVRAM, though. When a region of the NVRAM was selected, locks were established separately into read locks and write locks. Then either HMAC or PCR authentication could be used to unlock those. Strangely enough, locality is not a selectable authentication, but it is possible to additionally select those areas of NVRAM to be either readable or writeable only once per power on. Another useful property is that GPIOs of the chip can be selected to be on or off by writing a 1 or a 0 into specified reserved location handles of NVRAM.

Reserved NVRAM indices are

```
TPM_NV_INDEX_GPIO_xx              0x00011600
PC Client GPIO_Express_00         00
PC Client reserved                01-7F
PC Client VendorSpecified         80-FF
PC Client GPIO_Express_00_bit     0x01
```

## Commands

### Tspi_NV_DefineSpace

**Purpose:** This command sets aside a section of the NVRAM space to be used with a specific set of authorization values. The PCRs for read and write are set with this command directly. In order to set the authorization data to be used for read and write (should it be required), a policy object is used. The permissions needed are set with flags in the NV Storage object before using this command.

**Usage:** `Tspi_TPM_NV_DefineSpace ( TSS_HNVSTORE    hNVStore`
`                               TSS_HPCRS       hReadPcrComposite`
`                               TSS_HPCRS       hWritePcrComposite`
`                               )`

Here `hNVStore` is the handle of the NV storage object. You must set it up to have the correct values to make this object be set as "write once per boot" and "read once per boot."

**Returns:**

`TSS_SUCCESS`    The command completed successfully.

`TSS_E_INVALID HANDLE`    Can't find the TPM.

`TSS_E_BAD_PARAMETER`    One of the parameters does not meet the requirements.

`TSS_E_INTERNAL_ERROR`    The command failed.

**Context:** First, an NV storage object is created, and its permissions set. Then a policy object is created and associated with the NV storage object (if authorization data is needed for the object). Then this command is used, with PCR values set for read and write authorization, if they are selected in the policy object.

### Tspi_NV_ReleaseSpace

**Purpose:** This command reverses the `DefineSpace`, zeroing and releasing the space back to general usage.

**Usage:** `Tspi_TPM_NV_ReleaseSpace ( TSS_HNVSTORE   hNVStore`
`                                  )`

Here `hNVStore` is the handle of the NV storage object to be released.

**Returns:**

TSS_SUCCESS    The command completed successfully.

      TSS_E_INVALID HANDLE    Can't find the TPM.

      TSS_E_BAD_PARAMETER    One of the parameters does not meet the requirements.

      TSS_E_INTERNAL_ERROR    The command failed.

**Context:** You must have a handle to an NV storage object already assigned in order to release it.

## Tspi_NV_WriteValue

**Purpose:** This command fills in the values in an NV storage object inside the TPM.

**Usage:** Tspi_TPM_NV_WriteValue ( TSS_HNVSTORE      hNVStore
                                    UINT32            offset
                                    UINT32            ulDataLength
                                    BYTE*             rgbDataToWrite
                                    )

Here hNVStore is the handle of the NV storage object. The variable offset tells where to begin writing inside the storage object, DataToWrite is the data to write there, and ulDataLength is the length of that data.

**Returns:**

TSS_SUCCESS    The command completed successfully.

      TSS_E_INVALID HANDLE    Can't find the TPM.

      TSS_E_BAD_PARAMETER    One of the parameters does not meet the requirements.

      TSS_E_INTERNAL_ERROR    The command failed.

**Context:** You must have already used the DefineSpace command to use this.

## Tspi_NV_ReadValue

**Purpose:** This command reads the data stored in an NV storage object.

**Usage:** Tspi_TPM_NV_DefineSpace ( TSS_HNVSTORE      hNVStore
                                    UINT32            offset
                                    UINT32*           pulDataLength
                                    BYTE**            prgbDataRead
                                    )

Here hNVStore is the handle of the NV storage object. The variable offset tells where to begin reading. A pointer to the length of the data to read is ulDataLength, and prgDataToRead tells the TSS where to dump the data read.

**Returns:**

TSS_SUCCESS    The command completed successfully.

TSS_E_INVALID HANDLE    Can't find the TPM

TSS_E_BAD_PARAMETER    One of the parameters does not meet the requirements.

TSS_E_INTERNAL_ERROR    The command failed.

**Context:** You must have written some data in the NV storage object before it makes sense to use this command.

# Auditing Functions

The owner of a TPM ought to be able to tell how that TPM has been used. This is a basic property of security, since well before the rainbow series of books. In order to determine that a TPM has not been misused, it is necessary first to determine how it has been used. The 1.1 TPM had audit functions built in, but they were easily bypassed, and hence were not exposed by the 1.1 TSS. In the 1.2 TPM, those functions were completely replaced with a new set that has utility. Be warned, though, that the audit functions are not required in the PC-specific specification, so it is likely they will only exist on server TPMs.

The audit functions allow a TPM owner to select which TPM functions will be audited. It then keeps a running hash internal to the TPM of those functions (which are to be audited), to be used to validate the external history kept of the TPM functions. The monotonic counter (see the next section) is incremented every time the machine boots, and the audit function then uses that command to write out the data kept in the internal hash to make sure that an unbreakable chain of audit logs is kept.

## Tspi_TPM_SetOrdinalAuditStatus

**Purpose:** This command is used to define exactly which ordinals will be audited. The command itself is audited by default. Once set, any use of the command ordinal will be elected in the audit log.

**Usage:** Tspi_TPM_NV_DefineSpace ( TSS_HTPM          hTPM
                                     TSS_COMMAND_CODE  ordinalToAudit
                                     TSS_BOOL          auditStatus
                                     )

Here hTPM is the TPM handle, and ordinalToAudit is the ordinal whose audit status is being changed. The auditStatus will either be TRUE (to be audited) or FALSE (not to be audited).

**Returns:**

TSS_SUCCESS    The command completed successfully.

       TSS_E_INVALID HANDLE    Can't find the TPM.

       TSS_E_BAD_PARAMETER    One of the parameters does not meet the requirements.

       TSS_E_INTERNAL_ERROR    The command failed.

**Context:** This is used to select ordinals that should be audited.

## Tspi_TPM_GetAuditDigest

**Purpose:** This command gets an AIK signed audit log, along with necessary data to determine if it is correct. Audit is not required in the PC-specific specification, but will likely be required in the server specification.

**Usage:** Tspi_TPM_NV_DefineSpace ( TSS_HTPM            hTPM
                                              TSS_HKEY            hAIK
                                              TSS_BOOL            closeAudit
                                              TPM_DIGEST*         pAuditDigest
                                              TPM_COUNTER_VALUE*  pCounterValue
                                              TSS_VALIDATION      pValidationData
                                              UINT32*             ordSize
                                              UINT32**            ordList
                                              )

Here hTPM is the handle of the TPM, hAIK is the handle of the AIK that is to be used to sign the TPM information necessary to validate the audit log, TSS_BOOL is a means to close an audit session when it is read, the pCounterValue and pValidationData are used to validate the audit log, and the ordList is the list of ordinals being audited.

**Returns:**

TSS_SUCCESS    The command completed successfully.

       TSS_E_INVALID HANDLE    Can't find the TPM.

       TSS_E_BAD_PARAMETER    One of the parameters does not meet the requirements.

       TSS_E_INTERNAL_ERROR    The command failed.

**Context:** This command is used after a set of ordinals have been set to be audited, and then later it is checked. An example use would be if this set of commands was used to audit creation of a signing key followed by use of that signing key.

# Monotonic Counter

Another addition to the TPM was the monotonic counter. This counter has the property that it only increments in a step size of 1, and it will only increase—it can never be reset to zero. Obviously such a design is not entirely possible—either the counter will eventually "roll over" or it will stop incrementing. The design was set to make sure that the counter would not roll over for at least seven years, even if it were subject to a denial-of-service attack. This is achieved by throttling the speed at which the counter can be incremented. How much throttling is necessary is up to the TPM manufacturer, who presumably knows the capability of his process.

The monotonic counter was necessary to allow for auditing functions to work. Auditing functions are used by the owner of the TPM to determine exactly how it has been used. They also provide guarantees to the owner of a key that the key has not been used without permission.

Actually, there are four monotonic counters in the TPM. It is assumed that this provides the ability for four separate operating systems to each use their own monotonic counter. The counter that is in use is fixed at boot time—one cannot change between counters after the boot sequence. When a new counter is instantiated, it always starts at a value that is at least 1 more than the highest extant counter.

## Tspi_TPM_ReadCurrentCounter

**Purpose:** This command is used to read the current value of the currently chosen counter. There are no TSP layer commands to increment the counter or create new counters. This is because if two different applications were each to increment the counter without communicating, the counter would lose its "monotonic" character.

**Usage:** Tspi_TPM_ReadCurrentCounter ( TSS_HTPM     hTPM

　　　　　　　　　　　　　　　　　UINT32*     counterValue

　　　　　　　　　　　　　　　　　)

Here hTPM is the handle of the TPM and counterValue is the value of the currently selected counter.

**Returns:**

TSS_SUCCESS     The command completed successfully.

　　　　TSS_E_INVALID HANDLE     Can't find the TPM.

　　　　TSS_E_BAD_PARAMETER     The counterValue passed is invalid.

　　　　TSS_E_INTERNAL_ERROR     The command failed.

**Context:** It is probably the case that this command will only be used by the operating system, which will then provide a virtualized counter available to the applications.

## Tick Counter

A secure clock was still considered too expensive for a TPM during the 1.2 TPM time frame. Additional problems occur with a secure clock, including battery lifetime, voltage drift, and inaccuracies due to temperature variations. However, the function itself is useful, so a subset of the secure clock was added into the TPM. This is the tick counter. Every time the TPM is turned on, it generates a random number to associate with the tick counter, and starts an internal clock with a starting value of 0.

The TPM is then able to sign data and embed into the signature both the random number and also the current clock tick. By exchanging messages with a known correct time-stamping service, the ticks can be associated with a real time. Known accuracy, drift, and so on of the internal clock can then be used to associate any clock tick (associated with that random number) with a real time.

### Tspi_TPM_ReadCurrentTicks

**Purpose:** This command reads the current tick value of the tick counter.

**Usage:** `Tspi_TPM_ReadCurrentTicks ( TSS_HTP        hTPM`
`                                 TPM_CURRENT_TICKS*    pTickCount`
`                                 )`

Here `hTPM` is the handle of the TPM, and `pTickCount` is a pointer to where the tick count will be returned.

**Returns:**

`TSS_SUCCESS`    The command completed successfully.

`TSS_E_INVALID HANDLE`    Can't find the TPM.

`TSS_E_BAD_PARAMETER`    One of the parameters does not meet the requirements.

`TSS_E_INTERNAL_ERROR`    The command failed.

**Context:** This can be run any time.

### Tspi_TPM_TickStampBlob

**Purpose:** This command sets aside a section of the NVRAM space to be used with a specific set of authorization values. The PCRs for read and write are set with this command directly. In order to set the authorization data to be used for read and write (should it be required), a policy object is used. The permissions needed are set with flags in the NV storage object before using this command.

**Usage:** `Tspi_TPM_TickStampBlob (  TSS_HHASH        hHash`
                              `TSS_KEY_HANDLE   hAIK`
                              `TSS_VALIDATION*  pValidationData`
                              `)`

Here `hHash` is the hash being signed by the AIK, together with the current tick count and the random number that corresponds to the current tick counter. The `pValidationData` is a structure. Before calling this function, an anti-replay nonce should be put into the structure. On return, the structure will contain the signature and the buffer that was signed.

**Returns:**

`TSS_SUCCESS`    The command completed successfully.

| | |
|---|---|
| `TSS_E_INVALID HANDLE` | Can't find the TPM. |
| `TSS_E_BAD_PARAMETER` | One of the parameters does not meet the requirements. |
| `TSS_E_INTERNAL_ERROR` | The command failed. |

**Context**: Clever usage of this command can associate the tick count with an actual time. This can be done in a number of ways. For example, a tickstamped blob can be signed and sent to a Time Stamping Authority (TSA). The resulting signature is then tickstamped. Now it is easily shown that the tick stamp that corresponds to the TSA signature must lie between the two tick counts of the TPM. If one then knows the accuracy and precision of the TPM, one can easily associate any future tickstamp (or even a past tickstamp) with an actual time, with some error.

## SOAP

In 1.1, DCOM was the only interface defined for talking remotely to the 1.1 TCS stack. However, DCOM had problems—it was a Microsoft technology, so most Unix implementations could not take advantage of it, and it was getting long in the tooth on the OSs that did use it. SOAP is the defined replacement for DCOM, though DCOM will likely remain available in most implementations for some time.

Remote access to a TPM is a scary thing for privacy gurus, though. It is not wise to allow a remote user to have direct access to hardware that exists on a client platform. So by default, access to functions remotely is turned off, and the user is allowed a fine control over access to functionality he permits remote users to have on his platform.

This fine control is determined using an XML document, which the TCS stack can read. It allows an end user to control either by function the commands that are going to be available to the end user or by group of functions in a certain order.

## Transport Session

In the 1.1 specification, it was possible to securely authorize a command, using an HMAC, so that a listener on the line could not determine the authorization data used. However, if an UNBIND or

UNSEAL operation was securely authorized, the results of that command were released in the clear by the TPM. This is clearly a design mistake, as the unprotected released data (usually a key) was usually more valuable than the protected authorization data.

In the 1.2 TPM, this was fixed by creating a secure "tunnel" to the TPM using a transport session. Transport sessions are the default used to communicate remotely to a TPM through the TCS, but it is possible that a transport session would be used even in a local communication. The design is not particularly compute heavy, and it is usually better to be safe than sorry. On the other hand, when using a transport session, it is equally important that the programmer be aware that no 1.1 TPM will be able to understand the command.

## Tspi_Context_SetTransEncryptionKey

**Purpose:** This command is used to set up an encryption "tunnel" between an application and the TPM so that any software listening in at the TPM cannot view any sensitive data going in or out of the TPM.

**Usage:** `Tspi_Context_SetTransEncryptionKey ( TSS_HCONTEXT    hContext,`
`                                           TSS_HKEY        hKey`
`                                           )`

`hKey` will have associated with it a symmetric key used to create the secure tunnel. `HContext` is the context that is to use the secure tunnel.

**Returns:**

`TSS_SUCCESS`      The command completed successfully.

`TSS_E_INVALID HANDLE`    Can't find the TPM.

`TSS_E_BAD_PARAMETER`     One of the parameters does not meet the requirements.

`TSS_E_INTERNAL_ERROR`    The command failed.

**Context:** One must first set the symmetric key information into the key object addressed by `hKey` using `Tspi_SetAttribData` before calling this command.

## Tspi_Context_CloseSignTransport

**Purpose:** This ends the transport session started by `SetTransEncryptionKey`.

**Usage:** `Tspi_Context_CloseSignTransport ( TSS_HCONTEXT     hContext`
`                                          TSS_HKEY         hSigningKey`
`                                          TSS_VALIDATION*  pValidationData`
`                                          )`

**Returns:**

TSS_SUCCESS    The command completed successfully.

TSS_E_INVALID HANDLE    Can't find the TPM.

TSS_E_BAD_PARAMETER    One of the parameters does not meet the requirements.

TSS_E_INTERNAL_ERROR    The command failed.

**Context:** One first must have started a `SetTransEncryptionKey` session before one can end it.

# Administrative and Convenience Functions

One of the most important administrative functions in the 1.2 spec is the ability for the owner to "lock" keys in non-volatile memory of the TPM so that they are always available. This can provide a means for a pre-boot restricted environment to log on to a remote service securely. (Recall that SRKs, the only keys non-volatile in a 1.1 environment, can only be used for storage, not signing.) This is called "registering" a key.

Second, a byte of NVRAM has been set aside to keep information on how the owner of the TPM would like resources partitioned across VMs in the event that a hypervisor is being used to talk to the TPM. In this case, each VM will likely have its own communication path to the TPM, and so the only place where this data can reside that is available to the end user is in the TPM itself.

Third, some people were sure that TPMs must be designed to have a back door in them. (This is not true.) Because the EK was the only thing in the chip as it was shipped, they assumed that the EK was used as a back door. The real reason the EK was unerasable was that the credential that may ship with it would be difficult (and expensive) to replace. But rather than have people believe there was a back door, two new commands were added—one to erase the EK, and another to generate a new one.

Because DER and BER encoding are needed in various places, for convenience two functions were added to put a `TssBlob` in DER or BER encoding.

Some of these new functions are very specific to the hardware itself, and thus are only exposed in the TCS. Others are exposed all the way to the TSP layer.

## Commands

### Tspi_TPM_CreateRevocableEndorsementKey

**Purpose:** This requests the TPM to create an endorsement key and password. With knowledge of the password, the endorsement key can be revoked. If a certificate already exists for an endorsement key, it is recommended that the endorsement key not be revoked, as it costs money to create a new certificate.

**Usage:** `Tspi_TPM_CreateRevocableEndorsementKey (`

| | |
|---|---|
| `TSS_HTPM` | `hTPM` |
| `TSS_HKEY` | `hKey` |
| `TSS_VALIDATION*` | `pValidationData` |
| `UINT32*` | `pulEkResetDataLength` |
| `BYTE**` | `prgbEkResetData` |

`)`

Here `hTPM` is the handle of the TPM that is going to create a new EK. `HKey` is used to specify the attributes of the new endorsement key. The `pValidationData` is a pointer to a validation instruction. If the length pointed to by `pulEkResetDataLength` is zero, that means the TPM should self-generate the password used to revoke the EK, returning that value in `rgbEkResetData`, and its length in `pulEkResetDataLength`. Otherwise, the authentication data necessary to revoke the key stored in the pointer `rgbEkResetData` is used.

**Returns:**

| | |
|---|---|
| `TSS_SUCCESS` | The command completed successfully. |
| `TSS_E_INVALID HANDLE` | Can't find the TPM. |
| `TSS_E_BAD_PARAMETER` | One of the parameters does not meet the requirements (likely the number of sessions is too large). |
| `TSS_E_INTERNAL_ERROR` | The command failed. |

**Context:** This allows a user to decide to create an endorsement key that cannot be easily erased by a denial-of-service attack. (The password/auth data controls the removal of the endorsement key.) One suggestion for the use of this is by a manufacturer, who could set the revocation password to be the machine serial number hashed with a manufacturer secret. Another is if the EK is squirted, it could be the hash of the public EK with a manufacturer secret. This way, the revocation password could be given to end users who requested it, but it would not be susceptible to a general virus style denial-of-service attack.

## Tspi_TPM_RevokeEndorsementKey

**Purpose:** This requests the TPM to create an endorsement key and password. With knowledge of the password, the endorsement key can be revoked.

**Usage:** `Tspi_TPM_RevokeEndorsementKey ( TSS_HTPM    hTPM`

| | |
|---|---|
| `UINT32` | `ulEkResetDataLength` |
| `BYTE*` | `rgbEkResetData` |

`)`

Here `hTPM` is the handle of the TPM with the EK to be revoked, `rgbEkResetData` is the authentication data necessary to revoke it, and `ulEkResetDataLength` is the length of the authentication data.

**Returns:**

`TSS_SUCCESS`    The command completed successfully.

| | |
|---|---|
| `TSS_E_INVALID HANDLE` | Can't find the TPM. |
| `TSS_E_BAD_PARAMETER` | One of the parameters does not meet the requirements. |
| `TSS_E_INTERNAL_ERROR` | The command failed. |

**Context:** This allows a user to revoke an endorsement key, assuming he knows the correct password.

## Tcsi_Admin_TSS_SessionPerLocality

**Purpose:** It is clear that whatever decision is made for the apportionment of a limited number of concurrent sessions (minimum 16) among localities would be wrong. So this command allows the end user to put his request for the apportionment in NVRAM in the TPM itself. There is no way to enforce this, but it does register the user's wishes.

**Usage:** `Tspi_Admin_TSS_SessionPerLocality ( TSS_HCONTEXT   hContext`
`                                        UINT32         ulLocality`
`                                        UINT32         ulSessions`
`                                        TPM_AUTH*      pOwnerAuth`
`                                        )`

By default, all localities are given 0 sessions. This command is used to change the number of sessions given to a locality. If `ulSessions` is larger than the number of remaining unassigned sessions, then an error message is thrown. The memory region being used is a pre-allocated index (`TPM_NV_INDEX_Sessions`) and requires owner authorization for writing.

**Returns:**

`TSS_SUCCESS`    The command completed successfully.

| | |
|---|---|
| `TSS_E_INVALID HANDLE` | Can't find the TPM. |
| `TSS_E_BAD_PARAMETER` | One of the parameters does not meet the requirements. |
| `TSS_E_INTERNAL_ERROR` | The command failed. |

**Context:** This allows a user to register his preference for apportionment of sessions among localities.

## Tcsi_Admin_TSS_MaxTimePerLocality

**Purpose:** This command is similar to `SessionsPerLocality`—it allows the user to register how much time he would like the system to allow any locality to have exclusive use of the TPM. There is nothing that enforces this in the system, however.

**Usage:** `Tcsi_Admin_TSS_MaxTimePerLocality (` `TSS_HCONTEXT`    `hContext`
                                      `UINT32`          `ulLocality`
                                      `UINT32`          `ulMaxTime`
                                        `TPM_AUTH*`     `pOwnerAuth`
                                      `)`

The `hContext` is the context handle, the `ulLocality` is the locality in question, the `ulMaxTime` is the maximum amount of time that a locality should wait before releasing a PTM, and `pOwnerAuth` is a pointer to the owner authorization.

**Returns:**

`TSS_SUCCESS`    The command completed successfully.

    `TSS_E_INVALID HANDLE`    Can't find the TPM.

    `TSS_E_BAD_PARAMETER`    One of the parameters does not meet the requirements.

    `TSS_E_INTERNAL_ERROR`    The command failed.

**Context:** This allows a user to register his wishes for the amount of time a locality can have exclusive use of the TPM.

## Tspi_TPM_CheckMaintenancePolicy

**Purpose:** This checks to see if the maintenance public key is correct. It is used at manufacturing time to determine if the correct maintenance public key was used.

**Usage:** `Tspi_TPM_CheckMaintenancePolicy (`
                                       `TSS_HTPM`              `hTPM`
                                       `TSS_HKEY`              `hMaintenanceKey`
                                       `TSS_Validation*`     `pValidationData`
                                       `)`

A nonce is sent to the TPM, which hashes it together with the maintenance public key. The `pValidationData` is a pointer to the validation data, which consists of the hash of the maintenance public key together with the nonce. The maintenance public key was not returned lest it be considered a privacy problem (although it is likely that a large number of machines would have the same value).

**Returns:**

TSS_SUCCESS    The command completed successfully.

    TSS_E_INVALID HANDLE    Can't find the TPM.
    TSS_E_BAD_PARAMETER    One of the parameters does not meet the requirements.
    TSS_E_INTERNAL_ERROR    The command failed.

**Context:** This allows a user to check to see if the maintenance public key stored in his TPM (if it has one) is correct.

## Tspi_Context_RegisterKey

**Purpose:** This is used to put a key into non-volatile storage (persistent storage) in the TPM so that it is always loaded. This is useful in a low memory environment (like preboot).

**Usage:** Tspi_Context_RegisterKey ( TSS_HCONTEXT    hContext
                                     TSS_HKEY        hKey
                                     TSS_FLAG        persistentStorageType
                                     TSS_UUID        uuidKey
                                     TSS_FLAG        persistentStorage
                                                       TypeParent
                                     TSS_UUID        uuidParentKey
                                     )

Here hContext is the context handle, hKey is the key being registered, uuidKey is the UUID by which the key is registered in persistent storage (note that this may change after a boot), TSS_FLAG is used to note if the parent key has PCR restrictions, and uuidParentKey is the UUID of the parent key.

**Returns:**

TSS_SUCCESS    The command completed successfully.

    TSS_E_INVALID HANDLE    Can't find the TPM.
    TSS_E_BAD_PARAMETER    One of the parameters does not meet the requirements.
    TSS_E_INTERNAL_ERROR    The command failed.

**Context:** The user must have a key already created and have the system in the correct state to load the key when registering a key. It should be noted: If a parent key of the key being registered needed the PCRs to be in a particular state to load the key, and that state was being used to guarantee that the key being registered is also being used in that state, registering such a key would obviate that requirement. As a result, it is not possible to register a key that has a parent or ancestor that requires a particular set of PCR values. (Of course, this cannot be guaranteed of migratable keys as they can be created/wrapped entirely outside the TPM.)

## Tspi_Context_UnregisterKey

**Purpose:** This removes a key from the NVRAM of the TPM so that it is no longer available until it is loaded.

**Usage:** Tspi_Context_UnregisterKey ( TSS_HCONTEXT    hContext
                                        TSS_FLAG        persistentStorageType
                                        TSS_UUID        uuidKey
                                        TSS_HKEY*       phKey
                                        )

    Here hContext is the context handle, TSS_FLAG indicates if it is a user or system persistent storage, uuidKey is the UUID of the key being discarded, and phKey is a pointer to the handle of the key object containing the info (from the archive). Normally anyone can unregister a key, but KeyControlOwner can change that.

**Returns:**

TSS_SUCCESS    The command completed successfully.

    TSS_E_INVALID HANDLE    Can't find the TPM.

    TSS_E_BAD_PARAMETER     One of the parameters does not meet the requirements.

    TSS_E_INTERNAL_ERROR    The command failed.

**Context:** This can only be used after a key has been registered. It can't be used on the EK or the SRK—they each have their own command to get rid of them.

## Tspi_TPM_KeyControlOwner

**Purpose:** This command allows setting a "super user" control of a registered key. An owner can set a bit on a registered key such that the key remains in non-volatile storage inside the TPM. Only the owner is able to evict the key from the internal registry.

**Usage:** Tspi_TPM_KeyControlOwner ( TSS_HTPM     hTPM
                                      TSS_HKEY     hKey
                                      UINT32       attribName
                                      TSS_BOOL     attribValue
                                      TSS_UUID*    pUuidData
                                      )

    The hTPM variable refers to the TPM where the key is being semi-permanently stored. HKey is the key itself. The attribName and attribValue variables are used to set (or unset) the bit to keep the key in storage. (TSS_TSPATTRIB_KEYCONTROL_OWNEREVICT can be either TRUE or FALSE.) The pUuidData is the UUID by which the key was registered as a TPM resident key. Note that this UUID is volatile in the sense that with every new boot sequence, another UUID may be set to the key—if a key has been added or evicted from the TPM during the previous boot cycle.

**Returns:**

TSS_SUCCESS    The command completed successfully.

TSS_E_INVALID HANDLE    Can't find the TPM.

TSS_E_BAD_PARAMETER    One of the parameters does not meet the requirements.

TSS_E_INTERNAL_ERROR    The command failed.

**Context:** This command is used by the TPM owner typically to establish a signing key in the TPM, which can be used to establish that a platform in pre-boot state is the one it says it is.

## Tcsi_EnumRegisteredKeys

**Purpose:** This lists the keys that are currently loaded in NVRAM in the TPM. It is a TCS layer command, and usually used by the key manager to make sure that the correct key is pointed to when a TSP caller calls for a key.

**Usage:** Tspi_Context_CloseSignTransport(

| | |
|---|---|
| TSS_HCONTEXT | hContext |
| TSS_UUID* | pKeyUUID |
| UINT32* | pcKeyHierarchySize |
| TSS_KM_KEYINFO** | ppKeyHierarchy |
| ) | |

Here hContext is the context handle, pKeyUUID is NULL for all keys, and ppKeyHierarchy is a pointer to the array of structures in the key hierarchy.

**Returns:**

TSS_SUCCESS    The command completed successfully.

TSS_E_FAIL    The command did not complete successfully

**Context:** This is used to find out all the information of the keys currently registered in the TPM. If no keys are added or removed, the information will remain static.

## Tspi_GetRegisteredKeyByUUID

**Purpose:** Get a key handle for a UUID that belongs to a registered key. Works well for static registered keys. (If keys are registered or unregistered, all UUIDs may change.)

**Usage:** `Tspi_GetRegisteredKeyByUUID (  TSS_HCONTEXT    hContext`
                                        `TSS_FLAG        persistentStorageType`
                                        `TSS_UUID        uuidData`
                                        `TSS_HKEY*       phKey`
                                        `)`

Here `hContext` is the handle to the established context, `persistentStorageType` is either user or platform, `uuidData` is the UUID of the key we want a handle for, and `phKey` is a pointer to where the handle is placed.

**Returns:**

`TSS_SUCCESS`    The command completed successfully.

| | |
|---|---|
| `TSS_E_INVALID HANDLE` | Can't find the TPM. |
| `TSS_E_BAD_PARAMETER` | One of the parameters does not meet the requirements. |
| `TSS_E_PS_KEY_NOTFOUND` | No such UUID in registered keys. |
| `TSS_E_INTERNAL_ERROR` | The command failed. |

**Context:** This is one way to get the handle to a key in registered storage in the TPM so it can be used.

## Tspi_Context_GetRegisteredKeyByPublicInfo

**Purpose:** Get a key handle for a UUID that belongs to a registered key. Works well for static registered keys. (If keys are registered or unregistered, all UUIDs may change.)

**Usage:** `Tspi_Context_`
`GetRegisteredKeyByPublicInfo (  TSS_HCONTEXT      hContext`
                              `TSS_FLAG          persistentStorageType`
                              `TSS_ALGORITHYM_ID algID`
                              `UINT32            ulPublicInfoLength`
                              `BYTE*             rgbPublicInfo`
                              `TSS_HKEY*         phKey`
                              `)`

Here `hContext` is the handle to the established context, `persistentStorageType` is either user or platform, `algID` is the type of key (usually RSA), `rgbPublicInfo` is the public info of the key we want the handle for, and `phKey` is a pointer to where the handle is placed.

**Returns:**

TSS_SUCCESS    The command completed successfully.

     TSS_E_INVALID HANDLE    Can't find the TPM.

     TSS_E_BAD_PARAMETER    One of the parameters does not meet the requirements.

     TSS_E_PS_KEY_NOTFOUND    No such UUID in registered keys.

     TSS_E_INTERNAL_ERROR    The command failed.

**Context:** This is one way to get the handle to a key in registered storage in the TPM so it can be used.

## Tspi_Context_GetRegisteredKeysByUUID

**Purpose:** This is to get the entire array of TSS_KM_KEYINFO structures for the registered key hierarchy.

**Usage:** Tspi_Context_
GetRegisteredKeysByUUID ( TSS_HCONTEXT         hContext

                       TSS_FLAG            persistentStorageType

                       TSS_UUID*           puuidData

                       UINT32*             pulKeyHierarchySize

                       TSS_KM)_KEYINFO**    ppKeyHierarchy

                       )

Here hContext is the handle to the established context, persistentStorageType is either user or platform, puuidData is usually set to NULL to get everything, and ppKeyHierarchy is a pointer to where the results are put.

**Returns:**

TSS_SUCCESS    The command completed successfully.

     TSS_E_INVALID HANDLE    Can't find the TPM.

     TSS_E_BAD_PARAMETER    One of the parameters does not meet the requirements.

     TSS_E_PS_KEY_NOTFOUND    No such UUID in registered keys.

     TSS_E_INTERNAL_ERROR    The command failed.

**Context:** This is one way to get the handle to a key in registered storage in the TPM so it can be used.

## Tspi_Context_GetRegisteredKeysByUUID2

**Purpose:** This is to get the entire array of TSS_KM_KEYINFO2 structures for the registered key hierarchy.

**Usage:** `Tspi_Context_`
`GetRegisteredKeysByUUID2 (` `TSS_HCONTEXT` `hContext`
                                `TSS_FLAG` `persistentStorageType`
                                `TSS_UUID*` `puuidData`
                                `UINT32*` `pulKeyHierarchySize`
                                `TSS_KM)_KEYINFO**` `ppKeyHierarchy`
                                `)`

Here `hContext` is the handle to the established context, `persistentStorageType` is either user or platform, `puuidData` is usually set to NULL to get everything, and `ppKeyHierarchy` is a pointer to where the results are put.

**Returns:**

`TSS_SUCCESS`    The command completed successfully.

| | |
|---|---|
| `TSS_E_INVALID HANDLE` | Can't find the TPM. |
| `TSS_E_BAD_PARAMETER` | One of the parameters does not meet the requirements. |
| `TSS_E_PS_KEY_NOTFOUND` | No such UUID in registered keys. |
| `TSS_E_INTERNAL_ERROR` | The command failed. |

**Context:** This is used to get information about all the keys registered in the TPM. It is the same as `GetRegisteredKeysByUUID2` except that it returns `KEYINFO2` structures instead of `KEYINFO` structures. The only difference between a `TSS_KM_KEYINFO` and a `TSS_KM_KEYINFO2` structure is the addition of information as to whether the key (and its parent) are registered in the user hierarchy or the platform hierarchy.

## Tspi_EncodeDER_TssBlob

**Purpose:** This is a helper command in the TSS stack used to take a `TssBlob` and put it into the standard DER encoding used to transfer blobs between different machines.

**Usage:** `Tcsip_Context_CloseSignTransport (` `TSS_HTPM` `hTPM`
                                                    `)`

**Returns:**

`TSS_SUCCESS`    The command completed successfully.

| | |
|---|---|
| `TSS_E_INVALID HANDLE` | Can't find the TPM. |
| `TSS_E_BAD_PARAMETER` | One of the parameters does not meet the requirements. |
| `TSS_E_INTERNAL_ERROR` | The command failed. |

**Context:** One needs to check the header of a blob to see if it is already DER encoded before using this command.

## Tspi_DecodeBER_TssBlob

**Purpose:** This is a helper command in the TSS stack used to take a `TssBlob` and put it into the standard BER encoding used to transfer blobs between different machines.

**Usage:** `Tcsip_Context_CloseSignTransport ( TSS_HTPM  hTPM`

`)`

**Returns:**

`TSS_SUCCESS`   The command completed successfully.

   `TSS_E_INVALID HANDLE`   Can't find the TPM.

   `TSS_E_BAD_PARAMETER`   One of the parameters does not meet the requirements.

   `TSS_E_INTERNAL_ERROR`   The command failed.

**Context:** One needs to check the header of a blob to see if it is already BER encoded before using this.

# Example Program

1. Determine the level of a TPM and the TSS being spoken to.
2. Create a transport session to talk with the TPM.
3. Turn on auditing of creation of CMKs.
4. Delegate the use of the CMK to another user.
5. Create a CMK key locked to a particular locality, and register the values in PCRs 0 and 1.
6. Sign the CMK with an AIK.
7. Sign the AIK with DAA.
8. Check the audit log.

The TSS 1.2 specification was announced in February 2006 with the header files following shortly after. Machines with 1.2 TSS stacks began shipping before the end of 2006. At that point, these new functions became available. It was not possible for us to provide tested code for the book using the 1.2 functions, as the stacks were not available; however, we thought it important to provide an analysis of those functions—how they can be used, and why they are written the way they are—so that the programmer and architect will be able to make use of this book for the next several years.

## Summary

As the TPM specification is updated with new functionality, so the TSS must also keep pace. This section of the book provided a look at many functions that have not yet been taken advantage of, that exist in the new TSS 1.2 specification. In the future, the TPM specification will likely have more functionality added to it, but the intent of the TSS specification writers is that any code written using previous TSS APIs will continue to work with new TSS software stacks.

# PART IV

# Appendixes

# TPM Command Reference

Commands to the TPM go through an interface known as the TSS. There are two types of commands that go to the TSS: those that are known to be secure, and those that are not needed to be secure. Commands that need not be secure are not usually implemented in the TPM and are found in Appendix B, "TSS Command Reference." These include bind and verify signature. Commands that must be secure, and that therefore must be implemented in hardware, are prefixed with TPM.

Beyond this breakdown, there are several different kinds of commands. Some of them are designed to be used during setup of the system, some are designed to be used by the TSS to load and evict keys as necessary, some are designed to be used by an administrator, and some are designed to be used by application developers. There is no reason that the functions cannot be used by application developers, but they will not be as useful to them.

The following table lists the functions and categorizes them by their design point:

A = Application developer (or referenced in applications in this document).

B = For the BIOS.

S = Setup.

M = Middleware (such as loading/unloading keys as necessary).

D = Administration.

O = Optional command. These are unlikely to actually appear in any chip.

P = Command that would only be used by the manufacturer of the PC.

X = System or OS only.

| TPM Function Name | Version | Design Point | Description |
| --- | --- | --- | --- |
| TPM_Seal | 1.1 | A | Hide data / symmetric keys locked to a machine state. |
| TPM_Sealx | 1.2 | A | Hide data / symmetric keys locked to a machine state / locality. |
| TPM_Unseal | 1.1 | A | Recover data / symmetric keys locked to a machine state. |
| TPM_UnBind | 1.1 | A | Recover data /symmetric keys locked to a passphrase. |
| TPM_CreateWrapKey | 1.1 | A | TPM create and store a key (of any selected type). |
| TPM_LoadKey | 1.1 | M | Load a key into the TPM. |
| TPM_LoadKey2 | 1.2 | M | Load a 1.2 style key into the TPM. |
| TPM_EvictKey | 1.1 | M | Unload a key from the TPM. |
| TPM_GetPubKey | 1.1 | M | Get the public key of the SRK. |
| TPM_CMK_SetRestrictions | 1.2 | D | Set restrictions on a certified migratable key. |
| TPM_CMK_ApproveMA | 1.2 | D | Lets a TPM owner approve the migration authority picked for a certified migratable key. |
| TPM_CMK_CreateKey | 1.2 | D | Create a certified migratable key. |
| TPM_CMK_CreateTicket | 1.2 | D | Used to create a ticket either to perform migration to a intermediate migration authority approved by a migration selection authority, or to prove that a blob migrated by a migration authority was indeed approved by a migration authority and hence can be trusted to be a CMK. |
| TPM_CMK_CreateBlob | 1.2 | D | First step in migrating a CMK to a migration authority. |
| TPM_CMK_ConvertMigration | 1.2 | D | Final step in migrating a CMK blob into a new TPM. |
| TPM_MigrateKey | 1.2 | D | A command written to allow a TPM to be used as an intermediate migration authority. It is basically a rewrap command. |

| TPM Function Name | Version | Design Point | Description |
|---|---|---|---|
| TPM_CreateMigrationBlob | 1.1 | D / A | Create a new blob that can be read by a different TPM. |
| TPM_ConvertMigrationBlob | 1.1 | D / A | Convert intermediate blob to final blob. |
| TPM_AuthorizeMigrationKey | 1.1 | D / A | Decide which target TPMs keys can be moved to. |
| TPM_SHA1Start | 1.1 | S | Used to calculate PCR values in memoryless environs. |
| TPM_SHA1Update | 1.1 | S | Used to calculate PCR values in memoryless environs. |
| TPM_SHA1Complete | 1.1 | S | Used to calculate PCR values in memoryless environs. |
| TPM_SHA1CompleteExtend | 1.1 | S | Used to calculate PCR values in memoryless environs. |
| TPM_CertifyKey | 1.1 | D / A | Create a certificate for a non-migratable key signed by an ID. |
| TPM_CertifyKey2 | 1.2 | D / A | Create a certificate for a non-migratable key of type 1.2, signed by an ID. |
| TPM_Sign | 1.1 | A | Sign a message. |
| TPM_GetRandom | 1.1 | A | Get a random number. |
| TPM_StirRandom | 1.1 | S / M | Add entropy to the RNG. |
| TPM_SelfTestFull | 1.1 | S / M | Perform a full self test (for the paranoid or startup). |
| TPM_CertifySelfTest | 1.1 | A | Certify the results of a self test. |
| TPM_ContinueSelfTest | 1.1 | S / M | Finish off a self test (during startup). |
| TPM_GetTestResult | 1.1 | D / A | Get uncertified results of a self test. |
| TPM_Reset | 1.1 | S | Close sessions to allow a driver to start from known state. |
| TPM_Init | 1.1 | D | Initialize platform in a way that does not unload certain non-PCR locked keys. |
| TPM_SaveState | 1.1 | M | For power management. |

| TPM Function Name | Version | Design Point | Description |
|---|---|---|---|
| TPM_Startup | 1.1 | S | Command launched by root of trust during startup. |
| TPM_OwnerClear | 1.1 | D | Used to reset the TPM including the SRK. |
| TPM_DisableOwnerClear | 1.1 | D | Used to require physical presence to use Owner_Clear. |
| TPM_ForceClear | 1.1 | D | Used to reset the TPM including the SRK with physical presence required even if Disable_Owner_Clear is set. |
| TPM_DisableForceClear | 1.1 | D | Require a reboot and physical presence to clear. |
| TPM_SetCapability | 1.1 | M | This is a means of setting capabilities of a TPM. |
| TPM_GetCapability | 1.1 | M | This is a means of finding the capability settings of a TPM. |
| TPM_GetCapabilitySigned | 1.1 | M | Same as above, only signed by an ID (identity). Should not be used, as a security problem has been found with it. |
| TPM_GetCapabilityOwner | 1.1 | M | Same as above, but allows access to data that requires owner authorization. |
| TPM_GetAuditDigest | 1.2 | M | Get history corresponding to audited functions. |
| TPM_GetAuditDigestSigned | 1.2 | M | Same as above, signed. |
| TPM_SetOrdinalAuditStatus | 1.2 | M / D | Each function has an ordinal. Select functions to audit. |
| TPM_GetOrdinalAuditStatus | 1.2 | M / D | Find out the audit status for a given function. |
| TPM_SetOwnerInstall | 1.1 | S | Enable the process of taking ownership of a TPM. |
| TPM_OwnerSetDisable | 1.1 | S | Disable the process of taking ownership of a TPM. |
| TPM_PhysicalDisable | 1.1 | S | For the super paranoid, they can turn off the TPM. |
| TPM_PhysicalEnable | 1.1 | S | To turn on the TPM. |

| TPM Function Name | Version | Design Point | Description |
|---|---|---|---|
| TPM_PhysicalSetDeactivated | 1.1 | D | Deactivate physical presence requirement. |
| TPM_SetTempDeactivated | 1.1 | S | Disables the TPM until the next boot. This is used for privacy. |
| TPM_SetOperatorAuth | 1.2 | B | Allows an operator to act as though he has physical presence after a boot. Must be set with physical presence during the boot. |
| TPM_FieldUpgrade | 1.2 | D | Optional command. Not likely to be implemented. |
| TPM_SetRedirection | 1.2 | M | Optional command. For redirecting the output of a command to a special bus in some designs. |
| TPM_TakeOwnership | 1.1 | D | Basic command for creating an SRK and an owner for a TPM. Until this command is executed, the TPM can't do much of anything. |
| TPM_SaveKeyContext | 1.2 | M | For key caching. |
| TPM_LoadKeyContext | 1.2 | M | For key caching. |
| TPM_CreateEndorsementKeyPair | 1.2 | S | Done by manufacturer, or by user if he has first destroyed the old Endorsement Key. |
| TPM_CreateRevocableEK | 1.2 | M | Done to create an EK that is revocable by the end user. This of course destroys the certificate, reducing the value of the TPM some. Main use is for the paranoid. |
| TPM_RevokeTrust | 1.2 | M | Used to destroy the Endorsement Key (usually followed by creating another one). |
| TPM_ReadPubek | 1.1 | M | Returns the Endorsement Public Key. |
| TPM_DisablePubekRead | 1.1 | S / D | Disallow non-owner to read the Endorsement Key. |
| TPM_OwnerReadInternalPub | 1.2 | M | Owner-authorized reading of either the EK pub or the SRK public key. |
| TPM_OwnerReadPubek | 1.1 | M | Owner-authorized reading of Endorsement Public Key. |

| TPM Function Name | Version | Design Point | Description |
|---|---|---|---|
| TPM_MakeIdentity | 1.1 | M / A | Create a key that will become an identity. |
| TSS_CollateIdentityRequest | 1.1 | M / A | Create package to send to CA for an identity certificate. |
| TPM_ActivateIdentity | 1.1 | M / A | Obtain symmetric encryption key used to decrypt the CA provided certificate. |
| TPM_CreateMaintenance Archive | 1.1 | O / M | Provides means to create blob used to recover SRK to a new system. |
| TPM_KillMaintenanceFeature | 1.1 | O / M | Optional command; mandatory if previous command is present. |
| TPM_LoadMaintenanceArchive | 1.1 | O / M | Optional: Recover SRK to new TPM from maintenance archive. |
| TPM_LoadManuMaintPub | 1.1 | O / P | Optional: For manufacturer to load a public key used in maintenance command. |
| TPM_ReadManuMaintPub | 1.1 | O / M | Optional command to read the manufacturer public key in the chip. |
| TPM_PcrRead | 1.1 | M / A | Read the current PCR values from the TPM (not authenticated). |
| TPM_Quote | 1.1 | M / A | TPM signed the PCR values from the chip. |
| TPM_Quote2 | 1.2 | M / A | TPM signed extended PCR values from the chip. |
| TPM_DirRead | 1.1 | M / A | TPM read the Data Integrity Register (20 bytes; owner auth required to write it, but anyone can read it). |
| TPM_DirReadSigned | 1.1 | M / A | TPM signed values in the Data Integrity Register. |
| TPM_DirWriteAuth | 1.1 | M / A | Owner-authorized writing of data to a DIR. |
| TPM_Extend | 1.1 | B / M/ A | Used to update a value in a PCR. |
| TPM_PCR_Reset | 1.2 | A / M | Used to reset a resettable PCR. |
| TPM_SHA1Start | 1.1 | B | Used to help the BIOS calculate a SHA before the full processor memory is available. |

| TPM Function Name | Version | Design Point | Description |
|---|---|---|---|
| TPM_SHA1Update | 1.1 | B | Continue a SHA in case you hash something big. |
| TPM_SHA1Complete | 1.1 | B | Finish the SHA. |
| TPM_SHA1CompleteExtend | 1.1 | B | Finish the SHA and extend into a PCR. |
| TPM_OIAP | 1.1 | D / M / A | Create an authorization handle. |
| TPM_OSAP | 1.1 | D / M / A | Create an authorization handle used for multiple commands that use the same authorization. An authorization need only be provided once. |
| TPM_DSAP | 1.2 | D / M / A | Create an authorization session using delegation. |
| TPM_SetOwnerPointer | 1.2 | D / M / A | Used by 1.2 code to allow legacy software to use delegation. Probably will never be used. |
| TPM_ChangeAuth | 1.1 | D | Create a new blob for a key with a different authorization. |
| TPM_ChangeAuthOwner | 1.1 | D | Change the TPM owner authorization. |
| TPM_ChangeAuthAsymStart | 1.1 | D | Used to change authorization of an entity without the parent authorization. |
| TPM_ChangeAuthAsymFinish | 1.1 | D | Used to change authorization of an entity without the parent authorization. |
| TPM_SaveAuthContext | 1.1 | D | Saves an authorization session outside the TPM. |
| TPM_LoadAuthContext | 1.1 | D | Reloads a saved authorization session outside the TPM. |
| TPM_Delegate_Manage | 1.2 | D | Create, enable, or invalidate a family delegation table. This is used to delegate a group of commands to a particular authorization, which are normally only owner authorized. |
| TPM_Delegate_Create KeyDelegation | 1.2 | D | Used to create a delegation of authority to use a particular key. |

| TPM Function Name | Version | Design Point | Description |
|---|---|---|---|
| TPM_Delegate_CreateOwnerDelegation | 1.2 | D | Delegate a command that normally requires the owner's authorization by creating a blob instead of a family table. |
| TPM_Delegate_LoadOwnerDelegation | 1.2 | D | Load the delegation blob created by the CreateOwnerDelegation command, prior to using the blob-based delegation. |
| TPM_Delegate_ReadTable | 1.2 | D | Find out what is in the TPM internal family delegation table. |
| TPM_Delegate_Update Verification | 1.2 | D | When removing a delegation, one needs to increment the delegation table number, and then update the delegation table number for all the delegations that are *not* being removed. This command is used to update the still-valid delegations. |
| TPM_Delegate_VerifyDelegation | 1.2 | D | This command is used to verify that a delegation blob (used either for authorizing use of a key or in place of an owner authorization) is valid. |
| TPM_NV_DefineSpace | 1.2 | A | Set aside a piece of the NVRAM, establishing its authorization characteristics. Also used to remove such a space. Authorization characteristics can include PCRs, locality, authorization data, read or write once per boot. |
| TPM_NV_WriteValue | 1.2 | A | Write to the NVRAM space. |
| TPM_NV_WriteValueAuth | 1.2 | A | Write to the NVRAM space if it requires authorization data to write. |
| TPM_NV_ReadValue | 1.2 | A | Read from NVRAM space. |
| TPM_NV_ReadValueAuth | 1.2 | A | Read from NVRAM space if it requires authorization data to be read. |

| TPM Function Name | Version | Design Point | Description |
| --- | --- | --- | --- |
| TPM_KeyControlOwner | 1.2 | M | The owner can set a key into NVRAM inside the TPM, so that it isn't unloaded when the TPM is powered down. Useful to have some keys always handy, especially in low-memory situations (such as pre-boot). |
| TPM_SaveContext | 1.2 | M | Save out stuff from the TPM so that more things can be loaded, but save it so it can be reloaded quickly (symmetrically encrypted with a key only the TPM knows, and only valid until a reboot). |
| TPM_LoadContext | 1.2 | M | Load a saved context back into the TPM. |
| TPM_FlushSpecific | 1.2 | M | Remove a key that was saved into the TPM's internal NVRAM. |
| TPM_GetTicks | 1.2 | A | Get the current tick value. |
| TPM_TickStampBlob | 1.2 | A | Sign something with an ID and include the current tick value. |
| TPM_EstablishTransport | 1.2 | M | Establish an encrypted session to the TPM. |
| TPM_ExecuteTransport | 1.2 | M | Use a transport session. |
| TPM_ReleaseTransportSigned | 1.2 | M | End a transport session. |
| TPM_CreateCounter | 1.2 | X | Create one of four monotonic counters. It will start at the highest value of any counter. |
| TPM_IncrementCounter | 1.2 | X | Increment the current counter (chosen at boot). |
| TPM_ReadCounter | 1.2 | X | Read the value of the current counter. |
| TPM_ReleaseCounter | 1.2 | X | Remove a counter. |
| TPM_ReleaseCounterOwner | 1.2 | X | Remove a counter that requires owner authorization. |
| TPM_DAA_Join | 1.2 | A | Protocol used to create and join the group signature used in DAA |
| TPM_DAA_Sign | 1.2 | A | Used to sign something with a DAA certificate. |

# TSS Command Reference

This appendix provides a list of the TSS commands that are available in either 1.1 or 1.2 TCG software stacks. Those listed as 1.2 will only be available for machines with a 1.2 TSS. Along with the list is a brief description of what each command does, so that a user can quickly find the correct command to use:

A = Application developer (or referenced in applications in this document).

B = For the BIOS.

S = Setup.

M = Middleware (such as loading/unloading keys as necessary).

D = Administration.

O = Optional command. These are unlikely to actually appear in any chip.

P = Command that would only be used by the manufacturer of the PC.

C = Core service—not typically used unless one is talking remotely to a TPM.

X = System or OS.

| TSS Function Name | Version | Design Point | Description |
|---|---|---|---|
| Tspi_SetAttribUint32 | 1.1 | A/S | Set an integer attribute of an object. (First one must create the object using Tspi_Context_CreateObject.) |
| Tspi_GetAttribUint32 | 1.1 | A | Find out the value of an integer attribute of an object. |
| Tspi_SetAttribData | 1.1 | A/S | Set a non-integer attribute of an object. (First one must create the object using Tspi_Context_CreateObject.) |
| Tspi_GetAttribData | 1.1 | A | Get a non-integer attribute of an object. |
| Tspi_ChangeAuth | 1.1 | A/D | Create a new object with a different authorization. |
| Tspi_ChangeAuthAsym | 1.1 | A/D | Create a new object with a different authorization (but the same other internal parameters) without revealing knowledge of the new authorization to the parent key. |
| Tspi_GetPolicyObject | 1.1 | A | Find out the current authorization policy associated with the context. |
| Tspi_Context_Close | 1.1 | A | Close a context. |
| Tspi_Context_Connect | 1.1 | A | Connect to a context after it is created. |
| Tspi_Context_Create | 1.1 | A | Create a context. |
| Tspi_Context_FreeMemory | 1.1 | A | Free memory allocated by a Tspi-level function. |
| Tspi_Context_GetDefaultPolicy | 1.1 | A | Use the default authorization policy for the creation of an object. |
| Tspi_Context_CreateObject | 1.1 | A | Create an object, such as a key object. After creating the object, the fields in the object need to be set. |
| Tspi_Context_CloseObject | 1.1 | A | Destroy an object. |
| Tspi_Context_GetCapability | 1.1 | A | Get the current capabilities of the context. |
| Tspi_Context_GetTPMObject | 1.1 | A | Get the TPM object associated with a context. |

| TSS Function Name | Version | Design Point | Description |
| --- | --- | --- | --- |
| Tspi_Context_LoadKeyBlob | 1.1 | A/D | Load an encrypted key blob into the TPM, used when you have the key blob file. |
| Tspi_Context_LoadKeyByUUID | 1.1 | A/D | Load a key into the TPM when you know its UUID. |
| Tspi_Context_RegisterKey | 1.1 | A/S/D | Register a key into either a user's key store or a system's key store and returns the UUID. |
| Tspi_Context_UnregisterKey | 1.1 | A/D | Remove a key from a user or system key store. |
| Tspi_Context_DeleteKey ByUUID | 1.1 | A/D | Remove a key from the TPM referenced by UUID. |
| Tspi_Context_GetKeyByUUID | 1.1 | A/D | Search for a key by its UUID, and returns a handle to it. |
| Tspi_Context_GetKey ByPublicInfo | 1.1 | A/D | Search for a key by its public data and returns a handle to it. |
| Tspi_Context_Get RegisteredKeysByUUID | 1.1 | A/D | Return a list of all the registered keys in a registry, along with their UUIDs. |
| Tspi_Policy_SetSecret | 1.1 | A/S | How one associates authorization data with a policy, to be used, for example, in creating or using a key. |
| Tspi_Policy_FlushSecret | 1.1 | A | Remove the authorization data from memory. |
| Tspi_Policy_AssignToObject | 1.1 | A | How one assigns a policy to an object— for example, a key. |
| Tspi_TPM_Create EndorsementKey | 1.1 | S | Used by manufacturing to create the initial endorsement key. In 1.2, it can also be used to create a new endorsement key after the old one has been destroyed. |
| Tspi_TPM_GetPub EndorsementKey | 1.1 | A/S/D | Return the public portion of the endorsement key. |
| Tspi_TPM_TakeOwnership | 1.1 | S | The first command one uses to become owner of the TPM. It also causes the TPM to generate an SRK. |

| TSS Function Name | Version | Design Point | Description |
|---|---|---|---|
| Tspi_TPM_Collate IdentityRequest | 1.1 | A/S/D | Gather all the information a certificate authority will need in order to provide a certificate for an AIK. |
| Tspi_TPM_ActivateIdentity | 1.1 | A/S/D | Take the encrypted returned data from the certificate authority, and use it to determine the decryption key used to return the certificate for an AIK to the owner. |
| Tspi_TPM_ClearOwner | 1.1 | D | Remove the owner auth and wipes the SRK from the TPM. |
| Tspi_TPM_SetStatus | 1.1 | A/S/D | Set bits in the TPM. |
| Tspi_TPM_GetStatus | 1.1 | A/D | Find out how bits in the TPM are set. |
| Tspi_TPM_SelfTestFull | 1.1 | A/S/D | Tells the TPM to execute a full self test. |
| Tspi_TPM_CertifySelfTest | 1.1 | A/M | Tells the TPM to use an AIK to certify the self-test results. |
| Tspi_TPM_GetTestResult | 1.1 | A/M | Get the self test result, unsigned. |
| Tspi_TPM_GetCapability | 1.1 | A | Get the set of capabilities of the TPM. |
| Tspi_TPM_GetCapabilitySigned | 1.1 | -insecure | This command is eliminated in the 1.2 TPM and should not be used due to a discovered insecurity. |
| Tspi_TPM_SetCapability | 1.1 | A | Set capabilities of the TPM. |
| Tspi_TPM_Create MaintenanceArchive | 1.1 | S/D | Optional command for creating a means of recovering a SRK to a new system upon death of the old chip. Because it is optional, it is unlikely to be in any actual chips. |
| Tspi_TPM_Kill MaintenanceFeature | 1.1 | S/D | Kill (permanently) the ability of the chip to create a maintenance archive of a particular SRK. |
| Tspi_TPM_Load MaintenancePubKey | 1.1 | S/D | Used in manufacturing to load in a maintenance public key into the TPM. Because maintenance is seldom (if ever) actually implemented, this command is unlikely to be used. |

| TSS Function Name | Version | Design Point | Description |
|---|---|---|---|
| Tspi_TPM_Check MaintenancePubKey | 1.1 | S/D | Checks to make sure the maintenance public key really got loaded. It exports the hash of the maintenance public key. |
| Tspi_TPM_GetRandom | 1.1 | A | Return a random number of the specified size. |
| Tspi_TPM_StirRandom | 1.1 | A | A means of adding entropy to the internal random number generator. It is a good habit to call it with the current time. (Because it only adds entropy, it can never hurt.) |
| Tspi_TPM_Authorize MigrationTicket | 1.1 | S/D | Allows the owner to authorize target public keys to be used for migration. |
| Tspi_TPM_GetEvent | 1.1 | M | List a PCR extend event. |
| Tspi_TPM_GetEvents | 1.1 | M | List a group of the PCR extend events. |
| Tspi_TPM_GetEventLog | 1.1 | M | Gives the entire PCR event log. |
| Tspi_TPM_Quote | 1.1 | A/D | Uses an ID to sign the PCRs currently in the TPM. A nonce is used to guarantee freshness. |
| Tspi_TPM_PcrExtend | 1.1 | A/S | Extend a particular PCR. |
| Tspi_TPM_PcrRead | 1.1 | A/S/D | Read a particular PCR. |
| Tspi_TPM_DirWrite | 1.1 | D | Not likely to be used—it writes a particular 20 byte field in all 1.1 (and 1.2) TPMs. Only 20 bytes of NVRAM is guaranteed in a 1.1 TPM. |
| Tspi_TPM_DirRead | 1.1 | D | Read the register above. |
| Tspi_Key_LoadKey | 1.1 | A.M | Load a particular key into the TPM. |
| Tspi_Key_GetPubKey | 1.1 | A | Get the public key of a key pair. |
| Tspi_Key_CertifyKey | 1.1 | A/S/D | Create a certificate of a non-migratable key by signing it and its characteristics with an AIK (ID). |
| Tspi_Key_CreateKey | 1.1 | A/S/D | Create a new RSA key. |

| TSS Function Name | Version | Design Point | Description |
|---|---|---|---|
| Tspi_Key_WrapKey | 1.1 | A/S/D | Wrap an already extant RSA private key. |
| Tspi_Key_CreateMigrationBlob | 1.1 | A/S/D | Create a migration blob from a migratable key. |
| Tspi_Key_ConvertMigrationBlob | 1.1 | A/D | Import a migration blob from a migratable key. |
| Tspi_Hash_Sign | 1.1 | A | Hashes and signs data with a given key. |
| Tspi_Hash_VerifySignature | 1.1 | A | Verifies the signature of given data. |
| Tspi_Hash_SetHashValue | 1.1 | A | Set a particular hash value if you don't happen to want to use SHA-1. |
| Tspi_Hash_GetHashValue | 1.1 | A | Determine the current value of a hash object. |
| Tspi_Hash_UpdateHashValue | 1.1 | A | Add new data into a hash object, which continues the hash in the way defined by the hash algorithm. Currently only SHA-1 is supported, but this is likely to change in the future. |
| Tspi_Data_Bind | 1.1 | A/S | Bind data to a TPM by encrypting it with a public storage key. This takes place outside the TPM. |
| Tspi_Data_Unbind | 1.1 | A | Unbind data by decrypting with a private storage key. This takes place inside the TPM. |
| Tspi_Data_Seal | 1.1 | A/S | Encrypt data to a TPM key and PCR values. It can be done only inside the TPM because it also registers historical data as to the PCR values in the TPM when the command is done. |
| Tspi_Data_Unseal | 1.1 | A | Decrypt data sealed to a TPM when PCRs are in a determined state (and optional authorization data is present). |
| Tspi_PcrComposite_SelectPcrIndex | 1.1 | A | Select a particular set of PCRs in a PcrComposite object. |

| TSS Function Name | Version | Design Point | Description |
|---|---|---|---|
| Tspi_PcrComposite_SetPcrValue | 1.1 | A | Set what values the PCRs in a PcrComposite object should have. This is preparation for doing a seal. |
| Tspi_PcrComposite_GetPcrValue | 1.1 | A | Returns the current value of a PCR in a PcrComposite object. |
| Tspip_CallbackHMACAuth | 1.1 | A | Used by an application if it doesn't want to use the default mechanism for creating an HMAC for proving knowledge of authorization data. |
| Tspip_CallbackXorEnc | 1.1 | A | Used to provide a means of inserting a secret to a TPM object (such as when doing a change auth) without allowing sniffing software to see what the new authorization is as it goes by. |
| Tspip_CallbackTakeOwnership | 1.1 | A | Take ownership of a TPM using a callback mechanism. |
| Tspip_CallbackChangeAuthAsym | 1.1 | A | Use a callback mechanism to change authorization. |
| Tspi_EncodeDER_TssBlob | 1.2 | M | Helper function to encode a blob using DER encoding. |
| Tspi_DecodeBER_TssBlob | 1.2 | M | Helper function to decode a blob using BER encoding. |
| Tspi_Context_SetTransEncryptionKey | 1.2 | M | Set the encryption key used by a transport session. |
| Tspi_Context_CloseSignTransport | 1.2 | M | Finish a transport session. |
| Tspi_Context_GetRegisteredKeysByUUID2 | 1.2 | M | Get the list of the 1.2 keys that are in the registered key hierarchy. |
| Tspi_TPM_KeyControlOwner | 1.2 | S | Set a key to be in NVRAM inside the TPM so it doesn't disappear when power is removed (can also remove this property). |
| Tspi_TPM_CreateRevocableEndorsementKey | 1.2 | S | Create an endorsement key that can later be removed. |

| TSS Function Name | Version | Design Point | Description |
|---|---|---|---|
| Tspi_TPM_Revoke EndorsementKey | 1.2 | S | Discard an endorsement key (of course, this will also make the certificate disappear, which is not a good idea). |
| Tspi_TPM_SetOperatorAuth | 1.2 | X | Used in preboot to set an authorization that can be used postboot to invoke physical presence. |
| Tspi_Data_SealX | 1.2 | A | Just like Seal, except that it can also use locality and record historical PCR values for PCRs other than the ones it is locking to. |
| Tspi_TPM_Quote2 | 1.2 | A | Provide more information (including locality stuff) than Tspi_TPM_Quote does. |
| Tspi_PcrComposite_ SetPcrLocality | 1.2 | A | Set the locality settings for a PcrComposite structure. |
| Tspi_PcrComposite_ GetPcrLocality | 1.2 | A | Return the locality settings of a PcrComposite structure. |
| Tspi_PcrComposite_ GetCompositeHash | 1.2 | A | Return the Composite hash of the PcrComposite structure. |
| Tspi_PcrComposite_ SelectPcrIndexEx | 1.2 | A | Because the new Pcr_long structure independently sets which PCRs to record historically and which to use for release, this command was needed to set them individually. |
| Tspi_Key_UnloadKey | 1.1 | M/A | Remove a key in the TPM. |
| Tspi_TPM_CMKSetRestrictions | 1.2 | M | Determines if it will be possible to delegate the ability to create CMKs. This is necessary because an implied contract is made between the end user and the entities listed on the msalist of a key. |
| Tspi_TPM_CMKApproveMA | 1.2 | M | Allows the owner to create a ticket that allows a particular migration selection authority or migration authority to be used. |

| TSS Function Name | Version | Design Point | Description |
|---|---|---|---|
| Tspi_TPM_CMKCreateTicket | 1.2 | M | Used by a migration selection authority to approve a migration authority and by a TPM to prove to itself that a migrated CMK key was indeed approved by a migration selection authority that is on its list. |
| Tspi_Key_MigrateKey | 1.2 | M | Used by a migration authority to migrate a CMK blob to a new TPM. |
| Tspi_Key_CMKCreateBlob | 1.2 | M | The blob created when the migration of a CMK is started. |
| Tspi_Key_CMKConvertMigration | 1.2 | M | Import a migrated CMK blob. |
| Tspi_TPM_ReadCurrentCounter | 1.2 | A | Read the value of the current counter. |
| Tspi_TPM_ReadCurrentTicks | 1.2 | A | Read the current tick value (which corresponds loosely to time) of the TPM. |
| Tspi_Hash_TickStampBlob | 1.2 | A | Sign data together with the current tick value and tick nonce. Uses an AIK. |
| Tspi_NV_DefineSpace | 1.2 | A | Create a section of NVRAM and associates it with specific authorization (such as authorization data, PCR values, locality, or once per power on). |
| Tspi_NV_ReleaseSpace | 1.2 | A | Put NVRAM space previously allocated back into the pool. |
| Tspi_NV_WriteValue | 1.2 | A | Write a value to the NVRAM space previously allocated. |
| Tspi_NV_ReadValue | 1.2 | A | Read a value from NVRAM space previously allocated. |
| Tspi_TPM_Delegate_AddFamily | 1.2 | M | Create a new family of delegates. |
| Tspi_TPM_Delegate_GetFamily | 1.2 | M | Get a handle to a family of delegates. |
| Tspi_TPM_Delegate_InvalidateFamily | 1.2 | M | Invalidate a family of delegates—after this is performed, the delegations of this family will no longer work. |

| TSS Function Name | Version | Design Point | Description |
|---|---|---|---|
| Tspi_TPM_Delegate_CreateDelegation | 1.2 | M | Create a new delegation in a family table. |
| Tspi_TPM_Delegate_CacheOwnerDelegation | 1.2 | M | Load a delegation table. It is typically used in manufacturing to pre-populate a delegation family (which will not be active unless the owner authorizes it). |
| Tspi_TPM_Delegate_UpdateVerificationCount | 1.2 | M | Remove a particular delegate from a table. All the members that need to still be valid are updated, and the one that is not will not be updated. |
| Tspi_TPM_Delegate_VerifyDelegation | 1.2 | M | Check a particular delegation. |
| Tspi_TPM_Delegate_ReadTables | 1.2 | M | Read all the delegation tables in a TPM to find out the current status. |
| Tspi_TPM_DAA_Join | 1.2 | M | Get a DAA credential. |
| Tspi_TPM_DAA_Sign | 1.2 | A | Use a DAA credential to verify either a message or an AIK. |
| Tspi_TPM_DAA_VerifySignature | 1.2 | M | Step 2 of verifying a DAA credential on a TPM. |
| Tspi_DAA_ARA_RevokeAnonymity | | | Used by a DAA issuer to revoke a DAA credential. |
| Tspi_TPM_GetAuditDigest | 1.2 | A | Get the current audit digest of the TPM. |
| Tspi_TPM_SetOrdinalAuditStatus | 1.2 | A | Set an ordinal to be audited. |
| Tspicb_CallbackSealxMask | 1.2 | A | Used when masking or unmasking data sent or returned with Data_SealX or Tspi_Data_Unseal operations. |
| Tspicb_CollateIdentity | 1.2 | A | Because it isn't clear what encryption algorithms will be required by a certificate authority, this command can be used to encrypt the collated information with any encryption algorithm. |

| TSS Function Name | Version | Design Point | Description |
|---|---|---|---|
| Tspicb_ActivateIdentity | 1.2 | A | Similarly, when a certificate is encrypted by the certificate authority, the decryption will be done entirely in software, so this command allows any decryption algorithm trusted by the certificate authority to be used. |
| Tspicb_DAA_Sign | 1.2 | A | Extend properties of the DAA protocol. |
| Tspicb_DAA_VerifySignature | 1.2 | A | Extend the usefulness of the DAA protocol. |
| Tspi_TPM_ReturnPlatformClass | 1.2 | M | Return what kind of platform the TPM is on—for example, PC platform, cellphone, or server. This is useful if the trust properties of such platforms are very different (which they likely will be) and if the PCR properties (for example, which are resettable) are different. |
| Tcsi_OpenContext | 1.1 | C/A | Start a context with the core services. |
| Tcsi_CloseContext | 1.1 | C/A | Close a context with the core services. |
| Tcsi_FreeMemory | 1.1 | C/A | Free memory used in a context. |
| Tcsi_RegisterKey | 1.1 | C/A | Put a key in a registry (user or system). |
| Tcsi_EnumRegisteredKeys | 1.1 | C/S/D | Return a list of registered keys. |
| Tcsi_GetRegisteredKey | 1.1 | C/S/D | Return a handle to a particular registered key. |
| Tcsip_LoadKeyByBlob | 1.1 | C/A/S | Load a key when only the blob is known. |
| Tcsip_LoadKeyByUUID | 1.1 | C/A/S | Load a key when the UUID is known. |
| Tcsip_EvictKey | 1.1 | C/M | Get rid of a key from the TPM. |
| Tcsip_CreateWrapKey | 1.1 | C/A/S | Create a key in the TPM. |
| Tcsip_GetPubKey | 1.1 | C/A/S | Get the public portion of a key. |
| Tcsip_MakeIdentity | 1.1 | C/A/S | Create an AIK (owner authorized operation). |
| Tcsip_LogPcrEvent | 1.1 | C/M | Update the log of PCR events. |

| TSS Function Name | Version | Design Point | Description |
|---|---|---|---|
| Tcsip_GetPcrEvent | 1.1 | C/M | Get a particular PCR event from the log. |
| Tcsip_GetPcrEventsByPcr | 1.1 | C/M | Get the PCR events for a particular PCR. |
| Tcsip_GetPcrEventLog | 1.1 | C/M | Get the entire log of PCR events. |
| Tcsip_SetOwnerInstall | 1.1 | C/S | Check to see if the TPM is currently "owned." |
| Tcsip_TakeOwnership | 1.1 | C/S | Take ownership of the TPM. |
| Tcsip_OIAP | 1.1 | C/A | Start up an OIAP session. |
| Tcsip_OSAP | 1.1 | C/A | Start up an OSAP session. |
| Tcsip_ChangeAuth | 1.1 | C/A/D | Change the authorization of a blob (by creating a new blob with a new authorization). |
| Tcsip_ChangeAuthOwner | 1.1 | C/A/D | Change the owner authorization of the TPM. |
| Tcsip_ChangeAuthAsymStart | 1.1 | C/A/D | Change an authorization while masking the data traveling to the TPM. |
| Tcsip_ChangeAuthAsymFinish | 1.1 | C/A/D | Finish a change authorization session. |
| Tcsip_TerminateHandle | 1.1 | C/M | Clear out authorization data in a left-over session. |
| Tcsip_ActivateTPMIdentity | 1.1 | C/S | Get the symmetric key from the TPM necessary to decrypt the certificate returned by the certificate authority. |
| Tcsip_Extend | 1.1 | C/A/B | Extend a PCR. |
| Tcsip_PcrRead | 1.1 | C/A | Read the current value of a PCR. |
| Tcsip_Quote | 1.1 | C/A/M | Sign the current value of a set of PCRs. |
| Tcsip_DirWriteAuth | 1.1 | C/A | Write the DIR register. |
| Tcsip_DirRead | 1.1 | C/A | Read the DIR register. |
| Tcsip_Seal | 1.1 | C/A/M | Create a SEAL blob of data, encrypted so that it can only be decrypted when particular PCRs are in a particular state. |
| Tcsip_Unseal | 1.1 | C/A | Decrypt data that has been sealed. |

| TSS Function Name | Version | Design Point | Description |
|---|---|---|---|
| Tcsip_UnBind | 1.1 | C/A | Decrypt data that has been encrypted (in software) and locked to authorization data only. |
| Tcsip_CreateMigrationBlob | 1.1 | C/A/S/D | Create a migration blob for a migratable key. Requires knowledge of the migration authorization and approval of the owner of the TPM for the target public key. |
| Tcsip_ConvertMigrationBlob | 1.1 | C/A/S/D | Import a migratable blob (only necessary if it has been doubly encrypted with a random number). |
| Tcsip_AuthorizeMigrationKey | 1.1 | C/S/D | Used by the TPM to authorize a migration target. Creates a ticket that can thereafter be used. |
| Tcsip_CertifyKey | 1.1 | C/A/S | Use an AIK to certify a non-migratable key. |
| Tcsip_Sign | 1.1 | C/A | Sign data with a signing key. |
| Tcsip_GetRandom | 1.1 | C/A | Get a random number. |
| Tcsip_StirRandom | 1.1 | C/A | Add entropy to the random number generator (always a good idea). |
| Tcsip_GetCapability | 1.1 | C/A/S | Get capabilities of the TCS. |
| Tcsip_GetCapabilitySigned | 1.1 | | Should not be used (it has a security hole). |
| Tcsip_GetCapabilityOwner | 1.1 | C/A/S/M | Get owner-authorized capabilities. |
| Tcsip_CreateEndorsementKeyPair | 1.1 | C/S | Used in manufacturing to create an EK. |
| Tcsip_ReadPubek | 1.1 | C/A/S | Read the public portion of the EK (used to assemble data necessary for the CA to produce a certificate). |
| Tcsip_DisablePubekRead | 1.1 | C/S/D | Don't let anyone except the owner to read the public portion of the EK (lest it be considered a privacy problem). |
| Tcsip_OwnerReadPubek | 1.1 | C/S | Owner read of the public EK. |
| Tcsip_CertifySelfTest | 1.1 | C/M | Sign the self-test values. |
| Tcsip_GetTestResult | 1.1 | C/A | Get the results of the self test. |

| TSS Function Name | Version | Design Point | Description |
|---|---|---|---|
| Tcsip_OwnerSetDisable | 1.1 | C/A/S | Set the TPM to disabled. |
| Tcsip_OwnerClear | 1.1 | C/D | Erase the owner auth; remove SRK. |
| Tcsip_DisableOwnerClear | 1.1 | C/S | Don't allow owner clear to be done during this power cycle. |
| Tcsip_ForceClear | 1.1 | C/M | Use physical access to authorize clearing the owner. |
| Tcsip_DisableForceClear | 1.1 | C/S | Don't allow ForceClear to be used until a restart. |
| Tcsip_PhysicalDisable | 1.1 | X | Set physical presence to off. |
| Tcsip_PhysicalEnable | 1.1 | X | Set physical present to on. |
| Tcsip_PhysicalSetDeactivated | 1.1 | X | Doesn't allow physical presence to be activated until power is reset. |
| Tcsip_SetTempDeactivated | 1.1 | C/A/M | Set TPM deactivate for one power cycle. |
| Tcsip_FieldUpgrade | 1.1 | C/S/D | Upgrade the firmware of the TPM. |
| Tcsip_SetRedirection | 1.1 | C/S/D | Redirect where code sent from the TPM. |
| Tcsip_CreateMaintenanceArchive | 1.1 | C/S | Create a backup maintenance archive used to re-create a TPM in the event that the TPM or the motherboard on which it resides dies. Only can be done with cooperation of the owner and the manufacturer of the TPM, neither of whom is given access to the secrets inside the TPM. |
| Tcsip_LoadMaintenanceArchive | 1.1 | C/D | Uses a maintenance archive, re-wrapped by the manufacturer to recreate a TPM (SRK, owner auth). |
| Tcsip_KillMaintenanceArchive | 1.1 | C/S | Kill the ability of the TPM to create a maintenance archive. |
| Tcsip_LoadManufacturer MaintenancePub | 1.1 | C/M/F/G | In manufacturing, load the public key used to create the maintenance archive. |

| TSS Function Name | Version | Design Point | Description |
|---|---|---|---|
| Tcsip_ReadManufacturer MaintenancePub | 1.1 | C/M/F/G | Read the hash of the manufacturing public key that would be used to create a maintenance archive. |
| Tcsip_UnregisterKey | 1.1 | M | Remove a key from the registry. |
| Tcsip_KeyControlOwner | 1.2 | A/M | Put a key into NVRAM inside the TPM so it isn't lost on a power cycle. |
| Tcsi_GetRegisteredKeyBlob | 1.2 | M | Return a key blob from the registry given its UUID. |
| Tcsip_GetRegistered KeyByPublicInfo | 1.2 | M | Return a key blob from the registry given its public data. |
| Tcsip_EstablishTransport | 1.2 | M | Part one (of three) of getting a transport session. |
| Tcsip_ExecuteTransport | 1.2 | M | Part two (of three), using a transport session. |
| Tcsip_ReleaseTransportSigned | 1.2 | M | Part three (of three), finishing off a transport session. |
| Tcsip_Quote2 | 1.2 | A | Just like Tcsip_Quote, but it returns more information, including locality information. |
| Tcsip_SealX | 1.2 | A | Seal data so that it can be released only when PCRs are in specified values and localities are in certain states. |
| Tcsip_LoadKey2ByBlob | 1.2 | A | Load a 1.2 type key (which has more information, including extended information on PCRs and localities) into the TPM. |
| Tcsip_SetOperatorAuth | 1.2 | X | Set the operator authorization value of the platform. |
| Tcsip_CertifyKey2 | 1.2 | A | Create a certificate for a key just like CertifyKey, but provides additional information for 1.2 style keys. |
| Tcsip_SelfTestFull | 1.2 | A | Perform a full test of the TPM. |
| Tcsip_ContinueSelfTest | 1.2 | X | Finish a self test of the TPM of those commands that aren't automatically tested when the TPM is turned on. |

| TSS Function Name | Version | Design Point | Description |
|---|---|---|---|
| Tcsip_SetTempDeactivated2 | 1.2 | A | Same as SetTempDeactivated, but accepts an optional authorization. |
| Tcsip_PhysicalPresence | 1.2 | M | Used when Operator Auth is in use. |
| Tcsip_DSAP | 1.2 | M | Start an authorization session where the authorization is delegated. |
| Tcsip_Delegate_Manage | 1.2 | A/M | This is a multipurpose command used to perform most of the operations of creating, enabling, locking, unlocking, and invalidating a delegation table. |
| Tcsip_Delegate_CreateKeyDelegation | 1.2 | A/M | Delegate authorization of a key. |
| Tcsip_Delegate_CreateOwnerDelegation | 1.2 | A/M | Delegate owner authorization. |
| Tcsip_Delegate_LoadOwnerDelegation | 1.2 | A/M | Load a delegated owner authorization into the TPM so it can be used. |
| Tcsip_Delegate_UpdateVerificationCount | 1.2 | M | Re-authorize individual delegations after a delegation table has been incremented. Those not re-authorized thereby become unauthorized. |
| Tcsip_Delegate_VerifyDelegation | 1.2 | M | Check to see if a delegation blob is valid. |
| Tcsip_Delegate_ReadTable | 1.2 | M | Determine what the TPM delegation table currently is. |
| Tcsip_NV_DefineOrReleaseSpace | 1.2 | A | Create or delete a region of NVRAM, along with the authorization necessary to either read or write to that memory. |
| Tcsip_NV_WriteValue | 1.2 | A | Write data to an NV region. |
| Tcsip_NV_WriteValueAuth | 1.2 | A | Write data to an NV region that requires authorization to write. |
| Tcsip_NV_ReadValue | 1.2 | A | Read data to an NV region. |
| Tcsip_NV_ReadValueAuth | 1.2 | A | Read data to an NV region that requires authorization to read. |
| Tcsip_CreateRevocableEndorsementKeyPair | 1.2 | A | Create a revocable endorsement key. |

| TSS Function Name | Version | Design Point | Description |
|---|---|---|---|
| Tcsip_Revoke EndorsementKeyPair | 1.2 | A | Revoke a revocable endorsement key pair. |
| Tcsip_PcrReset | 1.2 | A | Reset a resettable PCR (only certain PCRs are resettable, and those only under defined locality conditions—see the Platform specific spec). |
| Tcsip_ReadCounter | 1.2 | A | Read the value of the current monotonic counter. |
| Tcsip_CreateCounter | 1.2 | X | Create one of four monotonic counters. |
| Tcsip_IncrementCounter | 1.2 | X | Increment the current counter. |
| Tcsip_ReleaseCounter | 1.2 | X | Discard the current counter. |
| Tcsip_ReleaseCounterOwner | 1.2 | X | Owner-authorized discard of the current counter. |
| Tcsip_TPM_ReadCurrentTicks | 1.2 | A | Read the current tick value (like the time). |
| Tcsip_TickStampBlob | 1.2 | A | Sign data with the current tick count and tick nonce. |
| Tcsip_TPM_DAA_Join | 1.2 | M | Get a DAA certificate. |
| Tcsip_TPM_DAA_Sign | 1.2 | A | Sign data or an AIK with a DAA certificate. |
| Tcsip_MigrateKey | 1.2 | M | Used by a migration authority to rewrap a CMK migration blob to a target TPM. |
| Tcsip_CMK_SetRestrictions | 1.2 | M | Used by the owner to allow delegation of the function of creating a CMK. This function is necessary because an implied contract is being made when a CMK is created with the entities listed on the msalist. |
| Tcsip_CMK_ApproveMA | 1.2 | M | Used by the owner to approve a list of migration selection authorities and migration authorities. |

| TSS Function Name | Version | Design Point | Description |
|---|---|---|---|
| Tcsip_CMK_CreateKey | 1.2 | A | Create a Certified Migratable Key (CMK). |
| Tcsip_CMK_CreateTicket | 1.2 | M | Used by an MSA to approve an MA for migration or to approve import of a CMK into a TPM. |
| Tcsip_CMK_CreateBlob | 1.2 | M | First step in migrating a CMK is to create a blob encrypted with an MA's public key. |
| Tcsip_CMK_ConvertMigration | 1.2 | M | Last set in migrating a CMK, where the migrated blob is imported into a TPM. |
| Tcsip_GetAuditDigest | 1.2 | M | Get the current audit digest. |
| Tcsip_GetAuditDigestSigned | 1.2 | M | Get a signed version of the current audit digest. |
| Tcsip_SetOrdinalAuditStatus | 1.2 | M | Set which ordinals are being audited. |

# Function Library

In reviewing the various software programs that are listed in this document, it became clear that a few subroutines that make use of the base functions of the TCG TPM would be useful. These functions would either separate out functionality from TPM functions that are so overloaded with function as to make them hard to use, or they would provide function that is an aggregate of functions defined in the TPM. This appendix is a list of those functions (which are not in the standard itself) and a description of their functionality.

| Function Name | Description |
| --- | --- |
| EncryptFile(HFILE *fileHandle, hkey *UserPublicKey) | Generate a 256-bit random number. |
| | Use AES to encrypt the file using the random numbers as the key. |
| | Bind the 256 random number to the user's default key. |
| | Attach the bound random number to the file. |
| | Store the file with the new .enc extension. |
| DecryptFile(HFILE *encrypted FileHandle fh, hkey *UserPublicKeyPassphrase) | Strip the bound key out of the encrypted file. |
| | Use UserPublicKeyPassphrase to decrypt the 256-bit random number. |
| | Use AES to decrypt the encrypted file, using the 256-bit key. |
| | Store the file with the .enc extension removed. |

| Function Name | Description |
|---|---|
| DecryptFileLoad( HFILE *encrypted FileHandle, hkey *UserPublicKeyPassphrase) | Strip the bound key out of the encrypted file. Use UserPublicKeyPassphrase to decrypt the 256-bit random number. Use AES to decrypt the encrypted file, using the 256-bit key. Load the file into memory with the .enc extension removed. |
| CreateSecureMigratableKeyBlob( *parentKeyBlob, UsePassphrase, MigratePassphrase, LoadPassphrase) | Load parentKeyBlob. Issue a TPM_CreateWrapKey to create a 2048-bit migratable RSA key with UsePassphrase and MigratePassphrase. Migrate the resultant blob to the same parentKey, obtaining random number, R. Create a 256-bit AES key with the LoadPass phrase with SHA256. Encrypt R using the AES key. Store the encrypted R and the migrationBlob on the hard disk. |
| LoadSecureMigratableKeyBlob( *migratableKeyBlob, LoadPassphrase) | Load parentKey of Migratable Key Blob. Create AES key from LoadPassphrase with SHA256. Decrypt R from the encrypted R using the AES key. Load MigratedKeyBlob using R. Take returned KeyBlob and load it directly back into TPM (without saving it to disk). |

# TSS Functions Grouped by Object and API Level

Although the TSS specification is written in C, the overall philosophy of the architecture is object based. As a result, it is useful to group functions together with the objects they interact with. The following table gives the list of objects, together with the functions that can be used with them at both the Tspi and Tcsip level of interaction.

**Tspi Functions**

| Object | Function | Functions | Description |
|---|---|---|---|
| TPM Object | Setup | Tspi_TPM_TakeOwnership<br>Tspi_TPM_ClearOwnership<br>Tspi_TPM_ClearOwner<br>Tspi_TPM_CreateMaintenanceArchive<br>Tspi_TPM_KillMaintenanceArchive<br>Tspi_CheckMaintenancePubKey<br>TPM_FieldUpgrade | These commands are used when a TPM is first being setup or being turned off |
| | Administration | Tspi_TPM_SetOperatorAuth<br>Tspi_TPM_SetStatus<br>Tspi_TPM_GetStatus<br>Tspi_TPM_GetCapability<br>Tspi_SetAttribUint32<br>Tspi_GetAttribUint32<br>Tspi_SetAttribData<br>Tspi_GetAttribData<br>Tspi_TPM_SetCapability<br>Tspi_TPM_SelfTestFull<br>Tspi_TPM_CertifySelfTest<br>Tspi_TPM_ReturnPlatformClass | These commands are used to determine the state a TPM is in. |

## Tspi Functions

| Object | Function | Functions | Description |
|---|---|---|---|
| TPM Object | Using the random number generator | Tspi_TPM_GetRandom<br>Tspi_TPM_StirRandom | These commands either use the internal random number generator to get a random number, or can be used to add entropy to the internal state |
| | Auditing Commands | Tspi_TPM_GetAuditDigest<br>Tspi_TPM_SetOrdinalAuditStatus | These commands are used to create a log of every time that a command is used. It is possible to use it to obtain a signed audit trail. It is not yet implemented in any TPM shipping. |
| Context and Key Objects | Used to get a key into the TPM and ready to use | Tspi_Context_LoadKeyByBlob<br>Tspi_Context_LoadKeyByUUID<br>Tspi_Context_GetKeyByPublicInfo<br>Tspi_Context_GetKeyByUUID<br>Tspi_Context_RegisterKey<br>Tspi_Context_UnregisterKey<br>Tspi_Context_GetRegistered<br>  KeysByUUID<br>Tspi_Context_GetRegistered<br>  KeysByUUID2<br>Tspi_Key_LoadKey<br>Tspi_Key_UnloadKey<br>Tspi_Key_GetPubKey<br>Tspi_Key_CertifyKey<br>Tspi_Key_CreateKey<br>Tspi_Key_WrapKey<br>Tspi_ChangeAuth<br>Tspi_ChangeAuthAsym<br>Tspi_SetAttribUint32<br>Tspi_GetAttribUint32<br>Tspi_SetAttribData<br>Tspi_GetAttribData<br>Tspi_GetPolicyObject<br>**Certified Migratable Key Commands**<br>Tspi_Key_CMKCreateBlob<br>Tspi_Key_CMKConvertMigration | These commands create load and register and find keys in the TPM and TSS contexts. They also allow you to change the password of a given key. |

| Object | Function | Functions | Description |
|---|---|---|---|
| | | Tspi_Key_MigrateKey<br>Tspi_TPM_CMKSetRestrictions<br>Tspi_TPM_CMKApproveMA<br>Tspi_TPM_CMK_CMKCreateTicket<br>Tspi_Key_CreateMigrationBlob<br>Tspi_Key_ConvertMigrationBlob<br>Tspi_TPM_AuthorizeMigrationTicket | |
| | Signing Commands | Tspi_HashTPM_Sign<br>Tspi_TPM_TickStampBlob<br>Tspi_Key_CertifyKey<br>Tspi_TPM_CertifySelfTest<br>Tspi_TPM_Quote<br>Tspi_TPM_Quote2<br>TSS_VerifySignature | These are the various types of signing commands: general-purpose signing, signatures of time, PCRs, self tests, and using a signature to certify a non-migratable key. These commands provide general-purpose cryptographic services. |
| PCR Object | Commands that change, read, or utilize the PCR values | Tspi_TPM_PcrExtend<br>Tspi_TPM_PcrRead<br>Tspi_PcrComposite_SelectPcrIndex<br>Tspi_PcrComposite_SetPcrValue<br>Tspi_PcrComposite_GetPcrValue<br>Tspi_TPM_PcrReset<br>Tspi_Data_Seal<br>Tspi_Data_Sealx<br>Tspi_TPM_Quote<br>Tspi_TPM_Quote2<br>Tspi_PcrComposite_SetPcrLocality<br>Tspi_PcrComposite_GetPcrLocality<br>Tspi_PcrComposite_GetCompositeHash<br>Tspi_PcrComposite_SelectPcrIndexEx<br>Tspi_TPM_GetEvent<br>Tspi_TPM_GetEvents<br>Tspi_TPM_GetEventLog | These commands can be used to determine what a current PCR value is, or to lock data to a particular PCR state. Additionally, they are used to read the EventLog, which has its contents extended into a particular PCR. |

## Tspi Functions

| Object | Function | Functions | Description |
|---|---|---|---|
| Hash Object | Commands to do hashing. Although the TPM is able to do hashing, this function typically does the hash in software because it is faster. | Tspi_Hash_Sign<br>Tspi_Hash_VerifySignature<br>Tspi_Hash_SetHashValue<br>Tspi_Hash_GetHashValue<br>Tspi_Hash_UpdateHashValue<br>Tspi_SetAttribData | These are the various types of signing commands: general-purpose signing, signatures of time, PCRs, self tests, and using a signature to certify a non-migratable key. These commands provide general-purpose cryptographic services. |
| Endorsement and Identity Key Objects | Commands used to establish Identities | Tspi_TPM_CreateEndorsementKeyPair<br>Tspi_TPM_GetPubEndorsementKey<br>Tspi_TPM_CollateIdentityRequest<br>Tspi_TPM_ActivateIdentity<br>Tspi_TPM_CreateRevocable EndorsementKey<br>Tspi_TPM_RevokeEndorsementKey<br>Tspicb_CollateIdentity<br>Tspicb_ActivateIdentity | These commands are used to create identity keys, which in turn can testify on behalf of the TPM to things the TPM can know are true: counter state, non-migratability of a key, time stamps, PCR values, and so on. |
| DAA Object | DAA Commands used for Direct Anonymous Attestation | Tspi_TPM_DAA_JoinInit<br>Tspi_TPM_DAA_JoinCreate DaaPubKey<br>Tspi_TPM_DAA_JoinStoreCredential<br>Tspi_TPM_DAA_Sign<br>Tspi_DAA_IssuerKeyVerification<br>Tspi_DAA_IssueSetup<br>Tspi_DAA_IssueInit<br>Tspi_DAA_IssueCredential<br>Tspi_DAA_VerifyInit<br>Tspi_DAA_VerifySignature<br>Tspi_DAA_RevokeSetup<br>Tspi_DAA_ARDeEcrypt<br>Tspicb_DAA_Sign<br>Tspicb_DAA_VerifySignature | These commands are all used in the DAA protocol that was defined to provide anonymity to the certification of TPM keys. |

| Object | Function | Functions | Description |
|--------|----------|-----------|-------------|
| Data and Non-Volatile Random Access Memory (NVRAM) Objects | Data Storage and Access Commands | Tspi_Data_Bind<br>Tspi_Data_Unbind<br>Tspi_Data_Seal<br>Tspi_Data_Sealx<br>Tspi_Data_Unseal<br>Tspi_NV_DefineSpace<br>Tspi_NV_ReleaseSpace<br>Tspi_NV_WriteValue<br>Tspi_NV_ReadValue<br>Tspi_TPM_DirWrite<br>Tspi_TPM_DirRead<br>Tspi_SetAttribUint32<br>Tspi_GetAttribUint32<br>Tspi_SetAttrib<br>Tspi_GetAttrib | These commands are used to securely store data, either encrypted, outside the TPM, or inside the TPM (in NVRAM or DIR locations). |
| Context Object | Context and Policy Management Commands | Tspi_Context_Create<br>Tspi_Context_Close<br>Tspi_Context_Connect<br>Tspi_Context_FreeMemory<br>Tspi_Context_GetDefaultPolicy<br>Tspi_Context_CreateObject<br>Tpsi_Context_CloseObject<br>Tpsi_Context_GetCapability<br>Tspi_Context_GetTPMObject<br>Tspi_Context_SetTransEncryptionKey<br>Tspi_Context_CloseSignTransport<br>Tspi_Policy_SetSecret<br>Tspi_Policy_FlushSecret<br>Tspi_Poloicy_AssignToObject | These commands are used to start a conversation with a TPM. |
| Counter Object and Tick Object | Monotonic Counter and Time-Stamping Functions | Tspi_TPM_ReadCurrentCounter<br>Tspi_TPM_ReadCurrentTicks<br>Tspi_TPM_TickStampBlob | These commands allow the user to determine the current value of the two internal counters in the TPM: the tick counter, which measures time, and the monotonic counter. Additionally they allow association of a tick value with an event. |

## Tspi Functions

| Object | Function | Functions | Description |
|---|---|---|---|
| Delegation Table Object | Delegation | Tspi_TPM_Delegate_AddFamily<br>Tspi_TPM_Delegate_GetFamily<br>Tspi_TPM_Delegate_InvalidateFamily<br>Tspi_TPM_Delegate_CreateDelegation<br>Tspi_TPM_Delegate_Cache OwnerDelegation<br>Tspi_TPM_Delegate_Update VerificationCount<br>Tspi_TPM_Delegate_VerifyDelegation<br>Tspi_TPM_Delegate_ReadTables | These commands allow authorization to use a command or object to be delegated to another authentication using a table kept inside the TPM. |

## Tcsip Functions

| Object | Function | Functions | Description |
|---|---|---|---|
| TPM Object | TPM setup | Tcsip_SetOwnerInstall<br>Tcsip_TakeOwnership<br>Tcsip_ChangeAuth<br>Tcsip_ChangeAuthOwner<br>Tcsip_ChangeAuthAsymStart<br>Tcsip_ChangeAuthAsymFinish<br>Tcsip_CreateMaintenanceArchive<br>Tcsip_LoadMaintenanceArchive<br>Tcsip_KillMaintenanceArchive<br>Tcsip_ReadManufacturer MaintenancePub<br>Tcsip_OwnerSetDisable<br>Tcsip_OwnerClear<br>Tcsip_DisableOwnerClear<br>Tcsip_ForceClear<br>Tcsip_DisableForceClear<br>Tcsip_PhysicalDisable<br>Tcsip_PhysicalEnable<br>Tcsip_PhysicalSetDeactivated<br>Tcsip_SetTempDeactivated<br>Tcsip_SetTempDeactivated2<br>Tcsip_PhysicalPresence<br>Tcsip_FieldUpgrade | These are basic commands for administrating the TPM itself. They are used to find out the TPM's capabilities, take ownership of it, transfer ownership, and set flags in the hardware. |

| Object | Function | Functions | Description |
|---|---|---|---|
|  | Administration | Tcsip_OIAP<br>Tcsip_OSAP<br>Tcsip_TerminateHandle<br>Tcsip_ActivateTPMIdentity<br>Tcsip_SetOperatorAuth<br>Tcsip_SelfTestFull<br>Tcsip_ContinueSelfTest<br>Tcsip_GetTestResult<br>Tcsip_SetRedirection<br>Tcsip_GetCapabilityOwner<br>Tcsip_GetCapability<br>Tcsip_SetCapability<br>Tcsip_GetPubKey<br>Tcsip_OwnerReadInternalPub |  |
|  | Random Number Commands | Tcsip_GetRandom<br>Tcsip_StirRandom | These commands obtain random values, or add entropy to the internal random number generator. |
|  | Auditing Commands | Tcsip_GetAuditDigest<br>Tcsip_GetAuditDigestSigned<br>Tcsip_SetOrdinalAuditStatus | These commands are used to create a log of every time that a command is used. It is possible to use it to obtain a signed audit trail. It is not yet implemented in any TPM shipping. |
| Key Objects | Key Management Commands | Tcsip_LoadKey2ByBlob<br>Tcsip_LoadKeyByBlob<br>Tcsip_LoadKeyByUUID<br>Tcsip_EvictKey<br>Tcsi_EnumRegisteredKeys<br>Tcsi_GetRegisteredKey<br>Tcsi_GetRegisteredKeyBlob<br>Tcsi_GetRegisteredKeyByPublicInfo<br>Tcsi_RegisterKey<br>Tcsip_UnregisterKey<br>Tcsip_KeyControlOwner<br>Tcsip_CreateWrapKey<br>Tcsip_GetPubKey<br>Tcsip_OwnerReadInternalPub | These commands create load, migrated, and register keys for the TPM. They also allow you to change the password of a given key. |

## Tcsip Functions

| Object | Function | Functions | Description |
|--------|----------|-----------|-------------|
| | | **Certified Migratable Keys**<br>Tcsip_CMK_SetRestrictions<br>Tcsip_CMK_ApproveMA<br>Tcsip_CMK_CreateKey<br>Tcsip_CMK_CreateTicket<br>Tcsip_CMK_CreateBlob<br>Tcsip_CMK_ConvertMigration<br>Tcsip_CreateMigrationBlob<br>Tcsip_ConvertMigrationBlob<br>Tcsip_AuthorizeMigrationKey<br>Tcsip_MigrateKey | |
| PCR Object | Commands which change, read or utilize the PCR values | Tcsip_Extend<br>Tcsip_PcrRead<br>Tcsip_Quote<br>Tcsip_Quote2<br>Tcsip_PcrReset<br>Tcsi_LogPcrEvent<br>Tcsi_GetPcrEvent<br>Tcsi_GetPcrEventsByPcr<br>Tcsi_GetPcrEventLog | These commands make use of the Platform Configuration Register values. |
| Endorsement and Identity Key Objects | Commands used to establish Identities either using the EK or DAA | Tcsip_CreateRevocableEndorsement KeyPair<br>Tcsip_RevokeEndorsementKeyPair<br>Tcsip_CreateEndorsementKeyPair<br>Tcsip_ReadPubek<br>Tcsip_DisablePubekRead<br>Tcsip_OwnerReadPubek<br>Tcsip_TPM_DAA_Join<br>Tcsip_TPM_DAA_Sign<br>Tcsip_MakeIdentity\<br>Tcsip_ActivateTPMIdentity | These commands are used to create identity keys, which in turn can testify on behalf of the TPM to things the TPM can know are true: counter state, non-migratability of a key, time stamps, PCR values, and so on. |
| Data and Non-Volatile Random Access Memory (NVRAM) Objects | Data Storage and access Commands | Tcsip_NV_DefineOrReleaseSpace<br>Tcsip_NV_WriteValue<br>Tcsip_NV_WriteValueAuth<br>Tcsip_NV_ReadValue<br>Tcsip_NV_ReadValueAuth<br>Tcsip_Seal<br>Tcsip_Unseal<br>Tcsip_Unbind<br>Tcsip_Sealx<br>Tcsip_DirWriteAuth | These commands are used to securely store data, either encrypted, outside the TPM, or inside the TPM (in NVRAM or DIR locations). |

| Object | Function | Functions | Description |
|--------|----------|-----------|-------------|
| Context /Transport Object | Context /Transport | Tcsi_OpenContext<br>Tcsi_CloseContext<br>Tcsi_FreeMemory<br>Tcsip_DSAP<br>Tcsip_OIAP<br>Tcsip_OSAP<br>Tcsip_ChangeAuth<br>Tcsip_ChangeAuthOwner<br>Tcsip_ChangeAuthAsymStart<br>Tcsip_TerminateHandle<br>Tcsip_EstablishTransport<br>Tcsip_ExecuteTransport | These functions establish a session for talking to the TCS or the TPM. They are set up to require different kinds of authentication, whether delegated, needed for each function, or having authentication take place once and continue. |
| Counter Object and Tick Object | Monotonic Counter and Time-Stamping Functions | Tcsip_ReadCounter<br>Tcsip_CreateCounter<br>Tcsip_IncrementCounter<br>Tcsip_ReleaseCounter<br>Tcsip_ReleaseCounterOwner<br>Tcsip_TPM_ReadCurrentTicks<br>Tcsip_TickStampBlob | These commands control the use of the two internal counters in the TPM: the tick counter, which measures time, and the monotonic counter. |
| Delegation Table object | Delegate | Tcsip_Delegate_Manage<br>Tcsip_Delegate_CreateKeyDelegation<br>Tcsip_Delegate_CreateOwner Delegation<br>Tcsip_Delegate_LoadOwnerDelegation<br>Tcsip_Delegate_UpdateVerification Count<br>Tcsip_Delegate_VerifyDelegation<br>Tcsip_Delegate_ReadTable | These commands are used to delegate authorization for a TPM function or object to another authorization. |

## Device Driver Level Commands

| Object | Function | Command Name | Description |
|---|---|---|---|
| TPM Object | Device Driver Library Interfaces | Tddli_Open<br>Tddli_Close<br>Tddli_Cancel<br>Tddli_GetCapability<br>Tddli_SetCapability<br>Tddli_GetStatus<br>Tddli_TransmitData<br>Tddli_PowerManagement<br>Tddli_PowerManagementControl | These functions are used to talk to the TPM driver at the lowest level of the TSS stack. If there is no TSS stack available, these are the commands that you will have to use to talk to the TPM. |

# Index

**BOOKS ONLINE**
**ENABLED**

# THIS BOOK IS SAFARI ENABLED

## INCLUDES FREE 45-DAY ACCESS TO THE ONLINE EDITION

The Safari® Enabled icon on the cover of your favorite technology book means the book is available through Safari Bookshelf. When you buy this book, you get free access to the online edition for 45 days.

Safari Bookshelf is an electronic reference library that lets you easily search thousands of technical books, find code samples, download chapters, and access technical information whenever and wherever you need it.

**TO GAIN 45-DAY SAFARI ENABLED ACCESS TO THIS BOOK:**

- Go to **http://www.awprofessional.com/safarienabled**

- Complete the brief registration form

- Enter the coupon code found in the front
  of this book on the "Copyright" page

If you have difficulty registering on Safari Bookshelf or accessing the online edition, please e-mail customer-service@safaribooksonline.com.

Addison
Wesley